30117 004404329

D0513671

VICTORIAN BANBURY

The Borough of BANBURY 1825

From a plan made by J. Davis
(with additions)

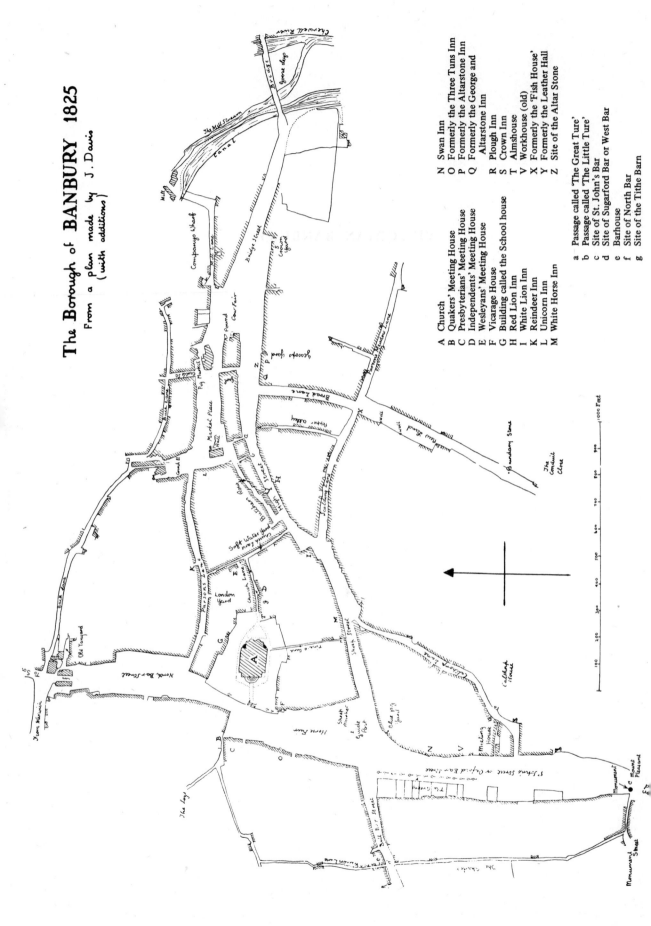

A Church
B Quakers' Meeting House
C Presbyterians' Meeting House
D Independents' Meeting House
E Wesleyans' Meeting House
F Vicarage House
G Building called the School house
H Red Lion Inn
I White Lion Inn
K Reindeer Inn
L Unicorn Inn
M White Horse Inn

N Swan Inn
O Formerly the Three Tuns Inn
P Formerly the Altarstone Inn
Q Formerly the George and
   Altarstone Inn
R Plough Inn
S Crown Inn
T Almshouse
V Workhouse (old)
X Formerly the 'Fish House'
Y Formerly the Leather Hall
Z Site of the Altar Stone

a Passage called 'The Great Ture'
b Passage called 'The Little Ture'
c Site of St. John's Bar
d Site of Sugarford Bar or West Bar
e Barhouse
f Site of North Bar
g Site of the Tithe Barn

VICTORIAN BANBURY

Barrie Trinder

PHILLIMORE

WESTMINSTER
CITY LIBRARIES

1982

Published by
PHILLIMORE & CO. LTD.
Shopwyke Hall, Chichester, Sussex

© Barrie S. Trinder, 1982

ISBN 0 85033 433 0

8302

DR
942.571
BANBURY

-9 FEB 1983

Typeset in the United Kingdom by
Fidelity Processes, Selsey, Sussex

Printed in Great Britain by
THE BOWERING PRESS LTD.,
Plymouth, Devon

CONTENTS

Literary Appendix:

LIST OF PLATES

(between pages 80 and 81)

LIST OF TEXTUAL FIGURES

Frontispiece: The Borough of Banbury, 1825

PREFACE AND ACKNOWLEDGEMENTS

This is a study which has extended over many years and taken many different turnings. It has been set aside from time to time in favour of more urgent tasks, but never totally abandoned. Over such a long period I have received generous help from a great many people.

My interest in 19th century Banbury and my awareness of the richness of the sources for its study dates from 1957 when I worked for a spell at the town library before going to Oxford. By chance it was at this time that the Banbury Historical Society was established, and I owe much to the Society as a whole and to individual members of it who have aided my researches. Jessie and the late Alan Pain and Mrs. Barbara Harry kindly transcribed a variety of documents for me. The late John Langley provided me with many insights into Banbury society in the 1890s from the depths of a rich store of reminiscences. I learned a great deal from a variety of contributors to the Society's magazine during the period of my editorship between 1962 and 1973. Jeremy Gibson, the founder-secretary and editor of the Society has for a quarter of a century given me unstinted assistance, and kindly loaned me a family heirloom without which it would have been much more difficult to work on the history of an Oxfordshire town while living in Shropshire. My work on the history of Banbury was improved beyond measure by the quietly sceptical and deeply learned mind of the late Dr. E. R. C. Brinkworth, and it is a matter of great personal regret that he did not live to see the study completed. Finally, the Banbury Historical Society has generously aided the publication of this volume by including it in its Records Series.

My first paper on 19th century Banbury was presented to the Dean Kitchen Society at St Catherine's, Oxford, in the Michaelmas Term 1959, and it is a pleasant irony, particularly to one whose subsequent career has been in adult education, to have discovered that Dr. G. W. Kitchen, after whom the Society was named, taught the first adult education classes in History in Banbury in the 1870s.

In the late 1960s my work on Banbury was greatly aided by attendance at Edward Thompson's seminar at the Centre for the Study of Social History at the University of Warwick, by many fruitful contacts with Colin Bell, then of the Banbury Social Survey, and by a stimulating and harmonious partnership with Dr. Brian Harrison, now of Corpus Christi College, Oxford, which produced *Drink and Sobriety*.

Like all historians I am indebted to many librarians and archivists, and in particular to the staff of the Bodleian Library, the Oxfordshire and Northamptonshire Record Offices, the Public Record Office and the Newspaper Library at Colindale, all of whom at various times have accorded me help beyond the mere obligations of duty. I also owe much to my students in Shropshire and elsewhere, many of whose ideas and suggestions are incorporated in the book. I am particularly grateful to the members of my seminar on Victorian market towns at Rewley House Summer School in Oxford in 1979 whose discussions proved particularly stimulating.

The final form of this study has been shaped by a thesis submitted for the degree of Doctor of Philosophy in the University of Leicester in 1980. I record with pleasure my gratitude to Professor A. M. Everitt, for his wise and perceptive advice during four years of study at Leicester, and to my employers, the Shropshire County Council, who provided assistance for part of my period of study. I owe a vast debt to my wife without whose patience and encouragement the thesis would never have been completed.

My deepest gratitude as far as this particular study is concerned is to my parents, who were considerate enough to bring me up in a town with an absorbing history, and have always assisted my researches. My mother, who first encouraged my interest in things historical, would, I hope, have enjoyed, this book, had she lived to see it, and it is to her memory and to my father, that it is dedicated.

BARRIE TRINDER

Shrewsbury
January 1982

For my father and in memory of my mother

'. . . those less marked vicissitudes which are constantly shifting the boundaries of social intercourse and begetting new consciousness of interdependence. Some slipped a little downward, some got higher footing: people denied aspirates, gained wealth, and fastidious gentlemen stood for boroughs; some were caught in political currents, some in ecclesiastical, and perhaps found themselves surprisingly grouped in consequence; while a few personages or families that stood with rock firmness amid all this fluctuation were slowly presenting new aspects in spite of solidity, and altering with the double change of self and beholder. Municipal town and rural parish gradually made fresh threads of connection — gradually, as the old stocking gave way to the savings-bank, . . . Settlers, too came from distant counties, some with an alarming novelty of skill, others with an offensive advantage in cunning'.

GEORGE ELIOT
Middlemarch

ABBREVIATIONS

BA	*Banbury Advertiser*
BCR	*Banbury Co-operative Record*
BG	*Banbury Guardian*
BH	*Banbury Herald*
BHS	Banbury Historical Society
BFTS	British and Foreign Temperance Society
Bod.Lib.	Bodleian Library
B of H Mins.	Minutes of Banbury Board of Health
BPL	Banbury Public Library
BPLC Mins.	Minutes of Banbury Paving and Lighting Commissioners
BPP	*British Parliamentary Papers*
BRA Mins.	Minutes of Banbury Reform Association
C & CH	*Cake and Cockhorse*
CSU	Complete Suffrage Union
GWR	Great Western Railway
JOJ	*Jackson's Oxford Journal*
JRSE	*Journal of the Royal Agricultural Society of England*
LBR	London and Birmingham Railway
LNWR	London and North Western Railway
LWMA	London Working Men's Association
MI Mins,	Minutes of Banbury Mechanic' Institute
NALU	National Agricultural Labourers' Union
NH	*Northampton Herald*
OC & CC	*Oxford City and County Chronicle*
OH	*Oxford Herald*
ORO	Oxfordshire Record Office
ORS	Oxfordshire Record Society
PC	Potts Collection
Pol.Corres.(1832)	Political Correspondence (1832)
PRO	Public Record Office
RC	Rusher Collection
SPCK	Society for Promoting Christian Knowledge
VCH	Victoria County History
YMCA	Young Men's Christian Association

Banbury Fashions for July,

FROM

"PYE'S ENTERTAINING MUSEUM,

AND

Compendium of *Useful* Knowledge."

"H. J. P. has also made a discovery likely to be of great utility in these hard times, of giving a knap and gloss to *Turned Coats*, so that they may have the appearance of being on the right side; among some of his more immediate friends, the economical plan of wearing two Faces under one Hat, has been introduced with striking effect."

Notwithstanding all the recent inventions, the **True Blue** on the **Right** side, and the good old **English Fashion** of wearing one face only, are and will be the prevailing Fashions in **Banbury.**

FOLL , PRINTER, ALBION OFFICE, BANBURY.

A reformer's poster from General Election Campaign, 1832.

I

A MATURE MARKET TOWN

'The old market place ... is ... all alive with the busy hum of traffic, the agricultural wealth and the agricultural population of the district. From the poor farmer with his load of corn, up to the rich mealman and the great proprietor, all the "landed interest" is there, mixed up with jobbers and chapmen of every description, cattle dealers, millers, brewers, maltsters, justices going to the Bench, constables and shopmen, apprentices, gentlemen's servants, and gentlemen in their own persons, mixed with all the riff-raff of the town, and all the sturdy beggars of the country, and all the noisy urchins of both'.[1]

THE 19th-CENTURY MARKET TOWN was a place of rendez-vous, the venue for the aristocratic assembly or the bourgeois soirée, for the circuit meeting or the synod, a gathering-place for ardent Protestants or outraged Protectionists, a point of convergence for carriers' carts, a place of muster for volunteer riflemen or dissident radicals. At the wharves and warehouses of the market town calicoes and fustians from the Miltons and the Coketowns were unloaded, to pass through the hands of drapers, tailors and dress-makers, to become the apparel of both townspeople and agriculturalists. Iron from Shutt End, Blaenavon or Old Park passed to foundrymen and millwrights who transformed it into chaff-cutters or threshing machines for the innovating agriculturalists of the district and for a wider world. It was in market towns that most of the consumer goods of mid-Victorian England were manufactured. As parliamentary constituencies such towns decided the composition of governments. In most market towns it was possible to observe almost every shade of the complex spectrum of English religion, as well as a profusion of voluntary associations providing enlightenment, sustenance or amusement. The Victorian market town has not received from historians the attention that has been given to the urban metropolis, the manufacturing town or the countryside, yet a study of such a town is capable of illustrating the whole range of English society, urban and rural, aristocratic, bourgeois and proletarian, Liberal and Conservative, Dissenting and Anglican, puritan and libertarian.

For some English market towns the first half of Victoria's reign was a period of unusual prosperity and communal self-confidence. During the previous century the larger market towns, particularly those served by water transport, had grown at the expense of the smaller centres.[2] The prosperity of agriculture in the era of high farming created a demand for the shoes, the suits, the saddles and the sideboards made in market towns, as well as for the iron, coal and cloth delivered to them from the manufacturing districts. The religious and political tensions of market town society could stimulate innovation and enterprise. The Municipal Corporations Act of 1835 and the Public Health Act of 1848 increased the opportunities which townspeople had to govern themselves, and in

1

some towns, the political influence of neighbouring aristocrats was extinguished by the 1832 Reform Act. The proliferation of jobbing printers, and the growing numbers of provincial newspapers, particularly after the repeal of the Stamp Duties in 1855, together with the building of institutes, corn exchanges, town halls and other meeting places, enabled the citizens of small towns to debate with one another at great length. While the state provided only a minimum of relief for the needy, and the commercial provision of recreational activities was insignificant, voluntary societies influenced the lives of townspeople more profoundly than the actions of governments, and their numbers grew rapidly from the 1830s. The establishment of poor law unions, the building of railways and the founding of voluntary associations covering wide areas all increased the influence of market towns as regional centres.

Some market towns remained 'sleepy hollows', small agglomerations of shops, visited by mere handfuls of carriers, with infrequent and declining markets, only one or two weak dissenting causes, and a few struggling voluntary societies.[3] Many such towns lost their parliamentary representation, if they ever enjoyed it, in the 1832 Reform Act. They were places which had declined, relative to the larger centres, in the 18th century, and except in special circumstaces, this decline continued in the 19th. Such towns, the Brackleys, the Bishops' Castles and the Beaminsters, may be defined as 'immature' market towns.

This study is concerned with what may be termed a *mature* market town, a community which blossomed and flourished in the 19th century. Such communities are best defined by functions rather than by the size of their populations. They stood at the intersections of turnpike roads and were, within their own regions, dominant centres of country carrying. They had access to water transport, and, by the 1850s, to railways. Such towns were capable of producing any commonly-used consumer goods, except those like pottery or hosiery for which there were already national markets. Locally controlled banks provided sources of venture capital and opportunities for investment. Jobbing printers, newspapers and meeting rooms provided facilities for communal debates and entertainments. Such towns were self-governing, with their own corporations, parliamentary representation and boards of health, and were usually the centres of poor law unions. They had many voluntary organisations and congregations of all the major religious denominations. Some such communities were cities, which combined the functions of a regional market centre with those of a manufacturing, resort, university, seaport or county town. The status of a market centre is probably best indicated by the number of carriers who served it. Table One shows how places which differed considerably in the size of their populations, could be remarkably similar in terms of their market functions. The mature market town was not *dependent* on resort dwellers, county or diocesan administration, or large scale manufacturers, although such activities might flourish there. Places like Cambridge, Exeter, Leicester or Cheltenham were in every sense mature market towns, but their roles as regional centres were combined with others, so that it is as difficult to see them just as market towns as it is to see Birmingham and Manchester purely as canal ports.

Banbury is a town which is particularly worthy of study because it was a major market centre which had no other significant functions. It stands on the frontiers of southern England and the Midlands, of the Cotswolds and the eastern counties, in Oxfordshire, but on the borders of Northamptonshire and Warwickshire, and within a short distance of Buckinghamshire, Worcestershire and Gloucestershire. It had a population of less than 9,000 in 1851. Towns of this size were often no more than local centres, places with one main street and only two significant shops of each trade,[4] but Table One shows that as a market centre Banbury was comparable with Ipswich, Leicester or Northampton, places of much greater size. As late as 1916 John Orr found it remarkable that a town with so many inhabitants could subsist almost entirely by the services which it provided for its region.[5] Banbury was *primarily* a regional market centre, an excellent anatomical specimen of the genus. It was not pampered into corpulence by aristocratic bounty, nor was it lulled into indolence by providing goods and services to rich, elderly spinsters or fundholding survivors of merchant adventuring or colonial wars. Its back was not bowed by obeisance to sheriffs, grand jurors and deputy lieutenants. Its muscles were not over-developed by undue concentration on one manufacturing industry, nor were its limbs stunted by obstacles of water or mountains. What happened in Banbury between 1830 and 1880 has a significance which is more than local. Just as towns like Ludlow, the model of the medieval planted town, or Bath, the archetypal resort, powerfully illuminate the history of most towns, so 19th-century Banbury, because it was a pure and unadulterated market town, exemplifies its type, and expands our understanding of market towns in general, the Nottinghams and the Northamptons as well as the Bridgnorths and the Brackleys.

Banbury would have been a different community if it had not enjoyed its own parliamentary representation. It was one of about 170 roughly similar constituencies, places which largely determined which party controlled the House of Commons.[6] A study of politics in Banbury shows how certain types of MP came to be elected, and how their behaviour at Westminster was influenced by their constituents, but politics are accorded a prominent place in this study for other reasons. Margaret Stacey remarked of Banbury in the late 1940s:

> 'parliamentary election campaigns appear to perform a most vital function of the "safety valve" variety. They provide a licence to say in public about a political opponent or his policies what it is otherwise taboo to say'.[7]

This was as true in the 19th century as in the 20th. Banburians' minds were not permanently obsessed with politics, but the groups formed and the language used at elections revealed the underlying division within the community and the tensions which existed between different groups.

As well as being a good anatomical specimen of a market town, Banbury was also an archetypal polarised community, one where, in the dynamic areas of society, the vertical divisions were of more consequence than the horizontal. Between 1830 and 1880 the rift between Liberals and Dissenters on one side, and Anglicans and Conservatives on the other[8] was productive of more creative and destructive energy than any divisions of society based on economic functions. In Banbury, as elsewhere, the horizontal division between the respectable and the non-respectable, the 'one line which ran right through Victorian society',[9] was always in evidence, but the division was not, in essence, one of economic function, and it was, for the individual, surmountable. The flash-points between respectable and non-respectable, the fairs, the race meetings, the boundary between the borough and Neithrop, produced class skirmishes rather than class warfare, and the non-respectable were never a coherent social force in the period under review.

Above the respectability line, divisions between masters and employees were generally of less importance than those between the two principal politico–religious groups. The polarisation of bourgeois society had important consequences in politics and religion, it considerably influenced the local economy, and profoundly affected the activities of voluntary associations.

Mid-19th century literature confirms that polarisation within market town communities was not unusual. Such conflict, brutal and stultifying as it may have been to those who suffered from it, and insensitive and mystifying as it may appear in a more secular, less highly politicised age, could be creative and even satisfying, and it was a stimulus to democratic responsibility. The ironmonger who proposed his banker for election to parliament, the solicitor who argued against a clergyman's efforts to enforce Sabbath observance, the chemist who set down in a pamphlet his reasons for opposing ritualism, the shoemakers, weavers and railwaymen who penned publicity for a co-operative society, were all members of a community in which every public action had to be justified. The fruits of this conflict may be seen in the proliferation of voluntary societies, in the critical view which was taken of every action by public bodies, and in the excellence sought by tradesmen seeking to lift themselves above the pressure of faction.

Literary evidence also suggests that the experiences of Banburians in the 19th century reflected those of market townspeople in general. Mark Rutherford's description of the town where he first served as a minister is of a less prosperous place than Banbury, but the sense of polarisation which comes from his writings matches the situation in Banbury.[10] The ironmongers and lawyers who appear in Rutherford's novels could well have been Banburians. Hollingford in Elizabeth Gaskell's *Wives and Daughters*,[11] which was modelled on Knutsford, was superficially a very different town from Banbury, yet there is much in the novel which reflects the nuances of Banburian behaviour. Hardy's Casterbridge was also a town whose rhythms were very similar to those in Banbury.[12] At several points in English history relations between Banbury and Coventry, some 25 miles distant, have been particularly close, and of all English novelists it is the Coventrian George Eliot who best mirrors the feelings, hopes and experiences which can be perceived from various sources to be those of 19th-century Banburians.[13]

The word 'Banbury' represented several different things in the 19th century. The *parish* of Banbury was of ancient origin, probably pre-dating the definition of counties in the south Midlands since it overlay the boundary of Oxfordshire and Northamptonshire.[14] The parish consisted of more than 4,500 acres, divided into the townships of Neithrop, Calthorpe, Wykham and Hardwick in Oxfordshire west of the Cherwell, and Grimsbury and Nethercote in Northamptonshire to the east of the river. The *borough* of Banbury, which was in existence by 1167 and received its first charter in 1554, consisted of rather more than 80 ill-defined acres around the church. Until the early 19th century the *town*, the built up area, was entirely within the borough, with the exception of the middle portion of Calthorpe Lane, but between 1800 and 1830 building land in the borough was exhausted, and development began in the adjacent non-municipal portions of the parish. The townships of Wykham and Hardwick were severely shrunken settlements by the end of the Middle Ages, and in the 19th century consisted only of a few farms, whose occupiers, as substantial ratepayers, could, if they chose, considerably influence the affairs of the town. Calthorpe did not have its own fields in the Middle

Ages, and may have been the remnant of the original vill of Banbury which assumed a separate existence after the creation of the borough. The township of Neithrop had its own field system, and a distinct nucleus, a group of ironstone farmsteads some 600 yards west of the parish church, but from the 16th century onwards the name Neithrop was often applied to the whole of the Oxfordshire portion of the parish outside the borough. Banbury was the centre of a poor law union of 51 townships, with a population of 26,705. It was also the centre of a hinterland of about 140 villages and hamlets within a circuit of ten miles, containing between 40 and 50,000 people who regarded the town as their natural centre. Banburians were conscious in the 19th century that they formed an urban community distinct from the surrounding agricultural region, and it is with this urban community, the *town* of Banbury, that this study is concerned, but everything that happened in Banbury reflected to some extent what happened in the countryside, and the history of the town is in some senses the history of those who lived in the hinterland as well as the ten thousand or so who formed the market town community.

The sources for the study of 19th-century Banbury are unusually rich. The collections of ephemera made by four Banbury printers have survived, thus preserving many of the posters, broadsheets and handbills by which arguments in the town were conducted.[15] One collection includes 163 items published during the five-month election campaign of 1832, and another has 25 posters and pamphlets issued during a Sabbatarian controversy in 1856 which lasted for little more than three weeks. Poll books, most of them recording occupations and addresses, were published after every contested parliamentary election between the Reform Act and the Ballot Act. One printer published an annual directory from 1832 onwards which listed the town's tradesmen in occupational groups, and officers of many voluntary associations.[16]

Banbury's first newspaper was the *Banbury Guardian*, founded in 1838 as a four-page sheet explaining the new poor law.[17] It became a stamped, weekly newspaper in 1843, and remained throughout the century the voice of the Liberal Reformers who came to power in the 1830s. The *Banbury Advertiser* was launched in 1855 after the repeal of the taxes on newspapers, and represented the views of militant dissenting radicals. The *Banbury Herald*, published between 1861 and 1864 provided a well-written Conservative view of life in the town, but was subsequently incorporated in the *Oxford Times*. The press was an integral part of Banbury society. Accounts of most events were written by those who attended as participants not just as reporters. In consequence, the local newspapers sometimes deliberately avoided controversy which might cause offence. The *Advertiser* declared during the Sabbatarian dispute of 1856 that:

'On some questions which from time to time have agitated the town, we have deemed it right to maintain a discrete silence. The Sabbath Question has been thus passed by, because thought unsuitable to the columns of a newspaper'.

The *Guardian* brusquely commented that a great feud had arisen about the Sabbath, the letters on which would not be published.[18]

It is fortunate that such reticence is largely compensated by reports on Banbury in newspapers published in the surrounding towns, *Jackson's Oxford Journal* and the *Northampton Mercury* included short reports on the town in most issues, but the most revealing insights are provided by the most avowedly political newspapers. The *Oxford Herald* in its Liberal period between 1831 and 1836 employed as its correspondent the printer, William Potts, subsequently editor of the *Banbury Guardian*, and after it turned to Conservatism, published reports on the town from the historian Alfred Beesley. The radical *Oxford City and County Chronicle* treated affairs in Banbury with a racy, irreverent scurrility. The best outside commentary was provided by the ultra-Tory *Northampton Herald*, one of whose founders, Francis Litchfield, incumbent of Farthinghoe, filled the Banbury column with incisive vituperation from 1831 until 1859.

The documentary sources for the study of 19th-century Banbury are also rich and profuse. The archives of the most important firm of local solicitors are in the Oxfordshire Record Office.[19] Two important collections of political correspondence survive in Banbury Library,[20] and the records of the town's churches are remarkably full.

The town has also been well served by its past historians. The *History of Banbury* by Alfred Beesley, published in 1841, is a work of outstanding quality, written by a polymath son of Quaker parents, whose 'easy pecuniary circumstances' enabled him to devote most of his life to literary and scientific pursuits and to public affairs. He joined the Church of England in 1825, and after being an active Reformer in the early 1830s, became an ardent Conservative.[21] Several important memoirs of 19th-century Banbury have been published,[22] and there are some valuable modern works which deal with the town, chief amongst them Margaret Stacey's classic sociological study of the local community in the late 1940s, which is fruitfully suggestive about the 19th century.[23] Since Banbury's hinterland extended to Juniper Hill, Barford and Tysoe, the town was the market centre for Flora Thompson, Joseph Arch and Joseph Ashby, and thus features in three of the most evocative books on the English countryside.[24]

A study of Banbury between 1830 and 1880 can throw light on a wide range of questions concerning the common experiences of many 19th-century Englishmen, and about a certain type of urban community in particular. Such a study has also a local context. It is concerned with incidents in a town established before the Norman Conquest, to which Alexander, Bishop of Lincoln, added new streets in the 12th century,[25] where the puritan William Knight gloated over the destruction of a cross in 1600,[26] where an aluminium factory was established in 1931,[27] and to which an instant coffee plant was re-located in 1965.[28] Banbury is a good anatomical specimen of a particular type of town at a particular period in history, but it is also an individual town, shaped by its past, and its consciousness of its own history, as well as by the topography and resources of its region.

Arms of the Corporation.

CIVIC PRIDE AND PAROCHIAL SQUALOR:
BANBURY AND NEITHROP 1830-1850

'The situation of Banbury is low; and though it exhibits a bustle of business . . . there is something forbidding in its general aspect, owing to the narrowness and dirtiness of the streets'.

William Mavor, 1805[1]

'One of the cleanest, best regulated and most orderly towns in the kingdom'.

Martin Billing, 1854[2]

BANBURY WAS A TOWN at a cross-roads. In origin it was a Saxon manor of rather more than 4,500 acres, the centre of the north Oxfordshire estates of the Bishops of Dorchester which comprised the Banbury Hundred. The parish church, doubtless the centre of the original settlement, stood near the point where the ancient Jurassic Way crossed the main road from Oxford to Coventry, about half a mile from the bridge where the prehistoric route crossed the Cherwell. In the early 12th century Alexander, Bishop of Lincoln,[3] built a castle between the church and the river, in front of which he laid out a market place and new streets where there had previously been fields.

Banbury's topography is best interpreted as a series of market places. Along the main north-south route were the wide streets of South Bar, the Horsefair and North Bar. The east side of the Horsefair was the traditional selling place for sheep. Bishop Alexander's Market Place was used for the general market, by butchers, and for the sale of pigs. Cattle were sold in the wide part of Bridge Street known as the Cowfair.[4] Banbury's defences in the Middle Ages consisted of the castle, its moat, four gates, and possibly a ditch linking them.[5] The last of the gates, the North Bar, was pulled down by a team of waggon horses in 1817. The position of the South Bar, demolished about 1785, was marked by an obelisk called the Monument, which was destroyed in 1843 because it was an 'eyesore' where weavers and tailors congregated in their lunch hours.[6] The castle, twice besieged in the Civil War, had been obliterated by 1685, and the site given over to vegetable gardens.[7]

The borough of Banbury consisted of some 81 ill-defined acres.[8] A parliamentary commissioner observed in 1832:

'The extent of the borough is unusually limited, being confined (with the exception of one small field and a very inconsiderable property of garden grounds) to the space occupied by the streets and buildings of a part of the town. The limits of the borough, although well-known and admitted, do not appear to be very accurately defined'.[9]

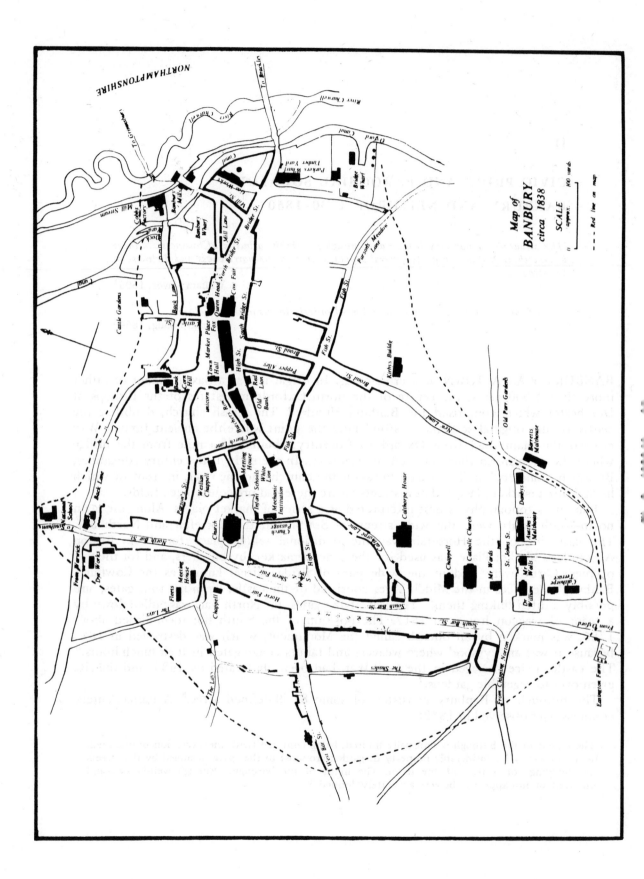

Map of
BANBURY
circa 1838

SCALE
0   approx.   100 yards

- - - - Red line on map

NORTHAMPTONSHIRE

The tithe map of 1852 shows a line of crosses approximating to the boundary, but it was not until the first edition of the 25 in. Ordnance Survey map was published in 1881 that it was precisely recorded.[10] Every three years, usually on Guy Fawkes' Day, there was a beating of the bounds, when white arrows were painted on walls to mark the limits.[11] The boundary incorporated the whole of Banbury Bridge up to the main stream of the Cherwell. It followed the mill stream northwards, excluded the buildings of Banbury Mill, and then kept to the line of the Cuttle Brook westwards along Back Lane, excluding the site of the Castle, until after crossing the road to Coventry, it turned south, enclosing what appear to have been the burgage plots of North Bar, the Horsefair, West Bar and the western side of South Bar. On the eastern side of the latter, it took in seven tenements south of the junction with Calthorpe Lane, and then followed the backs of the properties in South Bar and High Street before cutting across the eastern end of Calthorpe Lane. It incorporated the medieval suburb of Newland before making its way back to the river.

Until the late 18th century the built-up area of Banbury was probably no larger than it had been in the middle ages, but between 1801 and 1831 the population of the borough rose by 36 per cent from 2,755 to 3,737, and the population of Neithrop grew by 106 per cent, from 1,055 to 2,169. Building land in the borough was almost completely exhausted, and its population increased by only 8 per cent between 1831 and 1851, while that of Neithrop rose by 93 per cent. In 1801 Neithrop housed 26 per cent of the population of the parish, a proportion which increased to 34 per cent in 1831, and 48 per cent in 1851.[12]

Banbury was a town of small landowners, where property was minutely sub-divided. A chief rent book for the borough in 1831 lists 179 properties, which were owned by 117 different people and institutions. Only two solicitors, with 11 and 9 plots respectively, and a brewer with 14 had more than four properties. Neithrop was similarly a township of small proprietors.[13]

Banbury was in no sense a town of resort. Only 113 of the adults given occupations in the 1851 census, 2.74 per cent of the total, lived on investments, and the majority of them were widows of local tradesmen. If there were no pseudo-gentry in the town, there were no Georgian terraces to accommodate them. Several of Banbury's handsome 18th-century houses were empty for long spells around 1830,[14] and the magnificently formal appearance of South Bar is due not to Georgian planning, but to the realignment of the road in the 1820s and '30s and to Victorian in-filling.

There were several notorious haunts of criminals, drunkards and prostitutes, among them Crown Yard in Bridge Street, Lodging House Yard in Calthorpe Lane and Blue Pig Yard at the west end of High Street. In 1837 charitable societies were praised for extending their aid 'to the poor *of the yards*', and in 1859 a brothel keeper from Blue Pig Yard who had formerly resided in Lodging House Yard insisted that he had 'generally worked for a living when living *in these yards*',[15] as if the yards comprised a particular kind of place where the poor were expected to live and where working was exceptional. The buildings in Mill Lane comprised a well-known 'rookery', which was doubtless in the mind of the editor of the *Northampton Herald* in 1843 when he doubted the suitability of Bridge Street as a location for a school:

'those dens of filth and of immoral pollution which are no less disgraceful to the town than discreditable to the police ... and to the owners of the property that has long been so grossly and so degradingly abused'.[16]

Prostitution was continuously obtrusive. In 1849 the borough bye-laws provided for a fine of five shillings to be imposed on any common prostitute soliciting to the annoyance of passers-by, just as they laid down penalties for selling butter under weight or shaking carpets in daylight.[17] The 1851 census recorded two 'nymphs of the pave' at the Royal Oak beerhouse in Calthorpe Street.

A particularly notorious source of moral infection was Waterloo, a terrace constructed in the second decade of the century at the bridge foot in Northamptonshire. In May 1834 'persons of bad character, pickpockets &c.' gathered in 'that great public nuisance called Waterloo'. In 1836 'that intolerable nuisance on the other side of Banbury gate, Waterloo Place' was blamed for a series of robberies. A court case in 1844 revealed that lodging houses at Waterloo, kept by Thomas Ward, a native of Westport, Co. Mayo, accommodated criminals visiting Banbury races. Gentry from Northamptonshire considered buying and demolishing Waterloo, but this task was accomplished by the Great Western Railway in 1846. The destruction of the terrace, 'one of the greatest nuisances in the neighbourhood, for years the resort of vagrants and thieves', was widely welcomed.[18] The Wards moved their lodging house to Rag Row in Neithrop and it was from 'that low, wretched place' that a wooden-legged man, a one-armed man and a certain Elizabeth Wright operated a begging letter racket in 1850.[19] The yards, Waterloo and Mill Lane were all close to the town centre, and the zeal of Banbury's social reformers has to be seen against a background of insulting behaviour by drunkards and persistent soliciting by unsavoury prostitutes in the very heart of the business area.

The suburbs of Banbury displayed many features characteristic of most medium-sized towns of the period. There were several large houses surrounded by pleasure grounds which sealed considerable areas from development. Close to the town centre were the grounds of Calthorpe House, those behind John Wake Golby's house in High Street, and the gardens and fish ponds of Neithrop House which served as a barrier between the hamlet of Neithrop and the town. 'Beechfields', the home of the solicitor John Munton, built in West Bar about 1830, had grounds large enough to accommodate flower shows.[20] There were gardens on the castle site, off the Warwick Road, and to the south and west of the town centre, which were let to such tenants as George Herbert's father, who was a weaver.[21] By 1832 brickmakers were digging clay along the Drayton, Broughton and Middleton Roads.[22] Sand was also quarried, and a poor quality roadstone was dug from pits off the Bloxham Road. About 1830 the costs of bricks and local stone seem to have been about equal, and brick was regarded as the more fashionable material.[23] Working-class cottages in Constitution Row and Southam Road built in the 1820s and '30s have brick fronts and back walls in Hornton Stone. The elegant 'Beechfields' has a stuccoed front, and a rear elevation of stone. Substantial numbers of bricks do not appear to have been imported before the closing years of the 19th century, but Welsh slates seem to have been used from the time the Oxford Canal was opened. On the edges of the town were timber yards on the Green and in North Bar, drying racks for dyers in Warwick Road, osier beds on the Hardwick Road, and heaps of manure and offal off South Bar.[24] The town was surrounded by fields enclosed in the 18th century or earlier, and the only open spaces available for recreation were the cricket ground on the Oxford Road and the meadows on the Northamptonshire side of the Cherwell which were used as a racecourse.

Most of the new middle class houses constructed in Banbury in the early 19th century were in the South Bar area. In about 1839 Crouch Street was laid out on the western side of South Bar. One of the first buildings on the new road was the British School, designed by J. M. Derrick, who may also have been responsible for villas in the Gothic style in Crouch Street.[25] Terraces in the classical style were built in South Bar itself. In the late 1830s there was a boom in the building trade. Bricklayers struck for an extra sixpence a day in May 1840, when a newspaper reported that 'a considerable quantity of buildings have recently been or are now in progress'.[26] The working class cottages in Constitution Row were built about 1840 by Joseph Garrett who had brickyards in the vicinity.[27] In the town centre, J. A. Gillett the banker built 21 working class cottages in Back Lane, Broad Street and Pepper Alley in the 1830s.[28] There was also ribbon development along the Southam and Warwick Roads. In Neithrop two classical villas, Cedar Villa and Neithrop Villa, were built in the immediate vicinity of some particularly insanitary cottages. There were several in-filled folds in the hamlet, small fields or stackyards which had been randomly filled with ironstone cottages. One was euphemistically called John Pain's Square. Richard Gould, a surveyor, converted the one-time Neithrop parish work-house into cottages called Gould's Row, and north of the Warwick Road the Neithrop pound was filled with cottages with took the name of Pound Yard.[29]

If Banbury was a town of small landowners, it was also a town of small speculators. Many of its cottages were built in short terraces and courts which took their names from the local traders who built them. A list of properties made in 1850 includes Golby's Yard, Miss Wyatt's Cottages, Hobley's Lane, Armitt's Cottages and Gunn's Row.[30]

The largest development of working class houses before 1850 was on the meadows south of Bridge Street, where by 1843–44 Upper and Lower Cherwell Streets ran south to Fish Street. The Neithrop Jury List for August 1843 named three residents in the two streets, and by 1848 the directory included 32 traders in the area. By 1847 two terraces in the vicinity, Spring Cottages and Victoria Terrace were occupied. By 1851 the development extended south of Fish Street and comprised nearly 300 households.[31] The houses were constructed by several speculators. Robert Gillett, one-time landlord of the Crown Inn, a milkman, farmer and grazier, built for himself a six-bedroomed house and a dairy in Upper Cherwell Street about 1843–44, and subsequently erected four brick cottages on adjacent land. William Hobley, a builder constructed other cottages in the area.[32] James Gardner's small foundry was situated on the perimeter of the development, but only 7.45 per cent of the employed population of the new streets were working in engineering in 1851,[33] The houses in the Cherwell streets were both cheap and profitable. The poorest type cost only £35 to build, inclusive of land costs, and yielded £6 10s. 0d. per annum rent. The better type cost £70, and brought in between £8 and £10 a year. It was reckoned that the whole cost could be recovered within 12 years.[34]

There were few houses of architectural distinction in Banbury. A fire in 1628 and long spells of fighting in the Civil War had destroyed almost every medieval building, although several 16th-century timber-framed buildings survived, among them the Red Lion, the Reindeer and the Original Cake Shop. Otherwise most of the oldest buildings were built within a few years of 1650, usually of stone, although some had elaborate street frontages in timber.[35] George Herbert remarked that only two houses in the town were alike, that most of the buildings in the centre had low walls of crumbling ironstone, and roofs of thatch or Stonesfield slate, and that the town was built 'in a straggling and irregular manner' with no notice taken of bow windows or flights of steps which encroached into the public way. Alfred Beesley, born in 1800, remembered when the streets were rain-sodden hollow ways, with stepping stones to cross them, ridden with dung heaps, ash heaps and standing pools of water.[36]

Water was one of the dominant elements in the townscape. The inhabitants of Calthorpe Lane petitioned for a culvert to relieve flooding in 1835, and in 1846 blamed deaths in the street on 'the stench arising from the stagnant water and filth accumulating in the drains'. Sections of two streams which flowed eastwards across the town to the Cherwell ran in part in the open and served as sewers. Pure drinking water was scarce. There were several free pumps but it was still profitable to sell soft water obtained from pumps off Church Lane.[37]

The transformation of the appearance of Banbury began in 1825 when a Paving and Lighting Commission was established.[38] The Commission first met in June 1825 when John Davis of Adderbury was appointed engineer and commissioned to make a map. Land between Bridge Street and the canal was acquired for a stone yard, and served the Commissioners and their successors until 1974. Money was raised by loans, among the mortgagees being the historian Alfred Beesley. The Commissioners' efforts met with considerable opposition. One of their first objects was to improve the impression of Banbury gained by travellers on the main Oxford-Coventry road. The act granted them authority to plant trees 'in the wide parts of the streets and other public places' and the setting out of saplings in South Bar was authorised at one of the first meetings. Some were pulled up, and when the Commissioners persisted there was a riot led by a baker in which the trees were burned on a bonfire. The resentment of the rioters was shared by wealthier citizens, among them Richard Austin, the brewer, who told the Commission:

'We think it impossible that a market town dedicated to the purposes of trade can be a fit place to blend the larger ornaments of nature with those of commercial utility, either the body or the head must be in disproportion'.[39]

The process of rationalising the town was carried further after the election of the new municipal corporation in 1835-36 when many streets were re-named.[40]

The Commission transformed the appearance of the borough. When new houses were erected, it insisted that no bow windows or projections of other kinds would be permitted, and that plated doors should be placed above coal cellars. Householders who allowed privies to become full were reprimanded. In 1840 an engineer from Birmingham informed the Commission that the Gornal stone curbing they had obtained in the 1820s was useless. The deficiencies in the pavements were set right during the 1840s, when the mean annual expenditure of the Commission was £564 per annum. A sanitary inspector was appointed, who, when he presented his third report in 1848, was able to claim that the remaining public health problems in the borough were marginal. Three yards remained filthy, there were dung heaps by the British Schools and in Calthorpe Lane, and an offensive bone store at the Queen's Head, while three houses in Cherwell remained undrained. Even the yards where the poorest lived were being cleaned by the

Commission's scavengers. The Commissioners had, as Alfred Beesley remarked, 'removed all the characteristic traces of the once "dirty Banbury"'.[41]

The Commission had powers to employ watchmen, which passed to the Borough Corporation with the coming into effect of the Municipal Corporations Act in 1835. The corporation's Watch Committee first met on 11 January 1836 and decided to establish its own police force. William Thompson, a chairmaker, was appointed part-time Superintendent, two full-time constables were engaged, and six watchmen, formerly employed by the Commission, were retained. A police station was established in the lobby of the Theatre in Church Lane. The constables had a salary of £1 per week, and were provided with batons and a Uniform 'of the same description as the London Police'. The police were instructed to visit lodging houses to ensure that vagrants were not harboured, and prohibited from entering public houses except in the course of duty. Drunkenness on duty was nevertheless the occasion of numerous reprimands, and three dismissals in the ensuing decade. In 1840 the night watch was abolished, and two additional full-time constables appointed. The effectiveness of the force was limited by the borough boundary which malefactors could cross to escape arrest. There were no police in Neithrop until 1857. The police were the object of derision from the Corporation's political opponents, but it was due to them that there was a noticeable difference between the standards of public order in the borough and those in Neithrop.[42]

The Commission agreed to illuminate the town with gas in 1825, but subsequently oil lamps were erected. The Banbury Gas Light and Coke Company was formed in 1833, began to supply private homes in March 1834, and lit its first street lamp on 29 August 1834. A gasworks was erected by the canal, adjacent to the stone yard in Bridge Street.[43]

In Banbury, as in the nation at large, the threat of disease was a powerful stimulus to sanitary reform. In 1831 there was an outbreak of a severe disorder nicknamed 'Banbury Fever'. In 1832 and 1833 there were typhus epidemics, the latter originating in a dung heap in Monument Street. In 1845 there was a serious epidemic of smallpox. By the late 1840s one sixth of all deaths in the town arose from epidemic, endemic and contagious diseases.[44] The threat of disease sharpened class differences. In November 1831 the Mayor and Magistrates warned inhabitants 'particularly the lower classes' to take precautions against cholera.[45] Banbury's middle classes were certainly frightened by the squalor in which some of their neighbours lived, and their fears stimulated both sanitary reform and the building of suburban villas. There was considerable support for public health reform because the problems in Neithrop were so manifest, and because the Paving and Lighting Commission, with its limited powers, had brought about obvious improvements within the borough. The *Banbury Guardian* in 1848 called for stronger public health legislation because it considered permissive laws had been ineffective.[46] After the Public Health Act of 1848 came into effect, 163 residents in Neithrop petitioned the Central Board of Health for an enquiry into the sanitary condition of the town. Since Neithrop had a death rate of 26 per 1,000, compared with 21.6 per 1,000 in Banbury, it could have been the subject of an enquiry even without a petition, since the Central Board was empowered to order an investigation in any locality where the rate exceeded 23 per 1,000.[47]

The Inspector, T. W. Rammell, took evidence in Banbury in the spring of 1849.[48] He found examples of defective sanitation in the borough which the Paving and Lighting Commission had been unable to eradicate. In Crown Yard there was one privy to 43 people, and there was one for 47 in Mill Lane. There were dung heaps in Soft Water Yard and Catherine Wheel Yard. He concluded that privy accommodation presented 'perhaps as extreme cases of the kind as are to be found in the filthiest and most crowded towns in England'. Nevertheless he thought that the borough was tolerably well paved, cleansed and policed.[49] He was unable to reach the same conclusions about Neithrop.

'Neithrop', Rammell observed, was 'so situated and of such a form that it almost entirely surrounds the Borough of Banbury and the boundary between them is extremely intricate and ill-defined'. He was told of the social differences between the two parts of the parish. Thomas Pain, the solicitor, said that the back streets of Neithrop were 'inhabited by the poor and persons of bad character'. Dr. R. S. Wise observed 'the poorer classes chiefly reside in Neithrop'. Neithrop was badly if at all paved. Refuse accumulated in its streets, and its high mortality rate was caused by the neglect of drainage and by polluted water supplies. Thomas Pain told Rammell of his frustration when there were men and women fighting and calling blue murder outside a beerhouse in Back Lane near his home, with whom the borough police were powerless to interfere.[50] Before 1835 the contrast between Banbury and Neithrop had extended to the administration of poor relief. The Banbury poor house was 'neat and clean in the extreme', and the paupers had meat every day if they wished, but 'a more wretched habitation was never beheld' than the Neithrop workhouse.[51]

The most disturbing evidence which Rammell discovered concerned the Cherwell streets, built within the previous six years on land which was obviously ill-drained. Dr. Rye said the area was subject to fever and had been the seat of a smallpox outbreak in 1845. Richard Brazier, a whitesmith and Primitive Methodist who lived in Cherwell, told him that a group of six houses shared one privy, and that the contents of cess pits were often left in the streets for several days.[52] The foul living conditions in Cherwell were not, like those in Blue Pig Yard or Calthorpe Street, the result of topographical constraints dating from the middle ages, of immemorial custom, or of a concentration of the most feckless classes. They had been created between 1843 and 1849 by respected citizens.

Rammell's report defined many urgent problems. Some were practical questions, which awaited the importation of the appropriate expertise for their solution. Some were rendered insoluble for the time being by administrative immobility or the lack of political will. Meanwhile the political, religious and recreational activities of respectable Banbury took place on a well-lit stage, with dirt, disease, drunkenness, crime and prostitution flourishing in the wings. Banbury's problems were magnified by the division between the borough and Neithrop. The two portions of the parish, Rammell observed, 'form one town, though not with unity of social interests'.[53] Still, in 1850, the nocturnal traveller approaching Banbury would see from a distance the lights of the borough, but before reaching them would have to stagger and stumble through the puddles, dung heaps and waggon ruts of the unpaved, unpoliced and unilluminated streets of Neithrop.

Figure 3. The Boundary of the Borough of Banbury.
(From M. D. Lobel, ed., *Historic Towns*, I, 1969).

III

TOWN AND COUNTRY:
THE LOCAL ECONOMY BEFORE THE RAILWAYS

As I was going to Banbury
Upon a summer's day,
My dame had butter, eggs and fruit,
And I had corn and hay;
Joe drove the ox, and Tom the swine,
Dick took the foal and mare,
I sold them all — then home to dine
From famous Banbury Fair.[1]

THE TERM 'BANBURYSHIRE', much used in the 1830s, was not just an affectation for Banbury's economy was in many respects comparable with that of most county towns. In 1831 some 44,000 people lived within eight miles of the town, and regarded Banbury as the main focus of their economic activities.[2] Countrymen from further afield sent orders to Banbury tradesmen through their weekly carriers, or annually visited its fairs. The nearest places of comparable size, the county towns of Oxford, Northampton and Warwick, the city of Coventry and the resort of Leamington, lay 20 or more miles away. None of the smaller market centres between ten and fifteen miles distant, Bicester, Brackley, Shipston-on-Stour and Chipping Norton, had facilities to match those in Banbury, while Deddington, Hook Norton and Aynho, between five and seven miles away, which had been regarded as markets in the 17th century, could no longer claim to be towns. Like market towns in other regions, Banbury had grown between 1700 and 1830 at the expense of its smaller rivals.[3]

Banbury's hinterland was well defined by the editor of the *Banbury Guardian* in 1843:

'The town of Banbury is situated at the northern extremity of the county of Oxford, twenty-two miles from the city of Oxford. It is so near to the county of Northampton that a portion of its outskirts are within the limits of that county: the town of Northampton being twenty-eight miles distant. The county of Warwick, Warwick itself lying at a distance of twenty miles, comprises a considerable portion of what may be termed the Banbury district, and reaches within three miles of the borough of Banbury. Portions of Worcestershire and of Gloucestershire are also in much nearer neighbourhood and in much more intimate connection with the town of Banbury than with either of their respective county towns. The county town of Buckingham is distant only nine miles, while the nearest place in it in which a newspaper is published is distant thirty-four miles. Thus remotely situated from any place of central importance, in a fertile, wealthy and highly populous district; having the advantage of direct water communication with London, Birmingham, and other commercial marts, it is of natural consequence that the town of Banbury has become distinguished as a market for almost every description of merchandise. To the 140 places within a circuit of ten miles it may be said to be a metropolis'.[4]

16

The Poor Law Commissioners in 1835 found Banbury the only place in the region which could be considered as the centre of a union.[5] Several outlying parishes were added after the original designation of the union, which eventually consisted of 51 townships, including Banbury, Neithrop and Grimsbury. Seven other townships were included in poor law records with their mother parishes or adjacent, larger townships. Four of the 46 rural townships, Adderbury, Middleton Cheney, Bloxham and Hook Norton, had populations of over a thousand in 1831. Seven had between 500 and 1,000; 27 between 200 and 500, six between 50 and 200, and two, the shrunken villages of Prescote and Clattercote, less than 20. Most of the union was in Oxfordshire, but it included six Warwickshire parishes to the north west of Banbury, and eight in Northamptonshire to the east and north east. To the south east the large Northamptonshire parish of King's Sutton, only four miles from Banbury, was placed in the Brackley Union, as were the closed villages of Aynho, Farthinghoe and Thenford, only a little further away. The union did not therefore include the whole of Banbury's hinterland, but as an easily definable unit, it is a useful means of measuring statistically the changes which were taking place in the countryside.

The extent of Banbury's economic influence is shown by the routes of the carriers' carts which travelled to the town. Carriers went to Banbury from every settlement of significance within ten miles, and there were weekly services from many villages between ten and fifteen miles away, like Enstone, Fringford, Charwelton and Harbury. Some places even further away also had services, most of them small market towns like Buckingham, Bicester and Daventry. Within ten miles the influence of Banbury was unrivalled by that of any other market town. In villages between ten and fifteen miles away the town shared customers with Northampton, Coventry, Oxford, Stratford-upon-Avon and Warwick. Its influence was felt in places as much as 20 miles distant.[6]

The pattern of migration into Banbury also shows the extent of the town's regional influence. In 1851 there were 1,317 migrants born in the parishes which comprised the Poor Law Union living in the town, some 15 per cent of the population. By expressing the total from each parish as a percentage of the population of that parish in 1851, an index figure can be obtained which enables crude comparisons to be drawn between the parishes. The average figure for the union was 6.27, but as Table Four shows, there were many more migrants from the villages nearest Banbury than from those at a greater distance. Most of the parishes on the edge of the union had index figures between three and four. Only from parishes more than ten miles away were the numbers of migrants insignificant, and the town's hinterland defined by this means is remarkably similar to that shown by the carriers' cart routes.

Banbury stands in the centre of one of the most fertile farming regions in Europe. The strong, deep, red ironstone soils have been praised by agricultural commentators from the time of Camden to the present.[7] Arthur Young concluded:

'a finer district of soil is not often to be met with whether in grass or arable. This red district, in respect of soil, may be considered as the glory of the county. It is deep, sound, friable, yet capable of tenacity; and adapted to every plant that can be trusted to it . . .'.[8]

The region dependent on Banbury extended beyond the redlands to the Stonebrash and other less fertile areas, but the rich red soils created the essential character of the hinterland. By 1830 the process of enclosure in the region was all but complete. On the dryer uplands wheat and barley were grown, while roots and green crops were cultivated for dairy and beef cattle, sheep and pigs. Only on the flood-prone meadows of the Cherwell Valley was there any concentration on livestock.[9] The Banbury region could present a prospect of beauty, plenty and peace. Alfred Beesley wrote in 1841:

'A more thoroughly English landscape, or a spot more rich in arable or pasture land, thickly overspread with trees, watered by many streams and ornamented at short intervals with villages, spires and towers, can perhaps hardly be found elsewhere'.[10]

The social climate of Banbury's hinterland in the 1830s and 40s was less idyllic. In 1830 the average wage of a farm labourer was only 9s. a week, while single men in winter sometimes earned as little as 3s. In 1838 farm workers' wages were between 9s. and 10s. a week, lower than they had been 30 years earlier.[11] As Cobbett observed in the Isle of Thanet, nowhere was less hospitable to the poor than the best arable districts, where land was so valuable that none was left as common.[12] A major cause of rural poverty was the collapse of the local textile industries, which had provided employment for considerable numbers of male weavers and many more female spinners in the 18th century. Plush-weaving declined in most Banburyshire villages between 1830 and 1850. There were 27 plush weavers at Middleton Cheney in 1841, but only five in 1851. The number at Adderbury fell from 44 to 11 in the same period.[13] In 1844 there were 24 stocking frames at Middleton Cheney and 25 at Chacombe, but the industry was utterly depressed. Middleton Cheney in 1835 presented 'a complete picture of a decayed manu-facturing district', and in 1839 eleven families from the village were on poor relief in Leicester.[14] Pillow lace was still made at Moreton Pinkney in the 1830s, but the lace-makers were poorly paid. At Juniper Hill in the 1870s the days when lacemaking regularly occupied the women of the hamlet, and the products were taken annually to Banbury Fair, were a distant memory.[15] There was no regular work for women in the countryside outside the harvest and haymaking periods, and a wife who sought to supplement her husband's earnings was likely to be drawn to Banbury, where she could work as a seamstress, laundress or charwoman.

Underemployment in the Banbury region was reflected in heavy expenditure on poor relief. In most parishes a peak of expenditure had been passed by 1830, and spending was declining in the years before the Poor Law Amendment Act, probably as the result of more efficient, less humane administration rather than because needs were diminish-ing. The Speenhamland system was widely used, and in Adderbury, Hanwell, Hornton, Shennington, Tadmarton, Cropredy and Claydon the roundsman system was employed.[16] Social discontent was openly manifest in the 'Swing' riots of 1830. The rioting in Banbury on 29 November 1830 may have arisen from tensions within the town, but in the countryside the causes of disorder were agrarian, arising from the threats to employ-ment posed by the introduction of machinery. On 30 November a mowing machine was destroyed at King's Sutton and a threshing machine at Bodicote. The next day two machines were burned at Tadmarton, and on 3 December a threshing machine was set alight at Upper Boddington.[17] The riots of 1830 drew some national attention to the social tensions of the Banburyshire countryside, but only the riotous nature of the machine burning was unusual. There were constant undercurrents of less open forms of social protest. In 1835 the district was said to be very distressed and highly pauperised.[18] Incendiarism was very common. Poaching was prevalent, both as a means of succour and as a form of social protest. In the winter of 1846–47 sheep stealing was endemic in Middleton Cheney, Adderbury and Deddington. In 1845 a black-faced gang of burglars from Culworth was captured, after committing a series of robberies well into Warwickshire.[19]

Joseph Ashby observed that villages had 'their own special ways and dispositions, as men do'. He contrasted the extrovert conversation of the men of the open village of Tysoe with the guarded suspicion of the estate villagers of Upton, and the taciturnity of the work-absorbed quarrymen of Ratley.[20] Similar contrasts could be discovered in the 1830s. In May 1833 after a new overseer reduced poor law expenditure in Middleton Cheney, the state of the village was reported as 'alarming'. Seven sheep were stabbed and left 'in a horrid condition', ricks and barns were destroyed by incendiary fires, and anonymous letters were circulating. In 1832 the parish was 'in a very unsettled state'. In 1832 a group of thieves from Charlton was caught after plundering many barns in the district.[21] Moreton Pinkney, nine miles from Banbury, was a particularly lawless open village. The young Tractarian Thomas Mozley found it a place of numerous freeholders, many public houses and two much-encroached-upon commons, a 'village of misery and dirt, of pigs and paupers'. A neighbouring landowner complained in 1849 that 'the Moreton dictionary does not include such words as morality, honesty, truth, gratitude &c. . . . at least half the grown-up population are . . . fit for any crime from lying to murder'.[22] Other heavily pauperised open villages to the east of Banbury were King's Sutton, Marston St Lawrence, Culworth and Sulgrave.[23] Some seven miles south of Banbury was a ring of peaceful, sparsely populated closed villages, Worton, Glympton, Rousham and Sandford St Martin. In Northamptonshire the Drydens had, long before the 1830s, cleared the cottages of Canons Ashby, while the labouring poor of Edgecote had been despatched to the adjacent parish of Chipping Warden. Thenford was an archetypal closed village, where the Severne family who lived at the Hall distributed beef to the poor every Christmas, and held dinners for farmers and cottagers at which traditional English songs were sung.[24] The most orderly village in the region was Farthinghoe, ruled by Francis Litchfield, who was rector from 1817 until 1876. He was a Conservative, a racegoer, an antagonist of Thomas Arnold, and a founder of the *Northampton Herald*, who made his once unruly village into one which was renowed for its 'content, joy and gladness'. He attributed his success to his village clothing society, deposits for which were collected weekly after divine service, so that members were compelled to attend church. Members who were convicted, or who became pregnant while unmarried were expelled. Through the influence of the society the number of Christmas communicants was raised from an average of 15, to a total of 110 by 1837. Litchfield introduced allotments for labourers and insisted upon the whitewashing of cottages, and was praised in 1838 for ending the 'squalid poverty and wretchedness' which had once characterised the village.[25]

Seven turnpike roads linked Banbury with neighbouring towns.[26] The turnpikes included all the present main roads out of the town except the route to Northampton through Thorpe Mandeville, the ancient Banbury Lane, which was still a drovers' route in the early 19th century, and was never subjected to tolls. A census taken in March 1845 of the traffic crossing Banbury Bridge revealed that over a five day period there were 1,008 pedestrians per day, 132 horses being ridden, 55 carts or waggons and 36 private carriages. Some 372 beasts were driven over the bridge in the five days, a total

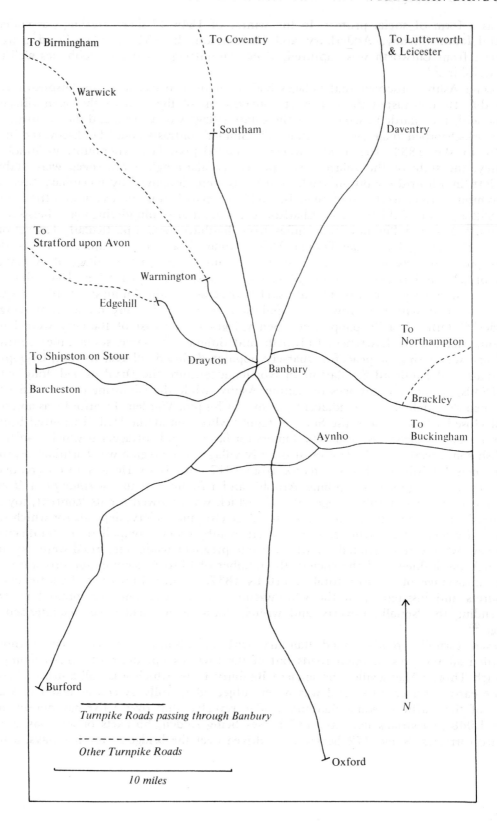

Fig. 4. Turnpike Roads passing through Banbury.

Figure 5. Banbury Bridge (Alfred Beesley, History of Banbury, *Plate XVIII.)*

which would have been much greater in the droving season when as many as 2,000 cattle a day from Wales and Herefordshire crossed the Cherwell.[27] A survey taken in 1845 found, on the basis of observations over a 14-day period, that the busiest road out of Banbury was that to Southam and Coventry, with an estimated 4,966 tons of freight passing per year, followed by that to Oxford with 4,108, the Bicester road with 2,886, and that to Stratford with 2,626. The density of passenger traffic was in the same order. It was calculated that 2,704 tons of general merchandise a year went to London by road, compared with about 4,000 tons by water.[28]

In 1834 Banbury had one cart and two waggon services to London each week, doing the journey in about 40 hours, and two weekly waggon services to Birmingham which travelled overnight. By 1836 there were three van and two waggon services to London each week. The ponderous London waggons, 18 ft. long, 7 ft. 6 in. wide and 12 ft. high were each drawn by eight horses. A punt was suspended from the bottom of the vehicle between the wheels, in which live lambs, pigs and poultry could be carried. Heavy goods were placed in the centre, and butter, and carcasses of sheep and pigs piled on top, the load being closed up with heavy mohair curtains.[29] Banbury was on two long distance cart circuits, providing weekly links with Worcester, Gloucester, Stratford, Coventry and Leicester. Three carts a week went to Northampton, and country carriers offered connections to other towns. Evesham could be reached via Shipston-on-Stour or Brailes, Cheltenham via Lower Swell or Stow-on-the-Wold, and Bedford via Buckingham.[30]

Stage coach services through Banbury improved rapidly in the early 1830s. In 1830 there were 16 journeys a week to London, 13 to Birmingham, six to Leicester and Oxford and three to Northampton and Kidderminster. Most were worked from the *Flying Horse*, which was kept by John Drinkwater, a partner in the Birmingham–Oxford *Regulator* coach. By 1836 most of the coach services had moved with Drinkwater to the *White Lion*. In that year there were 22 services a week to London, 19 to Birmingham and 12 to Oxford. The fastest coach reached London in seven and a half hours.[31]

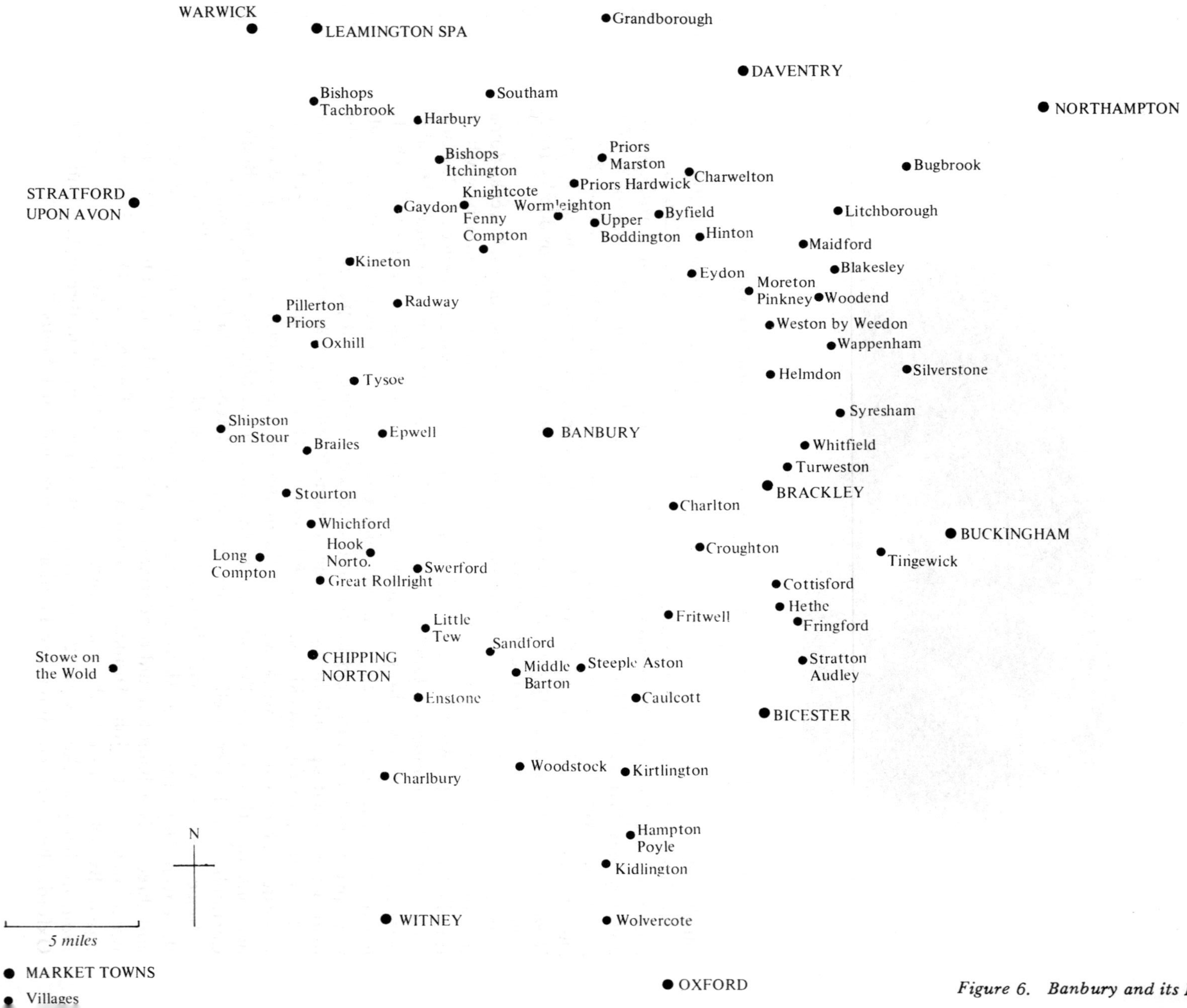

WARWICK

STRATFORD
UPON AVON

LEAMINGTON SPA

Grandborough

DAVENTRY

NORTHAMPTON

Bishops
Tachbrook

Southam

Harbury

Bishops
Itchington

Knightcote

Gaydon

Fenny
Compton

Wormleighton

Priors
Marston

Priors Hardwick

Upper
Boddington

Byfield

Charwelton

Hinton

Bugbrook

Litchborough

Maidford

Blakesley

Moreton
Pinkney

Woodend

Weston by Weedon

Wappenham

Silverstone

Kineton

Radway

Pillerton
Priors

Oxhill

Tysoe

Eydon

Helmdon

Syresham

Whitfield

Turweston

BRACKLEY

BANBURY

Charlton

Cottisford

Hethe

Fringford

Stratton
Audley

BICESTER

Croughton

Fritwell

Tingewick

BUCKINGHAM

Epwell

BraILES

Stourton

Whichford

Hook
Norto.

Swerford

Great Rollright

Little
Tew

Enstone

Sandford

Middle
Barton

Steeple Aston

Caulcott

Woodstock

Kirtlington

Hampton
Poyle

Kidlington

Wolvercote

Shipston
on Stour

Long
Compton

CHIPPING
NORTON

Charlbury

WITNEY

OXFORD

Stowe on
the Wold

N

5 miles

● MARKET TOWNS
● Villages

Figure 6. Banbury and its Hinterland.

The most important road vehicles servicing Banbury were neither the lumbering waggons nor the speedy stage coaches, but the humble carriers' carts which brought in country people and their produce, and distributed merchandise from the town to the agricultural districts. 'Some idea may be formed of its commerce', wrote one observer of Banbury market in 1854, 'by the fact of nearly 300 carriers attending it, many of whom visit it on two other days in the week'. In 1831, 167 carriers made 367 journeys per week into the town. By 1841, 192 carriers made 437 journeys.[32] Banbury well deserved the appellation 'the metropolis of the carriers' carts'. Its services bear comparison with those of much larger Midland county towns, like Northampton which had 290 services in 1849, or Derby which had 465 in 1846.[33] In 1847 the carriers were described as 'those who earn a hard liveliehood by their two or three days a week attendance at Banbury and upon whose care the traders are, most of them, dependent for the regular transaction of a good portion of their business'.[34]

The most popular day for carriers' visits to Banbury was Thursday, the principal market day, on which about 190 carriers entered the town. In 1835 business on Thursdays was said to be very brisk, while the rest of the week was a time of comparative leisure for traders.[35] Most services on Tuesdays, Wednesdays and Fridays were provided by carriers from nearby villages who operated daily. About a quarter of the weekly calls were made on Mondays, and the popularity of Saturday, with about 15 per cent of the calls, grew steadily.[36] The carrying trade was concentrated at certain public houses. Most popular in 1831 were the *Plough* and the *Waggon and Horses*, each of which received 40 calls per week. Twenty-six public houses were involved in the trade in 1831 and 24 in 1851. The *Bear*, which had 11 services in 1831 and 31 in 1851, and the *Old George* whose total of nine rose to 31, both substantially increased their trade, while the *Talbot*, an important carrying inn in 1831, did not cater for the trade 20 years later.[37]

The year 1836 marked the zenith of stage coach and waggon services from Banbury. In October 1837 the London and Birmingham Railway was opened from London to Tring. Some London coaches then ran to Aylesbury to connect with an omnibus which met the trains at Tring. Early in 1838 Banburians were concerned that the LBR would be detrimental to the town, and the building of a new turnpike road to Weedon station, or a horse tramway to Blisworth were considered.[38] It was feared that such projects would be rendered redundant by the North and South Junction Railway, projected to run from Basingstoke to Stonebridge near Coventry.[39] In 1838 the turnpike trust improved the road between Middleton Cheney and Brackley which formed part of the route from Banbury to several stations on the LBR.[40]

After 1838 road services from Banbury underwent a series of kaleidoscopic changes, responding feverishly to the opening of railways, which continued until Banbury's own lines began to operate in 1850. On Monday 9 April 1838 the LBR was opened to Denbigh Hall, north of Bletchley, about 31 miles from Banbury. A coach called *The Railway* began to run from the *Red Lion* to Denbigh Hall, bringing the time for a journey to London down to six hours. In May 1838 freight services commenced between London and Banbury through Denbigh Hall. Later in the year the LBR was opened throughout, and Wolverton station became the railhead for Banbury. In October 1838 the Royal Mail coach service from London to Birmingham which had run through Banbury was transferred to the railway, and a feeder mail coach began to run to Wolverton.[41] In 1838 there were 13 departures a week for London via Wolverton, but 15 services a week still

24   VICTORIAN BANBURY

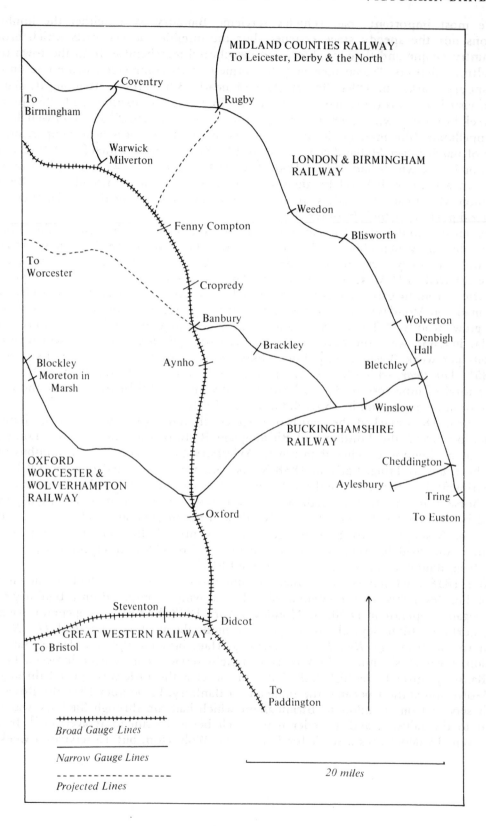

Fig. 7. Banbury's Railheads and Railways, 1838-53

did the whole journey by road. On 10 June 1839 a branch from the LBR at Cheddington to Aylesbury was opened, and in April 1840 a new coach and rail service from Banbury to London in six and a quarter hours was inaugurated by this route. Another service to London connected with the trains at Weedon. In 1840 the Midland Counties Railway was opened from Derby to Rugby, and the *Regulator* service to Leicester was diverted to Rugby station, where it connected with trains to York. On 1 June 1840 the Great Western Railway was completed from Paddington to Steventon, ten miles from Oxford. An omnibus to Oxford connected with another which ran to Steventon, where passengers joined a train to Paddington. On 12 June 1844 the Great Western branch from Didcot to Oxford was opened, and coaches from Banbury began to connect at Oxford station with trains to London. Also in 1844 a branch was opened from the LBR at Coventry to Milverton Station, Warwick, which then became the terminus for the *Regulator* coach from Oxford and Banbury which had previously run to Birmingham.[42] In 1845 one through coach service to London survived, but most passengers went by coach and rail, either through Oxford, or by way of Weedon, Wolverton or Aylesbury on the LBR. The best time by the LBR route was 5 hr. 30 min., but the GWR claimed that one service did the journey in 5 hr. 25 min. By 1848 the long distance stage coach routes through Banbury had all been abandoned, and services were entirely orientated on the railway stations at Milverton, Rugby, Weedon, Wolverton, Aylesbury and Oxford. Most freight was directed to the railways, but some waggons ran direct to London until 1850, and the Birmingham services continued until 1852.[43]

The Oxford Canal was opened from its junction with the Coventry Canal at Hawkesbury to Banbury in 1778, and was completed to Oxford in 1790. Banbury became a canal town of repute, with three wharves, canal-side limekilns and timber yards, and a dock for building and repairing boats. In the 1830s Banbury had six or seven fly boat services a week in each direction, taking small consignments southwards to Oxford and London, and to destinations throughout the north and Midlands. During the 1840s some services were transferred to road and rail, but one company continued to operate a daily fly boat in each direction. Two market boats a week sailed to Oxford.[44] There was a heavy through traffic of bulk loads along the canal to the Thames. In 1842, 9,900 boats, an average of 190 a week, passed over Claydon summit north of Banbury. The main traffics were minerals southward-bound from the Midlands, and agricultural produce passing northwards. William Ward whose company traded at the Old Wharf, Banbury, said in 1841 that their trade was principally the carriage of coal, slate and salt from Staffordshire and Leicestershire, and of grain in the opposite direction. In 1845 about 30,000 tons of coal a year, brought by canal from South Staffordshire, were consumed in the Banbury area, and some 50,000 tons used around Oxford would have passed through. Each year 3,000 tons of general merchandise left Banbury by canal for Birmingham, Liverpool and Manchester, and 10,000 tons of grain and hay was sent to Birmingham and the Black Country.[45]

On the night of 30 March 1851 seven canal boats were moored at Banbury with their crews sleeping on board, and 33 boatmen spent the night in the town. Many were natives of Banbury or of canalside villages like Bletchington, Thrupp and Shipton. The majority stayed in Mill Lane and Cherwell Street near the wharves, but two passed the night in the notorious *Royal Oak* beerhouse in Calthorpe Street.[46]

Banbury's market was one of the principal trading centres in the Midlands. A dealer told a government commissioner in 1845 that it was the largest market he knew, and when asked 'In all respects do you consider Banbury to be a very important place?', he replied 'Just so'. C. S. Read described Banbury in 1854 as 'the most businesslike and thriving town in the county', and compared it favourably in this respect with Oxford. In the mid-1840s about 350,000 quarters of corn were annually despatched northwards from Banbury by canal, and grain traffic to Birmingham was quoted as evidence of the need for a railway. Barley was sent to brewers in Dudley, and wool to Leicester and Kidderminster. Waggons and vans took butter, pigs, sheep and poultry to the London markets, and one Banbury carrier retained an agent at Newgate to handle his butter business. Cattle were driven from Banbury to Smithfield, and the brothers Buckett purchased fat sheep in the district to be driven to London.[47] The wholesale trade in agricultural produce was Banbury's most important economic activity, but it employed only 64 people, 1.58 per cent of the town's workforce.[48] The turnover in milling, woolstapling and seed businesses seems to have been substantial, and it is possible that such concerns operated at lower profit margins than most retailers. The transactions of one firm of millers and mealmen who banked with Gilletts occupied 42 ledger pages in three years, a quite exceptional figure.[49]

Banbury's economy revolved around its two long-established banks. The Cobb family had been active in the weaving trade and the Presbyterian congregation since the early 18th century. Their Old Bank in High Street, founded in 1783, was administered successively by Timothy Cobb (1755-1839), and by his sons Timothy Rhodes Cobb (1797-1875) and Edward Cobb (1806-1899). It was amalgamated in 1853 with banks from Buckingham and Aylesbury to form the Buckinghamshire and Oxfordshire Union Bank, which was absorbed by Lloyds Bank in 1902.[50] The New Bank in Cornhill was founded by Richard Heydon in 1784, and on his retirement in 1819 it was bought by the Tawney family, who in 1822 sold it to Joseph Ashby Gillett, a Quaker from Shipston-on-Stour, who had acted as an agent for Cobbs. Henry Tawney, then a minor, retained a partnership in the concern. Gillett purchased the bank with the aid of a loan from his brother-in-law, Joseph Gibbons, whose family had holdings in banks in Birmingham and Swansea. The New Bank only narrowly survived the financial crisis of 1825, but by the 1830s it was prospering.[51]

Both banks were owned by Dissenting families whose wealth originated in weaving. Both families lived in imposing houses in the town centre. Both owned property in the town. Yet the two banks epitomised the polarisation of local society. The Cobbs were conscious of their long Dissenting lineage, and their radicalism, and were proud that their family motto 'God with us' was that of the New Model Army.[52] They were active in many organisations identified with Liberalism and Dissent. Joseph Ashby Gillett was circumspect in his political views, but his partner Henry Tawney was a Conservative parliamentary candidate, and it was believed that Gillett himself was a Tory. He supported such Dissenting causes as the British Schools, but his customers included Anglican charitable societies, the Poor Law Union, the Agricultural Association and several Conservative landowners, all of which identified the bank with the Church of England and the Conservative Party. It is doubtful whether majority of either bank's customers decided where to deposit their money for reasons which were primarily ideological. Banbury Conservatives often complained that farmers and gentry behaved treasonably by banking with Cobbs. Nevertheless organisations which had political or religious affiliations deposited their money accordingly, and the banks stood on either side of the deepest division in local respectable society.

The profession of attorney was one of the traditional occupations of all market towns. Between 1653 and 1723 eight different attorneys are recorded in the Banbury baptisms and burials register.[53] The market town solicitors were the principal local agents of the major insurance companies. They channelled the savings of the moderately wealthy into profitable investments. They facilitated transfers of land and businesses. They were sometimes entrepreneurs in the development of property. Their creative instincts are largely obscured by their traditional professional reticence, but their role in the community in the early 19th century was essentially positive rather than passive. The number of legal practices in Banbury between 1830 and 1851 varied between seven and ten, the fluctuations being caused by amalgamations, and the attempts of newcomers to establish themselves.[54] The practices of the Bignell and Alpin families were linked with the North family of Wroxton Abbey and the old corporation, and their traditions were continued by Conservative solicitors like George Moore, clerk to the Poor Law Union. In the early 1830s there came to prominence a group of solicitors who influenced the development of the local economy at many critical points, dominated local government, and provided leadership and direction for many important voluntary organisations. The oldest among them was James Wake Golby, senior partner in the practice of Golby, Munton and Draper, a Unitarian, who was aged 60 in 1830. His partner, John Munton, an Anglican, was 46 in 1830, and a native of Bow, Middlesex. Their junior was Thomas Draper, aged 27 in 1830, a native of Kenilworth, whose family had land at Culworth. In 1831 he married the daughter of another Banbury solicitor, Thomas Tims, and was for some years tenant of the Vicarage. Tims was born in Cropredy, was 51 in 1830, and had been in Banbury since before 1810. He was an Anglican, and it was said at the time of his death in 1860 that he was 'a devoted supporter of liberal views before liberalism became fashionable'. Francis Francillon, great-grandson of a Huguenot refugee, and son of a purser in the Royal Navy, moved to work in Thomas Tims's office in 1838 after a spell in Chipping Norton. He professed no religion, but his wife was a Quaker and he was buried in the Friends' graveyard at Adderbury. Two other lawyers were connected with the group but were not active in public affairs until the late 1830s. John Munton's son William was aged only 15 in 1830. Edward, younger son of Timothy Cobb, qualified as a solicitor as well as a banker, but he was only 24 in 1830 and at that time had no interest in public affairs. The reputations of the various partnerships varied. Like Cobbs Bank, the firm of Golby, Munton and Draper was a prestigious concern which attracted the custom of many wealthy men who did not share the partners' political views. By contrast, Francis Francillon was renowned as an expert in electoral registration, and as an eloquent and passionate advocate for disadvantaged or unpopular defendants. He made a magnificent declaration of the rights of the meanest defendants to legal representation when acting for two prostitutes in 1859.[55] This group comprised less than half the solicitors in Banbury but their influence was out of all proportion to their number. They were the source of much of the movement towards change in the town. Like most market town lawyers they had considerable funds at their disposal. As a Banbury clergyman remarked, 'the country attorney's office was often the office of a money lender — money lent on land or furniture or even on stock on farms or in workshops'.[56] The solicitors actively promoted railways, housing developments and public utilities. As political and administrative innovators they shaped the character of the town. They can well be likened to the groups of native lawyers who in the 20th century have guided ex-colonial territories into independence.

The number of medical practices in Banbury between 1830 and 1850 varied between four and eight, and in 1851 there were 12 doctors in the town. The doctors had many family connections with the legal profession. The much-respected Robert Brayne was succeeded by his nephews Henry Robert and Thomas Brayne, both of whom married into solicitors' families. John Wise was succeeded by his son Robert Stanton Wise, and his daughter was the second wife of Thomas Draper. Charles Brickwell married the daughter of John Munton. The evidence which the doctors presented to the Board of Health enquiry in 1849 shows that they were well acquainted with the conditions in the poorest parts of the town, and the profession provided numerous councillors, several mayors, and officers in many voluntary societies. Eighteen men and 49 women were engaged in teaching in Banbury in 1851, in establishments which ranged from dame schools, through the publicly accountable institutions, to exclusive boarding schools. There were 82 pupils at five boarding schools in the town. Most of their scholars were drawn from the locality, but the schools run by Rebecca Eason and Genevieve Dupins attracted support from a wider area. At the principal boys' school, Samuel Hill's Banbury Academy, 18 of the 27 boarders were the sons of farmers.[57]

Retailers and craftsmen formed over 30 per cent of the working population of Banbury. It is impossible to draw a clear distinction between the two. Most self-employed craftsmen sold the shoes, suits, saddles or sofas which they had made, just as grocers, ironmongers, butchers and drapers sold goods produced by others. The variety of goods made in Banbury was remarkable, including clay tobacco pipes, organs, wood carvings, barometers, guns, pumps, trunks, gloves, umbrellas, candles and soda water. Appellations like 'cabinet maker', 'watchmaker' and 'tinplate worker' obscured numerous specialisms. Apart from cloth, hosiery and imported foods, there were few goods on sale in Banbury that could not have been produced in the town.

It is also difficult to distinguish masters from employees. Many shoemakers and tailors who worked on their own accounts, also undertook tasks for other masters, while men on the tramp constantly swelled the number of journeymen in the town. Shoemakers paused on their way to work in Oxford in term time, and in 1851 there were seven tailors staying at the *Catherine Wheel*, which may have been the tailors' trade house.[58] Eighteen shoemakers were listed in the directory in 1832, 26 in 1841, and 29 in 1851, but the number of people working in the trade rose from 84 to 166 between 1841 and 1851. Only one Banbury shoemaker in 1851 employed as many as six people, and 11 of the journeymen in the town appear to have been on the tramp. There were 13 master tailors listed in the 1832 directory, 23 in 1841 and 24 in 1851. The censuses show 94 men in the trade in 1841 and 107 in 1851. There were 211 dressmakers in 1851, nearly twice the number of tailors.[59]

Most of the principal retailers in Banbury, together with the main inns and the two banks, were grouped in the Market Place and adjacent parts of High Street, Parson's Street and Bridge Street. There were few shops of importance to the west of Church Lane or east of the junction of Bridge Street and Mill Lane. Within this central area, and among the less fashionable tradesmen of Broad Street, Calthorpe Lane and Fish Street, it was the universal practice for craftsmen or shopkeepers to live on the premises where they worked. Only a few bankers and solicitors lived in houses separated from their workplaces in the 1830s.

On average the drapers, grocers, chemists and ironmongers employed less than two people each, but the leading men in each trade employed six or even more. In 1851

James Austin, a chemist, employed an assistant and two apprentices who lived in and three porters who did not. Joseph Malsbury, a grocer, employed six, of whom two male assistants and two apprentices lived in. In 1841 Robert Kirby, a draper, had seven warehousemen and an assistant living in, and his household in 1851 included two sons in the trade, two assistants, a clerk and an apprentice. Retailing was not dominated by long-established family firms. Of 43 drapers, grocers, ironmongers and chemists in the town centre in 1851, only 14 had been born in Banbury, 11 came from nearby villages and 18 from such distant places as Bath, Eardisley (Herefs.) and Staines (Middx.). In 1857, when Banbury was more prosperous than it had been in earlier decades, a newspaper said the town was 'overstocked in every department of business'.[60] This was much more the case in the 1830s. Rivalry between traders was fierce, but competition was inhibited by trade regulations and unwritten conventions. Hours of opening were long but regulated. In 1845 it was agreed that shops should close at 7.00 p.m. in winter,

Figure 8. Shops in High Street (Alfred Beesley, History of Banbury, *Plate XXIII)*

but this closure time was not being observed in 1857, and it was always ignored on Saturdays.[61] The shoemaker who wished to exceed the regulated hours had to complete his hammering before closure time, and continue with less noisy tasks in a blacked-out room.[62]

Shopping habits were closely observed. To Elizabeth Gaskell's Miss Browning the opportunity to furnish a house was welcome, because 'the disposal of money involved the patronage of tradespeople'.[63] To shop was to choose, not just between competing merchants, but between Tories and Liberals, between churchmen and Dissenters. In the town of Mark Rutherford's first pastorate there were 'two shops of each trade, one which was patronised by Church and Tories and another by Dissenters and Whigs'.[64] There were many more shops in Banbury in 1832, 16 butchers, 17 grocers, and 18 bakers, and the man seeking to buy a watch or have a haircut had the choice of four jewellers or six hairdressers. Nevertheless the situation was essentially that which Rutherford described. Religion, politics and membership of voluntary societies could substantially affect a trader's business. As late as 1874 a Banbury co-operator summed up the unenviable lot of the market town trader:

'Look at the shopkeeper, willingly or unwillingly compelled to sacrifice every vestige of manly independence, especially he whose lot is cast in a country town. He worships his Maker, not after the dictates of his own conscience, but of that of his customers. He votes at an election, not to serve his country, or to save her from ruin, but to please his customers; in short, his every action is governed by his till. He . . . depends upon the will and caprice of others for bread and is a slave'.[65]

Pressure could be exercised by the organised working-class as well as by the wealthy. The political power of the working-class shopper in Huddersfield was summed up in the song title 'Non-electors can Vote on a Saturday Night'.[66] In Banbury threats of exclusive dealing were commonplace. When the shoemaker George Herbert attracted aristocratic patronage his rivals claimed it was because he was a Tory.[67] The position of the trader was further weakened by the long credit which was customarily given to upper and middle-class customers. Herbert related that he was never so poor as when his business was at its most successful:

'I could have got along well if I could have got in the money, but my customers were all noblemen, parsons, lawyers and doctors, and the parsons were the worst of all to pay. I used now to go out into the country . . . not for orders, but to look up money for wages &c.'[68]

In 1847 it was proposed to make half-yearly rather than annual tendering of accounts the regular practice in the town, and the *Banbury Guardian* quoted with approval the remarks of a Somerset contemporary:

'Tradesmen look forward with keen solicitude to the end of the year when they may without fear of offence present yearly or half-yearly bills. On their success in receiving these accounts, much of their personal comfort and that of their families depends'.[69]

In such circumstances the pressures of working-class customers who paid cash or were granted only short credit were naturally powerful.

The inhibitions of retailing in Victorian market towns may explain the popularity of the doctrine of Self-Help, not as a creed for action, but as a testament of achievement from which vicarious compensatory pleasures could be sought. Orators who extolled men who rose to greatness from humble origins probably had much appeal for tradesmen who faced many competitors, but were forbidden by convention to compete aggressively with them. For the retailer there were few escape routes from such frustrations, but there were possibilities open to craftsmen which were of great significance in the market town economy.

One was a horizontal method of escape, the spreading of the trader's energies into additional occupations. Many trades could be combined with part-time government posts which were eagerly sought. There was fierce competition for the most menial jobs offered by the Poor Law Union in 1835.[70] J. G. Walford, a watchmaker, was Registrar of Marriages. William Thompson, chairmaker, was Superintendent of the Borough Police. William Hutchings, basket maker, was High Bailiff to the County Court. William Brain, the postmaster, sold leather to shoemakers.[71] Robert Gardner, the gaoler, 'embarked in trade and filled numerous lucrative employments during his gaolership'.[72] Innkeeping could easily be combined with other jobs. Several Banbury public houses took their names from their landlords' trades, and may have served as trade houses. In the Bridge Street area in 1851, a butcher ran the *Railway Inn*, a millwright the *Millwrights' Arms*, a coal merchant the *Steam Packet*, a boatman the *Jolly Waterman*, a farmer the *Leathern Bottle*, a hairdresser the *Britannia* and a plasterer the *Fox*. The landlord of the *Swan* was a rose grower, lattice wire maker, auctioneer and sheriff's officer. The licensee of the *Woolpack* was a sausage maker, gingerbread dealer, tripe seller, cork cutter, baker and brewer.[73]

Secondary occupations, which demanded no formal qualifications, like photography, the selling of newspapers and insurance and the operation of servant registries expanded considerably in the 1830s and '40s. George Herbert, a shoemaker, adopted his hobby, photography, as his means of livelihood. Toy dealing and selling stationery were common secondary occupations. William Bunton, foundry fitter and Chartist, was a newsagent and toy dealer. Richard Hale, a saddler, was a newsvendor, and his wife and daughter were dressmakers. Thomas Willetts, a hairdresser, sold toys, while his wife made breeches and gloves. Insurance was one of the retailer's easiest means of horizontal expansion. The 1851 census reveals only one full-time insurance official in Banbury, but the directory in that year lists 23 agents for fire and life offices. Seven were solicitors, but the remainder included a chemist, a dentist, two ironmongers, a draper, a printer, a grocer, a timber merchant and a bank clerk. An insurance agency could provide extra income for a man who subsisted largely on private means. James Cadbury held two agencies after he gave up his grocery business in 1846, and Alfred Beesley, the historian, was agent to the Norwich Union when he was not following literary and scientific pursuits.[74] Servants' registration offices were first listed in the Banbury directory in 1843. In 1854 a newspaper claimed that they were rendering useless the traditional hiring fairs.[75] This was not the case, but they certainly attracted some business. There were six offices in 1851, kept by a hosier, a grocer, a shoemaker, an eating house proprietor and two milliners.

Several bank clerks had secondary occupations. John Conworth, clerk at Cobbs, lived at the bank, where his daughter ran a school. William Sutton Owen, a clerk at Gilletts, had a hatter's business. Sylvester Caines of the London and County Bank ran an insurance agency. The most enterprising bank clerk was William Barrett, who, by 1825, was earning £100 p.a. as a clerk at Gilletts. Two years later he was expelled from the Society of Friends for being married by a priest. In 1841 he was living at the bank, and operated an insurance agency, a corn and malt business and a milk-selling concern. During the 1840s he began a steam saw mill and a brickyard. In 1851 he was still clerk for Gilletts and employed six men and a boy on his own account.[76]

The other means of securing independence from political and religious pressures was by vertical development, the production of articles of such originality or such high quality that they could be sold beyond the confines of Banbury, or were indispensible to townspeople. The market town community could thus stimulate innovation and excellence. The Mayor boasted in 1850 that the townspeople had 'taken out more patents for their own inventions and improvements on the inventions of others, than, perhaps, any town of its size in the kingdom'.[77] One Banbury watchmaker built a machine for tagging laces, while another drew the wires which were used for cutting the pile of plush. A cutler made such excellent buckshorn-handled knives that country people reckoned to buy no others. In a letter from upstate New York in 1833, an emigrant pleaded with his father to 'bring a pocket knife for me, of Thomas's make, Banbury'.[78] William Bigg, chemist, and founder of the Mechanics' Institute, invented a well-known sheep dipping composition.[79] No less than 12 Banbury tradesmen exhibited in the Crystal Palace in 1851.[80] Many succeeded in reaching national markets. The printer and publisher, J. G. Rusher, sold children's books all over the country.[81] The makers of Banbury Cakes sent their wares 'by coach, chaise, waggon, cart horse and foot into all parts of this kingdom'. Samuel Beesley sent Cakes to America and, once, to Australia, and in 1838 Daniel Claridge despatched 400 dozen to the East Indies.[82] Cakes were usually despatched in wickerwork baskets made from willows in the local osier beds by Banbury's 16 basket makers.

There were two major manufacturing industries in Banbury. One, the making of plush was long-established. The other, the manufacture of agricultural implements, was in the process of emerging from the local ironmongery and millwrighting trades.

Textiles had flourished in Banbury since the Middle Ages. In the early 18th century the parish registers recorded garter, jersey, silk, linen, woollen and worsted weavers.[83] The manufacture of girth cloth was of some importance by 1750, but the speciality of the region became the making of shags or plush, a fabric with a double warp of two twisted threads of worsted or cotton, and a weft of a single thread of silk or mohair. It was used for upholstery, hats and liveries, and for finishing processes in the manufacture of other high quality fabrics. Plush was sold in an international market, and in the 1790s it was suggested, with some exaggeration, that most of it went to Russia.[84] The trade was characterised by a strong weavers' club. One master complained in 1787, 'Banbury is not the place for a manufactory, the Masters being so much under the control of the workmen', and a JP reported in 1793, 'they have associated . . . formed laws of their own, and set those of the country at defiance'. The club was re-constituted in 1822 when it still controlled entry into the trade.[85] Throughout the first half of the 19th century there were three or four firms active in the trade, although amalgamations and changes in the partnerships were frequent. When trade was plentiful, wages reached 30s. and even 40s. a week, but slumps were frequent, and plushmaking was often said to be in decline.

In 1838 the Banbury plush trade was controlled by three firms, Gilletts with 150 looms, the brothers Baughen with 120, and Harris, Banbury and Harris with 160. There were about 300 weavers in the district, many of whom worked several looms. In 1841 there were 105 resident in the town, 18 at Brailes, 35 at Shutford, 34 at Bloxham, 27 at Middleton Cheney and 34 at Adderbury.[86] Most of the worsted yarn was brought in from elsewhere. Baughens had a factory in which there were 30 hand-looms, but most weavers worked at home, and the masters' premises were used chiefly for commissioning and taking orders. Most of the cloth was dyed and finished in Banbury. In 1837 Gilletts purchased an embossing machine from Henry Bessemer, which enabled them to supply orders for Windsor Castle and the House of Commons. The trade club formed a lodge of Robert Owen's Grand National Consolidated Trades Union in 1834, but the masters refused to employ those involved, the lodge was dissolved, and the club was never again so powerful. In 1838 it had only 21 members, although it was still able to forbid the entry of women to the trade, to restrict entry to the eldest sons of weavers, and to ensure that each man took only one apprentice. Wages averaged £30 a year in 1838, a lower level than in the 1790s.[87] Plush-weaving was severely affected by the economic crisis of 1839-42. Gilletts suffered a heavy loss in 1842, when the family home was surrounded by about 100 demonstrating weavers. They gave up plushmaking in 1848-49, and were disappointed to receive only £6,000 for the business. Harris, Banbury and Harris gave up in 1843-44.[88] In 1851 there were 123 plush weavers in Banbury with 16 women and unskilled men employed in hair combing, winding, harness-making, shaving and portering. The trade employed 4.5 per cent of the working population. About half the weavers in Banbury had been born in the surrounding countryside, seven at Middleton Cheney, eight at Bloxham and six in Adderbury, but none in Shutford, where the trade still prospered. Among the weavers in Neithrop were several recent migrants. James Wright had several children, one aged only four, who had been born in Adderbury. Henry Hunt had children of four and two born at Little Bourton. Fewer plushmakers worked at home. By 1851, 88 people were employed at Baughens' factory in North Bar, where only 30 had worked in 1838. Worsted and mohair yarns were spun on 1,056 spindles with a 12 h.p. steam engine, but no attempts were made to introduce power looms at Banbury.[89]

The weavers had a reputation for their skills, their education and their political maturity. George Herbert's father was proud of his ability to turn to any branch of the trade.[90] They strongly supported the old Dissenting denominations. In Neithrop almost 40 per cent of the weavers were Dissenters, compared with 25 per cent of the tradesmen and 10 per cent of the labourers. Many weavers lived in overcrowded houses on The Bank in Neithrop or in Monument Street. Their living conditions were no better than those of the rest of the working-class nor were their wages higher. Their claim to be the labour aristocracy of Banbury was based on skill, education and prestige. By 1851 there was evidence that weavers were steadily leaving the trade. Thomas Caroll made his living by carrying a basket, two had become tailors and four were labourers. The conditions regulating entry to the trade had been discarded. Four families in Neithrop had two sons who were weavers. Yet the average age of weavers in 1851 was lower than in 1841. Only 12 of the weavers in Banbury were over 60, while there had been 25 in that age group in 1841. Nearly 80 per cent of the weavers in 1851 were under 50 and 19 were under 20.[91]

The Cobb family's weaving business catered for a national market, but the estimate in 1838 that it employed 40 people seems an exaggeration, although a substantial factory had been built the previous year. Nine girth weavers were recorded in the 1841 census and seven in 1851, which suggests that the trade was not of major significance in the town's economy.[92]

The proportion of the working population engaged in engineering was small, 90 individuals, or 2.21 per cent, but the industry in 1851 was on the eve of a period of expansion, a development of the skills which had been growing among Banbury's ironmongers and millwrights since 1800. Ironmongers sold agricultural implements made by millwrights, and sometimes sponsored the production of particular items, or took up ironfounding themselves. At the Banbury Agricultural Association meeting in 1838 Richard Edmunds, the ironmonger, attracted attention with a chaff-cutter made for him by a Mr. Riley, a member of a well-known Banbury family of millwrights, and the implement won for Edmunds the silver medal of the Agricultural Society of Scotland in 1841.[93]

The most important of the Banbury ironmongers was James Gardner, born in 1785, a Baptist, and a member of a family who had long been in the trade. In 1839 he leased land in Parson's Meadow Lane from Lyne Spurrett and Edward Cobb, and set up a small foundry for the manufacture of a hay and straw cutter patented in 1815, a fat cutter for soap and candle makers, and the Banbury Turnip Cutter, patented in 1834. He acquired a considerable reputation. When another firm produced a turnip cutter at the 1845 Royal Show, a critic commented, 'Mr. Gardner of Banbury has at length met formidable rivals'. He purchased the freehold of the foundry site in 1844, and by the time of his death on St Stephen's Day 1846 he was employing between 20 and 30 people. An obituarist described him as: 'the inventor of many clever pieces of mechanism', and claimed there was a demand for the turnip cutter from the continent and the colonies far beyond any possible supply. Gardner himself had boasted 'no machine has ever been offered to the public that will cut turnips into pieces of the same size with so little labour or that is so little liable to get out of repair'.[94]

The other important engineering concern was that of Charles and John Lampitt who had a millwright's shop at the junction of Paradise and Water Lane in Neithrop which dates from 1796. About 1837 they set up the Vulcan Foundry on the opposite side of the Warwick Road. Soon afterwards they supplied a steam pumping engine to John Hunt's brewery, and in 1847 one of their engines was demonstrated working a threshing machine.[95]

Engineering in Banbury was based on the workshop rather than the factory. In Neithrop there were 27 skilled men, but only seven foundry labourers. Ten of the 27 were Banburians, almost all of them Lampitts or Rileys, one came from a local village, and the rest from as far away as Devon, Essex and Newcastle-upon-Tyne. They were predominantly young men, who, if they were married, lived in comfortable houses, and they showed greater indifference to religion than any other occupational group.[96]

The scale of the engineering industry changed radically after the death of James Gardner. His son, also James, was only 18, and his executors, A. B. Rye the surgeon and his kinsman Benjamin Gardner, decided to retain the ironmonger's shop in High Street but to sell the foundry, which, with the rights for the turnip and chaff cutters, 'patented machines in great request', was put on the market in January 1847. It was not until August 1849 that Rye and Gardner agreed with Bernhard Samuelson, the 29-year-old son of a Jewish mercantile family, with interests in Hull and Liverpool, to lease the foundry for seven years from 1 September 1849, from which time it was called the Britannia Works. Samuelson had served a commercial apprenticeship, and in 1841 took charge of the continental business of Sharpe, Stewart and Co. the Manchester engineers. In 1846 he established a locomotive works at Tours, but was driven back to England by the French Revolution of 1848. His first contacts with Banbury probably came through his brother Martin, who worked as an engineer on the Buckinghamshire Railway, and married a surgeon's daughter from Middleton Cheney in March 1849. By local standards Gardner's foundry was a substantial business, and the difficulties encountered in selling it may have caused concern to the town's rulers. A. B. Rye was closely identified with the Liberal élite, and it is likely that Cobbs' Bank were involved in the sale. Many years later Samuelson referred to 'Mr. (T. R.) Cobb . . . my oldest friend in Banbury'.[97]

The only industry comparable with textiles and engineering in Banbury was brewing and malting, in which 48 people were directly employed in 1851. The most important brewery was that in North Bar which had belonged to James Barnes, the canal engineer, who was twice mayor of Banbury. In 1803 his daughter married Richard Austin, who by 1808 was a partner in the brewery. The following year Austin built the substantial house now number 51 The Green. In 1814 the whole business became his property on payment of 5 per cent per annum to Barnes on his share. It was valued at £37,061, and included 23 public houses and two malthouses. In 1832 the brewery was assessed for the Poor Rate at £96 10s. 0d., by far the most valuable property in the borough. The *Red Lion* hotel, by comparison, was worth £72 10s. 0d. In 1840 hops and spirits were being purchased from dealers in London and conveyed to Banbury by canal. George Herbert recalled that ale was exported to India, and, on two consecutive days in 1840, 63 and 66 casks were despatched to Liverpool. Other consignments were sent to Birmingham, Brierley Hill and London. The value of the concern declined between 1814 and the time of Austin's death in 1840, when it was assessed at £29,000. Only five of the 21 properties were then free of mortgage obligations. Control of the brewery passed to Barnes son of Richard Austin, who sold some of the property in 1842. In 1848–49 a partnership was negotiated with John Nixon Harman, and from 1850 the name Austin was dropped from the business. Cobbs Bank were probably involved in the merger, since Edward Cobb's father-in-law was one of the mortgagees, and the deal was negotiated by their associated solicitors, Draper and Munton.[98]

The other large brewery was that of Thomas and John Hunt. In 1807 Thomas Hunt the elder bought the *Unicorn* inn where he ran a malting business. By 1832 it had passed to his grandson John, who, about 1839, built a brewery in Bridge Street. By 1841 he had taken another Thomas Hunt as his partner. John Hunt died in 1848 and in 1850 William Edmunds entered the concern, which was employing 16 men the following year.[99]

Farming was an important part of the economy within as well as around Banbury. In 1851, 288 people in the parish were directly involved in farming and market gardening, and some of the 302 general labourers doubtless worked on farms. In the 1840s there were about 30 farms in the parish. The 1851 census records 29 farmers of whom 26 were working. They occupied some 3,432 of the 4,634 acres of the parish, and employed 140 people, less than 70 per cent of the farmworkers identified on the census. Banbury obviously functioned as an open village, providing accommodation for labourers on farms in nearby closed parishes. Most farm workers were born locally. There were only a few labourers from Ireland and distant parts of England in the town's lodging houses. Farm labouring was a largely hereditary occupation. In Neithrop, of 16 boys under 20 working on farms, only one was the son of a father employed outside agriculture, and few sons of farm workers followed any other occupation. Most started regular work about the age of 13, and few reached an active old age, only three of the 91 labourers in Neithrop being aged over 60.[100]

Banbury was a base for many hawkers who toured its hinterland. Flora Thompson recalled those who visited Juniper Hill: a fish and fruit salesman, a baker, a brewer's outrider, tinkers, grinders, gypsies with cabbage nets and clothes pegs, tramps with shoelaces, matches and lavender bags, and packmen and pedlars with haberdashery.[101] Many such travellers stayed in Banbury. In 1841 the *Queen's Head* accommodated nine clothmen and a silk mercer, all of them Irish, and three Irish linen dealers slept there ten years later. Most of the 42 hawkers staying in Banbury in 1851 were Irish. There were three silk mercers at the *Waggon and Horses*, and five travelling drapers at the adjacent house. James Killin of Crouch Street, born in Co. Down, was a silk mercer who had lived in Banbury since at least 1835. A hawker of toys born in Carlisle and a travelling jeweller born in Surrey stayed at the South Bar lodging house. Parked in Back

Lane was a cart from which Charles Hands, a native of Birmingham, conducted a travelling bazaar. At the *Crown* was Joseph Marks, a travelling jeweller, born in Poland. Banburians were involved in these trades through the 'swag' shops, like that of Jabez Thompson, where toys and cheap jewellery were supplied to hawkers.[102]

Banbury's major fairs were celebrated throughout the Midlands. The calendar of fairs was rationalised in 1836 by the new corporation. There were 13 annual fairs, most of which were cattle sales and had no other functions. Some hiring of farmworkers took place at the March fair, wool was sold in July, and the December fair featured fat cattle for the Christmas trade.[103] The Holy Thursday Fair was traditionally a holiday, but its recreational functions declined after a smallpox epidemic broke out at the event in 1827.[104] The horse fair held around Old Twelfth Day remained an important occasion throughout the 19th century. In 1850 the presence of many London dealers was reported, prices were high, and 'few who had a carthorse to sell did not get more money than they expected for it'.[105]

The Michaelmas Fair which attracted farmers, labourers, dealers, showmen, cheap jacks and pickpockets from all over England had a compelling magic which none of the other fairs could rival. The young Joseph Ashby, on his first visit in 1870, muttered 'Nijni Novgorod'. A few years later as he worked on the roadside at fair time, an aged traveller told him, 'I shall know I be an old man when I can't get to Banbury Fair'.[106] As a cattle sale the fair declined in the 1830s and '40s as more business was conducted at regular weekly and monthly markets. In 1832 there were 4,600 sheep, 1,220 cattle, 300 pigs and 200 horses on offer, and in 1834 over 1,500 cattle and 3,000 sheep. Such levels were not maintained. In 1846 there were only 1,000 cattle and 200 sheep.[107] The fair was the occasion for the sale of the soft, shallow, pale Banbury cheese, but supplies diminished during the 1840s. Only one cartload arrived in 1847 and none at all in 1848.[108] In other respects the fair flourished. It remained the occasion when farmers sold their grain crops. It was the greatest hiring fair in the south Midlands, and such crowds of grooms, waggoners, shepherds and dairymaids waited to be hired in the Market Place between Butchers Row and Parsons Street that shop windows had to be boarded up to avoid damage from the crush of humanity on the pavements.[109] The fair drew celebrated entertainments like Hilton's and Wombwell's menageries, and was a festival for pickpockets and swindlers. For Banbury shopkeepers, particularly the drapers, the fair began immediately after Michaelmas Day, as servants flocked to Banbury:

> 'Experience has taught them that there are few places which are accessible to them where they are so likely to get their money's worth for their money, or find so extensive a choice'.[110]

Some shopkeepers could do little business during the fair itself, since their windows were boarded up or blocked by stalls, but the fair period, when crops were sold and labourers were paid, was clearly the peak of Banbury's trading year.

The Michaelmas Fair epitomised the complexities of the relationship between Banbury and its hinterland. Countrymen demonstrated by their attendance the importance they attached to the market town, and the town's economic dependence on the countryside was clearly evident. It was an occasion on which townsmen liked to feel their superiority, to be ironic about the lightness of foot of rustic dancers in the fair's ballrooms, to express disgust at the way in which labourers paraded for hire like slaves, to be shocked at how easily they were swindled by metropolitan tricksters. At fair time, as on the occasion of the gentry's annual ball, or the Wesleyan quarterly meeting or the Agricultural Association show, Banbury was the stage on which the dramas of the rural population took place. It was possible to see Banbury whether as a community of ungrateful traders who made money from farmers and landowners and refused them the political support which was their due, or as an oasis of political and cultural enlightenment in a desert of reaction. No one doubted that the town and the countryside were economically interdependent, but there were many points at which their cultures clashed. There was a fashion in the late 1830s for calling Banbury 'the Manchester of Agriculture'. Its relationship with its hinterland was as complex as that of 'the Manchester of Trade' with the nation at large.[111]

IV

TWO DISTINCT CAMPS:
THE CHURCHES IN BANBURY 1830-1851

*'There is no day in the week on which more general notice is taken than on Sunday:
there is no day on which differences are more apparent'.*[1]

'MR. EDMUNDS, Burgess and Methodist preacher', seconded the Reform candidate for Banbury in the election of 1831. 'Mr. Samuel Beesley, a member of the Society of Friends' helped to nominate the Liberal candidate in 1837.[2] To speak of a man's religion in Banbury in the 1830s and '40s was utterly unremarkable. The numbers of churchmen and dissenters on the borough council were sometimes quoted, like football scores, in the newspapers.[3] Church rates, Maynooth, Sabbatarianism and the toleration of Catholics were matters on which all active citizens had opinions. To say that a Banburian was a Calvinist, a Churchman or a Quaker revealed as much about him as to call him a butcher, a draper or a weaver.

Figure 9. Old St Mary's Church (from Alfred Beesley, History of Banbury, *Plate XIV)*

All of the major English denominations and a variety of sects were represented in Banbury in the early 19th century. The level of religious observance in the town was high. On the Sunday of the Ecclesiastical Census in 1851, 6,920 attendances were recorded at ten places of worship.[4] No sizeable meetings were excluded from the census,

38

but no returns were made for several minor gatherings, and the totals for four congregations were obviously rounded off. Using the formula devised by W. S. F. Pickering, expressing the number of people at the most numerously attended service at each church as a percentage of the population, the index figure for Banbury is 35.17, rather below the highest county figures, like Bedfordshire with 57, or Huntingdonshire with 55, but far above urban areas like Lancashire, which recorded 27, or London with 21.[5] The index figure for Banbury obtained by using the formula employed by Professor Inglis, reached by expressing the total attendances at all services of the day as a percentage of the population, is 78.7, well above the national index for England and Wales which is 61, and also above the national figure for rural areas, which is 71.4, and for towns with more than 10,000 people, which is 49.7.[6]

Banbury's medieval church was a magnificent Gothic structure, but by the late 18th century its north aisle and crossing were almost ruinous, and the best architectural opinion of the time was that restoration was not feasible.[7] An Act of Parliament was obtained in 1790 for its replacement, under which a trust was established to raise money for and carry out the work.[8] The church was demolished in the latter part of 1790, and early in 1791, before sufficient money had been raised or estimates obtained, the construction of a new church to the design of Samuel Pepys Cockerell was begun. It was decided to raise 75 per cent of the cost in bonds at five per cent interest. The church was opened in 1797, with its uncompleted tower untidily covered with boards, three years later than the Act specified, encumbered with debts, and for more than two decades a standing reproach to the town's ruling class.[9] In the years which followed the churchwardens often failed to collect the rate authorised by the Act of Parliament, and sometimes embezzled the proceeds when they did. Charles Robert Cockerell, the distinguished son of the original architect, completed the tower and portico in 1822. Rating assessments were changed in 1825, but the trustees were advised that, under the Act of 1790, they could collect money only under the old assessments. Some persisted in an attempt to try to use the new assessments, but many parishioners refused to pay. For a time no interest was paid to bondholders, but in 1827 the trustees admitted their inability to use the new assessments. The faction which insisted that the trust was bound by the 1790 Act included four Unitarians, and it formed one of the nuclei of the party of reform in Banbury. It was not until 1840 that the accounts of the architect and the builder were settled, and two further years elapsed before all the liabilities were met and the trust was wound up.[10]

S. P. Cockerell's church was an austere preaching box. The chancel was square-ended and blocked-off by the east gallery, whose occupants had their backs to the altar. The walls and pillars were whitewashed, and the windows filled with frosted glass. Seats for the charity schoolchildren were in the gallery by the organ, while the poor and the servants of the middle-class had 290 free sittings under the gallery from which it was almost impossible to hear what was said at the reading desk or in the pulpit. Morning prayer was a civic as well as a religious ritual. During the mayoralty of John Golby Rusher in 1834–35, the corporation assembled at Rusher's house for wine and biscuits before processing to church, where the mayor sat on a raised seat in the curtained corporation pew, facing the congregation.[11]

Thomas William Lancaster was Vicar of Banbury from 1815 to 1849, the longest incumbency in the history of the parish. He was born, the son of a clergyman, in 1787, and after taking his BA at Oriel, became Fellow of the Queen's College in 1812. On ordination as priest in the same year, he became curate at Banbury, and was preferred to the vicarage three years later. About 1823, nervous disorder, and perhaps also his academic ambitions, led him to leave the church in the charge of curates and to live in Oxford. Lancaster was a competent scholar, who won some of the consolation prizes of the academic world, the chaplaincy to the Lord Mayor of London in 1828, and the Bampton Lectureship in 1831, but failed in spite of many sychophantic letters to gain such prizes as the librarianship of the British Museum or the chair of classics at King's College, London. He augmented his income by publishing theological works, by tutoring in the university, and, in the 1840s, as under-master of Magdalen College School. His appearances in Banbury were sufficiently infrequent for a newspaper to refer in 1840 to 'that great stranger, the Vicar'.[12] Lancaster had a remarkable ability for making himself appear ridiculous. In the 1840s he still dressed in the high fashion of the days of his youth, in a tight black coat with pantaloons and knee-high Hessian boots adorned with tassels at the shins. In 1820 he was marooned in the Town Hall during an election riot. He climbed into the loft below the clock, then fell through the ceiling of the floor below, ending up bestriding a beam in mid-air. He shunned enthusiasm, yet he was fierce in controversy, and was removed from the list of preachers at the Queen's College for describing Renn Dickson Hampden as 'that atrocious professor' during a University Sermon. Dr. Edward Burton, Regius Professor of Divinity, regarded him as 'a learned but odd man'.[13] He was certainly ill-suited to represent the Established Church in a community in which religious controversy was becoming endemic.

The resident curate of Banbury throughout the 1830s was John Richard Rushton, a zealous Evangelical, and a 'resolute opponent of ritualism'. When, in 1840, his parishioners presented him with a silver plate towards which 370 people had subscribed, he was praised for his concern for the old, the young and the sick. Within a fortnight in the summer of 1839 he presided over the annual meetings of the National Schools, the Visiting Charitable Society and the Auxiliary Bible Society, and preached on thrift to the friendly societies on Club Day.[14] He established a Sunday School in 1834 and in 1838 endeavoured to provide an evening service at St Mary's.[15] Mass confirmations, a much-publicised activity in the Oxford diocese in the 1850s, were no novelty in Banbury. Five hundred were confirmed at St Mary's in May 1840, and over 600 in August 1843.[16] The church choir, founded in 1835, was a social institution of some consequence. In 1840, 1841 and 1842 festivals were arranged to raise money for rebuilding the organ. In 1841 *Messiah* was sung, and full cathedral services were performed.[17]

J. R. Rushton made no secret of his political allegiances. He told the Banbury Conservative Association in 1840 that 'he attended the meeting, not as their pastor . . . but as a brother Conservative . . . ready at all times to come forward in support of those Conservative principles which he felt proud to confess'. The following year he informed another Conservative meeting that in the 11 years he had been in Banbury, 'it had never occurred to him that he was acting inconsistently by aiding the good cause'.[18] The duty of upholding the Established Church against Dissent, Popery and infidelity was one of the foundations of political Conservatism in Banbury. Conservatism could be combined with a desire for the reform of abuses. Alfred Beesley, poet and historian, who resigned from the Society of Friends in 1825 to join the Church, and later the Conservative Party, upheld the Establishment with all the vigour of a convert.[19] He had a romantic view of the Church, combining it with a love of the Gothic, which led him to repudiate St Mary's as architecture which was un-Christian.[20] He had great respect for Rushton, to whom he wrote:

'May those sober days of temperate but sincere reform which we both hope are now about to beam upon the Church we love, present one of their chief benefits in the bringing together of such men as you to fill, alike in her proudest and humblest situations, the high duties and callings of her faithful ministers'.[21]

The Church of England in Banbury remained strong because it could call upon loyalties which overlay divisions of party and social class. Many of the Reform Party, the Muntons, Thomas Tims and the Braynes, were churchmen. The Church was the most popular denomination amongst the religious poor. In Neithrop in 1850 nearly 40 per cent of those actively committed to a church were Anglicans, and the proportion was highest among the least skilled.[22] Early in the 1840s there were up to 240 communicants in Banbury and as many as a thousand people attended some services.[23] The 1851 census reveals congregations at morning and evening services of about 1,300.[24] When Lancaster's successor claimed in 1854 that 'almost all the poor receive our ministrations and about half the other classes',[25] he was exaggerating, but the Establishment did enjoy the support of many of the poor.

Clergy from rural parishes considerably influenced the Church in Banbury. Local incumbents participated in the foundation of the Diocesan School, and in the Church Missionary Society, the British and Foreign Bible Society, the SPCK and the Society for Promoting Christianity amongst the Jews.[26] They ranged from arch-reactionaries, like Francis Litchfield, Rector of Farthinghoe, to Evangelical Liberals like John Jordan of Somerton. Whatever the attitudes of the clergy in Banbury on any issue, there were always local incumbents, some from the neighbouring dioceses of Lichfield and Peterborough, who took a contrary view. It was impossible for the Vicar of Banbury to enjoy the unchallenged authority of the incumbent of a rural parish for in the market town community the ambiguities of this Church were mercilessly exposed.

Fear of the Church of Rome was a strong motivating force amongst Anglicans in Banbury. In December 1939, 700 attended a lecture on Popery by the Revd. John Jordan of Somerton, at which nearly £5 was collected for the Martyrs' Memorial in Oxford.[27] In the public excitement which followed the apostasy of John Henry Newman in 1845, the Banbury Protestant Institute was established. It was a largely Anglican body which organised a programme of lectures in defence of the Church.[28] The proposal to build a second Anglican church in Banbury, conceived before 1840, was primarily a reaction against the Church of Rome. In 1850 members of the Establishment were urged:

'to give this substantial proof of your consistent and principled opposition to the Church of Rome . . . while affording church accommodation to your poorer brethren, have the pleasing satisfaction of speedily raising a memorial of your own opposition to Romish errors and superstitions'.[29]

In December 1840 J. R. Rushton was preferred to the vicarage of Hook Norton and replaced by Thomas Mardon, who was assisted by an evening lecturer, the Revd. J. Sanders, who was succeeded in 1845 by Charles Forbes who ultimately became vicar of the new parish of South Banbury. Samuel Wilberforce was appointed Bishop of Oxford in 1845, and quickly recognised 'the greatness of our needs in Banbury'.[30]

In 1849 he arranged an exchange of livings between the ageing Lancaster and William Wilson, an energetic priest, 27 years old, who held his family's living at Worton.[31] Wilson was able to build on a solid foundation. The Church in Banbury in the 1830s and '40s exhibited many abuses but it was neither thoroughly corrupt nor wholly ineffective.

The Presbyterians assembling at the Great Meeting were the aristocrats of Banbury's dissenters. The congregation had its origins in the ejection of the Puritan Samuel Wells from the vicarage of 1662. By 1716 meetings were held in a double-roofed chapel off the Horsefair. Under the leadership of the Cobb family the congregation flourished, and during the pastorate of C. B. Hubbard between 1814 and 1845 Unitarian theology was gradually adopted. Members had been influenced by the writings of Joseph Priestley, and by the example of Joseph Jevans, the Presbyterian minister at Bloxham.[32] In 1830 the Great Meeting included many of Banbury's trading and professional élite. Apart from the Cobb family, the trustees included James Wake Golby, the solicitor, Bernard and Lyne Spurrett, ironmongers, and William Potts, printer, and publisher of the *Banbury Guardian*.[33] In 1843 Hubbard was succeeded as minister by Henry Hunt Piper, father-in-law of Edward Cobb, and previously chaplain to the Shore family of Norton Hall, Sheffield.[34] In 1851 the congregation comprised between 100 and 150 adults,[35] only about six per cent of the worshippers in Banbury, but its influence far outweighed its lack of numbers. The Unitarian Sunday School, founded in 1802, was the oldest in Banbury and gave the first elements of education to 'some of the first gentlemen of business' in the town.[36]

The Banbury Quaker Meeting also originated in the 17th century. It endured severe persecution during the Interregnum and in the post-Restoration period.[37] A new meeting house was erected in 1750, but during the second half of the 18th century it was admitted that 'too many indulge themselves in a spirit of ease and indifference'.[38] There were signs of renewed vitality by the beginning of the 19th century. In 1829 the Quaker Evangelical, J. J. Gurney, remarked of the Banbury meeting:

'In the *country* Friends are reduced and scattered. *Here* they are an increasing and very comfortable Society, & it has been *pleasant* to become acquainted with them. We seem to me to flourish better in the middle class than in those below them'.[39]

The banker Joseph Ashby Gillett became clerk of the meeting in 1830 and was acknowledged as a minister in 1841.[40] Other Quakers included Samuel Beesley, confectioner and Reformer, the Head family, woolstaplers, drapers and sponsors of teetotallism, Jeremiah Cross, a grocer, and James Cadbury, uncle of the founders of Bournville and son-in-law of Joseph Sturge, who set up as a grocer in Banbury in 1840. Banbury's principal Friends were in no sense a peculiar people, cut off by their beliefs from society at large.[41] There were some poor members who were occasionally relieved from the meeting's funds, but most were prosperous tradesmen. Discipline was severe, and several Friends were excluded for marrying outside the Society, for bankruptcy and drunkenness. The meeting scrupulously observed the resolution of the national yearly meeting of 1834 that 'The Best Recreation of a Christian is the relief of distress'.[42] Friends visited Banbury gaol, and Samuel Beesley died from an infection he contracted there.[43] In 1846 Martha, daughter of J. A. Gillett, was authorised to visit distressed families, and in 1849 to go to lodging houses, beerhouses and the cottages of the poor.[44] The meeting entertained American Quakers and maintained links with members who had emigrated.

It was attended in 1851 by about 60 people, less than two per cent of Banbury's worshippers, but its place in society was measured by its influence not its numbers.

The Wesleyan Methodist society presented many contrasts with the Unitarians and Quakers. It was easily the largest Noncomformist church in Banbury, with about 17 per cent of the worshippers in the town, and a morning congregation of 558 on 30 March 1851, yet few of its members were active in public life.[45] Methodism arrived late in Banbury, the first society having been established no earlier than 1784 when John Wesley preached in the Presbyterian meeting house.[46] In 1791, when 'many of the common people were inclined to Methodism', a chapel was built in Calthorpe Lane. The congregation moved in April 1812 to a new building in Church Lane which cost over £2,000, much of which was not paid off for half a century. Further debts were incurred by extensions in 1818 and 1839-41, and financial embarrassment dominated the history of the society until the 1860s.[47] The Wesleyan society was the centre of a large circuit through which Methodism was exported from the town to the countryside. Enthusiasm aroused at revivals such as that of 1821 was channelled into evangelism in the villages.[48] In the immediate vicinity of Banbury were cottage meetings at Grimsbury and Nethercote which served as nurseries for young local preachers.[49] Membership in the Banbury circuit (separate figures for the Banbury Society are not available) rose from 565 in 1830 to 813 in 1836 and reached 870 in 1845. In 1847 the societies around Kineton were formed into a separate circuit with 270 members. The total in Banbury was then 561, which increased to 641 by 1851.[50] Wesleyans included men of all shades of political opinion. Richard Edmunds the elder, an ironmonger, had been a churchman, but on his conversion at about the age of 33 in 1827, he began to interject Hallelujahs' into the liturgy at St Mary's, and was advised to join the Wesleyans.[51] As a member of the Old Corporation he voted for the Reform candidate in the 1831 election, although he was later a Conservative. He was active in the Bible Society, the anti-slavery movement and the British Schools. No other Wesleyan could match this level of public activity before 1850, although members tended to be upwardly mobile. John Walshaw, outrider to a tailor, became a grocer. John Kilby, a clerk in the office of Benjamin Aplin, later practised as a solicitor on his own account. Charles Drury, clerk to a woolstapler, became a surveyor. In 1850 the Wesleyans attracted fewer members of the middle-class than any other Noncomformist denomination, but more of the poor and unskilled.[52]

Primitive Methodism appeared in Banbury as the result of missioning in 1835 by the Revd. Joseph Preston of Witney, who hoped to enlarge an existing and isolated society at Chacombe. In 1836 the venture was renamed the 'Banbury Mission'. Services were held in a cottage in Newland until 1839 when a small chapel was erected behind two cottages in Broad Street, and a minister took up his station in the town.[53] The Banbury Primitive Methodist Circuit was formed in 1840 with 262 members, a total which increased to 689 within ten years, of whom about a hundred belonged to the Banbury society[54] The enlargement of the chapel in 1847 increased the congregation, and there were 212 people, about seven per cent of the worshippers in the town, at the most numerously attended service on 30 March 1851.[55] The principal laymen in the congregation was Richard Brazier, a whitesmith from Stourport, who moved to Banbury about 1837. He prided himself on being 'a working man', but by 1850 he had acquired some land from which he worked as a coal merchant and milkman. He was active in the temperance movement, and served as a Poor Law Guardian. The congregation was emphatically working class. Between 1842 and 1852, 42 children were baptised. The fathers of 18 were labourers, the rest including wheelwrights, shoemakers, weavers and boatmen.[56] The Primitives' more important meetings were held in Baptist or Independent chapels, and were often attended by ministers of those denominations, and by Wesleyans.

The remaining Protestant congregations in Banbury all sprang from a single source, a series of Thursday evening meetings begun by 'a few serious people' in 1772-73, which were followed by Sunday evening meetings at the home of Thomas Ainge, a tailor and Baptist. About 1780 a meeting room was fitted up, and the congregation began to be visited by ministers of the Countess of Huntingdon's Connexion. In 1792 a domed building seating 500 and called the New Chapel (perhaps to distinguish it from the Old Meeting) was erected in Church Passage.[57] The congregation included Protestants of many hues, Baptists, Independents, Antinominians, disciples of William Huntington the converted coal-heaver, and followers of the Countess of Huntingdon, who used the Anglican liturgy. Minister followed minister in rapid succession, and members were continually excluded and re-admitted. About 1812 the link with Lady Huntingdon's Connexion was broken, and the Baptist elements began to hold separate meetings. In 1813 a new building was opened for 'the Friends of the Gospel separated from the Chapel in Church Passage', on property belonging to Richard Austin, the brewer, on the west side of South Bar, which was licensed in 1815.[58] By 1816 the New Chapel was a distinctly Independent institution, where Baptists and others attended on sufferance, the congregation being divided into 'members', 'members of other churches' and 'hearers only'.[59] In 1818 Thomas Searle was ordained at the start of an eight year ministry, the longest in the history of the church to that date.[60] In the same year a Baptist chapel was opened at Bodicote which attracted some Baptists from Church Passage. When Robert Radford became the minister, about 1822, the Bodicote congregation split, part meeting at the village chapel and part in Banbury. For the latter group, Joseph Gardner the ironmonger built a chapel in West Bar in 1829, where Radford remained as minister until the early 1840s.[61] In 1834 Richard Austin built a chapel on the east side of South Bar to accommodate the Calvinistic Baptists who since 1813 had been meeting on the other side of the road. The congregation was served by regular ministers until 1851.[62]

In 1831 Caleb, son of the Revd. Richard Clarke of the Baptist church at Weston-by-Weedon in Northamptonshire, settled in Banbury as a hosier. He had unusual gifts for preaching and healing, and began to hold services in his own home. Those who assembled there formed one of the elements which made up the Particular Baptist church formed in 1840, which occupied a new classical chapel in Bridge Street the following year.[63] The congregation also included Baptists who had remained with the New Chapel, some from Austin's congregation, and a few Banburians who had previously attended village chapels. It was acknowledged that the building of the Bridge Street chapel was due to Clarke's influence, but he did not become its minister, and in 1846 he revived services in his own home.[64]

Thus by 1850 the meeting which began in 1772-73 had evolved into an Independent Church assembling in the New Chapel, two Calvinistic Baptist congregations meeting in the buildings erected by Gardner and Austin, the Particular Baptist Chapel in Bridge Street, and the meetings held in Clarke's house. The Disciples of Christ, a group of schismatic Baptists founded in the United States by Alexander Campbell and established in Banbury in 1840, probably sprang from the same source.[65] The Baptists and

Independents attracted about 15 per cent of the worshippers in Banbury in 1851.[66] They were mostly shopkeepers and skilled tradesmen, and included notable figures like James Gardner, inventor of the Banbury turnip cutter, Richard Austen the brewer, and Richard Goffe, a tailor who was five times mayor. Baptist and Independent dissent spread from the countryside into the town. Most of the leading members of the two denominations were immigrants to Banbury, many from villages where there were old-established dissenting congregations, although a significant proportion came from London.

The rebirth of Roman Catholicism in Banbury in the early 19th century was entirely a revival of the Roman faith among the native population, which owed nothing to Irish immigration. There were only 78 people of Irish birth in Banbury in 1851, less than one per cent of the population.[67] In the 17th and 18th centuries a Catholic presence in the district had been maintained by the Holman family of Warkworth Castle. There were some Catholics in Banbury by 1798 when a baptismal register was begun, and in 1802 an emigré French priest, Pierre Julien Hersent, settled in High Street. In 1804 he returned to Warkworth, and after the demolition of the Castle in 1806 built a chapel in Overthorpe which served local Catholics until he began to hold meetings on private premises in Banbury. He was joined in 1830 by Fr. Joseph Fox, who took charge of the congregation after his death in 1833, and acquired land for a church. Fox died in 1835 by which time the crypt was vaulted and parts of the walls erected.[68] Dr. William Tandy, who went to Banbury after Fox's death, was responsible for completing the church. He had attended the English college in Rome and knew Augustus Welby Pugin, who designed the sanctuary and the presbytery.[69]

The church of St John was opened with much ceremony on 19 June 1838. A large crowd gathered before the opening service and in a rush to enter the church several ladies were roughly pressed. Many of the congregation were curious Protestants, among them the Unitarian minister. The quality of the music was admired, but the sermon preached by the Hon. and Revd. G. Spencer, younger brother of Lord Althorpe, was less well received. 'The meanest Methodist cordwainer could have done better' wrote a not-wholly unsympathetic correspondent.[70] The church was regarded by Protestants with the same mixture of shocked horror and intense curiosity with which they would have contemplated a pornographic book. Churchmen were careful to describe it as a 'chapel', while Quakers, reviving the language of the 17th-century forebears, called it a 'mass-house'. In the autumn of 1838 Dr. Tandy engaged in pamphlet warfare with George Harris, a Baptist coal-dealer, who attacked image worship, transubstantiation, infallibility, the Latin mass and the veneration of the saints, and accused the Catholics of trying to seduce respectable Protestants with good voices to join their choir.[71] For a time almost every public gathering in Banbury became an occasion for the expression of opinions about Roman Catholics. A Wesleyan minister lecturing on popery objected to the presence of Catholic 'spies' in his audience. On 5 November 1838 about 1,000 people marched with squibs and crackers to burn an effigy of Dr. Tandy. A few days earlier one of the pinnacles of St John's Church had blown down, it was said, because George Harris had prayed to a Protestant St. Boreas.[72] The pinnacles or 'ears' were particularly offensive to Protestant sensibilities, and were reduced in size after they were found to be unsafe.[73] By 1851 Catholics numbered about seven per cent of the worshippers in Banbury and there were 480 people at the most popular mass on Sunday 30 March.[74] A holy guild, in effect a friendly society, was set up, a school opened, and a nunnery established.[75] The social composition of the congregation resembled that of other Non-conformist churches. In Neithrop there were about as many Catholics as Unitarians, Baptists or Independents. The Catholic congregation included several wealthy people, including the Perry family who had large market gardens, H. A. Dalby, a timber merchant, and George Craddock, a leading shoemaker.[76] *De facto* Catholic emancipation had yet to be achieved in Banbury. Catholics were active in some local societies, and sided with other Nonconformists in some controversies, but they played no part in municipal affairs. The emergence of a Catholic community in the town was perhaps one of the principal stimuli towards religious toleration. After the excitement of 1838 there were further occasions when anti-Catholic feelings were expressed, but in every case they were stimulated by outside factors. While Catholics were fellow tradesmen, it was difficult to harbour about them the fantasies and fears which could be entertained about plotting Jesuits or hordes of drunken Irishmen.

Protestant Dissenters comprised about half the worshippers in Banbury in 1851, while the Established Church could only claim the allegiances of about 42 per cent. Antipathy between the two had grown during the previous two decades, most notably on the issue of church rates. The national campaign against the rate began in 1834. In 1838 the Banbury Dissenters asserted that they would only allow the rate to be approved at the Vestry meeting if they were promised that they would not be called upon to pay. In 1839 a Calvinistic Baptist was elected to the chair of the Vestry meeting. George Harris, the anti-papist, proposed a motion to nullify the rate, and was seconded, ironically, by Dr. Tandy. The motion was carried, but at a subsequent poll the rate was adopted by 405 votes to 260. It was alleged that Quaker bankers and the Cobb family sustained the opponents of the rate, although James Wake Golby, the Unitarian solicitor, insisted that the issue was not one of church or dissent, and that the rate was an obligation of landownership which should be paid.[77] A group nicknamed the Banbury Thorogoods, after John Thorogood of Chelmsford, one of those imprisoned for opposing church rates, refused to pay.[78] Baptists, Quakers and Catholics suffered distress of their goods, but in 1840 there was negligible support when a Baptist tailor and a Quaker shoemaker tried to nullify the rate.[79] In 1841 the property of four Baptists was seized when they refused to pay the rate, and at the Vestry meeting 'Chartists, Baptists and others' tried to prevent 'the buzzing of the organ' by objecting to the rate. It was rumoured that Catholics had been ordered to cease their objections, and in 1842 and 1844 only Quakers refused to pay. For a decade the issue remained dormant.[80]

There were many issues on which the divisions of religious opinion in Banbury were far from clear-cut. Most practising Christians had an opinion on Temperance, but apart from Quakers and Primitive Methodists, no group was unanimous about it. Some Anglicans co-operated with Dissenters in philanthropic organisations, and in bodies like the British and Foreign Bible Society. While there were some tendencies towards religious toleration in the 1840s, there were other movements in the opposite direction. More societies became distinctively Anglican or Nonconformist, and clergy with intransigent temperaments came to occupy several pulpits. Religion for all but the very poor or the very rich was a means of self-identity, an aid to the absorption of newcomers into the town community, a way of easing social mobility, and one by which the class element in alms-giving could be disguised. Religion provided a series of vertical divisions within society which for many were as important as the horizontal divisions of social class.

V

THE POLITICS OF REFORM 1830-1850

'A strange spectacle has been presented to the reflecting mind in the history of the last eighteen months. A prosperous, happy and contented nation of money-getting people is converted in a twinkling into a community of restless, dissatisfied politicians'.[1]

THE SOCIAL AND ECONOMIC TENSIONS of Banbury society were reflected in the politics of the town between 1830 and 1880 with unusual clarity. There were strongly-held differences not only on national questions, the status of the Church of England, the Corn Laws or the continuance of slavery, but also on the functions and responsibilities of the town, questions which revealed profoundly different concepts of the nature of English society. Throughout the period local politics were conducted in the shadow of the epic struggle for the Reform Bill. Liberals were proud that they were among the labourers 'engaged in the momentous task of accomplishing the nation's reform', and of their contribution to 'the overthrow of political corruption'.[2] For decades afterwards a man's standing in politics was judged by his role in 1831-32. Like Agincourt, the Easter Rising or the siege of Troy, it was a perpetual point of reference, remembered with advantages by all who could recall their feats upon those memorable days.

The North family of Wroxton Abbey dominated the politics of Banbury throughout the 18th century. They regularly provided lavish dinners for the close corporation, who, before 1832, elected the member for Banbury. Between 1770 and 1782 Banbury was represented in the Commons by the Prime Minister. The eldest daughter of Lord North's son, the third Earl of Guilford, married John Stuart, second Marquess of Bute, who made Wroxton his home, became High Sheriff of Banbury and exercised the traditional North influence. In 1806 William Praed, chairman of the Grand Junction Canal Company, was elected MP in opposition to the North candidate, and in 1820 there were riots during the election, but there were few signs between 1800 and 1830 of principles opposition to the North interest. Banbury remained a pocket borough, generally content to accept the paternalistic bounty of the Norths, although the Norths did not own substantial properties in the town, and even at Wroxton they were but the lessees of Trinity College.[3]

The election of 1830 was the last in which the Wroxton influence was exercised with success. Henry Villiers Stuart, nephew of the Marquess of Bute, was returned unopposed, being greeted by the largest crowd which had ever assembled for a Banbury election.[4] In 1831 he voted against the Reform Bill on the grounds that his constituents opposed it. Popular feelings in Banbury were deeply aroused. On 22 April 1831, the day after parliament was dissolved, an address to the Corporation urging the return of a member pledged to support the Reform Bill was open for signature. It was reported on 30 April that 'a most disorderly feeling has manifested itself in sundry tumultuous acts'. Six of the corporation invited Timothy Rhodes Cobb and William Spurrett to find a Reform candidate. Others brought forward Colonel Henry Hely Hutchinson of Weston Hall, Northants, who had married the widow of F. S. N. Douglas, grandson of Lord North and MP for Banbury between 1812 and 1819. Cobb and Spurrett recommended John Easthope, a stockbroker,[5] and together with John Munton, Thomas Tims, Thomas Gardner and Samuel Beesley, issue a bill on 28 April regretting that Hutchinson was standing, and urging the corporation not to vote for him. On election day, 2 May, North Bar was barricaded to keep out non-resident voters, and as a precaution against military intervention. The Mayor, Thomas Brayne, was a Reformer, and on the advice of the deputy recorder, Andrew Amos, he decided that troops should not be brought in. Hutchinson stayed at Castle House, and when he emerged into Cornhill he was set upon by about 100 people, who jostled him as he fled under the protection of the parish constables towards the bridge. Attempts were made to duck him in the canal, but the Reformer, Francis Francillon, intervened, and the crowd was satisfied with a token immersion of his hat. Hutchinson described the incident as part of a reign of terror. Two members of the corporation voted for Hutchinson, but six supported Easthope who was duly returned. He stopped his celebration procession outside Cobbs Bank, and told young men that he had once worked there, and that by industry and probity they might rise in the social scale as he had.[6]

The cause of Reform received almost universal support in Banbury in 1831. Five of the six members of the Corporation who voted for Easthope were subsequently Conservatives, and Alfred Beesley later recalled that 'almost every Conservative in the place supported the Reform Bill'. Liberals claimed that, the moral and intellectual power of the town' had been raised against the Wroxton interests.[7] The election was interpreted as a victory of national significance:

> 'Thus has a triumph been gained which will create a sensation throughout the kingdom. It proves that the spirit of reform is so fully aroused that the borough patrons may be defeated in their strongest holds'.[8]

There was a sense of relief that aristocratic rule was ending:

> *'No more they'll enjoy*
> *Their old corporat dinners,*
> *And guttle, and guzzle,*
> *And quarrel, poor sinners;*
>
> *No more haughty nobles*
> *Will ride on our backs,*
> *To whip us and spur us*
> *And work us like hacks.*[9]

Nevertheless the Reformers laid much stress on the King's support of the Reform Bill. 'Proud faction', claimed one handbill, 'and her Rebel crew, insult their sovereign, and bid defiance to his power. The people in justice will then defend his cause'. The alternative to Reform, claimed its proponents, was despotism, and an end of liberty of the press. Anti-reformers forecast threats to property and the Corn Laws.[10]

The campaign of 1831 took place four months after the machine-breaking riots of 1830, when the yeomanry fought in Banbury against stone-throwing farmworkers and townsmen who carried an effigy of Villiers Stuart, MP.[11] At the Lent Assizes, 13 Banburians had been charged with rioting, nine of them gaining acquittals.[12] Reformers were concerned to avoid disorder which might provide an excuse for military intervention. 'Soldiers cannot make a bad cause a good one' asserted one poster.[13] A decade later Liberals were still justifying the blockading of the town:

'the barricades were raised, not for the purpose of attack, but for defence against an armed force, unconstitutionally, because uncalled for by authority, hovering around the town on an election day; barricades, which it required only on word from a chief magistrate in whose courage, talent and integrity the People had confidence, to cause to be removed by the people themselves'.[14]

The townspeople were urged to acquiesce should an MP be elected contrary to the wishes of the majority, because it would ultimately do much for the cause of Reform.[15] Samuel Beesley wrote to a friend on the evening of election day, with some evident relief, that 'peace was completely restored, and there is no cause to apprehend any further break in it'.[16] Among the supporters of the Wroxton interest there was resentment that 'might, in the case, proved stronger than right'.[17] There was much bitterness in the aftermath of the Reformers' victory. In September 1831 Thomas Brayne resigned as mayor and alderman, complaining of 'much notorious abuse and imbecility in the management of the local jurisdiction'. The Bute family secured the dismissal of Andrew Amos as deputy recorder. The Marquess of Bute was hissed and stoned in Banbury at the end of October, and declared that he would no longer reside at Wroxton.[18]

The second reading of the Reform Bill in the House of Lords on 14 April 1832 was greeted in Banbury by the bells of the parish church, but when the government was defeated in committee on 7 May there was talk in the town of an appeal to arms. When Earl Grey returned to office a Union Jack was hoisted on the church tower amid the firing of small arms, and it remained there until the Bill became law.[19] The Royal Assent was given on 7 June, and on 13 July the Reformers celebrated with a public procession in which the trade companies escorted the 'Champion of Reform', in white armour on a charger.[20] They also faced a general election, and consequently a crisis. For some time previously John Easthope had intended to retire as member for Banbury, but the Reformers had not tried to find another candidate.[21] The Conservatives learned of his retirement, and on 8 June Benjamin Aplin, agent to Lord Bute, visited Henry Pye the recently-arrived tenant of Chacombe Priory, taking the promise of Bute's support should he contest Banbury, and the Marquess's approval of his campaigning as a Reformer. The following day Pye issued a manifesto full of Reforming promises. The Reform Party hurriedly asserted that Easthope had not resigned, and that if he did, 'a gentleman of high character and known and tried principles' would be put forward.[22] They had no such person in mind, and the same day T. R. Cobb and John Munton hastened to London with instructions to persuade Easthope to stand, or to secure 'some gentleman whose name is eminent and his Whig politics notorious'.[23]

'Getting through business with the great men in the Whig interest is awkward' wrote Cobb to William Spurrett on 16 June; 'I shall be very glad to see a neighbour's face'. He suspected Lord Althorpe of trading Banbury for the Northamptonshire county seat, and complained that 'the lukewarmness and villainy connected with Politics is almost incredible'.[24] In Banbury the unity which had prevailed in 1831 had been dissipated. The Reformers were attacked as 'a self-appointed and secret committee of disunited dissenters', Conservative allegations that Cobbs Bank used Easthope's MP's franks to send money to London were proving wounding.[25] On Thursday 14 June William Spurrett instructed Cobb to go to Oxford by the following Sunday with a new candidate. This proved impossible, but Joseph Parkes, the most effective of parliamentary brokers, arranged an introduction on Sunday 17 June to Henry William Tancred, a barrister, son of a Yorkshire baronet, and author of a pamphlet on parliamentary representation. On 18 June, Cobb, Munton and Tancred left London to spend the night at Oxford.[26] The same evening the first public meeting of the Banbury Reform Association took place. A committee of 30 was formed, which the following morning heard letters from Cobb and Munton recommending Tancred, and listing notable Whigs who approved him. Cobb, Munton and Tancred had already moved to the *Fox* at North Aston, about eight miles from Banbury, whence they were summoned to appear at a meeting in the Market Place that evening. The committee formally adopted Tancred the following morning.[27] They had feared the candidature of an extremist backed by the Birmingham Political Union.[28]

The election campaign of 1832 lasted from early June until mid-December. The Reformers knew nothing of electioneering and the Conservatives had experience only of a very different system. The Tories still controlled the local administration, and obstructed Reformers who tried to find out who might qualify for the franchise. The Reform Act enlarged the constituency to include the whole parish of Banbury, and the candidates were escorted through the hamlets by supporters who had influence there.[29] The Conservatives sought to show that Pye was the better reformer of the two candidates, and that the Reform Committee was discredited and prone to extremism.[30] The Reformers sought to connect Pye with Lord Bute. A poster wryly commented that 'the Reform Bill has produced more conversions than the greatest saint in the Roman Calendar'.[31] Superficially Pye was an attractive candidate, 'independent of the party which has enjoyed the honours and advantages of office and of that which seeks them'.[32] His supporters suggested that his election would soothe the wounds caused by party faction: 'the storm which has so long agitated our borough . . . has greatly interrupted those feelings which as neighbours and Christians it should be our duty to maintain'.[33] He posed as the friend of the poor and his charity towards the disadvantaged of Chacombe was frequently cited.[34] He alleged that Tancred was an untried man of no reputation whose employment as a boundary commissioner made him a placeman.[35] Tancred equivocated about Slavery, on which it was acknowledged that there were unusually intense feelings in Banbury, while Pye supported immediate abolition. Tancred met members of the Banbury Anti-Slavery Society, after which he defined 'immediate and total abolition' to mean the fixing of a time limit to the continuance of slavery.[36] The Conservatives emphasised that Tancred was the creature of a clique, the nominee of Cobb, Golby and Co.:

> 'Although he walks in silk attire
> The COB webs are about him spread'.[37]

The Conservatives made a tactical error by publicising an endorsement of Pye's candidature by Thomas Attwood between 3 and 14 September. On 13 September the Reformers proved that Attwood was unacquainted with Pye and that he had written in the belief that there was no other Reform candidate.[38] The Reformers' tactics were defensive. They could not claim, as in 1831, that they were moving with the spirit of the times, with the whole community on their side. They had to stand and fight on the ground which they had won the previous year. With some effect they sniped at Pye, suggesting that his much-lauded expenditure on charity was insignificant, that he was not a resident country gentleman, but one 'who comes like an owl and takes lodgings in an old mansion . . . whom nobody knows anything of'. They reiterated Pye's past record on Reform, and his links with Conservative lawyers and the Marquess of Bute.[39]

Conservatives argued that Banburians should follow their economic interests rather than their ideological predilections, that it was in the interest of the town to accept the legitimate patronage of the landed classes. Banbury, it was maintained, was sustained by farmers, whom Pye, as a landed proprietor, would be bound to support.[40] After the Reform Act, it was suggested:

> 'all the large, newly-enfranchised towns will be careful to send to Parliament men versed in all the interests and bearings of Trade and Manufactures, which will actually predominate. Men of Banbury, it now behoves you to look well to your own interests in selecting a man able to advocate and watch over the interests of Agriculture . . . for by such interests does Banbury flourish'.[41]

Another Conservative argued:

> 'Banbury is solely dependent on Agriculture and its ramifications for every shilling we possess . . . Our duty and interests alike teach us to support Agriculture as pointedly as if we individually held the Plough. Manufacturers will be acute enough to send men to Parliament to advocate their interests; let us with becoming care defend our own'.[42]

The Reformers defended their ground ruggedly, occasionally allowing the Conservatives, as in the Attwood incident, to advance into perilous salients. They did not reject the premise that the town was dependent on Agriculture, but utterly denied that it owed any kind of fealty to the landed interest.

The campaign was one of attrition. The main incidents were the rumours and denials of Tancred's retirement in August, the claim by Pye that he had Attwood's support, and a riot during a dinner held by Pye's supporters at the *Flying Horse* on 25 September. A gang of youths shouted 'No Pye' as the candidate arrived to deliver his first public speech since the beginning of the campaign. The inn was stormed and the landlord alleged that several citizens attacked the house with the intention of destroying it, a capital charge which was subsequently dropped, although lesser charges were preferred.[43] Ultimately the Reformers won their defensive battle. As the campaign progressed and it became clear who would comprise the electorate, it was realised that the Reformers would have a majority. On the eve of nomination day, 10 December 1832, Pye's agent announced his retirement, and the next day Tancred was returned unopposed.[44]

In the years after the Reformers' victory there was increasing polarisation in public affairs. At the Oxford Lent Assizes in 1833 six of the rioters of 25 September were tried, found guilty and given short terms of imprisonment. Liberals insisted that innocent men had been charged in 'an odious prosecution which will never be thoroughly forgotten during the lifetime of the present inhabitants'. Support for James Hill, one of those imprisoned, was shown by electing him a churchwarden, although the archdeacon declared the election void. The prisoners were subsequently granted pardons by the Home Office.[45] Party conflicts dominated vestry meetings. Dissenters tried in 1834 to prevent the levying of a rate for an extension to the parish churchyard, and in 1833 the new democratic spirit was recognised by a decision to toll the same bell at funerals of rich and poor.[46]

Party manoeuvring pervaded the establishment of the Banbury Poor Law Union. Townsmen objected in principle to agricultural Guardians participating in the management of the poor of Banbury. The first meeting of the Board of Guardians was held on 6 April 1835. Banbury was represented by the Liberals, William Potts, Lynn Spurrett and Timothy Rhodes Cobb, but they were overwhelmed by Conservatives from the rural parishes.[47] Tory solicitors were elected to the offices of auditor and clerk after intensive canvassing, and even the post of relieving officer was fiercely contested.[48] In December 1835 an assistant rate collector was appointed for the borough, a publican being chosen in preference to an old retainer of the Cobb family. 'Mr. Cobb is not quite the man out of Banbury that he is in it', commented the *Northampton Herald*.[49]

Party spirit also affected the corporation. The Reformers provided information for the commissioners enquiring into municipal corporations in 1833 and petitioned for reform during the parliamentary discussions of the Municipal Corporations Bill in 1835. Conservatives argued that Liberals abstained from the affairs of the old corporation by choice.[50] The first election after the Municipal Corporations Act took place on 26 December 1835, when all 12 of the councillors elected were 'opponents of the former system'. After the elevation of four councillors to the aldermanic bench, a by-election was held on 8 January 1836, when three of the four successful candidates were Reformers.[51] The *Northampton Herald* observed that the noble and illustrious family which once *influenced* Banbury had been exchanged for the Cobbs, a vulgar, mean-minded family, which *governed* it, and showed that all 12 of the original councillors had links with Cobbs Bank and J. W. Golby the solicitor. A meeting was held at the Theatre to endorse the Reformers' candidates. The lowest number of votes cast for one of the elected candidates was 136, whilst the highest polled by any other candidate was eleven. It is evident that the Conservatives abstained from the election.[52] Town council elections continued to be a Liberal monopoly. Only 70 burgesses voted in the contest of 1836. In 1839 a newspaper reported apathy over the elections, and said that the Tories were refusing to take part. Chartist intervention in 1841 failed to make the election lively, and in 1842 it was called an annual farce.[53] In 1847 the Conservatives put forward John Drinkwater and James Danby, to 'attract the votes of those who think that the town council should not be composed exclusively of one party'. They received Chartist support and topped the poll, and succeeded again the following year.[54] In 1849 the Conservatives and Liberals each proposed two candidates who were returned unopposed.[55] The period of one-party rule on the corporation was over, but Liberal domination in the years after municipal reform had symbolised a dramatic shift of political power.

The unreformed corporation of Banbury was not especially corrupt, but it was subservient to the North and Bute families, and symbolised an unpopular *ancien régime*.[56] Dramatic changes followed its takeover by the Reformers. The most important tasks of the new corporation were the recovery, after temporary loss, of its own Quarter Sessions and Court of Record, and the administration of the borough's inadequate gaol.[57] A variety of superficial changes symbolised the shift of political power. The names of many streets were altered and displayed on large signs. It was rumoured that St John's Street had been re-named South Bar because Quakers objected to the old name.[58] Corporation attendance at St Mary's church ceased, and the corporation pew was 'sheep-penned into two and hired out for profit'.[59] The new council refused until 1850 to make an appointment to the post of High Steward.[60] A police force was established, which critics complained provided places for dependents of the Cobbs.[61] Two Conservative magistrates were excluded from the Bench, and replaced by three Liberals. One Tory, Henry Tawney, remained a justice, but he was an ineffective speaker, and by 1840 was too ill to carry out his duties. In 1842 after the formation of Peel's Conservative government, the two Conservatives were re-instated,[62] but Liberal control of the Bench between 1836 and 1842 had been a potent symbol of the change in political power. The new town council adopted an attitude of condescending moral superiority towards its predecessors. Shortly before Municipal Reform the old corporation sold their silver maces and bowls. Reformers alleged for many years that this was done to pay tavern debts.[63] In 1842 it was claimed that under the new corporation 'none of the Bridge or charity money has been spent on food and drink', and that no political influence was shown in the choice of contractors, the bridge having been repaired by a Tory.[64] In 1846 it was asserted that the new corporation did not 'eat and drink at the expense of the borough funds, the bridge money is laid on the bridge and not in swill'.[65] The magistrates re-appointed in 1842 were alleged to be those 'under whom the town was as notorious for disorder as for its quietness and order in late years'.[66]

The first parliamentary contest in Banbury after the Reform Act was in the general election held in the first week of 1835. The only opposition to Tancred came from a Birmingham Conservative, Edward Lloyd Williams, who posed as 'a sincere reformer', accepting the Reform Act and the need to relieve Dissenters of Church Rates.[67] Conservatives warned against him as the associate of 'notorious Whigs and radicals', while Birmingham Reformers provided evidence that he was a Tory. Williams limply claimed that he kept aloof from party politics, and openly offered to the poor tickets for coal, tea, sugar and currants.[68] After an ill-tempered performance on the hustings, which 'disgusted his staunchest friends', he gained only 43 votes against Tancred's 203. The *Morning Chronicle* concluded that the Banbury Reformers had slain 'a wolf in sheep's clothing'.[69]

The election which followed the accession of Queen Victoria in 1837 was more spirited. Tancred was opposed by Henry Tawney, the banker, who was described as 'an influential inhabitant and a magistrate, with every prospect of success'. He canvassed timorously, and seems to have regarded his candidature as an unpleasant duty thrust upon him.[70] At the nomination he was heard attentively 'in considera-tion of his nervous feelings', but his speech was punctuated by guffaws of laughter, and he soon put on his hat and retired.[71] Francis Piggott, a lawyer who had family connections with Banbury, came forward as a second Liberal candidate but he did not go to the poll.[72] With a poster headed 'Radical Charity', the Conservatives attacked the new Poor Law, pointing out that at the Bastille Union men and women were separated, poverty was treated as a crime, and relief was granted only on condition of perpetual imprisonment. Tancred's vote against the immediate abolition of flogging in the army was publicised, and Tawney's nomination proces-sion included a cart on which was a man being flogged. The Reformers reminded electors that Tories were responsible for the local administration of the Poor Law, and prevented workhouse inmates from attending their own place of worship.[73] They alleged Tory links with Ernest, Duke of Cumberland, King of Hanover, Victoria's uncle and her supposed rival for the throne:

'On then to the battlefield!
The sword for Queen Victoria yield!
Never! Never! will we yield!
Make the base ones flee.

Lay the proud King Ernest low!
Lyndhursts fall in every foe!
Peel bends beneath each freeman's blow!
Let us do or die!' [74]

There was disorder both at the nomination and on polling day. Tawney, it was suggested, was supported by 'a hired mob of wharfmen and boatmen', 'young farmers who seemed to have learned their manners from some of the quadrupeds in which they deal', prostitutes from Waterloo, and girls from the Church Sunday School, wearing bonnets paid for by public subscription, but trimmed with purple Tory favours. Tancred won by 181 votes to 79. After the declaration, Francis Litchfield, rector of Farthinghoe, tried to prevent the traditional chairing of the member.[75] Both parties had founded short-lived registration associations in 1835, and both responded to the result in 1837 by re-forming them.[76]

The Banbury Borough Conservative Association was established on 21 August 1837, a month after the election. Its principles were defined in a handbill:

'A True Conservative is fixed in his determination to preserve and add to the happiness of all, to preserve those Civil and Religious Institutions which have exalted us as a nation, to preserve the Constitution, with its limited Monarchy, to honour the Queen, to respect the Peers, and protect the People. If the Monarch needs support, the Conservative is to be found at the footsteps of the throne, if the Peers are threatened, they find him their supporter, if the Church is in danger, he flies to its rescue, but above all, if the liberties of the people are to be attacked, he is on foot in in their ranks, ready to fight hand in hand in their defence'.

All who professed the Gospel were invited, 'to take all measures . . . for upholding the civil and religious principles secured to us as Protestants at the Revolution in 1688'. A separate Protestant Conservative Association with identically defined principles was formed at the same time.[77]

Less than three weeks later, a Reform Association was formed and accepted a declaration of principles:

'. . . when the most strenuous efforts are being made in this borough as well as generally through-out the country, to retain for Toryism the ascendancy which has in former years cost this country so many millions of treasure, and has consequently entailed upon it a debt, the mere interest of which presses more particularly upon the industrious classes with almost paralysing weight; the members of the Banbury Reform Association feel that it behoves every man desirous of diminish-ing that burden or even of preventing its increase, and who wishes to obtain for every class of Her Majesty's subjects equal rights and privileges, to exert himself in order to prevent that ascendancy being regained'.[78]

The objectives of the Banbury Liberals were to protect and enlarge upon the concept of 'Civil and Religious Liberty' which was always toasted at their dinners. In 1847 Timothy Rhodes Cobb proclaimed that 'For twenty years some of us have been engaged in endeavouring to carry out what we believed to be for the interests of the People', and cited a catalogue of beneficial changes, culminating in the repeal of the Corn Laws.[79] The Reform Association was led by some of Banbury's wealthiest citizens. It was a bourgeois but also a radical body. Like the Anti-Corn Law League, it defined its position in class terms, both in relation to the aristocracy, who had betrayed their trust, and to the proletariat, for whose interests it felt responsible. In 1837 the Association resolved:

'That the Upper Classes thus losing the love and respect of the people . . . the Nation is less able to resist its common enemies, and if freedom of election be not obtained, the constitution of our beloved country will be endangered and perhaps destroyed'.

In a petition against the Corn Laws in 1839 the Association declared that its members:

'cannot close their ears to the numerous complaints of the working class of the privations endured by them, in consequence of the high price of bread; or to the demands of the manufacturers for an enquiry into the causes of the increasing advantages, which, they allege, foreign nations are annually gaining over this country as a commercial community; your petitioners, considering that the success of Agriculture is promoted by the prosperity of Trade . . . while to the landlord, Manufacturer or Tradesman, or the master employing the poor, the price of bread for his family is of but little moment as part of his general expenditure, to the Labouring Classes it is comparatively a question of starvation, half or more of their income being often expended in Bread alone'.[80]

The Reformers hoped to further their objectives by extending the franchise by legislation or registration, In 1845 Francis Francillon praised efforts to register the occupiers of new houses worth between £10 and £15 p.a., most of whom were dependent upon their own industry, and 'deeply interested in good and economical government'. The following year he urged the enfranchisement of the £5 householder, because independence increased the further you went down the social scale.[81] 'Independence' was second only to 'civil and religious liberty' as an epitome of Liberal thinking. It implied the independence of the town from obligations to the gentry. In 1837 the Association called for 'protection against the menaces, undue influence and tyranny of men of power'.[82] Reformers often depicted Banbury as a star of enlightenment in a dark Tory sky. In 1841 Tancred referred to the town as 'a cradle of liberty, a little island, an oasis of freedom in a waste, howling wilderness of Toryism'.[83] The Reformers were proud that their achievements owed nothing to friendly aristocrats, proclaiming in 1846 that 'We, without a Whig squire, or a Whig parson, and surrounded by Tories, have beaten Toryism'.[84]

Conservatives considered that the interests of the market town were identical with those of the countryside, and that consequently the townsmen owed the Agricultural Interest their political support. Aristocratic patronage was accepted as part of the natural social and economic order. In 1844 the draper R. T. Haynes stated:

'the aristocracy did not want of them a slavish bowing down to the ground, but they did expect that becoming and respectful treatment which, as Banbury tradesmen, they owed to that class of of society. They should be proud to have so many gentlemen engaged in the cultivation of their estates in the neighbourhood . . . They ought to do what they could for the prosperity of the town, and they should unite together to return to Parliament some highly influential neighbour'.[85]

Francis Litchfield said in 1846 that:

'when he walked through Banbury and saw so many splendid houses erected, and how many large and small fortunes had been made, and all by means of the money received from the neighbouring agriculturalists, he could not bring himself to belief that in Banbury the destruction of Agriculture could be desired, still less promoted'.[86]

Aristocrats and farmers did not always reciprocate such sentiments. A Conservative complained in 1844:

'there are in this borough a bold and valiant set of Conservatives who ought to be supported, and the only reason they are not successful is because they are not supported by the neighbourhood as they ought to be'.[87]

The Banbury Conservatives were regarded by the landed classes in rather the same way that the Red Army looked upon the leaders of the rising in the Warsaw Ghetto in 1944. The Conservatives complained that aristocrats did not mix socially in the town with those who shared their political opinions, and that rural Conservatives inconsiderately patronised Liberals, particularly Cobbs Bank and the solicitors Golby, Munton and Draper.[88]

'The party is strongest in point of fact', wrote Sir Robert Peel, 'which has the existing registration in its favour'.[89] When the Reform Association was formed in 1837 its committee was instructed 'to secure the registration of every entitled Liberal and prevent Tories with no right from registering', and the practical basis of Liberal superiority in Banbury was meticulous attention to the register. In most years the Association was represented at the registration court by Francis Francillon, who rarely failed at Association dinners to commend Banbury's 'pure' register, and to remind Reformers of the need to ensure the election of 'proper persons' as overseers to ensure fairness in compiling the register.[90]

The division between Reformers and Conservatives was one within Banbury's respectable middle class. During the late 1830s the organised working-class became an important factor in local politics. In 1834 the plush weavers formed a short-lived lodge of the Owenite Grand National Consolidated Trades Union, and the Temperance Society in its teetotal phase after 1836 was essentially a proletarian movement.[91] The Banbury Working Mens' Association was founded in October 1838 'to promote the moral, intellectual and political advancement of the working class, to promote the education of the rising generation and the extirpation of those systems which tend to future slavery'. Its leaders included Alexander Spooner, landlord of the *Fleur-de-Lys*, and Peter Layton, a tin plate worker.[92]. The formation of the Association was probably prompted by delegates from the London Working Mens' Association. Among the LWMA's most successful missionaries was Henry Vincent, then aged 23, a compositor with an unusual talent for oratory.[93] On Tuesday 27 November 1838 Vincent spoke at noon to a large audience in the Market Place. He later lectured at the Town Hall and the Theatre, and on 29 November addressed an audience of women. He showed sensitivity to the traditional prejudices of Banburians by coupling his advocacy of the Charter and his denunciation of Tory tyranny, Whig treachery and the new Poor Law, with an attack on the University of Oxford:

'Am I to be told that the people of Oxfordshire have not sufficient knowledge to elect members to represent them in Parliament when they have the light of the colleges shining continually upon them? Am I to be told that they are not moral enough when collegiate morality is before them as an example?[94]

A similar awareness of what would please an audience in Banbury Market Place was shown by the teetotal blacksmith, John Hocking, who in 1836 announced that he was going to Oxford 'to hammer and rivet Temperance principles into every student and inhabitant of that metropolis of learning'.[95] Vincent's criticism of the Poor Law led to his being invited to the workhouse which he had to confess was above criticism.[96]

Vincent introduced three new factors into Banbury politics. He impressed upon his listeners the need for working-class unity. As a recent convert to teetotallism he commended sobriety and refused to speak in public houses. He also brought women into politics:

> 'The men of Britain are combining in large masses in order to wring from a reluctant government their just share of political power. What have women to do with politics? My answer is "everything".'[97]

During 1839 Chartism became well-established in Banbury. In March a subscription of £3 was sent to the National Convention following a lecture by John Collins.[98] By August regular meetings were being held in a schoolroom on The Green belonging to the Austin family. Speakers called for exclusive dealing and incautiously advised Chartists to 'arm for the fray'. There was an ignominiously unsuccessful attempt to stage a run on the Savings Bank.[99] In 1840 most of the national Chartist leaders were in prison, and subscriptions were collected for them and their wives in Banbury. The Chartists maintained contacts with Henry Vincent while he was incarcerated. In November 1840 they were preparing a reception for him in Banbury, and on 21 November he issued a 'Letter to the Men of Banbury' from Oakham Gaol, portraying his conversion to moral force:

> 'The mists of ignorance, intemperance, vice, producing as they do dependent habits, serfish feelings, a crawling slavish disposition, a propensity to extol wealth rather than religion and virtue, a love of murderous war and its vain and empty glory, these are the things that enslave a people. Men of Banbury, let us assail the vice and ignorance of the people; let us root out the rank weeds of servility which our rulers have been planting; let us convince our countrymen that God has made them with capacities and feelings for the enjoyment of the most exquisite happiness; for the realisation of intellectual pleasure; for the exercise of the moral virtues, and has spread equally before all who accept the conditions, a rich banquet of eternal felicity when the storms and turmoils of this life are past'.[100]

Vincent was released on 31 January 1841. He married on 27 February and on 1 March began a five-day visit to Banbury, during which it was resolved that he would fight the constituency at the imminent gelection. He continued to advocate teetotallism, and described his visit as a recommencement of 'my assaults upon the system'. He told a friend that he had impressed many of the wealthy classes, and predicted that if elected he would sit in 'the Den' for not more than two sessions, since 'no respectable working man could associate with such bad characters without losing his reputation'.[101] On 3 June he told Francis Place that if three candidates should stand his return was certain, and asked Place to seek assistance from 'those who are favourable to Chartism and would treat the House of Commons to a working man'. Place reminded Vincent that honesty and patriotism were not the most marked characteristics of voters in small boroughs, rebuked him for the excited tone of his letter, and urged him to work at his printing business for a decade, after which he might be in a condition to do some public service.[102] Vincent ignored Place's advice, and issued an election address on 4 June. He canvassed vigorously, made two speeches a day, and spent each evening with his committee. 'He was not quiet one minute throughout the contest' remarked one observer.[103]

On most major issues there was little difference between Vincent and Tancred. Against the six points of the Charter, Tancred proposed household suffrage, the ballot and three year parliaments. Vincent's appeals to 'radical and free trade electors' were matched by

Tancred's promises of 'free trade, cheap bread, sugar, coffee and timber'. The Chartists referred to the inhumanity of the Poor Law, but it was difficult to establish Tancred's personal responsibility for abuses, and Vincent had previously been embarrassed after exaggerating the shortcoming of the Banbury workhouse.[104] Vincent complained that Tancred had failed to support proposals to put some financial responsibility on to the fathers of illegitimate children, that he had voted money for the royal stables and kennels, but Liberals could point out that Tancred had opposed Church Rates, that he favoured investigation of the Pensions List, and that he had a long record of voting for some of the points of the Charter. When Vincent appealed for 'cheap, good and responsible government' he was speaking in the language of the Liberals. It was only on foreign policy, on Canada, Syria, China and Spain that Vincent found his opponent vulnerable.[105] Vincent's attempts to show that he had the better radical credentials backfired when Henry Warburton and Thomas Duncombe publicly refused to support him.[106] He concentrated on attacking 'the system' and on arousing class feeling. 'This is an era', he proclaimed, 'in which the Democracy of England will trample down the aristocracy'. He saw himself as 'one of the industrious classes, with no aristocratic prejudices to corrupt and enslave me', and told a ladies' meeting that food and clothing were 'heavily taxed to support the profligacy of our rulers'.[107] The Banbury Liberals were not unpractised in the art of denouncing the aristocracy. Tancred referred to 'class interests which have hitherto obstructed every effort that has been made to diminish the burdens and to extend the privileges of the people'.[108] Vincent's expressions of class antagonism were tempered by his proclamation that the interests of middle and working classes were identical, but he was embarrassed when reminded of his past denunciations of 'shopocrats'.[109] He challenged Tancred to a pre-nomination ballot, but like most such challenges, it was refused by the stronger party.[110]

On 23 June, only six days before the nomination, the Conservatives brought forward Hugh, eldest son of William Holbech of Farnborough Hall, the very model of the candidate for whom the more thoughtful Tories had yearned since 1832. 'Banbury will do well', commented one newspaper, 'to support one who resides in the Hall of his fathers, and dispenses in the neighbourhood the blessings which may be conferred by a real English gentleman, who has the cause of his country and the neighbourhood at heart'.[111] Holbech did not fight a vigorous campaign and issued only a few posters, proclaiming that he opposed hasty change, upheld the constitution, and favoured a mixed duty on the import of corn.[112] Tancred's supporters publicised the severity with which the game laws were applied at Farnborough, but their concern as nomination day approached was with Vincent. They started rumours that he would not go to the poll, and emphasised that, wittingly or not, the Chartist was the ally of the Tory.[113] After a rowdy election on 30 June, Tancred polled 124 votes, against 100 for Holbech and 51 for Vincent.[114] The Conservatives had a candidate who fulfilled the aspirations of local party leaders, a national movement of opinion was in their favour, and the opposition was divided. Brave prophecies that Holbech would win next time could not disguise their failure.[115] For the Reformers, the result was a relief, if scarcely a triumph, while the performance of the Chartist seemed creditable.

After the election Vincent's committee held a festival in a malthouse belonging to Barnes Austin, 'who had supported Mr. Vincent with his vote and interest'. Eight hundred sat down to tea. Speeches were made by Joseph Osborn and the Revd. John Clarke, and it was forecast that Vincent would be at the head of the next poll. The Society of Journeymen Tailors presented him with a green velvet vest, and in his speech he 'illustrated democratic principles with great effect and made a most powerful attack upon ignorance, injustice and vice'.[116] Chartists continued to play a lively part in local politics. In September 1841 they disrupted a Liberal meeting on the Corn Laws. The following month open air meetings were addressed by Peter Murray M'Douall, who had just been released from prison, and at the registration court, W. P. Roberts, the Chartist solicitor from Bath, represented 32 Chartists who claimed the vote. In the municipal election in November, Barnes Austin, Joseph Stuttard, Robert Cockerill, George Thomas and Archibald Dods stood without success in the Chartist interest.[117]

Vincent attracted the allegiance of most working-class radicals, including Thomas Brewer, a whitesmith, and the recipient of the letter from Oakham Gaol,[118] Edward French, a journeyman shoemaker who was forced on account of his Chartist views to emigrate to Waterloo, Iowa, where Vincent found him a prosperous farmer in 1868,[119] and John Buswell, a shoemaker who later settled on the Chartist estate at Snigs End. Some, like Brewer, were teetotallers. Vincent was also supported by some trade unions like the Society of Journeymen Tailors. Yet the ability of the Chartist to fight an effective election campaign, with posters, pamphlets and meetings on hired premises, depended on the support of the wealthy, particularly of Barnes Austin who had inherited his father's brewery in 1840. Five of the nine landlords of his public houses who voted in 1841 supported Vincent. His head brewer, Frederick Fleet, his clerk, Joseph Osborn, and the minister of his Baptist chapel, John Clarke, were active at Vincent's post-election tea party. Austin voted Conservative in 1835, and had a reputation as a 'fast man'. He was an unlikely patron of a Chartist, particularly of a teetotaller.[120] His conversion to radicalism may have arisen from a personal antagonism to Francis Litchfield, the most eloquent local apologist for Conservatism. Litchfield's love of hunting did not prevent him from trying to put down sports which threatened public order. In April 1837 a prize fight between Palmer and Luckett took place near Banbury 'at the instigation of some brewers and beerhouse keepers'. A return match was planned for Tuesday 18 April, but Litchfield and other magistrates obtained warrants preventing it from taking place in Northamptonshire, Oxfordshire, Buckinghamshire or Warwickshire. They pursued the huge crowd of fight followers from Adderbury to Cottesford Heath, to Whittlewood and on through Paulerspury and Fenny Stratford to Brickhill Heath near Woburn, where the contest took place a few yards over the Bedfordshire border. As the devotees returned westwards, Barnes Austin was involved in a scuffle with Litchfield and other magistrates at Stony Stratford, and eleven months afterwards was fined £10.[121] Two months after the prize fight Austin failed to support Henry Tawney in the 1837 election, soon after the court hearing the Banbury Working Mens' Association was formed at one of his public houses, and not long afterwards the Chartists were assembling in his schoolroom in South Bar.

During 1842, the year of the Second Chartist petition and the Plug Plot riots, Thomas Cheney, the printer, acted as local agent for Vincent's newspaper, the *National Vindicator*, which was published in Bath. In March the Banbury branch of the National Charter Association had 40 members. In April the *Northern Star* reported, with some exaggeration, that the Banbury Chartists' meeting room held a thousand.[122] On 23 May Vincent spoke to 1,500 people outside the town hall,[123] but incurred some criticism for delivering

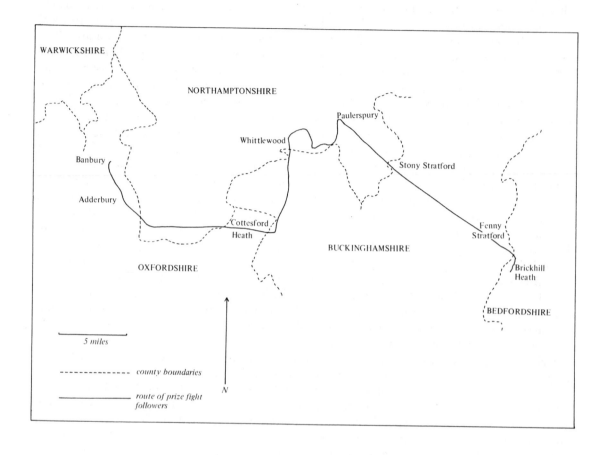

Figure 10.   Sketch map of route of prize fight followers, 18 April 1837.

most of his speeches to a paying audience in the Theatre. He was accused of 'filling his pockets out of the hard earnings of the poor'.[124] In July, 13 representatives to the general council of the National Association were nominated.[125] Banbury remained peaceful during the Plug Plot riots but Chartism seems to have benefited from the agitation elsewhere, for 50 membership cards for the National Association were issued in the quarter ending on 30 September. Some Banbury Chartists formed a branch of Joseph Sturge's Complete Suffrage Union, and sent three delegates to the conference in Birmingham in December 1842 called to bring together the CSU and Feargus O'Connor's National Charter Association.[126] One of them was Robert Kemp Philp, a Cornish printer who had edited the *National Vindicator* with Vincent in Bath. He moved to Banbury late in 1842 and ran a Chartist News Room in Church Lane. He was elected to the committee of the Banbury Mechanics' Institute in May 1843, but withdrew the following

September. By 1845 he had moved to London where he edited 'useful knowledge' publications. He was a teetotaller and in March 1844 lectured to the Banbury Temperance Society.

Locally, as nationally, much radical energy was directed away from Chartism in 1843. Banbury radicals were attracted by a variety of alternative causes. At least four Chartists were drawn into millenarian religion by the Disciples of Christ. Many had links with the local temperance movement, which at the time of the Plug Plot riots in 1842 entered on the period of its greatest prosperity.[128] Nevertheless some formal organisation continued, and Chartism survived to influence the general election of 1847 and various municipal contests, and to be a point of reference for radicals in subsequent decades. And for 30 years, Henry Vincent drew huge audiences whenever he lectured in Banbury.

The registered electorate in Banbury in the 1830s varied between 329 and 386.[129] In 1835 only 246, or 64 per cent, of the electors went to the hustings but the turn-out for the more closely-fought contests of 1837 was respectively 72 and 73 per cent. Banbury was one of 94 boroughs, about half of those represented in the Commons, which had electorates of between 300 and 1,000. There were 31 boroughs with less than 300 electors.[130] The 1835 election, in which the Liberals won 82.5 per cent of the poll, is an inadequate indication of the occupational and class basis of support for the parties since the Conservative challenge was so weak. In 1837 the Conservatives won 29.3 per cent of the poll. Only 23 of Tawney's votes came from those who had supported Williams in 1835. He attracted the support of 14 new voters, five who had voted Liberal in 1835 and 33 who had been neutral, which shows conclusively that many Conservatives had failed to vote for Williams. Most of the Conservatives of 1835 who failed to support Tawney in 1837 had died or gone away. Tawney's supporters included his partner, J. A. Gillett, and at least two of Gillett's fellow Quakers. Three other Friends who had voted Liberal in 1835 remained neutral. Tancred lost support among craftsmen and retailers, but Liberal support in these two crucial sectors of the electorate remained at over 75 per cent. More than half of the farmers voted for Tawney, and while farmers comprised less than 5 per cent of the Liberal vote, they made up over 13 per cent of Conservative support. In the drink trade support for the Conservative rose to over 40 per cent, comprising 22.67 per cent of the Conservative vote. Drink traders made up on 13.81 per cent of the Liberal vote. The 1841 election saw a substantial erosion of Liberal support. Tancred's vote fell from 181 in 1837 to 124, or 45.09 per cent of the vote. It is doubtful whether all of the 51 votes cost for Vincent would have gone to the Liberal in the absence of Chartist candidate. Tancred was supported by 98 voters who had voted for him in 1837, five previously neutral and three who had voted for Tawney, one of whom was a Quaker, perhaps drawn to favour the banker in 1837 by links with the Gilletts, while another was Thomas Ward of the Waterlooo lodging house whose vote was assumed to be purchasable. Only 32 of the 89 electors lost to the Liberals between 1837 and 1841 were dead or removed from the town. Eighteen were attracted to the Chartist, while seven voted Conservative and 26 remained neutral, an indication, perhaps, of disillusion with the Liberal government and with Tancred's performance as MP. Tancred gained the votes of only 18 of the 67 electors who polled for the first time in 1841. Holbech's hundred voters included 47 who had voted for Tawney, and seven converts from Liberalism, among them two farmers, two prominent drapers who were Anglicans, and two publicans. Three had once been members of the Reform Association committee.

The growth of Conservative support was due to Holbech's appeal to new electors, from whom he gained 25 votes. He had the support of half of those engaged in the drink trade, and 61.54 per cent of the farmers. More than half the 51 Chartist votes in 1841 came from new electors. Three had voted Conservative in 1837, two of whom, keepers of low lodging houses, were probably attracted by bribes rather than radical principles. Three Chartist voters who had been Liberals in 1837 were landlords of Barnes Austin's public houses. The majority of the Chartist voters were drawn from the poorer ranks of Banbury's craftsmen, 30.51 per cent of whom supported Vincent. The Chartist gained the votes of 19.57 per cent of the drink trade, comprising over a fifth of his support, an astonishing proportion for a teetotaller.

The accession to power of Sir Robert Peel's Conservative government, the appointment of Conservative magistrates in Banbury in 1842, and their nearness to defeat in 1841, shook the confidence of the Banbury Liberals. Their leaders subsequently strove hard to present Tancred in a favourable light. In February 1843, for the first time for a decade, the Reformers dined together at the *Wheatsheaf*. Tancred was among the 150 present, and the occasion became an annual tradition. It was held in the early spring, and during the 1840s Tancred was normally accompanied by a 'bottle holder', a Liberal MP popular in Banbury, Dr. John Bowring in 1844, Edward Bouverie in 1845, and Sir Andrew Leith Hay in 1847. Usually up to 200 attended. Provision was always made for teetotallers to drink water or coffee. Toasts usually included 'Free Trade', 'Civil and Religious Liberty', 'the working classes' and 'the extension of the suffrage and vote by ballot'. Tancred's voting record was questioned at the dinners, and his visits to Banbury were used for meetings with influential or supplicant individuals. On one occasion he asked his agent for 'a list of names of persons whom I ought to see'.[131]

The summer counterpart of the dinner was the annual meeting of the British Schools Society, formed in 1840 at a meeting chaired by Tancred, who gave £100 towards the building of the school, subscribed £5 annually, and attended the first 16 annual meetings. The Liberal MPs William Ewart and Dr. John Bowring were among the guest speakers in the 1840s. The meeting was sometimes followed by a Liberal excursion into the countryside, usually to Edgehill, which was a place of special significance to the Reformers who saw themselves as heirs of the 17th-century Parliamentarians. In 1843 a group of Liberals travelled to Chalgrove Field for the inauguration of the John Hampden monument. Tancred observed in a speech at the celebration lunch that he was 'surrounded . . . by a band of my own warm-hearted constituents', and boasted 'In Banbury we warm ourselves by the reflection that we live on the confines of Edgehill, and we come here today to inflame ourselves, if that were necessary, for the same glorious cause'. His speech was remembered with particular pleasure by Edward Cobb some 15 years later.[132] Conservative social occasions appear to have been less successful. A dinner was usually held each autumn, but the attendance rarely exceeded 60.[133]

Tancred sustained his reputation amongst the wider body of constituents by his support of local causes and his ability to place local men in government jobs. In 1842 he made a donation to the Mechanics' Institute, following an appeal by Francis Francillon, who was troubled by the ethics of seeking money from an MP:

'I am sure that a donation would not only be popular, but useful, and, as I disdain soliciting it, it would be an unsolicited one if you thought right to make one'.

Figure 11.   Edgehill Round Tower (from W. P. Johnson, History of Banbury*)*

He subscribed to the Dorcas Society in 1842, to the races in 1845, the Horticultural Society in 1847, the Primitive Methodists in 1848, and to a fund for a sick Baptist minister in 1849. In the severe winter of 1845–46 he made £100 available for the poor.[134] During Peel's ministry between 1841 and 1846 he naturally had little influence in government appointments, but after 1846 he obtained jobs in the Excise for the sons of two prominent Liberals. He was unable to help a dissenting minister to become an Inspector of Schools, to find a post for a bankrupt chemist, or to assist a young plush weaver to become a letter carrier.[135] Appointments as letter carriers were of considerable political importance. When the Middleton Cheney walk became vacant in 1850 Tancred complained 'It rains messengers'. The knowledge that an MP could obtain positions of this kind probably did much to enlist the support of the deferential working-class although such appointments were few in number. The right to make them was jealously contested as late as the mid-1860s.[136]

The introduction of Income Tax in the 1842 Budget, the educational clauses of the 1843 Factories Bill, and the increased government grant to the Roman Catholic training college at Maynooth in 1845, were all the subjects of protest meetings in Banbury during Peel's ministry,[137] but while Tancred consistently supported the abolition of the Corn Laws, Liberals avoided open debate on Free Trade in Banbury. In February 1846 Francis Francillon admitted that Anti-Corn Law League lecturers had not been brought to the town to avoid upsetting the farmers. Nevertheless in 1847, repeal was seen as 'the greatest of moral triumphs'.[138] Several Protectionist meetings held in Banbury were supported by farmers rather than townspeople.[139]

Chartism revived in 1846 with the formation of a branch of the Chartist Land Company, whose membership was large in comparison with that of branches in other towns. Two Banbury families settled on the Land Company estate at Snigs End in Gloucestershire.[140] A Chartist offered to stand in the 1847 election, but after Tancred had accepted a series of demands, which included the support of universal suffrage, the Chartists, led by the shoemaker Robert Baxter, gave him their backing.[141] The Conservative candidate in the election was James MacGregor, a Liverpool banker, and chairman of the South Eastern Railway. He fulfilled Joseph Parkes's forecasts that he would prove 'green at electioneering'. He propounded strongly Protestant sentiments, and made much of his opposition to the Maynooth Grant, but clumsily confessed that his mind was not made up about the extension of the franchise.[142] He suffered from being readily identifiable with all that was disreputable about railway speculation, even to the extent of receiving turbulent support from unemployed navvies who had been engaged to build the Oxford and Rugby Railway. Both candidates made inflammatory speeches at the nomination and MacGregor's Protestant sentiments were expressed all over the town on huge orange and purple posters. Each side employed two bands. The Grand Duke Constantine of Russia passed through Banbury during the contest, and his attendants expressed surprise at what they saw.[143]

Tancred won the election, gaining 226 votes (57.95 per cent of the poll) against MacGregor's 164.[144] A comparison with the 1837 election shows that in every significant sector of the electorate there had been a substantial increase in the proportion of electors voting Conservative. The number on the register increased from 383 to 465 between 1841 and 1847, while the turn-out went up from 72 to 84 per cent. MacGregor gained over 70 per cent of the agricultural vote, and marginally increased the Conservative share of the votes of the drink trade and of the retailers. Tancred benefited most from the division of the Chartist vote. 36 of the 51 voters who had supported Vincent in 1841 voted in 1847, 27 for Tancred and 9 for MacGregor, the latter including Barnes Austin, who gave a celebratory party for MacGregor, exactly as he had done for Henry Vincent. MacGregor attracted only two voters who had supported Tancred in 1841, and lost two Holbech voters to the Liberal. 44 voters in 1847 had remained neutral in 1841, and divided almost evenly, 24 for Tancred and 20 for MacGregor. Of the 166 new electors, 93 supported Tancred and 72 MacGregor.

By 1847 Banbury was a safe Liberal constituency. Liberals could appeal to precedent, seeking the return of 'our faithful representative for 15 years', and to Banbury's sense of its own identity within a hostile hinterland, declaring, 'for the Liberal Borough of Banbury to return a Tory would be a sad disgrace to us'. Yet the Liberal position no longer appeared unassailable. Conservatives won the town council election of 1847, and their performance in the general election was creditable. One of the characteristics of a safe seat is that it contains an élite willing to strive for the success of their favoured party, and in Banbury Liberal leaders were still determined to maintain social cohesion among their followers and to keep a pure register. Nevertheless memories were fading of the discredited *ancien régime*, and of the bliss experienced by those alive at the dawn of the Reformers' triumphs. Banbury was still, in 1847, one of the small boroughs which were the seedbed of Victorian Liberalism, but the respectability of Conservatives had been re-established.

VI

A HABIT OF SPONTANEOUS ACTION

'Even if the government could comprehend within itself, in each department, all the most eminent intellectual capacity and active talent of the nation, it would not be the less desirable that the conduct of a large portion of the affairs of society should be left in the hands of the persons immediately interested in them'. [1]

THERE WAS A REVOLUTION in the government of Banbury during the 1830s when the townspeople secured for themselves a degree of control over their own affairs such as they had rarely enjoyed previously. At the same time many of the less formal ways in which the local community functioned were transformed. Opportunities for providing charitable assistance to the needy and for self-help were enlarged. Educational provision was extended and local culture re-vitalised. In some respects voluntary societies anticipated the functions of the formal institutions of government. At a time when the impact of government on many aspects of the life of the community was minimal, voluntary societies affected the lives of most people rather more than the decisions of the Home Secretary, the Mayor or the Board of Guardians. In the provision of sustenance in adversity, in education and in entertainment there were revolutions between 1830 and 1850 as profound as the contemporary changes in the institutions of government.

Some important organisations in Banbury, the National Schools Society, the Savings bank and the Visiting Charitable Society were formed about 1820, while the Old Charitable Society dates from 1782, but a high proportion of the societies which shaped so much of the life of the mid-Victorian town were founded in the 1830s.[2] Organisations like the Mechanics' Institute, the Temperance Society, the Choral Society and the Agricultural Association directly or indirectly affected the whole community. Some voluntary societies were centrifugal. They saw themselves as town-centred, and charged with a civilising mission to the countryside. Such groups tended to be Dissenting rather than Anglican, and radical rather than Conservative. Other groups were centripetal, gatherings of the like-minded from the countryside who assembled in the market town to pursue common objectives. Many Anglican organisations were centripetal and largely clerical in their membership. The country parson was often isolated, and he had an obvious need to meet with fellow enthusiasts to aid the mission to Jerusalem or plan the excavation of tumuli. Polarisation between Anglicans and Conservatives and Dissenters and Liberals was always evident among voluntary societies in Banbury. In several areas of activity there were competing societies, and there were disputes when one faction tried to appropriate for itself an institution which was alleged by the other to belong to the community at large. Religious and political divisions could be an incentive to additional provision, but in some spheres polarisation hindered worthwhile developments.

It was observed of voluntary organisations in Banbury in the 1960s that 'the more manifest the functions of an association, the wider the social range of membership — the more diffuse the aims, the more latent the functions, the narrower the social range of membership'.[3] This was also true in the 19th century. Co-operation between factions was possible when there were clearly-defined, non-sectarian objectives, but when an organisation's activities had obvious denominational implications, as in the provision of schooling, or when its social activities took precedence over its declared aims, it tended to recruit from only one politico-religious faction or social class. The latent functions of many societies are not obvious to the historian. It is evident from the correspondence of Henry Tancred that the annual meetings of the British Schools Society served as rallies for the Liberal Party, but this would not have been directly discernible from any other source.[4] Other organisations probably had similar latent functions which can no longer be perceived.

The celebration of Queen Victoria's coronation on Thursday 25 June 1838 was one of the peaks of voluntary achievement in Banbury, a point of reference for Banburians throughout the 19th century. It was regarded as an occasion when the middle classes triumphed over their political and religious differences to treat the poor on an unprecedented scale. Preparations for the event began less than a month beforehand, when there were forecasts of 'such a banquet of fun as would have made our Puritan Banbury forefathers of Cromwell's day look very oddly'. An official committee raised money for a dinner for the poor, while a group of young men sought subscriptions to provide entertainments. There was a procession of the trades similar to that which celebrated the triumph of reform in 1832, a tea for Sunday School children, dancing and sports. The committee earnestly tasted plum puddings in mid-June, believing the proof of the pudding to be in the eating. 1,700 lbs of such pudding comprised the first course of a meal served in the Horsefair for 'all the working-classes and poor who chose to partake of it'. 3,400 sat down at 45 tables, each of which had a tradesman as its superintendent, and four young men as waiters. The pudding was followed by 180 dishes of beef, weighing over 3,000 lbs, with 1,596 lbs of bread and 45 kilderkins of ale. 'Many who partook of the dinner', reported one observer, 'seemed absolutely entranced at the sight and enjoyment of such liberal fare'. There was much emphasis on class-mixing and on the participation of both sexes, but groups with religious scruples refused to join the procession, and sectarian differences were never far from the surface. There were disputes over the toasts to the royal family at a dinner given after the event for the organisers.[5] Such rivalries were less well-concealed on the occasion of the Queen's wedding in 1840. 'Everybody knows', remarked one newspaper, 'that the people of Banbury can do things well when they do but drop dirty politics', but the whole occasion vibrated with social tension. There was no celebration for the poor. The main event was a ball at the National School, attended by 400, equally divided between Liberals and Conservatives. A rather forced attempt was made to foster non-sectarian goodwill by arranging for the first dance to be led by William Munton, son of the Liberal agent, partnering Sarah Rusher, daughter of a leading Conservative.[6]

Some voluntary associations fulfilled some of the functions of the state or of local authorities, anticipating reforming legislation, and may be categorised as quasi-governmental associations. When such an organisation had a clearly defined non-sectarian purpose it could unite middle-class opinion. The association which did so most successfully was formed to prevent begging in Banbury. In 1832 a newspaper complained about beggars in the town, 'so many of whom are to be seen travelling about the county in all directions that it is obvious that their trade must be a profitable one'.[7] The Society for the Supression of Mendicity was founded early in 1834 with a committee representing all shades of bourgeois opinion. When mendicants applied to its superintendent, Thomas Taylor, he provided them with a night's lodging at the 'Mendicity House' near the bridge, on condition that they left the town the following day. Over 2,000 were thus accommodated in four years, most of whom were mechanics and labourers seeking work rather than vagrants. About 15 per cent were Irish and Scots, and in 1838 the society was wound up because people were said to be reluctant to spend money on 'beggars from other countries', The society was praised as 'the means of clearing the town of the swarms of vagabonds with which it was formerly infested'.[8] By 1838 its functions were being assumed by the new Union Workhouse, and it had anticipated the policies towards vagrants set out in the new Poor Law. It was the most effective quasi-governmental agency in the town because the divisions among the middle classes were bridged by a clear common purpose.

Societies formed to protect property may also be regarded as quasi-governmental associations. Their purpose, the better enforcement of the law, would appear to have been clearly manifest. Yet societies of this kind in Banbury exemplified the fundamental division within the middle classes, because their manifest aims became obscured by their social functions. The Neithrop Association for the Prosecution of Felons was formed before 1820, when it had 20 members, and was already holding an annual dinner. By 1833 membership had risen to 36, but it fell to 12 by 1837, and stood at only 17 in 1842. Prosecutions were rarely undertaken, and in 1843 only £3 14s. 2d. was expended, while accumulated funds totalled £84 10s. 0d. The association had become an exclusive, self-perpetuating body, largely Conservative and Anglican in membership, with undefined entry qualifications.[9] The Banbury Association for the Prosecution of Felons was formed at the suggestion of James Beesley, the town clerk, in 1835. The annual subscription was only five shillings with an entry fee of the same amount. Each member had to pay half a crown a year for a dinner whether he attended or not. In 1836 it had 62 members, 25 of whom lived outside the borough. Eighteen of the Banburians voted Liberal in 1835, when only five supported the Conservative. During the 1840s the association undertook about 40 prosecutions, posted bills and offered rewards.[10] It fulfilled more of its manifest functions than the Neithrop Association, and its foundation may be seen as part of the reform of the *ancien régime* in Banbury, but the place of the annual dinner in the constitution suggests that it also had a social role as the Liberal counterpart to what had become a Conservative dining club.

The education of the young was regarded in mid-19th century Banbury as the province of private enterprise and Christian philanthropy, but certainly not as part of the business of government. At least 50 private schools operated in the town between 1832 and 1850, ranging from the prestigious Banbury Academy to small classes taught by individuals in their own homes, some in houses as cramped as those in Monument Street or Spring Cottages.[11] The Blue Coat School, founded in 1705, catered for a minority of the children of the poor.[12] The most significant development of the early 19th century was the realisation that market forces were incapable of providing adequately for increasing numbers of children, and that the influence of the endowed charity schools was marginal. The response was to establish voluntary schools, linked to national organisations, and run by local committees, their income being a mixture of low fees collected from pupils, local subscriptions and some support from the national bodies, which in turn received government funds. The establishment of such bodies anticipated publicly-financed education for the poor in much the same way that the Mendicity Society anticipated the New Poor Law. The Banbury National School was founded in 1817, absorbing the old-established Thorpe Charity School, on whose land in Southam Road its buildings were erected. The Blue Coat Trustees, who administered another ancient charity, paid £30 p.a. to the new school, for which they were allowed to send to it as many children as the trust could clothe. Initially the school was supported by wealthy dissenters as well as by churchmen.[13]

In 1833 a government enquiry identified seven schools in Banbury in addition to the National School, although the local directory for that year listed sixteen.[14] Some of these private schools had denominational affiliations. The Banbury Academy was linked with the Unitarians, and the boarding school for young ladies run by the Misses Eason with the Baptists. The first public dissenting school was an Infants School established in Church Passage in 1835 following a meeting addressed by Samuel Wilderspin, the well-known advocate of infant education. Parents whose children had outgrown it were said to have called for the British School which was built in Crouch Street in 1839-40, supported by a body of dissenters described in a hostile newspaper as 'a company of shareholders, the *family* of Unitarians and Anythingarians'.[15]

While the Dissenters were extending their educational role from the infant to the elementary stage, the Anglicans became involved with a secondary school. In April 1839 the Oxford Diocesan Board of Education was formed, one of its aims being to establish 'boarding or other middle or commercial schools for the sons of the farmer and the trader'. Meetings in Banbury in 1840 resolved to raise £2,500 in £25 shares, and to advertise for a 'classical and commercial teacher'. Soon afterwards John Thomas Cooke, who claimed to have been Professor of English at the Imperial University of St Petersburg, became master of what was variously called the Diocesan School, the Middle School, or the Classical Commercial School, at Cherwell House in Bridge Street. Tuition in Latin, French, English, Geography, History, Arithmetic and Drawing was offered at £4 p.a. for day boys and £20 p.a. for boarders. There were 36 boarders in July 1841, and in December 1842 the school was said to be 'increasing in numbers and usefulness'. The venture faltered in 1843 or 1844. Cooke became master of a private 'classical and commercial' school in Crouch Street, and in the 1850s went to Aynho Grammar School and subsequently to Switzerland.[16] The failure of this attempt to provide a higher level of education through a public institution is perhaps an indictment of sectarian education. A non-denominational school might have succeeded in attracting sufficient able pupils, and such a school could considerably have influenced the development of the town. Banbury was rather too small in the 1840s to support rival establishments at this level. While sectarian enthusiasm had the effect of enlarging the provision of elementary schooling, denominational rivalries inhibited the growth of education at higher levels.

The Roman Catholics established their own educational system in the 1840s. Previously Catholic children had attended a private school run, with a variety of other enterprises, by one John Howell. In 1846 a new school was opened in a building adjacent to St John's church and Howell's establishment closed. In 1849 it provided free education for a hundred children of the poor, and taught about a dozen fee-payers. In 1852 it was taken over the the Sisters of Charity of St Paul.[17]

In 1851 some 1,668 children were attending school in Banbury, and about half of their places were provided by the four publicly accountable elementary schools, made up as follows:[18]

National School (1847)	240
Infant School (1854)	250
British School (1854)	270
Roman Catholic School (1849)	110
Total	870

The ages of children in school varied from two (nearly 30 per cent of two year olds were at school) to eighteen, although most children had left by the age of fourteen. Of those aged between five and ten, some 77.29 per cent were attending school, which suggests that the growth of voluntary schools since the 1830s had the effect of making elementary education available for all but the poorest children. In the 11–14 age group only 57.48 per cent of children were at school.[19] William Wilson's survey of Neithrop in 1850 shows that 113 out of 198 children in that very poor area went to the National Schools, regardless of the religious affiliations of their parents.[20] Thirty-four children went to the Nonconformist Infants School, but only two to the British School. Although the latter was some distance from Neithrop, it is probable that few children from the hamlet went there because it catered more for the middle class than the poor. Thirty-four Neithrop children, some the offspring of labourers, went to dames' schools.

In the sphere of adult education the outstanding innovation in early 19th-century Banbury was the formation of a Mechanics' Institute at a meeting of 61 people at the home of William Bigg, the Quaker chemist, on 12 March 1835, following a suggestion made after Samuel Wilderspin's lecture on infant schools. On 20 September 1836 a new Institute building was opened in Church Passage. A library was established, drawing and music classes began, a museum was founded, and in a manuscript magazine members recorded their interests and exercised their literary talents. Well-known lecturers were brought to the town, including J. S. Buckingham, who received 40 guineas for lectures on Palestine and Egypt in 1836. Some members spoke about their own interests. Francis Francillon lectured on the Battle of Edgehill, George Harris on 'Ancient Britons and Druidism', and Edward Cobb on the law of property. The Institute was primarily but not entirely a Liberal and Dissenting body, but members included such varied people as Dr. Tandy, the Roman Catholic priest, Alfred Beesley, the historian, and R. K. Philp, the Chartist. Sometimes conflicts with political implications arose within the Institute. In 1839 Alfred Beesley questioned whether John Minter Morgan's *Hampden in the Nineteenth Century* was suitable for the library, and it was withdrawn. The Institute affiliated in 1840 to the Midland Counties Literary and Scientific Association, and tried to spread its zeal into the countryside. A branch at Steeple Aston was established in 1837 and encouragement given to a new institute at Witney in 1838.[21]

In the 1840s the Institute fell into debt, and facilities in the reading room were reduced. The deliberations of the committee often appear petty and lacking in vision. In March 1851 the committee regretted that the Institute was 'so little valued by the classes for whose benefit it was established and is kept up'.[22] Mechanics' institutes can be criticised as organisations which failed in their declared objectives of enlarging educational opportunities for the working-class, and which, where they did attract working-class members, acted as de-politicising providers of entertainment and agencies of social control. In a society which was markedly polarised, the Banbury Institute sought to achieve limited cultural objectives while avoiding the minefields of political and religious controversy. The insistence in its rules that 'the Institute shall not at any time be perverted . . . to serve the purposes of any party, sect or establishment, in politics or religion; or be made the instrument of any party in questions of local politics' was very necessary in Banbury.[23] The Institute gave the town its first public library and museum. It provided an organisational framework for the promotion of lectures, and premises on which other organisations could meet. It encouraged a serious attitude towards learning. One prominent citizen recalled in 1878 that he was persuaded by William Bigg, 'to give up frivolous pursuits for the Mechanics' Institute, to his benefit'.[24] An eloquent tribute to the Institute in its early years was paid by Edward Cobb in 1876:

> '. . . some of the happiest days of my life were spent in its service, certainly the most useful and valuable to myself, for it brought me into contact with a class of persons with whom I had previously had very little commerce, from whom I not only derived a great deal of information of a kind I did not before possess, but was led by frequent discussion upon general subjects with some of the more intellectual members gradually to wipe off many erroneous views and prejudices which I had imbibed in some of the earlier years of my life when I can scarcely be said to have had any opinions at all. It completely changed my political views, if, indeed, I may be said to have had any before'.[25]

Whatever its failings, the Institute enabled members of different sects, parties and classes to mix on tolerably amiable terms. It remained part of the essential framework of local society for the rest of the century.

Banbury was notorious for its opposition to slavery, and the anti-slavery movement was one of the most effective voluntary agencies in the town. The issue was prominent in the election of 1832 and in subsequent parliamentary contests.[26] Opposition to slavery was the first question which turned the eyes of concerned Banburians overseas. The movement was successful because it was a cause and not an organisation. An anti-slavery meeting in August 1830 attracted an audience of 500, and led to the formation of a branch of the Anti-Slavery Society, which was wound up after the emancipation of slaves was achieved in 1833.[27] Subsequent activities were arranged on an *ad hoc* basis but were remarkably successful. A meeting in May 1838 called to protest against the apprentice system in the colonies was said to be the largest public meeting ever held in Banbury. The speakers included Liberals, Conservatives, Anglicans and Dissenters of many hues.[28] Because it lacked formal organisation, the anti-slavery movement provided few occasions for clashes of culture. The cause in Banbury was led by Quakers, but its aims were clear and widely accepted, and its strength lay in the diversity of its support.

Teetotallers were regarded with as much suspicion in Banbury as among the congregation at Mark Rutherford's Tanner's Lane chapel, where, 'If once a man differed so far from his fellows as not to drink beer and spirits, there was no knowing where the division might end'.[29] The temperance movement manifestly strove for social reform, although its aims were incapable of realisation by parliamentary bills, and until the 1850s legislation was not regarded as an appropriate objective. In practice, in Banbury as elsewhere, it developed a variety of latent functions.

The temperance movement first appeared in Banbury in 1834 when Samuel Beesley, Quaker, confectioner and Liberal, called together 15 'gentlemen of influence' to meet the Revd. William Fisher, agent of the British and Foreign Temperance Society, the London-based anti-spirits organisation, which already had several branches in Oxfordshire. A branch was formed in Banbury which, like the BFTS nationally, tried to achieve its objects by influencing the influential.[30] Just as the national temperance movement was set ablaze by an infusion of working-class teetotal zeal from Preston in 1834, so in Banbury the cause was transformed in April 1836 by John Hockings, the teetotal blacksmith from Birmingham. His humour and lecturing skill drew 500 to one meeting, and he gave a public demonstration that abstinence had not impaired his ability as a smith.[31] He won 20 teetotal pledges and transformed the Temperance Society from a discreet pressure group into a popular crusade. Within three months it had 120 members, of whom 71 were teetotallers, seven of them 'reclaimed drunkards'. Two years later membership had increased to 170, and experience meetings had become a central part of the society's activities.[32] There was friction between teetotallers and moderationists, but gradually the former predominated. The founder of the movement in Banbury, Samuel Beesley, retained wine and beer to the value of £50 on his annual inventory until 1840, when, it may be supposed, he became an abstainer.[33] Many teetotallers were also Chartists and worked for Henry Vincent in the election of 1841. After the failure of the Chartist challenge in the election, the Temperance Society entered a third phase. It ceased to be primarily an evangelistic body, and began to provide alternatives to established institutions. Early in 1842 a temperance hotel was opened, and John Head, a Quaker hosier, fitted up a 'large and commodious room' in Parson's Street which served the temperance movement for a quarter of a century. A ladies association was formed to distribute tracts and the society began missions in the villages. Membership rose to over 400 by the middle of 1842, and exceeded 500 twelve months later.[34] The typical activity became the middle-class tea party rather than the experience meeting listening to the confessions of reclaimed drunkards. The society functioned like a branch of the Anti-Corn Law League, and drew its strength from the same social forces. 'We have had our meetings of dissenting ministers', said Cobden in September 1842, 'we have obtained the co-operation of the ladies; we have resorted to tea-parties; and taken those pacific means for carrying out our views which mark us rather as a middle-class set of agitators'.[35] In September 1844 a Rechabite 'tent', a teetotal friendly society, was formed in Banbury, its first festival being modelled closely on the traditional Club Day celebrations.[36] In 1844 a Teetotal Brass Band was practising in the Temperance Rooms,[37] and the movement had sufficiently aroused feeling in the town to stimulate a publican to stand in the borough council election as an anti-Teetotal candidate. Coffee was by that time always provided for abstainers at Reformers' dinners.[38] After 1845 the income and membership of the society stagnated. Only meetings addressed by well-known speakers attracted large audiences. From 1846 an increasing emphasis was put on the advocacy of abstinence among children, as if the members had despaired of achieving their aims within their own generation.[39]

The Temperance Society received financial support from a wide section of respectable society. Subscribers in 1845 included Conservatives and Anglicans, as well as Liberals and Dissenters who were not teetotallers, but the active membership included no magistrates, councillors or Conservatives, and consisted for the most part of Liberals and Dissenters. The most prominent members were Quakers and Primitive Methodists, members of the only two denominations in Banbury who numbered no publicans among their adherents.[40] Temperance had become by the late 1840s a *weltanschauung*, a calendar of events for a portion of Banbury's dissenters. Its purpose, to bring sobriety to a society afflicted by a serious problem of public drunkenness, remained manifest, but it had developed many latent functions. It provided an alternative hierarchy of offices for ambitious Dissenters. With the Mechanics' Institute it popularised the public lecture. Through its meeting rooms, hotel and friendly societies, it provided facilities otherwise available only to those prepared to drink. It helped to break down the segregation of the sexes in public life. Yet in origin its purposes were more akin to those of the anti-slavery movement than the Mechanics' Institute, and as its contributions to local culture increased, so its effectiveness as a proseletysing pressure group was diminished.

The Banbury Agricultural Association was an organisation of very different social complexion from the Temperance Society, but there are curious parallels between the two bodies. The association was centripetal, an assembly in the market town of farmers and landowners from the hinterland. It was formed in 1834 to ensure that protection for agriculture was not diminished. Like many such societies it began to organise meetings at which cattle were judged and awards made to loyal labourers. The *Northampton Herald* pointed out in October 1842 that the purpose of the association was to protect the agricultural interest not to exhibit stock, and insisted that its committee should meet, according to the rules, on the first Thursday of each month that Parliament was in session.[41] As in the Temperance Society, the latent functions of the association were taking precedence over its manifest objectives.

Several religious societies met regularly in Banbury by the 1840s, their main social function, like that of the Clerical Meetings and Book Society in George Eliot's *Milby*, having been to provide meeting places for country clergymen.[42] The local auxiliary of the British and Foreign Bible Society was founded in 1817, and was supported by Wesleyans and Quakers as well as by Anglicans.[43] as was the local branch of the London Association for Promoting Christianity among the Jews, formed in 1842.[44] By the late 1840s the Society for Promoting Christian Knowledge, the Society for the Propagation of the Gospel, the Church Missionary Society and the Banbury Protestant Institute were all fulfilling similar functions.[45]

By 1850 the public lecture was an established part of the cultural pattern in Banbury, although it had been an unknown medium 20 years earlier. The promotion of lectures was pioneered by the Mechanics' Institute and the Temperance Society, and by 1850 other organisations were following their example. Women normally attended lectures, which led to agitation for meeting rooms which were not on licensed premises. The Mechanics' Institute and the Temperance Society provided such rooms and, when demanding a new town hall in 1850, one speaker called for better facilities for occasions when 'they wished to take ladies to lectures or what not'.[46]

Before the 1830s concerts and plays were part of the *ancien régime*. They were normally provided by professionals under the patronage of the town's traditional rulers, as in 1821 when *The School for Scandal* was produced under the patronage of the Earl of Guilford.[47] During the 1830s new institutions provided means of staging concerts without the help of wealthy individuals, and gave opportunities for local people to make their own musical entertainments. Banbury's theatre was a large building in Church Lane erected by James Hill.[48] For about two months at the beginning of each year a season of plays was staged there by Henry Jackman's itinerant company, which from 1805 until 1863 moved between the small towns of an area which stretched from the northern fringes of London to Ludlow and Market Harborough.[49] In 1838 one newspaper commented that 'his company of comedians have again come to waste their sweetness on the desert air of Banbury', and maintained that audiences were always thin, but in 1842 performances were well supported, and in 1848 the respectable way in which Jackman conducted the theatre was commended.[50] Performances were usually double or triple bills, appealing to many tastes and ranging from *King Lear* to displays by acrobatic dogs. Some performances were usually patronised by individuals or local organisations.

In October 1844 a concert was given at the Theatre under the patronage of Colonel and Lady North of Wroxton Abbey. A month later the Banbury Choral Society gave its first public concert, a selection from *Messiah*, at the British Schools.[51] The new style of promotion epitomised the changing pattern of artistic patronage in the town. The Choral Society was established with 33 members in May 1844, with the object of:

> 'stimulating the hard-worked mechanic to find a pleasing and grateful relaxation for the toilsome cares of life in the practice of Music, rather than, as now, waste the prowess of body and mind amid the debauchery of sensual indulgence'.[52]

An Amateur Musical Society was founded in the 1830s but seems to have languished. The Philharmonic Society founded in 1847 gave occasional public concerts,[53] and a town brass band was formed in 1836.[54] Increasing numbers of visiting musicians gave concerts in Banbury. In 1846 a Signor Morzini, a violinist somewhat improbably billed as a German, gave a recital at the *White Hart*, and in 1848 Mr. and Mrs. J. Pattinson performed 'operatic selections from the highly celebrated composer Rossini'.[55] A photograph of George Herbert, the shoemaker, and his musical friends in the 1850s shows how music could overcome sectarian barriers.[56] The group comprised a coal merchant, a grocer's commercial traveller, a shoemaker, a printer and a teacher of music who had once been a member of Henry Jackman's theatrical company. Two were Conservatives, and one a Liberal with Chartist sympathies. One was a Unitarian, one an Anglican and others attended no place of worship. Nevertheless no activity in Banbury was without its sectarian implications. When the Choral Society was founded it was thought necessary to declare that 'its rules can be scrutinised by all denominations'.[57]

Succour for the needy in early 19th-century Banbury was provided by paternal philanthropy, or by small and often financially unstable friendly societies. By 1850 most relief was given through larger organisations with a measure of public accountability. The main development among friendly societies in the period was the growth of the affiliated orders, represented in Banbury by the Manchester Unity and Independent Order of Oddfellows, and by the Rechabites.[58] In the Reform Procession in 1832, 22 different occupations were represented, grouped into 15 trade clubs.[59] The activities of such clubs were not well-publicised and few of their records have survived, but it seems that they declined during the following decades. Banbury's Club Day was on the first Tuesday of July, when friendly societies and trade clubs paraded to a church service before spending the afternoon feasting. In the evening they paraded the streets with banners, and serenaded honorary members, before closing the day with dancing at their club houses.[60] To some extent the old clubs were superseded by the Oddfellows, whose national organisation offered greater financial security, but it is difficult to establish the extent to which the Oddfellows' lodges were reincarnations of older societies. The Oddfellows organised a railway excursion to London via Wolverton in 1842, and there were three lodges of the Independent Order in Banbury by the following year. By 1848 the British Queen Lodge of the Manchester Unity order was established.[61] New politically-based friendly societies came into being, the Conservative Friendly Society in 1837 and a Reformers' society shortly afterwards.[62]

Another outlet for working-class savings was the Bank for Savings founded in 1818 which opened its own premises in 1839. Its bankers were the Cobbs, but a political balance was maintained by having Colonel North of Wroxton Abbey as its patron. In 1837 it held over 2,000 deposits.[63] The Banbury Small Savings Society was established in 1847-48 with the object of encouraging saving in the summer when work was plentiful, so that members would have money for essentials in winter. It was suspected of prying into the state of working-class savings.[64] The Medical Aid Society, founded by 1838, helped people to save for medical assistance, and the Refuge Society, formed in 1844 collected small sums weekly to give relief in case of sickness.[65] There were two chapel- rather than public house-based friendly societies in addition to the Rechabites. The United Christian Benefit Society, which met on Wesleyan premises, was founded with 30 members in 1841 and trebled its membership within six years. The Mutual Aid Society, a burial club founded by the Baptist Caleb Clarke in 1843, became one of the largest friendly societies in the town.[66]

Self-help groups could proliferate without causing sectarian strife since they did not appeal to the public for funds. The progress of societies which did raise money from the public for distribution to the needy was less smooth. The Old Charitable Society, established in 1782, was governed by a committee of deputies from the various congregations, and its income came from a special annual service at St Mary's attended by all denominations. This practice ceased in 1847 when special sermons were preached in all the churches and chapels in the town.[67] The Visiting Charitable Society was founded about 1820, and by 1843 was spending about £100 p.a. on distressed families. Both societies became the subject of bitter disputes between Anglicans and Dissenters in the 1850s.[68] Other bodies had clear denominational affiliations. The Banbury and Neithrop Clothing Society was a Church organisation, closely linked with the National Schools.[69] The Dorcas Society was formed by wives of leading Nonconformists in 1842, and was later connected with the Independent Church.[70] However illogical the duplication caused by the proliferation of charitable bodies, it is likely that more of the poor were relieved by the many competing organisations in Banbury than would have been helped under any more rational system.

Traditional recreation in Banbury was based on the occasion rather than the organisation, and was administered informally by groups who were not publicly accountable and rarely left records. By contrast, the new patterns of recreation which emerged in the 1830s and '40s were organised by publicly accountable bodies of middle-class citizens. The traditional forms of organisation were found at both ends of the social scale. One well-established traditional activity was the annual ball for the nobility at the *Red Lion* in January, which was attended by leading landed families, and from which the townspeople were exluded.[71] The gentry were also involved in the race meetings held in the meadows on the Northamptonshire side of the Cherwell. At the meeting in 1845 J. M. Severne, squire of Thenford, had his coat stolen.[72] On the first day of each race meeting the gentry were prominent, but in the evening and on the second day the criminal classes dominated the proceedings. In 1843 policemen trying to quell a riot were stoned and hissed, and in 1844 a man who had been seen in the company of hardened racecourse prowlers was found drowned.[73] The inquest revealed the presence of a whole company of criminals, including a couple called Gloucester Eliza and Bill, the former of whom decoyed men to remote places where the latter robbed them. The horse races were followed by pony and hurdle races of a rustic nature. There were booths, erected by publicans who subscribed £1, selling Newcastle salmon and gin mixed with cloves. Dancing and drinking went on through the night. A timber merchant always erected a temporary bridge over the Cherwell to give access to the course from the town centre.[74] After the 1846 meeting the course was taken over by the Great Western Railway. 'Before another season', commented the *Banbury Guardian*, 'we trust to see the fleeter locomotive where on Tuesday we expect the high-mettled racer'.[75] Race meetings continued spasmodically on other courses but they never became significant social occasions.

Another traditional activity was the annual wake in Newland in July, at which a mock mayor was elected. There were races for men and women, and the 'rough lot' who organised it were prone to steal from nearby gardens. After a night of hard drinking following the wake of 1843 a man was killed in a fight with a publican. A similar wake was held in Grimsbury but was not noticed in the press in the 1830s and '40s.[76] Elections too were recreational occasions of a traditional nature. During the 1841 contest Edward Cobb remarked that MPs should be chosen with 'no excitement, neither flags, nor banners, nor bands of music nor colours of any kind'.[77] These were exactly the festival trimmings which made elections like race meetings or fairs. The outstanding occasion in Banbury's traditional recreational calendar was the Michaelmas Fair, which gained importance as a festival as, with the growth of regular markets, it lost some of its specific economic functions.[78] It was an occasion when showmen, cheapjacks and criminals crowded into Banbury, and when disorder was always prevalent. The legal framework of the fair was the responsibility of the corporation, but its recreational aspects were entirely informal, depending on which showmen came to the town, and on the spontaneous decisions of thousands of pleasure seekers.

A new occasion which was formally organised by a voluntary association was the annual horticultural show. A Flori- and Horticultural Society was in existence in the 1830s, but a new society, in which the Munton family were prominent, was founded in February 1847, and held its first show on the *Flying Horse* bowling green on 14 September of that year, attracting over 800 people. The event became one of the principal occasions in the recreational year, and represented the antithesis of such traditional events as the fair, the wakes and the race meeting.[79]

The lack of public open spaces deprived most Banburians of the opportunity of taking part in sport in the early 19th century. Bowls was played on a green at the *Flying Horse* long before 1830, and there was a cricket ground on the Oxford Road, used by a club founded in 1836,[80] but there were few other facilities, and the most typical sporting events before 1850 were 'occasions', like the Palmer–Luckett prize fight or 1836, or the rat-catching in the tithe barn remembered with such pleasure by George Herbert.[81]

In Banbury before 1830 entertainment, schools and sustenance were provided as acts of individual philanthropy. During the 1830s and '40s there grew up a range of voluntary societies through which the bourgeoisie and the labour aristocracy came to exercise control over their own recreation, education and provision against adversity. They did this through voluntary associations, administered by committees responsible to annual meetings of subscribers. Some such societies dated from before 1830, and some paternalist means of provision survived after 1850, but the essential change, the great quickening in the rate of foundation of voluntary groups came in the '30s, and it was stimulated by the polarisation of local society, and by the constant background of vice, drunkenness and disorder in Banbury. By 1844 the *Banbury Guardian* could remark:

> 'There are few if any towns of the size of our own that can boast of so great a variety of societies for the amelioration of the condition of suffering humanity, and the promotion of the welfare of the different classes of the community',[82]

and it went on to cite the schools, the Mechanics' Institute, the Old Charitable Society and the Temperance Brass Band as examples. This represented as much of a revolution in local society as the change in parliamentary representation in 1831-32, or the takeover of the borough corporation by the Reformers in 1835. John Stuart Mill wrote in 1848:

> 'It is of supreme importance that all classes of the community, down to the lowest, should have much to do for themselves; that as great a demand should be made upon their intelligence and virtue as it is in any respect equal to; that the government should not only leave as far as possible to their own faculties the conduct of whatever concerns themselves alone, but should suffer them, or rather encourage them, to manage as many as possible of their joint concerns by voluntary co-operation'.[83]

Mill was not necessarily simply asserting what ought to happen in an ideal society. He could equally well have been making a descriptive statement about what had happened in towns like Banbury during the 1830s.

VII

A MARKET TOWN ECONOMY DURING THE
GREAT VICTORIAN BOOM

Substantial tradesmen here display
Their capital and skill:
May ample profits all repay,
And their just views fulfil.

Here such facilities combine
To augment the means of gain;
Conveyance quick, intelligence
By telegraph and train.[1]

THE MID-VICTORIAN BOOM is still evident in the streets and market places of
Banbury. In 1903 Thomas Ward Boss who had spent 78 years in the town calculated that
since his boyhood 60 new houses had been built in the High Street.[2] Seven new dissenting chapels, two corn exchanges, a town hall and arrays of suburban villas witness to the
prosperity of the 1850s and '60s, and a multitude of speeches and reports give an impression of increasing wealth. During the 1850s and '60s Banbury's communications
improved, new manufacturing industries developed, the old textile trades declined, rural
migration increased, and the sales of nationally-marketed consumer goods expanded.
A study of Banbury at this period is thus an examination at the local level of some of
the most significant forces which were affecting the national economy.

The population of Banbury rose from 8,793 in 1851 to 11,768 in 1871, growing by
16.4 per cent in the 1850s and by 14.9 per cent during the '60s, almost exactly the
national rate of growth. The population of the Poor Law Union outside the town
declined by 4.7 per cent in the 1850s and by 2.4 per cent in the '60s.[3] The proportion
of people living in Banbury who were born outside the town rose from 45.72 per cent
in 1851 to 50.67 per cent in 1871. This was due in part to increased migration from the
hinterland, particularly from adjacent parishes like Bodicote and Chacombe, but the
proportion of migrants from distant counties rose from 16.59 per cent in 1851 to 19.60
per cent in 1871. There were natives of every English county resident in Banbury in
1871, 39 from Devon, 37 from Kent, 58 from Lancashire, 36 from Lincolnshire, 72 from
Wiltshire and 257, or 2.2 per cent of the total population, from London.[4]

Banburians, like the citizens of similar towns throughout Europe, believed that
economic progress came on iron rails. Banbury's railways arrived relatively late, 12 years
after the London and Birmingham Railway, some twenty miles to the east, began to
affect the town's trade. Banbury was the focus of intense railway speculation in the
1840s. Two firm proposals emerged from a mass of conflicting schemes. One was for an

extension of the Didcot–Oxford branch of the broad gauge Great Western Railway through Banbury and Fenny Compton to Rugby, where it would make contact with the narrow gauge London and Birmingham and Midland Counties lines. At Fenny Compton this route was to be joined by the Birmingham and Oxford Junction Railway, to give direct access to the West Midlands. The other proposal was for a narrow gauge line from Tring on the London and Birmingham, through Banbury, to Worcester and Wolverhampton.[5] There was feverish railway activity in Banbury during 1844 and 1845. Robert Stephenson was seen surveying in the district in April and October 1844. A memorable meeting in July 1844 was attended by George and Robert Stephenson, Isambard Kingdom Brunel and Charles Saunders, secretary of the Great Western.[6] On hearing that his agent was 'over head and ears engaged with railroads', Banbury's MP regretted that he could not vote for both the broad and the narrow gauge schemes.[7] Parliamentary sanction was given for the broad gauge to advance north from Oxford, and in 1848 the GWR secured control of the Birmingham and Oxford line. The narrow gauge schemes were consolidated into the Buckinghamshire Railway, a subsidiary of the newly-formed London and North Western Railway, and the Oxford, Worcester and Wolverhampton Railway, a narrow gauge line which skirted the western edge of Banbury's hinterland.[8]

Public opinion in Banbury favoured the narrow gauge proposals. References to the London and Birmingham were cheered at the meeting in July 1844, and the *Banbury Guardian* argued for a narrow gauge route to the north.[9] Timothy Rhodes Cobb was a member of the management committee of the Buckinghamshire Railway, and held conclaves with Samuel Carter, solicitor to the London and Birmingham, in the Reform Club. At a dinner in 1850, Edward Watkin, then secretary to the company, said that the completion of the line owed more to Cobb than to any man living, and an obituary some 30 years later recalled that Cobb was 'particularly active in the promotion of the Buckinghamshire Railway'.[10] Both Banbury banks supported the Buckinghamshire line, but the committee of the Birmingham and Oxford lacked any local representatives.[11]

Construction of the Oxford and Rugby route began at Port Meadow in August 1845, but Banburians soon grew restive at the line's slow progress, and Charles Saunders had to counter charges that the Great Western might abandon it.[12] In May 1846 construction began at three points near Banbury, but the following summer the contractor ran into difficulties. Underemployed navvies played a boisterous part in the Banbury election in July 1847, and by the autumn the line 'presented a melancholy aspect of desolation'. In June 1848 the Revd. Thomas Mardon saved a sub-contractor from rioting navvies near Banbury bridge. The summer of 1849 was enlivened by spectacular blastings of rock in the cutting north of Cropredy, four miles from Banbury, which drew many spectators. A newspaper commented:

> 'It was pleasing to reflect that on the very spot where two centuries earlier the conflicting armies of the Royalists and the Parliamentarians were engaged in mortal combat, a troup of men were now engaged in using gunpowder for a far different and much nobler object — that of promoting a spread of commerce and speedy transit between the metropolis of England and the metropolis of the North'.[13]

For all this display, it was not until September 1850 that the Great Western was opened to Banbury, and not for a further two years did trains run through Cropredy cutting to Birmingham.

The broad gauge was beaten to Banbury by the Buckinghamshire Railway which by 1846 was envisaged as a route from Bletchley, on the LNWR main line, to Oxford and Banbury, the two lines diverging west of Winslow. An extension from Banbury towards Worcester and the Black Country was still anticipated.[14] Construction began near Bletchley in July 1846 and the line was marked out to Banbury in August 1847. In May 1848 a temporary brickworks was set up near Franklow's Knob.[15] The directors of the company agreed in 1849 to proceed first with the Banbury line, which was thought potentially more remunerative.[16] In April 1849 the engineer Robert Benson Dockray surveyed the site for the station, and a year later he accompanied the directors on an experimental journey from Bletchley to Banbury. During April 1850 he twice took government inspectors along the line, and on 1 May the passenger service began. When freight services commenced a fortnight later over a hundred waggons of coal were handled on the first day.[17]

Four months later, on Monday 2 September 1850, the first trains ran along the broad gauge rails from Oxford, into a station which for over two years was to remain a temporary terminus. Services to Birmingham did not begin until 1 October 1852, after a *contretemps* the previous day when a special train carrying dignitaries and hauled by the locomotive *Lord of the Isles*, which had been displayed in the Crystal Palace, collided six miles south of Banbury with a late-running mixed train.[18] The Great Western did not complete the Oxford and Rugby route north of Fenny Compton where an end-on junction was formed with the Birmingham and Oxford line. Nor was a third rail laid to enable narrow gauge trains from the Buckinghamshire line to continue north of Banbury. The connection between the LNWR and the GWR was not installed until 1863, and was never used for long distance traffic. Nevertheless it seems that the LNWR maintained some hopes of developing traffic to the west of Banbury since it built a substantial engine shed, capable of holding eight locomotives, far more than ever operated on the line at any one time, and the passenger station remained a flimsy, temporary structure, where until 1877 locomotives had to be detached from their carriages before the latter could enter the platforms.[19]

The Great Western route became an important main line, while the Buckinghamshire Railway was never more than a by-way, but for traffic to and from Banbury itself the two lines were competitive. The distance from Banbury to Paddington through Oxford was 86¼ miles, whereas from Banbury to Euston through Bletchley was only 78 miles. The fastest GWR expresses to and from Birmingham did not stop at Banbury. In 1855 there were eight services to Paddington, the fastest in 2 hr 45 min. There were four trains on the Buckinghamshire line, two with through coaches to Euston, one of which reached the capital in 2 hr 35 min. In 1863 there were five trains from Paddington to Birmingham and beyond which stopped at Banbury, which also enjoyed two services by slip coaches off non-stop trains, the first of which began in 1858. The fastest train did the journey in 1 hr. 55 min. The LNWR service was little changed from that of 1855, but it had been slightly accelerated.[20] There was agitation throughout the 1850s and '60s for an east-to-west line through Banbury, but when the two parts of this route were separately built, neither proved to be of more than local significance. It was not until 1900 that Banbury became a railway junction of national importance, and not until 1910 that the GWR decisively overcame the opposition of the LNWR for London traffic.[21]

'It will make quite a social revolution in the district, which until the opening of this line may be said to have been almost cut off from the world', wrote C. B. Dockray on the opening of the Buckinghamshire Railway.[22] As far as Banbury itself was concerned, Dockray exaggerated, but many agreed that the railway brought important benefits to the town. At the beginning of 1851 the *Banbury Guardian* spoke of 'the advantages of the railways opened to Banbury . . . so universally felt and admired', and cited the reduction of coal prices as one of them. In 1852 it was argued that the approach from the railway stations had become the main route into the town. 'In consequence of the railways', claimed Edward Cobb, 'the Oxford Road is no longer the chief entrance into Banbury. Now it is from the bridge . . .'. It was said that with existing market facilities, Banbury could not 'swallow day after day and every day the heaps and heaps of goods that both railways pour into the town', Fifteen years' satisfaction with the economic consequences of the railways were expressed by the ironmonger Richard Edmunds when

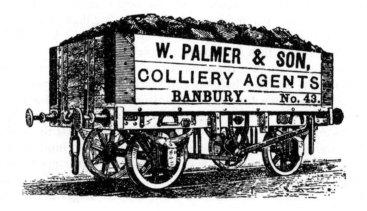

Figure 12. From Views and Reviews, *c. 1900.*

in 1865 he argued for a railway to the west by declaring 'We want as many railways as we can get'.[23] It is impossible to quantify the economic consequences of the railway at a local level, but occasional references in the press give some indications of the nature of the traffic. In 1869 it was estimated that the GWR took £29,000 in revenue at Banbury, of which £13,500 came from passenger traffic, and when the GWR station master absconded in 1866 he took with him the takings from the three largest goods accounts, which proved to be those of the Britannia Ironworks, Hunt Edmunds brewery and Messrs. J. and T. Davies, the builders.[24]

The railways did not deprive the Oxford Canal of the carriage of Warwickshire coal, for which it was particularly well suited, but coal from Cannock Chase and North Wales began to compete with that from Banbury's traditional sources. By the mid-1850s six of the town's 25 coal merchants had offices in the railway yards while seven operated from the canal wharves. Dividends on the Oxford Canal fell from 30 per cent in 1844 to 9 per cent in 1855, but traffic in bulk commodities remained buoyant, and until

he Oxford Canal at Banbury. The building to the right was part of the stoneyard established by the Paving and
ing Commission in 1825 and occupied by the Commission's successors, the Board of Health and the Borough
cil, until 1974. *(Photo: Author)*

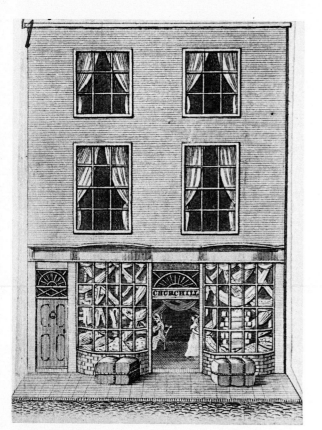

3. The County Tea Warehouse, according to Geo Herbert one of the largest grocery businesses in Ba bury. It stood in Cornhill, and was taken over by Jonathan Dury from Francis Broome and his partn *c.1836. (From the enlarged version of Alfred Beesley* History of Banbury. *Oxfordshire County Libraries, Banbury Library)*

2. The High Street shop of William Churchill, draper hatter and tailor, in the 1830s. *(From the enlarged version of Alfred Beesley's* History of Banbury. *Oxfordshire County Libraries, Banbury Library)*

4. *(left)* The London and Manchester Warehouse of Edward Shirt Philpots, draper, hatter and tailor, who had premises in both High St. and Market Place in the 1830s. *(Fr the enlarged version of Alfred Beesle* History of Banbury. *Oxfordshire County Libraries, Banbury Library)*

Cobbs Bank, High Street, probably built in the 1780s, ith alterations of the early 19th century and later. One the first brick buildings in Banbury. *(Photo : Author)*

6. Timothy Rhodes Cobb, perhaps the most influential man in Banbury between 1830 and 1860. *(Oxfordshire County Libraries, Banbury Library)*

7. *(below)* The Cobb family's girth weaving factory at the side of the Oxford Canal, built in 1837. *(Photo: Author)*

8. *(upper left)* The domed New Chapel in Church Passage, seen in a view of St Mary's Church. *(Oxfordshire County Libraries, Banbury Library)*

9. *(upper right)* James Gardner's Baptist Church at 34b West Bar (formerly No. 17½), constructed in 1829 and used until 1877. *(Photo: Author)*

10. *(lower right)* Richard Austin's Baptist Chapel in South Bar, built in 1834 and used until 1852. *(Photo: Author)*

TRIUMPH OF REFORM,
TO BE CELEBRATED IN

BANBURY,
Friday, July 13th, 1832.

PUBLIC PROCESSION.

Two HERALDS, on Horseback, with Trumpets.
Drapers and Grocers, six abreast,
WITH BANNERS, &c.

BUNDLE OF STICKS.

Reform Banner.　　MOTTO.　　*Reform Banner.*
"Union is Strength."

BAND OF MUSIC.

The Committee, five abreast,
WITH BLUE ROSETTES.

THE SOCIETY OF ODD FELLOWS, IN FULL REGALIA.

Waggon drawn by Oxen dressed in blue Ribbons,
CONTAINING

A PRINTING PRESS,

At which will be printed, during its progress, an account of the Procession,
IN FRONT,
A Banner.—"The Reformer's Artillery."
BANNER.

THE PRINTERS AND BOOKBINDERS.

A Car drawn by two Horses, containing

A Shepherd and Shepherdess,
WITH A DOG AND LAMB.

THE WOOL-COMBERS,
With Bishop Blaize, &c. &c.

BAND OF MUSIC.

THE WEAVERS,
WITH BANNERS, &c.

THE HATTERS, CORK-CUTTERS, & DYERS,
WITH FLAGS.

THE CURRIERS, SADDLERS, AND CORDWAINERS,
WITH FLAGS.

THE UNION FLAG.　　ST. GEORGE'S FLAG.
Magna Charta.　Petition of Rights.　Habeas Corpus.　Bill of Rights.

THE CHAMPION OF REFORM,
In White Armour, mounted on a Charger, bearing in his hand the Reform Act.

THE TAILORS,
WITH FLAG.

THE CARPENTERS AND SAWYERS,
WITH FLAG.

THE GARDENERS.
With Garlands, Bouquets, &c. &c.

THE MASONS.

The Slaters and Plasterers.

THE PAINTERS & GLAZIERS,
WITH EMBLEMS.

THE SMITHS AND COOPERS.

The Basket Makers, with Flags and Banner.

THE ADMINISTRATORS, WITH FLAGS, &c.

The Butchers and Bakers, with Flags and Banners.

THE PENSIONERS.

UNION FLAG.

BAND OF MUSIC.

Reformers, five abreast, with Flags, Banners, &c. &c.

CHENEY, PRINTER, HIGH-STREET, BANBURY.

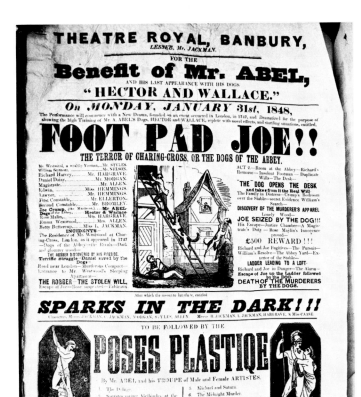

11. *(left)* The poster for the Triumph of Reform procession in Banbury on 13 July 1832. *(From George Herbert,* Shoemaker's Window, *ed. C. R. Cheney and Barrie Trinder, Phillimore, 1971, plate VII)*

12. *(above)* A bill for one of Henry Jackman's performances at the Banbury Theatre in 1848. *(Oxfordshire County Libraries, Banbury Library)*

EXTRAORDINARY
Rat-Catching.

HENRY JOHN PYE, Rat-Catcher to the *Marquis of Bute, Sir Charles Knightly, William Ralph Cartwright, Esq., &c. &c.*, begs leave to announce to the Public his great success in his calling, and to solicit their Patronage. His Traps, Snares, and little Engines of every sort, have been the admiration of all who have heard of them; and he may without boasting say that his mode of setting them is unequalled. He has an excellent parcel of Dogs, comprising amongst them Spaniels, Lurchers, and Setters, and a Newfoundlander of extraordinary size which he usually takes with him to guard his person. These animals, even against their natures, he has trained to be exceedingly good Rat-Catchers. He has also two or three fine Ferrets; one a clever one presented to him by the Marquis of Bute; and another which from the sleekness of its skin, its beautiful rotundity, a sort of smiling good-natured phiz, and certain noises made by it which some people call its joking, is considered an odd production of nature, and generally appears to be a great favourite of the Ladies who follow in the crowds to see its performances.

Henry John Pye yesterday exhibited his Dogs and Ferrets all over Banbury, and the Inhabitants were surprised to see how the Dogs, though followed and hooted at by a parcel of troublesome Boys, smelt out the slyest Rats where none were thought to be, and how nimbly and dexterously the Ferrets went into their holes and caught them.

There are amongst his Dogs two or three yelping and rather cross Curs, but they are weak and do not bite hard; and a sly Hound or two, but these are harmless. The rest are good-natured animals, and caress all who approach them. He intends shortly to exhibit his collection again in Banbury and the Hamlets, when the public are invited to see them. His success at Banbury was the more surprising, as one Tancred, a Catcher from London, had lately been over the ground; but as he had no traps or snares of any sort, the cunning Rats were all able to escape him, though he had a few good Dogs. Many of the Rats require a bait which Tancred does not know how to prepare, and not living in the neighbourhood he has not learnt their particular taste.

It is an extraordinary fact, but can be well attested, that Henry John Pye has lately caught several Rats in Banbury by bringing them even into the Public Houses, and causing them to drink various liquids prepared to entice them, in the presence of many persons. He has also been well nigh catching some by *simply* throwing money in the street.

With a well contrived trap called a Check, and four or five of his Dogs, he thought of catching a great number of Rats on Tuesday night last, but could not take one. Some of Tancred's Dogs frightened the Rats away, and even bit and drove out of its place one of his best Curs, which being hurt, and withal generally a little snappish, afterwards grievously snarled and shewed his teeth at them, with too little regard to the entirety of its own skin, as they gribbled in return very sharply and rather disabled the animal. Catchers should endeavour to keep their Dogs in temper as they may otherwise become useless and mischievous. Henry John Pye hopes that the Public will not consider the failure of this attempt as any disparagement of his ability, it being merely accidental.

Banbury, July 5th, 1832.

POTTS, PRINTER, ALBION OFFICE, BANBURY.

T. Tims

13.   A satirical account of the early stages of the 1832 election campaign in Banbury by Thomas Tims. *(Oxfordshire County Libraries, Banbury Library)*

ENERAL ELECTION
1841.

BANBURY

Vincent   52
Tancred   124
Holbech   100

TAVISTOCK

March 1843

Vincent   71
Trelawny   113

Universal
Suffrage

Rights
Man

IPSWICH!

August 16. 1842

Vincent   473
Thornbury   548
Gladstone   651
Fox (man)   611
Nicholson   2

4.   Henry Vincent, Chartist candidate for Banbury in the general election of 1841, and a popular lecturer in
he town for more than a quarter of a century afterwards. *(Author's collection)*

BARROWS AND STEWART'S
PORTABLE STEAM ENGINES

See "Note" page 4.

BARROWS & STEWART
ENGINEERS
BANBURY.

LANGTON Sc

The Boilers are multitubular, and constructed so as to secure unusual strength, and the greatest amount of steam space; the shell being continuous from end to end, avoiding the divisions known as fire-box, barrel, and smoke-box. They are made of best Staffordshire Iron; the fire-boxes of Low Moor, Bowling, or Farnley Iron, and of ample size for burning wood as well as coal. The cylinders are steam jacketed, and of full capacity. The Crank Shaft is bent out of one solid bar of first quality iron, and is long enough to admit a driving pulley on the free end. The governors have small balls, and act very quickly, being assisted by a spiral spring. The single slide bar and the horizontal pump are simple and neat arrangements; and everything can be got at without breaking any joints on the boiler, thereby saving much trouble and expense when repairs become necessary.

All the Engine Works are very strong, and arranged in the most simple manner, so that they can be seen and easily got at by the person in charge.

15. (*left*) A portable steam engine manufactured by Barrows and Stewart in 1876. *(Museum of English Rural Life, Reading)*

16. (*below*) Steam ploughing apparatus made by Barrows and Stewart, 1876. *(Museum of English Rural Life, Reading)*

LANGTON Sc MAN on

18. The steam engine from Hunt Edmunds' Brewery, made by Charles Lampitt at the Vulcan Foundry and installed *c*.1839. *(Photo: G.H. Starmer)*

17. A. Gardner's patent Turnip Cutter, made by Bernhard Samuelson & Co. in 1859. *(Museum of English Rural Life, Reading)*

19. A Samuelson reaper advertised in the firm's catalogue of 1859. *(Museum of English Rural Life, Reading)*

20. (*left*) George Herbert and friends, *c.*1850-54. Left to right: Charles Neighbour, violin; George Gardner, violoncello; George Herbert, viola; George Partleton, violin; John Cheney, flute. (*From George Herbert,* Shoemaker's Window, *ed. C. R. Cheney and Barrie Trinder, Phillimore, 1971, plate II*)

21. (*right*) Part of the Cherwell Infants School, which from 1856 was used as a meeting place for the Britannia Works Mutual Instruction and Recreation Society. (*Photo: Author*)

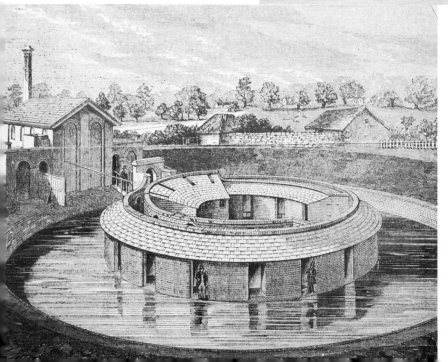

22. (*left*) The public swimming baths constructed by Thomas Draper in 1855. (*Oxfordshire County Libraries, Banbury Library*)

23. (*right*) One of the dilapidated cottages in the Tanyard, photographed c.1900. (*Oxfordshire County Libraries, Banbury Library*)

24. (*below*) Typical of the old style buildings in Banbury, the former Coachsmiths Arms in stone, brick and thatch at the corner of Broad Street and George Street (formerly Fish Street) replaced by the premises of the Banbury Co-operative Society in 1908. (*Oxfordshire County Libraries, Banbury Library*)

25. (left) Shops in the High Street typical of the many retail premises built in the 1850s and 60s in the classical style, in brick, with Bath stone dressings. (Photo: Author)

26. (right) Houses which defied the architectural norms of mid-Victorian Banbury. Nos. 23-24 Market Place (Cornhill), designed by the Oxford architect William Wilkinson and built for W. T. Douglas of Castle House in 1866 with the object of improving his view. No. 24 to the right was built as a residence, and No. 23 was intended as business premises for a spirit merchant. (Photo: Author)

7.   Cornhill. To the right are William Wilkinson's Gothic houses of 1866. In the centre is the building formerly occupied
y Gilletts Bank. The stone building to the right was formerly the *Plough* Inn, while on the extreme right is the facade of
1e Cornhill Corn Exchange of 1857. *(Photo: Author)*

8.   The rehabilitated frontage of the Central Corn Exchange of 1857. *(Photo: Author)*

29.	The landscape of a Freehold Land Society estate. Houses in Centre Street, Grimsbury, built in ones, twos and three by shareholders in the Banbury Freehold Land Society from 1853 onwards. *(Photo: Author)*

30.	The landscape of speculative building. Regents Place, The Causeway, a series of terraces built by William Wilkins between 1856 and 1871. *(Photo: Author)*

31. 'Soapy Sam'. The Rt. Revd. Samuel Wilberforce, Bishop of Oxford. (Author's collection)

32. The original design by Benjamin Ferrey for Christ Church, South Banbury, opened by Samuel Wilberforce, Bishop of Oxford, in 1853. The tower was not constructed until 1880, and the spire was never completed. (Oxfordshire County Libraries, Banbury Library)

33. The Metropolis of the Carriers' Carts, the Town Hall and Bridge Street, c.1885. (*National Monuments Record*)

1878 the company's dividend did not fall below 8 per cent. Flyboat services for sundries were maintained, although the Oxford market boat ceased to sail in 1852. Employment on the canal in Banbury declined by only four between 1851 and 1871, and in 1879, 74 vessels were registered in the town under the 1877 Canal Boats Act. By 1862 steam boats were appearing in the town, and recreational cruising had commenced. The canal remained a profitable concern, important to Banbury as a carrier of bulk commodities, and as a source of income from the servicing of vessels engaged in such trades as carrying coal from Coventry to Newbury, plaster from Barrow-on-Soar to Thatcham, and hides from Birmingham to Reading.[25]

By 1850 stage coach operators realised that they could not withstand direct railway competition, and all of the services through Banbury ended when the railways opened, those to London ceasing in 1850, and those in the Birmingham direction in 1852. The last stage coach service, from Chipping Campden, was withdrawn when the Oxford, Worcester and Wolverhampton Railway opened in May 1853. All stage waggons had ceased to run by the mid-1850s.[26] The railways gained much of the traffic in live cattle which had previously been tended by drovers. In 1852 a writer on the agriculture of Northamptonshire said of the Buckinghamshire Railway:

'Since the opening of these lines, the old mode of droving cattle and sheep to London has been nearly abandoned, and the surplus fatstock ... is now principally conveyed to Smithfield by railway'.

In 1865 a Herefordshire cattle dealer explained how he bought cattle in the Borderland and despatched them to Banbury market by rail through Gloucester and Swindon. It was feared that because there was no direct railway to the west, Moreton-in-Marsh might gain this trade from Banbury.[27]

The railways increased the prosperity of Banbury market. In 1854 the opening of the Birmingham line was said to have been a great stimulus to the corn trade. In 1856 Thomas Draper claimed that 520 farmers and dealers drove into Banbury market every Thursday. In 1863 the vendors of the *White Lion* boasted 'Banbury market is one of the best in the kingdom and the town is rapidly increasing in size and importance'. In 1864 an ironmonger described Banbury as 'the principal market for the whole district around it', and explained that great quantities of grocers' goods were sent westwards from the town by carriers' carts.[28] The number of people employed in road transport in Banbury increased from 47 to 48 between 1851, while the number of male employees at inns, most of whom cared for horses, remained stationary. When allowance is made for the undoubted decline of long distance traffic, these figures indicate a substantial increase in the number of local journeys, and a buoyant demand for vehicles is suggested by increases in the numbers of coachmakers from 13 to 24, and of wheelwrights from 13 to 17.[29]

Similar conclusions emerge from analysis of the carrying trade. The number of carriers serving Banbury declined from 192 to 167 between 1851 and 1861, while the total of weekly journeys fell from 437 to 370. This was due largely to the cessation of services which were directly duplicated by the railway, to such places as Abingdon and Hampton Poyle in the Oxford direction, and Leamington and Whitnash to the north. The number of weekly visits from Brackley carriers fell from 11 to four, of Buckingham carriers from six to two, and of those from Cropredy from 13 to six. Carrying from Shipston-on-Stour and Stow-on-the-Wold ceased, which gave some credence to the demands of those who sought a market to the west in order to consolidate the superiority of Banbury market. While some villages lost their services, carriers began to visit Banbury from places like Ladbrook, Ardley, Cherrington and Napton which had not been served in the 1840s.[30] It was acknowledged in 1866 that the number of carriers visiting Banbury had declined since the opening of the railways, but during the '60s the number of carriers remained stable, while the total of weekly journeys increased, exceeding 400 once more by 1871. A round figure of 400 weekly attendances was often quoted in the mid-60s. The carriers were seen as the symbol of Banbury's prosperity. In 1860 the *Banbury Advertiser* estimated that 167 carriers made 395 visits a week to Banbury, and asked 'Is any other little town so visited?'.[31] In 1865 Sir Charles Douglas was praised because 'he has helped . . . village carriers who tend so much to the prosperity of this town'. Banbury had many more carriers' services than county towns like Oxford, Newcastle-upon-Tyne and Shrewsbury, and only a few less than places like Nottingham, Leicester and Reading.[32] Carriers brought in agricultural, more particularly dairy and horticultural produce to shopkeepers, and on their return conveyed goods bought on behalf of customers from Banbury retailers. They also conveyed passengers, and in 1869 it was calculated that 166 carriers brought over a thousand people to Banbury Fair. The importance of the carriers was ironically symbolised in 1863 when Thomas Draper, the mayor, was attacked by a cow in High Street on Market day, but found his escape impeded because 'as usual, the left hand side was blocked with carriers' carts'.[33]

The railways apart, the most dramatic change in Banbury's economy in the 1850s and '60s was the rapid growth of the engineering industry, which in 1851 had employed only about 90 men, a mere 2.18 per cent of the employed population. By 1871 it gave work to more than 500, almost ten per cent of the town's labour force.[34] The true figure should be rather higher since some general labourers, carpenters and painters were probably not distinguished in the census as engineering workers. It would be easy to explain the rise of agricultural engineering in simple geographical terms. A speaker at a railway dinner in 1850 declared that Banbury 'lay between the immense iron district on the north west side, and a large agricultural district on the other, so that Banbury would become a species of entrepot by its natural position'.[35] This is exactly what did happen. For decades Banbury had sent farm produce to Birmingham and the Black Country. From 1850 this trade increased, as did the reverse traffic in coke and iron, and these materials were processed in Banbury into products useful to farmers. While the railways may have improved the supplies of raw materials, it was possible to bring them to the town by canal long before 1850, and one foundry received coke, pig-iron and sand by water throughout the 19th century.[36] Perhaps the railway was of more importance as a means of transporting machines to distant markets in Britain and to the docks. Yet the growth of engineering in Banbury was not shaped by geographical factors alone, but by the zeal of an entrepreneur whose horizons were not bounded by the limits of the town's hinterland. It demonstrates the social and economic forces which were affecting market towns throughout western Europe as the concepts of the entrepreneurs of the Industrial Revolution were extended from the coalfields to rural districts.

When Bernhard Samuelson gave a dinner for the employees of the newly-named Britannia Ironworks in 1849 they numbered only 27.[37] Within a decade the number of workers increased tenfold, their productivity was increased through the use of steam power, and the range of products of the works was extended. Samuelson had a commercial rather than an engineering background, and the internal management of the factory was left to others. From 1849 until 1854 it was in the charge of his brother Alexander, who had previously worked for Nasmyth Gaskell and Co. and for Boulton and Watt before joining Bernhard Samuelson at Tours. He was succeeded by John Shaw, who was followed from 1862 until 1874 by Danial Pidgeon, who patented eight new reaping and mowing machines while in Banbury and became a junior partner in the company in 1865.[38]

Samuelson had an international outlook, and sought to utilise foreign, particularly American technology. He exhibited his machines on the continent, and to the furthest reaches of the English-speaking world. In 1850 he won prizes at the Royal Show and elsewhere for a Gardner turnip cutter and for a churn made according to a patent of Charles Anthony of Pittsburg.[39] He displayed several machines in the Crystal Palace and won a prize for a turnip cutter, but his greatest achievement at the Great Exhibition was to gain a licence to manufacture the McCormick reaper. In October 1851 McCormick's British agents referred to 'the numerous machines which Mr. Samuelson, our manufacturer, is constructing for every part of the country'.[40] The great agriculturalist Philip Pusey described the reaper, the invention of a farmer's son from Rockbridge County, Virginia, as 'the most important addition to farming machinery since the threshing machine took the place of the flail', and compared it with the spinning jenny and the power loom.[41] One of the most consistent images of Banbury which remained in the minds of 19th-century visitors was that of rows of brightly-painted reapers loaded on to railway waggons and awaiting despatch.[42] The McCormick reaper was demonstrated in Banbury and exhibited at the Royal Show in 1852. The main agents for its production in Britain were Messrs. Burgess and Key, and Samuelson seems to have manufactured the machine on their behalf, although they themselves made it and showed their models in competition with his.[43] The turnip cutter usually won its class at the Royal Show in the 1850s. Samuelson also made a digging machine, mowing machines, chaff and linseed cutters and an oilcake breaker. Non-agricultural products included an American patent washing machine, lawnmowers, rollers and rustic garden seats.[44]

In 1859 the Britannia Works produced 18,000 implements, about a quarter of which were turnip cutters. Samuelson commenced production in 1858 of another American patent reaper, designed by Seymour and Morgan of Brockport, New York, which seems to have been named the Patent Britannia Self-Raking Reaping Machine, or the Banbury Reaper. It was extensively advertised in 1859 at a price of £32 10s. 0d. at the factory, and its good reputation in America was much publicised.[45] The reaper won respect at trials throughout Britain, particularly in the North East, and was the basis of the foundry's prosperity in the 1860s. In 1872 the works could produce 8,000 reapers a year. Prizes were won at Berlin in 1868, and at major French competitions in 1870 and 1876. Mowing machines gained awards at Quimper in Brittany, Francker in Friesland and Canterbury, New Zealand.[46] A visitor remarked that Banbury's chief trades were 'the manufacture of agricultural implements and steam engines, and . . . the Banbury reapers and mowers have long taken a leading position', and an Irish journalist called the mowing machine made by Samuelson 'the great time and labour saving mechanical contrivance which the current century has dawned on'. Numerous accounts confirm the export orientation of the Britannia Works, one of them remarking that Samuelson's machines were as well-known in Russia and Italy as they were in Kent and Sussex.[47]

The Britannia Works was divided into two halves. At Gardner's original workshops on the south side of Fish Street was a two-cylinder steam engine, powering machining shops, woodworkers' saws and blacksmiths' hearths. The lower works between Upper Windsor Street and the canal, built on land purchased from Thomas Draper, consisted of two cupola furnaces, with associated workshops and yards where assembled machines were painted. A 2 ft.-gauge tramway, sanctioned in 1870, linked the two sections, and ran on to the works depot adjoining the railway, where incoming timber was stored, and finished implements loaded on to waggons.[48]

The publicity for the Banbury Reaper in 1858-59 demonstrated the difference between the Britannia works and the millwrights' shops and small foundries from which engineering in Banbury had sprung. The Lampitts and Rileys built machines with great skill for specific purposes. Samuelson submitted his workers to the disciplines of mass production. Exporters and colonial farmers were assured that the reaper's driving mechanism was a complete unit which could be assembled by unskilled labour.[49] The Britannia works brought to Banbury the concepts of the American as well as the British Industrial Revolution.

The works labour force grew steadily between 1850 and 1871, although there were considerable seasonal variations. In September 1852 over 100 were regularly employed, but the total sometimes exceeded 200. In May 1854 there were 230 workmen, and by 1859 over 300 were in regular employment. Samuelson claimed in 1865 that 400 were employed, and that 113 were taken on between Easter and July for the summer trade. In January 1871 Daniel Pidgeon said that 500 had been employed during Christmas week 1870, an unusually large number for the season.[50] It was acknowledged that wages at the Britannia Works were high by local standards, and that the conditions of work were superior to those elsewhere. In 1858 a labourer received about a pound a week, sometimes as little as 12s. and sometimes as much as £1 2s. 0d. Early in 1859 Samuelson said the annual pay roll was £15,000 and the average wage £2 2s. 0d., the usual wages of labourers, included in the general average, being 15s. 0d. By the end of the year the annual bill was almost £20,000. In 1868 Samuelson said that his heart bled to see men on 11s. 0d. a week, which government reports show to have been commonplace at that time in the Oxfordshire countryside.[51]

The discipline at the foundry introduced new concepts into Banbury society. A visitor commented in 1859:

'everything is orderly and systematic, from the moment the workman enters the premises on Monday morning and sees his "number" entered by the doorkeeper, up to mid-day on Saturday, when the paymaster, by an excellent plan, pays the wages to all employees in less than five minutes'.

In 1871 two 'engineer's timekeepers' were recorded on the 1871 census in Banbury. The notion that time was a commodity to be kept and measured would have been alien in the town before 1850. As late as 1873 Banburians complained of the steam whistles which summoned employees to the engineering works.[52]

Samuelson was not simply an innovating entrepreneur in the tradition of Arkwright and Wedgwood, but a paternalist who cultivated loyalty and a sense of cohesion among his workpeople. He declared in 1850, 'I regard the whole of us as fellow workers, and I shall always be glad to do anything to oblige you', and coupled a toast to 'the progress of Knowledge and Liberty throughout the World' with the motto 'The Britannia

Ironworks expects every member to do his duty'. He advocated class mixing, declaring the objects of treats for workmen to be:

'to promote that fusion of classes, which . . . is "looming in the future". If this little entertainment has contributed in the least to take off the rough edges which have prevented us from dovetailing into each other, it will afford me the greatest possible satisfaction'.[53]

Subsequently he organised a mutual assistance fund, and provided recreational and educational facilities for his employees on a scale quite new to Banbury.[54] In 1871 Samuelson conceded a nine-hour day, reducing the working week from 60 to 55¼ hours. The decision was announced by Daniel Pidgeon to a meeting of workmen, who later processed to Samuelson's house at Bodicote as a mark of thanks, declaring 'We feel proud in being connected with the first as well as the largest firm in the district to confer this important benefit'.[55]

Work at the foundry gave men a common experience which hatters, locksmiths or tailors lacked. A third of the foundrymen came from outside the district, and many of those locally born were young. It was therefore easy to blame on foundrymen things which were normally blamed on immigrants or the young. Four men who drove a horse to death while going to Edgehill on the day following a works excursion there in 1858 were reprimanded in the press for disloyalty to their employer, and dubbed 'four drunken foundrymen'. In 1861 there were complaints that foundrymen insulted women in Church Lane, and in 1866 it was said that youths from the works jostled respectable people in the streets at night, and sang ribald songs which disturbed the congregation at St Mary's church.[56] Such rowdy youths could have been called residents of the Cherwell streets, former pupils of the National Schools or frequenters of particular public houses. That they were called 'foundrymen' shows how the foundry labour force was perceived from without as a cohesive body. Samuelson's political opponents claimed that foundrymen were ordered to disturb their meetings. Whether or not this was so, it is evident that they supported their master with enthusiasm. When charges were brought after the 1859 election riot, 25 of the 33 defendants were foundrymen.[57] The cohesion which Samuelson fostered was evidently effective.

The other engineering works in Banbury employed more than twice as many people in 1871 as the entire local engineering industry in 1851. Second after the Britannia works in order of size was the works of Barrows and Carmichael, which developed from the millwrighting business of J. E. Kirby, who began to make steam engines and threshing machines in North Bar in the late 1850s. About 1861 he moved to the Cherwell area in partnership with Thomas Barrows, a 28-year-old native of Birmingham. Shortly afterwards he retired, and Barrows was joined by one John Carmichael, who died in 1868, and was succeeded by a Scot, William Stewart. By the early 1870s Barrows employed about 200 people. The works manufactured portable and traction engines, threshing equipment, elevators and steam cultivating machinery. Barrows encouraged steam ploughing by offering prizes at agricultural shows for crops sown on land thus cultivated.[58] Charles and John Lampitt's Vulcan Foundry employed about 50 people in 1871, and produced steam engines and other machines of great ingenuity, the Lampitt geared engine being particularly famous.[59]

The craft tradition of the smaller engineering concerns throws into sharper relief the exceptional nature of the Britannia works, mass-producing standardised products with interchangeable parts for an international market, and utilising foreign technology in their design. But Samuelson's capital was potentially as mobile as his search for profitable innovations was wide-ranging. He invested in Banbury because political circumstances made it prudent to transfer his capital from Tours to the English Midlands. Within five years he had other interests. In 1852 while demonstrating a newly-patented digging machine at the Cleveland Agricultural Show, he was introduced to John Vaughan, the pioneer of the local iron trade, by C. B. Dockray, engineer of the Buckinghamshire Railway, whom he would certainly have known in Banbury. Samuelson built two blast furnaces at South Bank, Middlesbrough in 1854, and enlarged his concerns in Cleveland until by 1870 he was producing 3,000 tons of pig iron a week. In that year he commenced building the Britannia Ironworks, Middlesbrough, a forge with a capacity of 1,400 tons of puddled iron a week, which he sold in 1879. He lost over £25,000 in the early 1870s in an attempt to make steel by the Siemens-Martin process at the North Yorkshire Ironworks, South Stockton.[60] It is doubtful whether Cleveland iron was used at the Britannia works, Banbury, since most of the pig iron arrived by canal, probably from South Staffordshire, but Samuelson did consider building blast furnaces to smelt locally-produced ores in Banbury, and it was for this reason that he favoured a railway to South Wales.[61]

Less than half of those employed in engineering in Banbury were born in the town, and only just over 20 per cent came from the hinterland. About a third of the engineering workers had been born at a considerable distance, and among the highly skilled this proportion was much greater. Among those described as 'engineers', 61.6 per cent were from outside the hinterland, and 43.6 per cent of the fitters and 43.3 per cent of the moulders came from similar distances.[62] Only 14.2 per cent of the unskilled were born outside the hinterland, and nearly 30 per cent had come to the town from nearby villages. Many workers had doubtless been recruited from other trades. One ironworks labourer had previously been a tailor, and a coachmaker had become 'a painter at the works'. Many of the moulders and fitters in Banbury were born or had children born in well-known engineering centres. The railway towns may have served as staging posts for migrant engineers. Two moulders were born near Wolverton, and four other skilled workers in the vicinity of Swindon. An engine fitter aged 31 in 1871, living in Grove Street and working for Barrows and Stewart, was born at Bedlington, Northumberland, site of the ironworks where the Birkinshaw rail was invented and birthplace of Sir Daniel Gooch. His wife was born at Patricroft, Lancashire, where the Nasmyth steam hammer was made. His son aged seven was born at Swindon, home of the Great Western engineering works. His sons of four and two were born in Manchester, the latter at Gorton, site of the works of Beyer Peacock and Co. and of the Manchester, Sheffield and Lincoln Railway.

One consequence of the growth of engineering in Banbury was that steam power became more readily available. In 1857 it was estimated that there were 18 steam engines at work within a mile of the town centre. Those at the Britannia works, Hunt Edmunds brewery, Baughen's woollen mills and a wood-turning factory can readily be identified, but the number which cannot easily be located is impressive. Steam power was evidently being used by several quite small concerns.[63]

The textile industry, already in decline in 1851, contracted further during the next two decades. By 1871 the number of plush weavers was less than half that of 1851, and the total employed in textiles went down from 195, or 4.73 per cent of the working population, to 102, or 1.97 per cent. Fifty-two people were engaged in plush weaving, all of whom must have been employed by William Cubitt, once traveller for Gilletts.[64] In 1852, 88 plush weavers at Baughen's went on strike following a 25 per cent reduction in piece work rates. The average wage of a weaver was then 12s. a week, of which a quarter was deducted for shop rent, a level approximating to that of an Oxfordshire farm labourer, and less than could be obtained for menial labouring tasks at the foundries. The dispute lasted for over ten weeks. A co-operative was established but soon collapsed.[65] In 1857 the brothers Baughen became bankrupt after an explosion caused by frozen pipes at the former Cobb girth factory, which Thomas Baughen had taken over for spinning wool. Richard Baughen resigned as mayor, and Thomas as councillor. The factory stood empty until 1871.[66] The weavers, once the aristocrats of Banbury's working class, retained some sense of corporate identity as their trade declined, and they were the only occupational group to appear in the Reform Procession in November 1866, but their high status had disappeared.The restrictions which had sustained it had disappeared by 1871 when several weavers combined making plush with weaving worsted or girth, and in Foundry Square there lived a woman plush weaver.[67] The trade was evidently no longer worth protecting.

The numbers employed in brewing and malting increased from 50 to 79 between 1851 and 1871, due principally to the growth of Hunt Edmunds' premises in Bridge Street. Austin's brewery in North Bar was taken over by J. N. Harman in 1850, who, with his partner W. A. Bryden, operated it until the early 1870s when it was sold to Messrs. Dunnell. The brewing interests of William Barrett, clerk at Gilletts Bank, were taken over on his retirement about 1860 by his son. His Britannia Brewery in Newland was offered for sale in 1870. T. H. Wyatt's brewery in Bridge Street became the Banbury Brewery Co. in 1861, and in 1869 won a gold medal in Amsterdam for a brown stout which was claimed to be a favourite beverage on the continent. All three of these concerns were subsequently taken over by Hunt Edmunds. A reform document in 1866, which sought to define Banbury's working-class, put the breweries second only to the iron foundries as sources of employment.[68]

The building trade grew in the 1850s and '60s at a rate which reflects the large numbers of new houses, shops and chapels erected in Banbury in the period. The number employed increased from 184 in 1851 to 364 in 1871, although some of the 159 carpenters included in the latter total probably worked in the foundries. The number making and selling building materials increased from 45 to 62, and the total building labour force rose from 5.55 to 8.2 per cent of the working population. There were several quite large firms in Banbury. Albert Kimberley, a building contractor who had his own saw mill and brickworks, employed 90 men and five boys. Thomas and Stephen Orchard employed 40 men and three boys. J. and T. Davies employed 61. Kimberley gave treats to his workmen modelled on those provided by Samuelson. In 1866, 40 went to tea at Edgehill, and he entertained his employees when his son was married in 1875.[69]

The increased size of businesses in the 1850s and '60s encouraged the growth of trades unions. The local branch (No. 192) of the Amalgamated Society of Engineers was formed at the *Wheatsheaf* in 1859 with 15 members. Relative to the size of the skilled labour force at the foundries its growth was slow. There were 31 members in 1862 and 97 in 1880, rather less than a fifth of the engineers in Banbury.[70] Bernhard Samuelson was notoriously 'no great friend to Trades Unionism'. In 1859 he complimented his

employees that 'when the whole of England was agitated by the strike of the Amalgamated Engineers, you, my friends, remained staunch to your employer'. In 1867 he set
down his suspicions of the power of union leaders, displayed the previous year in a strike
at Beyer Peacock's in Manchester, where some of his own employees had once worked.[71]
When the much publicised nine-hour day was conceded in 1871, trades unions were
given no share of the credit for it. Samuelson nevertheless derived some support from the
trades unionists of the Reform League, and during the 1874 election promised to vote
for the repeal of the Criminal Law Amendment Act.[72]

Printing was the most strongly unionised trade in Banbury. Employment in the
industry increased from 26 to 38 between 1851 and 1871, all of whom worked in offices
of not more than five or six workers. The Banbury Typographical Association may have
dated from as early as 1849. By 1861 its club house was at the *Banbury Guardian* office,
but the following year the printers amalgamated with the bookbinders, and used the
latter's club house, the *Jolly Weavers*.[73] Unions were also active in the building trade.
In 1864 builders agreed to allow their workers to stop at four instead of five o'clock on
Saturdays, and 5.30 instead of 6 p.m. on other days, in return for a reduction of the
breakfast break to half an hour. In 1872 when the Banbury branch of the Amalgamated
Society of Carpenters and Joiners was founded, builders struck over the implementation
of a reduction of the working week from 59 to 56½ hours, and in another strike in 1873
the union achieved a farthing an hour increase in wages.[74] It would be wrong to over-
estimate the influence of unions in mid-Victorian Banbury. The carpenters and engineers
held joint dinners in the 1870s, apparently because neither union on its own could muster
sufficient to make up a worthwhile party. Nevertheless in building, engineering and
printing, where labour was skilled, mobile and able to pressurise employers during short-
term crises of production, unions were influential.

The workers in the major manufacturing industries in Banbury remained a small proportion of the total labour force. In 1871 less than seven hundred worked in engineering,
weaving and brewing, while 601 were directly employed in retailing and 843 in small scale
crafts.[75] The proportion in retailing increased from 10.71 to 11.58 per cent of the
working population between 1851 and 1871. Many shopkeepers rebuilt their premises
in this period. While the population of the town was rising and the hinterland was
prospering, the numbers of shops remained stable. The number of bakers increased from
27 to 28, while the number of grocers fell from 19 to 16, and of ironmongers from 14 to
12. Only the drapers increased significantly in numbers, from 16 in 1851 to 23 in 1871.
The numbers employed in many shops increased. On average each shop in the major
trades employed one more person in 1871 than in 1851, but this increase was
concentrated in shops which were already quite large.[76] Joseph Hicks, linen draper,
employed nine; John Mawle, ironmonger, eleven men and three boys, and Austen &
Payne, grocers, eight. Some shopkeepers by 1871 lived in the suburbs, but maintained
residential accommodation for their workers above their business premises. The home of
John Harlock, linen draper, was in St John's Road, but over his shop at 3 Parson's Street
lived three shopwomen and two shopmen in the charge of a housekeeper. Thomas
Coleman, grocer, who employed 14, lived in West Bay, but three employees lodged over
his shop at 56 Parson's Street with the family of William Green, his traveller. Above his
shop in High Street, Arthur Adams, draper, accommodated with his family two male assistants, three apprentices and eight female employees as well as two domestic servants.

Figure 13. Shops in High Street (from W. P. Johnson, History of Banbury*)*

Few of Banbury's major shops were established family businesses which continued in the same ownership from generation to generation. The shops of only six of the 16 drapers and six of the 19 grocers listed in the directory for 1851 were owned by the same families 20 years later. Many grocers and drapers came to Banbury from distant places. In 1871, 18 drapers occupied prime sites in Bridge Street, High Street, Market Place and Parson's Street. Four were born in Banbury, four in the hinterland, and 10 in such distant places as Ridgemount (Beds.), Leicester, and Havering (Essex). Of 13 grocers in the same area, four were born in Banbury, three in the hinterland, and the remainder in Birmingham, Guildford, Baldock, Bath and Durham. Similar patterns of movement can be observed among shopworkers. Arthur Adams's drapery staff came from as far afield as Lincolnshire, Norfolk and Cornwall. William Cowper, draper, had employees from Norfolk, Brighton and Portsmouth. Retailers employed growing numbers of specialist workers. Most of the large shops had a clerk, a traveller and several apprentices, while mechanics were employed by ironmongers and milliners by drapers. Women increasingly worked in shops. Only 18 worked in retailing in 1851, most of them the widows of tradesmen continuing their husbands' businesses. By 1871, 77 were employed in Banbury shops, including 29 working for drapers, 10 for bakers, five for grocers and three for butchers.

The most significant feature of retailing in 1871 was the growing number of shops selling articles manufactured outside the town. Ready-made clothes shops were first listed in directories in 1845, but until 1855 there were never more than three of them. There were 10 by 1861. Furniture and boot-and-shoe warehouses began to compete with local cabinet makers and shoemakers. The traditional small scale crafts declined during the 1850s and '60s, the number employed falling from 870 to 843, or from 21.09 to 16.24 per cent of the working population. The fall affected every section, except for the woodworkers whose numbers increased from 96 to 138, largely owing to increases among wheelwrights and coachmakers, and the growth of carving and gilding. Shoemaking

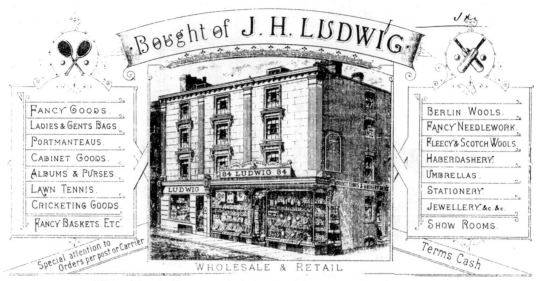

FANCY GOODS.
LADIES & GENTS BAGS.
PORTMANTEAUS.
CABINET GOODS.
ALBUMS & PURSES.
LAWN TENNIS.
CRICKETING GOODS.
FANCY BASKETS. ETC.

Bought of J. H. LUDWIG

84 LUDWIG 84

LUDWIG

BERLIN WOOLS.
FANCY NEEDLEWORK.
FLEECY & SCOTCH WOOLS.
HABERDASHERY.
UMBRELLAS.
STATIONERY.
JEWELLERY. &c. &c.
SHOW ROOMS.

Special attention to Orders per post or Carrier

WHOLESALE & RETAIL

Terms Cash

Figure 14.   J. H. Ludwig's fancy goods shop at 84 High Street, c. 1880.

expanded during the '50s until it employed 182 people by 1861,[77] but only 135 were employed in 1871. Some shoemakers had quite large establishments. William Shearsby employed nine men and four women, and Amelia Dumbleton had 13 employees, but there were no moves in Banbury, as there were in Northamptonshire, towards the establishment of a factory system of production. The reduction in the numbers involved in making clothing was more marked. The number of tailors fell from 107 to 82 between 1851 and 1871, of female dressmakers from 211 to 204, and of milliners from 56 to 37. A rise of 12 in the number of printers, and the advent of photography were responsible for a slight rise in the numbers engaged in the fine crafts.[78]

The progress of the early-closing movement in Banbury in the 1850s and '60s suggests that the masochistic competitiveness of earlier years was slowly mellowing. In 1852 the grocers began to shut at 8 p.m. each evening, and in the winter of 1856–57 shoemakers and leather sellers agreed to stop work at 7 p.m. In 1860 ironmongers and booksellers agreed to close early in winter, and the *Banbury Advertiser* remarked that few shops remained open after 7 p.m. In 1864 the town's two leading grocers extended early closing to Saturday nights, shutting at 9 p.m. from November to February. At Christmas 1867 it was still worth remarking that most shops in Banbury closed by 7 p.m. in mid-week. In 1868 and 1869 traders were petitioned to close their shops at 2 p.m. on the Tuesdays when the Mechanics' Institute fête took place, and Tuesday became a regular early closing day from 25 April 1871, when most shops began to shut at 4 p.m. Boxing Day 1870 was observed as a holiday at the request of the mayor, and the inauguration of Bank Holidays in 1871 was a legal recognition of what had gradually become an established practice in Banbury.[79]

The growth of a co-operative retail society in the late 1860s provides insights into the nature of retail trading in Banbury and into class relationships. The members of the weavers' co-operative formed in 1852 ran a retail store in Butchers' Row but it soon failed. At Christmas 1864 a beef club, largely formed of temperance activists, was so successful that a meeting was called on 18 April 1866 to consider setting up a co-operative society. Fifty members joined the Society, and on 7 June 1866 trading began, with volunteer assistants, from a lean-to building adjoining the *Leathern Bottle*. In spite of opposition from shopkeepers, the society flourished, and took £395 in its first year. A full-time assistant was engaged, and in November 1868 a new shop was opened on a freehold site in Broad Street. By June 1869 the Society had over 600 members. In the 1870s the movement became the way of life of many of Banbury's labour aristocracy. It was closely allied with temperance organisations, but while in the latter working men had worked closely with the middle classes, by setting up co-operative stores, they were challenging the very way of life of the traditional shopkeepers.[80]

The antipathy with which shopkeepers regarded the Co-operative Society, and the tenacity with which they adhered to late night opening on Saturdays, indicate the importance which they attached to cash paying or short credit working-class customers. They also faced competition from hawkers. Nothing is known of the traders at Banbury's retail market. There were no serious attempts to force them into a market hall, perhaps because such attempts had been successfully resisted in towns like Bridgnorth. A Saturday market, particularly for fish and vegetables, developed in the 1850s from informal gatherings of traders in the undercroft of the old town hall on Saturday evenings. They were warned by magistrates in 1851 that although they provided 'a great accommodation to the working class', they would be moved if they caused disturbances or traded after 10 p.m. Samuelson was given credit in 1859 for the establishment of the market.[81] There were 47 hawkers in Banbury in 1871. Many, including a group of 10 staying at the *Wheatsheaf*, were Irish; others were natives of Stockport, Sheerness and America. In May 1864 a cart ran over a small girl, whose parents, residents in Poplar, were travellers with 'one of those large vans which serve the purpose of a peripatetic store, where you can buy anything from a hearth rug to an armchair, which also serve as domicile and dormitory'. In June 1860 itinerant besom makers were encamped in Crouch Lane.[82] Pottery, haberdashery and cutlery were the goods most commonly sold by hawkers. At the Michaelmas Fair they traded in such diverse items as bear grease, concertinas, religious tracts, the works of the elder Dumas, pickled salmon and gingerbread.[83]

The number of agricultural labourers in Banbury fell from 217 to 122 between 1851 and 1871, probably because high wages in the foundries drew men away from farming in the neighbouring closed parishes. The number of farmers increased slightly due mostly to the settlement of retired agriculturalists in the suburbs. A slight decline in the number of horticulturalists masked the growth of Perry's nurseries into one of Banbury's most prosperous enterprises, which gave employment to about forty people.[84]

The polarisation of local society in the 1850s continued to be exemplified by the two principal banks. In Banbury itself Cobbs Bank remained dominant, through its involvement with the Britannia Works, the Buckinghamshire Railway, the development of Grimsbury and the varied speculations of Thomas Draper. Gilletts encountered difficulties in the 1850s, partially caused by the subvention of the unsuccessful engineering concerns of John Gillett of Brailes.[85] On two occasions rivalry between the banks and their political supporters emerged into open conflict. In 1851 under the sponsorship of Cobbs Bank a Freehold Land Society was formed to develop land in Grimsbury. It faced competition from a Banbury Permanent Benefit Building Society with J. A. Gillett and A. R. Tawney among its trustees, and a Conservative board of directors.

Protestations by adherents of both that their organisations were non-political were no more than confessions that they exemplified the polarisation of local society.[86]

Of greater moment was the rivalry between two schemes to build corn exchanges. In October 1856 a meeting attended largely by Conservatives, with Charles Gillett in the chair, sought support for an exchange in Cornhill. Newspapers soon warned against rivalry between competing projects, and in November a group backed by Cobbs Bank proposed a 'Central Corn Exchange' on the west side of the Market Place, with a new street of shops behind it. The vicar, William Wilson, tried to reconcile the two companies. The Liberal-controlled Board of Health demanded the removal of a minute encroachment by the Cornhill building. Both companies opened for business on Thursday 3 September 1857, the Cornhill Exchange without stands for merchants, and the Central with unplastered walls. The Cornhill company claimed in October to have let 30 stands and declared the rival scheme was 'begotten in envy and maintained in jealousy and revenge'. The shops associated with the Central Exchange were never built and Liberals were mocked at elections for not finishing the scheme and making the town appear ridiculous. The Central was subsequently recognised as the official exchange but the essential business of trading remained in less formal settings, and in 1879 the mayor was still appealing to traders to use the exchange rather than the street. T. R. Cobb's obituarist in 1875 recalled 'the battle of the Corn Exchanges which brought victory to neither side'.[87]

The Corn Exchanges affair was an awful warning of the waste which could occur when political and religious rivalries intruded into commercial affairs. In retailing there remained Whig, Tory and Radical shops, and Anglican and Dissenting craftsmen throughout the 1860s, but the professions became less involved in controversy. Cobbs Bank was amalgamated with an Aylesbury concern to form the Bucks and Oxfordshire Union Bank in 1853. Gilletts, under the talented management of the four sons of Joseph Ashby Gillett, who died in 1853, enlarged their activities in Woodstock, opened a discount house in the City in 1867, and in the '70s moved with great success into Witney and Oxford. Both the Cobbs and the Gilletts withdrew from the textile trade, and became more purely financial institutions than previously. Their horizons were lifted above the boundaries of the town and the limits of its factions.[88]

The generation of solicitors which had experienced the reform agitation of the 1830s remained active in the 1850s and '60s but their successors showed less enthusiasm for public controversy. The death of Thomas Draper in 1869[89] brought to an end a period when leading solicitors had been openly involved in every aspect of public affairs. In the election of 1859 the writer of a squib asked if Banbury would submit to dictation by 'DRAPER, lawyer or banker',[90] but such language would have seemed inappropriate a decade later when bankers and lawyers had come to occupy narrower professional roles than had previously been customary.

The proportion of those employed in the professions rose from 4.44 to 5.18 per cent of the labour force in the 1850s and '60s, due largely to an increase in the number of teachers from 67 to 114. The number of those involved with the legal profession rose from 26 to 40, and the total in banking fell by one.[91] The limited growth of the professions is probably explained by the narrower, more precise rules which professional men were coming to occupy. It is doubtful whether any bank clerk in 1871 had the same range of outside interests that William Barrett enjoyed 20 years earlier.[92]

It is not difficult to distinguish those features of economic life in Banbury in 1871 which would have appeared alien in 1850: the railway, the Britannia works, with its international connections, its paternalist management and its immigrant moulders and fitters, and the new 'warehouses' selling manufactured goods not made in the town. There were also changes in social attitudes. The class consciousness of skilled workers was expressed in trades unions and the co-operative movement, but it did not inhibit an acceptance of Samuelson's paternalist bounty. This attitude of deference did not extend to the rest of Banbury's ruling class. A proposal in 1863 to organise a gigantic dinner to celebrate the wedding of the Prince of Wales, modelled on that arranged for Queen Victoria's coronation, was dropped, because there had been 'a change in the habits and feelings of the English people', and men earning their livings were said to be loath to be the objects of 'eleemosynary hospitality'.[93] The hostility expressed towards shopkeepers by co-operators was never equalled by feelings against employers. It is possible that in the long run the growth of manufactures tended to create a fellow feeling between shopkeepers and the agricultural community, directed against both employers and workpeople in industry, which could well have been one of the foundations of small-town political Conservativism.

In some respects the likenesses between Banbury's economy in 1871 and that in 1850 are more striking than the differences. Domestic service occupied 17.87 per cent of the working population, almost exactly the same proportion as twenty years previously. The Michaelmas Fair still marked the peak of the year's trading. Banbury remained the 'metropolis of the carriers' carts'. It was still necessary for the bourgeoisie to organise soup kitchens for the poor in severe winters, and in a much publicised tragedy in 1857 the starved four-year-old daughter of a printer died after voraciously eating tripe broth on an empty stomach.[94] Least changed of all was the interdependence of town and countryside. The main reason for the flourishing state of Banbury's economy in 1871 was the relative prosperity of agriculture in the hinterland during the era of high farming. When agriculture declined in the 1870s, Banbury declined with it.

VIII

PUBLIC AUTHORITY AND PRIVATE ENTERPRISE 1850-1880

'We have indeed encouragement to pursue in spite of interested clamour and ignorant prejudice, the path which science and law marks out for us; satisfied that the time will come when our labours, now but timidly recognised, will be honourably remembered by all who wish well to the town'.[1]

HISTORIANS HAVE CUSTOMARILY WRITTEN about mid-Victorian government in terms of tension between *laissez-faire* and interventionist ideologies, between Liberty and Authority. The development of Banbury between 1850 and 1880 suggests that at the local level this is a false antithesis, and that, as the late Professor W. L. Burn believed, the problems faced by those in authority were more important than the labels which people attached to themselves or which posterity had attached to them.[2] Banburians did not refrain from expressing ideologies. Some were impatient at delays in improving the town and believed that the authority of government should be used to overcome private interests which caused them. Others saw the encroaching powers of government as a means of stifling enterprise, as unjustifiable restrictions on freedom, and as devices by which the town's ruling élite could extend its influence. Most developments in mid-Victorian Banbury were shaped by combinations of private interests and public authority. The occasions on which men set aside their principles as means of resolving practical problems were more significant than those when principles were put into practice.

In Banbury, as in other towns, power was shared by a multiplicity of *ad hoc* bodies, vestries, the borough and county magistrates, the borough corporation, the local Board of Health and the Poor Law Guardians. Some developments were the responsibility of public accountable but non-governmental bodies, like the committees which managed the principal schools or the boards of the water and gas companies. Others, like housing, were entirely private concerns.

After the effective abolition of Church Rates in 1853,[3] the vestries ceased to be political battlegrounds. The formation of the Banbury Poor Law Union made poor relief a regional rather than a town responsibility, and the views of Liberal Banbury never prevailed on the local Board of Guardians. After the first few elections in the 1830s, the town Guardians were mostly men without strong political attachments, and elections rarely aroused interest. The longest-serving Guardians were Francis Burgess, a retired Wesleyan minister, Henry Robert Brayne, a doctor, William Walford, a Neithrop landowner, and the Revd. Henry Back, the vicar, none of whom was a man of significant political standing. In Grimsbury the office of Guardian rotated between the principal

94

farmers until the 1860s when C. J. Brickwell, doctor and farmer, became chairman of the Board, was was regularly returned.[4]

Between 1851 and 1881 the population of Banbury rose by 38 per cent from 8,793 to 12,126,[5] and about 800 new houses were built. The death rate fell steadily, and the town centre was almost entirely rebuilt. Drainage, water and gas supplies were introduced or reorganised. Until 1870 the growth of population ran close to the national average, and the response of Banburians, in the face of the sanitary problems which it brought and the opportunities which it offered for development, was typical of that in many towns.

In 1850 the General Board of Health issued the report on the sanitary condition of Banbury compiled by T. W Rammell after his enquiry the previous year. A series of meetings led to the establishment of a local Board of Health, which, as Rammell recommended, covered the whole parish. The parliamentary order was made on 30 June 1852. The acceptance of Rammell's proposals was due largely to the advocacy of Edward Cobb, who envisaged the Board as a means towards the eventual unification of Banbury and Neithrop. He was opposed by farmers who objected to the rating of agriculture for town improvements, and by councillors who argued that the existing Paving and Lighting Commission was adequate for the needs of the borough.[6] The Board of Health was composed of 12 members. Six, seconded by the corporation, represented the borough, and were acknowledged to be the most important members of the council.[7] The others were directly elected to represent the non-corporate parts of the parish. The Board assumed the functions of the corporation with respect to sanitary matters.

The powers of the Paving and Lighting Commission were transferred to the Board of Health on 5 August 1852, and the first election for the non-corporate areas took place the following day. Twelve candidates stood for the six seats, all but one of which were won by Liberals, who included the foundrymaster Bernhard Samuelson. The first meeting of the Board elected Edward Cobb as chairman. There was optimism about the Board's prospects. The *Banbury Guardian* commented:

'The costly squabbles, turmoils and party contests which have been heard of in too many places are not likely to occur in this district. There has been in this district since the passing of the Act a unanimity and cordiality of feeling which augurs most favourably for the working of the measure'.[8]

The Board did not fulfil such sanguine expectations. It suffered from a rapid turnover in membership. Of those elected or appointed in 1852, only three remained members in 1860. Only one member served without a break through the 1860s. Between 1852 and 1880 some 66 different individuals served on the Board. The political balance on the Board varied with that on the Corporation. There was a Liberal majority throughout the 1850s, a small Conservative majority in the early 1860s, and Liberal dominance in the late '60s, and throughout the '70s. In 1858 two Conservative farmers won a contested election, but in 1881 it was alleged that for 20 years there had been no election, and that the Board was self-nominated and irresponsible.[9] The quality of leadership declined after 1853 when Edward Cobb left the town, and Samuelson ceased to be a member. The next chairman was the Quaker miller Robert Field, whose reputation was tarnished by his role in the Cemetery affair. He was replaced in 1856 by the chemist Thomas Beesley, who regarded his duties in a serious and professional manner, and produced a perceptive report on the Board's first five years. He was forced to resign in 1858, probably because he wished to move the cattle market out of the streets.[10]

In the early 1850s the Board was seen as a means of eliminating insanitary living conditions, of lowering rates, and of making Banbury into a beautiful as well as a healthy town. Richard Edmunds forecast that it would bring water to the areas which needed it, would eliminate bad accommodation which promoted immorality, and make Banbury a place of resort.[11] The Board failed to fulfil such aspirations because they were not accepted by the community at large, which saw many necessary measures as acts of petty tyranny, inimical to the economic interests of the town. Interference with time-honoured practices like keeping pigs and slaughtering cattle in the centre of the town, building bow windows and ignoring building lines, was the most frequent cause of contention. The Board lacked the competence to cope with major matters like sewage disposal, because the appropriate technology was only in process of development. Confusion over the roles of public bodies and private companies in the provision of utilities reflected national uncertainty about the role of government. On minor issues the debate revealed basic differences of opinion about the sort of town Banbury should be. Typical of such disputes was a controversy which arose over an order made in September 1857 instructing butchers to remove hooks from outside their shops, thus preventing the obstruction of pavements by hanging carcases. The clerk to the Board insisted that it was one of the first duties of the authority to keep the highway clear, but some members insisted that the public was against the Board on the matter, and that it should be dropped. One opponent said of the Board:

> 'instead of being a benefit and a blessing to the town, it is regarded not only as a nuisance, but as the greatest of all nuisances with which the town is cursed'.

Another argued:

> 'Banbury has risen to its present eminent business position from the *uncontrolled* energy and industry of its tradesmen and it especially behoves the Board to be careful of what it does inimical to the trading interests of the town, always bearing in mind that Banbury is a *business* town, and that the legislation suitable for a Leamington or a Cheltenham is quite out of place here'.[12]

In 1854 the houses were numbered, but the painter encountered so much opposition that the work was seriously delayed. In 1858 the Board found that a nameplace inscribed 'Queen Street' had been erected without authorisation at the end of Crouch Street, and ordered it to be removed, but it was still in place four years later. In 1861 an extensive re-naming of streets aroused fierce opposition.[13]

The Board came into conflict with many established market town practices. In 1871 it prosecuted two carriers for obstructing the highway, but the magistrates ruled in favour of the defendants who remained in 'the standings they had so long occupied'. In 1873 the Board's inspector found that many of the vans at the Michaelmas Fair were filthy, but could do nothing about it. In the same year George Cave was ordered to stop burning lime in his canal-side kilns, which produced an acrid fog which had been the subject of complaints since 1862.[14] During 1863 there was a dispute about slaughter-houses in Church Lane which the Board tried to close, thus, it was alleged, depriving butchers of their livings. In 1865 there was controversy over slaughter houses in High Street and Parson's Street, and pig sties in Fish Street.[15] In 1881 much ridicule was attracted by the 'White Lion Pig Case', when the Board tried to eradicate pig keeping in the very heart of Banbury.[16]

The Board's achievements in other spheres won respect. Plans for new sewers were completed by May 1854 when contractors were sought, and the clerk of works was appointed in July. As the sewers came into operation, huge dung heaps were removed from the Leys and the Shades. By 1857 three main sewers had been completed with a loan of £4,300 from the General Board of Health.[17] The effluent from the new sewers went into the Cherwell untreated, and Banbury gained a reputation for its foul smell, said to have been noticeable from passing non-stop trains. Plans for a filtration works were made by the Board's surveyor, Thomas Garrett, in 1858, but were not implemented. In his guide book written in 1859 W. P. Johnson quoted Shenstone's poem 'Cherwell's verdant side', and commented that the poet wrote before the establishment of Boards of Health and the concomitant nuisance of common sewers.[18] In 1861 Stephen Spokes of Twyford Mill, four miles downstream from Banbury, complained that sewage was contaminating his stretch of the river, and in November 1865 he began legal action. The following year the Board leased 137 acres of Spital Farm to the east of the town for a sewage irrigation scheme. A pumping engine was built, and the system came into operation in December 1867. The following season's meadow and rye grass realised over £200, and for a time the scheme came close to realising the ultimate aspirations of many Victorian sanitary reformers by making a profit. In 1871 Spital Farm was purchased for £23,000 by a consortium, and sold to the Board at the same cost.[19] The irrigation scheme gained national repute, with accounts of it being published in the *Gardeners' Chronicle, Land and Water, The Field,* the *Salopian Journal* and the *Bedfordshire Mercury.* It was so successful that in 1870 Spokes began to raise trout in the Cherwell at Twyford.[20]

The Board of Health quickly concluded that it could not raise the capital to provide the town with water. The formation of a water company was announced in August 1854 and a prospectus issued early in 1855, but it was not until the summer of 1857 that the company took shape. A meeting was held in June at which a scheme to take water from the Cherwell near Grimsbury Mill was announced, and by the time of the first annual meeting in August £7,000 had been subscribed. By March 1858 pipes had been laid, and water was being supplied although consumers were warned that it would be of poor quality until the pipes were cleaned out.[21] In 1864 the Board contemplated borrowing £17,200 to purchase the Water Company, but there were allegations that some individuals were involved on both sides of the transaction and the proposal was dropped.[22]

The canal-side gasworks in Bridge Street, established in the 1830s, was enlarged in 1850 and 1852 in anticipation of increased demand from the railway stations. In 1854 there was a prospect that a rival gas company would be formed, but Bernhard Samuelson intervened to prevent wasteful competitition. A new works was built by the existing company between the two railways. The old site was offered for sale in August and the first gas from the new works flowed into the mains in November 1854.[23] In 1852 when the Board of Health was constituted there were 50 street lamps in the borough, but only 10, all privately financed, in Neithrop. By December 1852 sites for 42 lamps in Neithrop had been recommended. By 1865 there were 96 lamps in Banbury, 54 in Neithrop and 9 in Grimsbury.[24] The Board contracted out the scavenging of the streets, and from 1867 each house was provided with a receptacle for rubbish.[25]

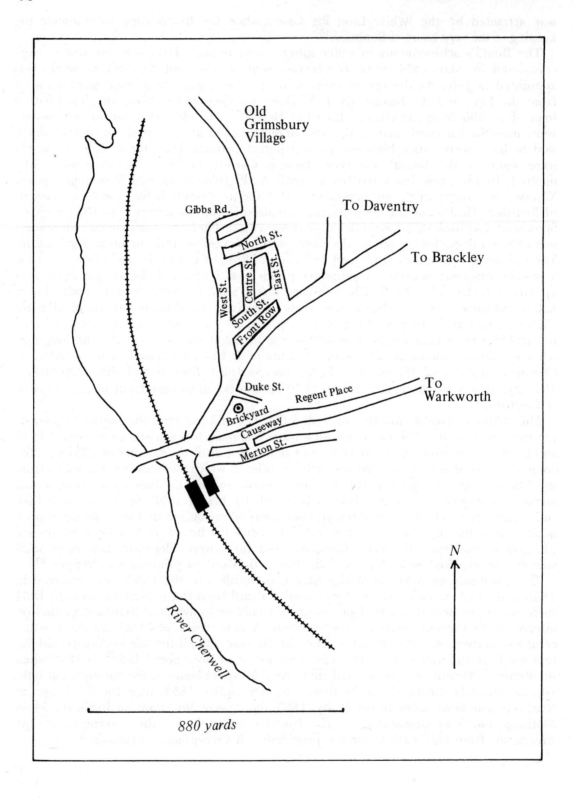

Fig. 15. The Growth of Grimsbury, 1850-80.

Housing was entirely the concern of the private sector, the role of the Board of Health being only to approve the laying-out of new streets, to inspect the building lines and drainage facilities of new developments, and, when appropriate, to take new roads into public control.

The development which most epitomised the ethos of Liberal Banbury was New Grimsbury, originally called Freetown. Early in 1851 an audience of 300 heard James Taylor of Birmingham lecture in Banbury on Freehold Land Societies. Taylor was a disciple of the Unitarian minister George Dawson, and a zealous crusader for working-class self-help. The principle of a freehold land society was that members should subscribe to buy land at wholesale prices, and distribute building plots among themselves at the same price. By creating freeholds, such societies extended the franchise in county constituencies, but Taylor denied that such consequences had a party object.[26] The formation of a Banbury Freehold Land Society was proposed by Francis Francillon. Henry Tancred became president, and headquarters were established at the Mechanics' Institute. Cobbs became the society's bankers, and Bernhard Samuelson joined the committee. A plot of 13 acres to the north of the turnpike road to Middleton Cheney, 300 yards east of Banbury Bridge, was purchased from Sloan Stanley by T. R. Cobb and sold to the society for the same price.[27] Three of the 13 acres were used for roads, and the remaining 10 divided into 151 plots. By April 1853 the roads and drains were under construction and the plots were allocated by ballot. The name of each shareholder was written on a piece of paper, together with an indication of how many lots he was entitled to. The member whose name was drawn first took plot No. 1, and so on, with plural shareholders taking as many consecutive lots as they held shares. The plots were divided between 101 shareholders, who were bound to observe covenants about building lines and the value of houses to be constructed.[28]

The subscribers included most of Banbury's Liberal élite, but few working men, and the estate became an area for small scale speculative building rather than owner occupation. Bernhard Samuelson subscribed for six shares and drew Nos. 41–46, the first two of which became the site of the *Prince of Wales* public house. In Centre Street, plot 37, allocated to William Cubitt, was developed by the builder William Wilkins who erected two houses there in 1861. Plots 66 and 67 won in the ballot by T. H. Wyatt, the brewer and Thomas Dumbleton, a saddler, were the site of three dwellings constructed by the builders Thomas and Stephen Orchard in 1858.[29] While the quality of building on the estate was higher than elsewhere in Banbury, there were few owner occupers and the pattern of ownership was not very different from that of purely private developments. The houses along the turnpike road formed the 'front row' of the estate and became a middle-class suburb. Many of the owners purchased the equivalent plots in South Street and thus obtained long gardens giving rear access to their premises. By 1861 there were 22 houses in the row, the inhabitants including clerks from the foundries, banks and breweries, commercial travellers, a baptist minister, the canal company surveyor, the master of the British School and an excise officer. Only one occupant, William Baker, a draper, was a working shopkeeper, and 10 years later there was still only one active trader in the row.[30] The estate grew slowly. Some plots were used as gardens and the area gained the name of 'The Diggings'. The inhabitants, outside 'Front Row', were mostly artisans. The occupants of the 25 houses in Centre Street in 1861 included a postman, a millwright, a railway porter, a bricklayer, a boat builder and a labourer at a coal wharf. In the early 1870s the east side of East Street and the west side of West Street, which were not part of the Freehold Land Society property, became available for development. They were filled in with terraces of up to twelve houses, whereas those on the estate were grouped in twos, threes and fours.[31] The Freehold Land Society stimulated other building in Grimsbury. Plots on the turnpike road to the east of East Street were sold for building in the early 1870s, and by 1871 most of the 300-yard gap between the Bridge and the estate had been filled with houses. To the north of the estate Robert Gibbs was authorised to lay out the road, which later bore his name, in 1873.[32] To the south west the ancient causeway to Warkworth was lined with working-class dwellings in the 1850s and '60s. On the north side several terraces of four-room cottages called Regents Place were built by William Wilkins, who purchased the site in 1852, and financed the construction of the houses by a series of 5 per cent mortgages, one of them from an illiterate shoemaker from Camberwell. Ten were constructed in 1856, 14 in the following year, eight more by 1860 and a further six between 1869 and 1871. Between the Causeway and Middleton Road, at the edge of Wilkins's brick pit, was Duke Street, a terrace of 30 houses built about 1870. Other cottages were built on the south side of the Causeway. Ebenezer Wall received sanction to construct eight in 1871, and one George Cary gained authorisation for four the following year.[33] South of the Causeway the first houses on a new road, later called Merton Street, were authorised in 1873 and various speculators had built 57 by 1882.[34]

The construction of houses on the Cherwell meadows continued after 1850, and by 1871 there were about 350 dwellings in the area. One of the first tasks of the Board of Health was to move the piles of filth which had accumulated in the ill-drained Cherwell Streets in the 1840s.[35] Most of the development after 1850 was the The Gatteridges, an estate purchased from the Spurrett family by Thomas Draper, who laid out streets and sold plots to developers. When the Board of Health considered the condition of Upper Windsor Street in 1864, it was noted that the road was built and drained by Mr. Draper, and that terraces had been constructed by three speculators. Gatteridge Street running eastwards from Newland was sufficiently developed in 1853 for an application to be made for street lamps. Plans for Britannia Road were drawn up in 1853, and houses were being built there in 1858.[36] Most of the streets in the Cherwell area were occupied by the working class. In 1871 the occupants of the 33 houses in Windsor Terrace included 17 skilled and six unskilled foundry workers, 13 builders, a shoemaker, a Post Office telegraph linesman, a railway porter, a canal boatman, a porter at an ironmonger's, a laundress and six women who made their livings by needlecraft. Gatteridge Street has more middle-class residents, including an excise officer, a coach builder employing 11 men, a decorator also employing 11, and several clerks.[37]

There was much building in Broad Street where the Board of Health complained in 1854 of obstruction by materials for new houses. In 1861 a cul-de-sac on the east side, later called Grover Street, was sanctioned. Ten of the houses were offered for sale as an investment in 1862, when attention was drawn to their 'quiet and cheerful situation' and their proximity to the principal foundries. They were let to 'respectable tenants' at 3s. 6d. a week. In 1870 the construction of Grove Place (later Newland Place) on the western side of Broad Street was sanctioned. Census returns show that the area was, as W. P. Johnson observed in 1859, made up 'chiefly of the dwellings of the working class'.[38]

To the west of the town the Gillett family extended Paradise Lane, previously a cul-de-sac off the Warwick Road, across the gardens called the Vineyards to the Broughton Road. Notice of intent to build the road was given in September 1855 and the contract for constructing it was let the following month. Plots were let to speculators, but the area developed slowly. By 1862 the new road was called Bath Road, and the following year another new road joining it was named Queen Street. Park Road was constructed during the 1870s. Some of the houses were meanly dimensioned two-storey brick cottages, while others were elegant Gothic villas. By 1871 only about 17 houses had been built in Bath Road and seven in Queen Street. In 1882 there were 27 in Bath Road, 48 in Queen Street and 24 in Park Road.[39]

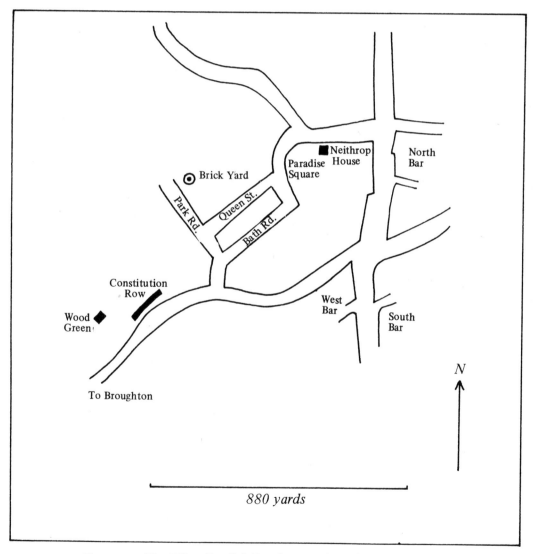

Figure 16.   The Gillett Family's Development in Bath Road, 1855–80.

The Calthorpe Estate, the property of Edward Cobb, to the south of the town centre, was gradually developed during the 1860s. In 1857–58 Cobb sold two portions of the pleasure grounds of Calthorpe House to Dr. R. Stanton Wise, who by 1863 had laid out Marlborough Road linking Newland with High Street. The new road was taken over by the Board of Health in 1870, and in 1872–73 the Board granted applications for houses in Marlborough Place, a cul-de-sac for which Wise had received sanction in 1866.[40] In 1861 Edward Cobb laid out Dashwood Road linking Newland and South Bar, and 11 building plots had been marked out between it and St John's Road by 1862. They were gradually filled with the residences of such wealthy citizens as William Edmunds the brewer.[41]

The southern edge of the town was already by 1860 the principal resort of the wealthiest of Banbury's middle classes. The mainspring of development was an attempt in 1852 to provide houses for 'respectable families not engaged in business'. Such families, argued the *Banbury Guardian*, would be of benefit to the town:

'We have workers and those who are seeking to get money in abundance; and it must be a wise step to encourage the residence amongst us of those who come to spend and not to get money'.

Fourteen plots were laid out on the Oxford Road and in St John's Road, and sold with designs for villas prepared by Edward Bruton, architect of the town hall. The 1871 census shows that several actually were occupied by people living on income from investments. Others were the homes of solicitors and senior clerks, and one was a boarding school.[42] Farther south Thomas Draper purchased the Hightown estate in 1861 with the intention of 'giving the inhabitants of Banbury an opportunity to buy three, two, one or half-acre sites at £300–£500 an acre for suburban or villa residences'. He laid out a new road, although most of the houses along it were not built until the 1880s and '90s. More attractive to the wealthy in the 1860s and '70s, because nearer to the town centre, were the Gothic terraces and villas of West Bar.[43]

To the north and west of the town centre terraces of working-class cottages were built off the New Road, following the clearance of dung heaps in the 1850s, and on the Castle Gardens where the Board of Health sanctioned a road linking North Bar with the Market Place in 1854.[44]

Most housing in Banbury was provided by small-scale speculators. Some were builders, like William Wilkins, bricklayer and brickmaker, who constructed most of the north side of the Causeway, the whole of Duke Street, several terraces on the Freehold Land Society estate, at least 19 houses in Castle Street and others in Marlborough Road, Gatteridge Street and Dashwood Road. His houses were, for the most part, small and ill-constructed and the despair of the medical profession. He was described by a doctor in 1870 as one who 'would lay down some bricks at night to find them houses in the morning . . . who made fortunes out of poor people while denying them pure water'.[45] William Aris, another builder and brickmaker, built numerous houses on the Gillett family's development in Bath Road, several terraces in Windsor Street, 18 houses in Broad Street and the whole of Grove Street. While Wilkins retained the ownership of the houses he built, Aris sold many of his to fellow-speculators. Albert Kimberley, another builder, constructed houses in Windsor Street, Britannia Road, Bath Road, Middleton Road and West Street. Other developers had no direct connections with the building trade. Joseph Mascord, an ironmonger who went bankrupt in 1870, owned various properties in the town centre, a terrace of 12 cottages in Windsor Street and five plots on the Freehold Land Society estate. Ebenezer Wall, ropemaker, Liberal and Disciple of Christ, was building throughout the 1850s, '60s and '70s, among his properties being a terrace in the Causeway, cottages on the Freehold Land Society estate and Britannia Terrace. Landowners like the Gilletts, the Cobbs, Thomas Draper and R. S. Wise brought land on the market in quantities which made development possible but the actual building was mostly undertaken by people of lesser standing and resources.[46]

The rate of house-building was uneven, although gaps in the records of the Board of Health prevent the formulation of complete series of statistics. In the nine years from 1857 to 1866, 289 houses were authorised, a mean of 28.9 per year, but half were sanctioned in the two years 1860 and 1861. In the nine years from 1870 to 1878, 353 houses were authorised, an average of 39.2 per year, but 62 were authorised both in 1873 and 1878.[47]

Much of the centre of Banbury was rebuilt between 1850 and 1880. The new town hall in Bridge Street, designed by Edward Bruton and completed in 1854, was seen as an ornament to the approach to the town from the new railway stations. It was a building indelibly associated with the Liberal Party which was often blamed for its appearance. The clock was not added until 1860, the year when the old town hall was removed from the Market Place, re-erected on a canal-side wharf by Thomas Draper, and used for the storage of artificial manure.[48] The Board of Health records show a continual process of alteration and rebuilding in Parson's Street, High Street, Market Place and Bridge Street. Few market towns are so dominated by Victorian frontages as Banbury. Most shop buildings of the mid-19th century had classical proportions, were of three or four storeys, and were constructed of local brick, with Bath stone quoins, sills and lintels, and sometimes with complete window surrounds in stone, with scrolls on the supporting sills. The high-ceilinged rooms on the first floors show that most were intended for accommodation as well as trade. Bath stone for coping was delivered by rail, and by 1853 was being sold below the price of the local Hornton stone.[49]

The establishment of the Board of Health removed some of the urgency for uniting Banbury and Neithrop, but it did nothing to improve public order. Thomas Draper, who lived at Calthorpe House, told the magistrates in 1859 that, following the murder of a prostitute in Calthorpe Street in October 1858, 'disgraceful scenes of drunkenness, cursing, swearing, obscene and beastly language' had increased, and that the borough police would not venture beyond 'the white mark on the wall', which indicated the Neithrop boundary.[50] Several attempts were made to unify the borough and Neithrop but they came to nothing.[51] Banbury retained its independent police force until 1925, although several attempts were made to merge it with neighbouring forces, and in 1860 Banbury was one of only two towns with populations below 5,000 to have its own force. Local councillors were proud of the borough's relative freedom from crime — it was claimed that there had been only two burglaries in 25 years — but others complained that Banbury's criminals operated outside the borough, and deplored the lack of watch between 5 a.m. and 7 a.m., the time when depredators returned from the countryside with their loot. A slight reorganisation took place in 1860. William Thompson became a full-time superintendent, with a brass plate on his door. He retired at the age of 79 in 1875, when one of the first tasks of his successor was to replace the constables' tall hats with helmets.[52] The non-corporate parts of the parish were policed from June 1857, when an inspector and two constables of the newly-formed Oxfordshire force took up their duties in Neithrop. A county police station was built in Newland in 1861–62.[53]

An inspector of prisons remarked in 1851 that he had never seen such a bad gaol as that maintained by the borough corporation in the Market Place. It was closed in 1852 when prisoners were removed to Oxford, and from 1854 its function as an overnight lock-up was taken over by the cells in the new town hall.[54]

Public authority and private enterprise were both involved in the provision of education in Banbury. The population of young persons between two and 18 in the town rose from 3,259 in 1851 to 4,544 on 1871, an increase of 39.43 per cent. Comparison of the two censuses suggests that the expansion of school places failed by a small margin to keep pace with this increase. In 1871 there were 2,199 young people recorded as scholars on the census, 48.39 per cent of the age group, compared with 51.18 per cent in 1851. It seems that at least one enumerator in 1871 was inconsistent in recording whether children were attending school or not, but even allowing for some under-recording it is clear that at best the provision of new school places can only just have matched the growth of population, and that the proportion of children at school did not increase in the 1850s and '60s. In 1870 it was estimated that there were 1,894 children attending school in Banbury, 1,484 at public and 410 at private establishments. By 1877, 1,999 children attended the six public schools. The 1871 census suggests a marked decline in the practice of sending very young children to dame schools. In 1851, 26.79 per cent of two year-olds were recorded as scholars, but the figure fell to 2.90 per cent 20 years later. The proportion of three-year-olds in school fell from 45.69 to 35.71 per cent, but the proportion of five-year-olds was almost the same. The proportion of children of 14 and over attending school was slightly higher than in 1851.[55]

Several new schools were provided. An Infant School, opened in Windsor Terrace in 1851, was absorbed 10 years later in the Cherwell British Schools, which were built by Bernhard Samuelson. Christ Church National Schools were opened in Grimsbury in 1862.[56] Although Samuelson advocated a School Board in Banbury after the passing of the 1870 Education Act, there was opposition on the grounds of increased costs, and in the 1870s increased capacity had to be provided in the existing schools.[57]

The British School provided rather more than the basics of education. J. H. Beale, its Canadian-born head master, who was appointed in 1854, was a school-master of exceptional talents. Matthew Arnold HMI reported in 1858 that 'Mr. Beale's great exertions and remarkable personal influence continue to produce more and more complete results in the school'. Another inspector commented on the eve of the introduction of the Revised Code in 1863, 'This is a most excellent school, and I should say there are few which are likely to pass so creditably under the new ordeal'. The school committee responded to the Revised Code by insisting that they considered reading writing and arithmetic to be no more than means to Education, and not Education itself, and expressed themselves satisfied that the teachers should persevere with a more liberal syllabus. Beale was constantly responsive to the quality of homework, frequently re-arranged the details of the syllabus, and was keenly interested in the progress of indivisual boys. His delight shines through the pages of his log book on such occasions as when, in 1866, Richard Wright, having completed his pupil teachership, gained a first class Queen's Scholarship and went to study at Borough Road College. Beale responded to every kind of education opportunity. In 1863 he took a party to the Crystal Palace, and in 1864 arranged for a Coventry weaver to demonstrate the manufacture of silk ribbons. His birthday on 13 May was always celebrated, and in 1865, when it fell on a Saturday, he was greeted outside the school by 60 boys and pupil teachers. He also organised the Science and Art classes, and used them to do advanced work with his school pupils. In 1862 Matthew Arnold commended his success:

> '... in the First Class of this British school, I found a boy, not 12 years old, who has carried off the Gold Medal for Physiology against several hundred competitors, many of them men of 30 and 40'.

Pupils won numerous prizes in such national competitions. The liberal, science-based syllabus which Beale taught was exactly that recommended by Bernhard Samuelson, one of the chief advocates in the House of Commons of scientific and technical education. Yet even in Samuelson's constituency, the educational constraints of the Revised Code, and the administrative limitations of the 1870 Education Act, prevented those with imagination from creating that kind of schooling which they knew to be necessary. Attempts in 1868 to establish a grammar school, funded by the town's educational charities, came to nothing, but the British School demonstrated that a high level of education could be achieved with limited resources in a provincial town. In 1878 Beale retired to concentrate on a private school which he had established some years previously at the Ark house. Some boys went with him and many more were withdrawn from the British Schools on his departure.[58]

The construction of Banbury Cross in 1859 was a curious example of the overlapping of public authority and private enterprise. It was built in celebration of the marriage of the Princess Royal on 25 January 1858. The official celebrations, financed by public subscription took the form of a dress ball on the wedding day, and a concert the following evening. Not all Banburians approved of this programme, and a further subscription was raised by Thomas Beesley and A. B. Rye, calling for a permanent memorial. At a meeting on 23 January, William Wilson, the vicar, called for a structure like the Martyr's Memorial. Others argued for something more useful, and the final design, a spire with conduit basins and a fire hydrant was a compromise. It was erected during the first half of 1859 after complaints about delays. The foundation stone was laid by a shoemaker, and the gilt cross at the top was inserted by T. W. Boss, the Mechanics' Institute librarian. The mayors of the time avoided all involvement in the project which nevertheless received quite widespread support from the town's ruling class, although some radicals opposed it. The Cross was only briefly discussed by the Board of Health, and it is some measure of the scope for private initiatives that a memorial could be erected at Banbury's principal traffic intersection by a committee of relatively obscure men, with no official status.[59]

Banbury, like most English towns, was transformed in many respects between 1850 and 1880. Substantial changes were made in public health, public order and education which marked decisive breaks with age-old practices. The death rate fell from 23.0 per 1,000 in 1850 to 13.5 in 1895. The town was drained and supplied with water, and its gas supply was extended, all in the face of a rapidly growing population. Some areas remained squalid. In 1870 Globe Court and Calthorpe Court were reported to be particularly offensive. In 1871, 26 people were crowded into the Rag Row lodging house, presided over by Bridget Ward, then aged 78, who had once kept the notorious Waterloo lodging house. Yet few really bad houses were built after 1850. Whatever the deficiencies of William Wilkins's Cottages, the Causeway never became as squalid as the Cherwell Streets had been in the 1840s, almost as soon as they were built. By the 1870s the Board of Health was beginning to use its powers to declare unfit for habitation some of the worst of the old houses in the town centre.[60]

The changes in the town are better interpreted as the achievements of a community, the outcome of tensions between principles, individuals and groups, than as an advertisement for either interventionism or *laissez-faire*. Many of those who were active as private individuals in the development of Banbury were also holders of public office. James Cadbury lived on his investments in property and was a member of the Board of Health, the British School Committee, and many other organisations. Thomas Draper was a member of the Corporation and the Board of Health as well as the developer of the southern part of the Cherwell area and Hightown Road. The considerable degree of common membership between the Board of Health and the Water Company in the 1860s raised suspicions of corruption, but such situations were almost inevitable, given the intimacy of society in Banbury. Almost all authority was exercised from within the town, and those who held power could see its effects immediately. In 1873 the magistrates ordered the police to stop open air meetings, after one justice complained about the violent language used by teetotallers. In 1866 the Board of Health heard a member complain that on the previous day Mr. Norton's son caused a nuisance by riding a velocipede, and he was warned about his future conduct.[61] The magistrates were overruled, and whether the Board had power over velocipedes is questionable, but such trivial incidents show how close were the decision makers to those affected by their decisions, and how relatively unimportant was the precise status of a particular authority. Banbury was ruled by an élite, and authority came as much from membership of that élite as from powers devolved by central government or conferred by democratic election. When William Wilkins was denounced in 1870 for the polluted water supplies of his cottages the rebuke did not come from a bureaucrat but from one of the town's doctors who was also a borough councillor,[62] and it is likely that the weight of the rebuke derived from the esteem in which the doctor was held rather than from his official position.

Private enterprise and public authority were inextricably mixed. One result of such confusion could be corruption, although there is no evidence of any particular scandals in mid-19th-century Banbury. Another result could have been that membership of public bodies exercised an educational function, and that councillors and Board members came to understand why sanitary regulations were necessary. Beneficial developments came not so much because individual entrepreneurs were free to exercise their talents, but because the town as a community was free to act responsibly. In some areas the powers devolved by central government made this possible. The town was drained, and its new building adequately regulated. In other respects they were inadequate. Private interests made it impossible to unite the borough with Neithrop, and fears of taxation and unimaginative legislation impeded the development of the liberal and scientific educational system which some townsmen saw to be necessary. The period between 1850 and 1880 was one when Banbury was self-governing to an unusual extent, and the achievements of those years suggest that its citizens responded wisely to their responsibilities.

IX

NAMES, SECTS AND PARTIES:
THE CHURCHES IN BANBURY 1849-1880

'... almost every sect in Banbury was represented, Unitarians, Methodists of all shades, Congregationalists, Hyper-Calvinists, and church people. Coming up to the chapel in the conveyance, he (C. H. Spurgeon) has asked me what denominations we had in Banbury. I told him I thought we pretty well had them all. Indeed, it had been said that if a man lost his religion, he might well find it at Banbury'.[1]

BANBURY'S PRE-EMINENCE as a market town was matched by the variety and strength of the religious affiliations of its citizens. In 1853 a newspaper estimated that there were 17 places of worship in the town, while a Baptist minister guessed that there were fifteen.[2] Religious controversy flourished in Banbury like a plant growing in a rich soil in a well-heated greenhouse. There was an element of exaggeration about religion in the town, which illuminates the basic tensions in towns where arguments were less openly debated.

The religious controversies of the 1850s took place in a situation of social and political equilibrium; one in which there was much that united Christians as well as much that divided them. There was little disagreement amongst Protestants about the need to contain the Church of Rome, to extend primary education, and to spread the culture and life style of the bourgeois church member. The privileges still enjoyed by the Established Church were balanced, locally, by the political dominance of the largely Nonconformist Liberal Party. There were two principal sources of religious division. One was related to what may be called social evangelism. While there was general agreement about the desirability of extending the social influence of the churches, opinions varied as to whether this should be done through legislation, the denunciation and confrontation of evil-doers, or a more specifically religious presence in politics. The other source of division was the continuing social disabilities of the Dissenters, which, though often trivial in themselves, could be inflated into profoundly destructive issues.

On 19 June 1849 William Wilson exchanged livings with T. W. Lancaster, and was instituted to the vicarage of Banbury, Lancaster taking the cure of 45 souls at Worton. Wilson's father was for 26 years Vicar of Walthamstow, and an influential figure in London Evangelicalism. His uncle, Daniel Wilson, was Bishop of Calcutta, and builder of that city's Gothic cathedral. In November 1849 Wilson appointed two curates, who, with Charles Forbes, Vicar of South Banbury, made up the largest clerical staff the parish had known since the Reformation. Rooms were hired for week-night meetings in Neithrop, Bridge Street and Upper Cherwell Street. Every Wednesday there was an evening service in St Mary's. A Church Communicants' Society was formed in

December 1849. Early in 1850 a new Sunday morning service was instituted, at which pewholders were requested to allow the poor to occupy their seats. In the summer of 1850 the church ceiling was whitewashed for the first time in half a century, the roof was repaired, and the rotting timbers of the pews renewed. In 1858 the organ was rebuilt and the east gallery removed.[3]

Samuel Wilberforce embarked on his first Lenten mission in 1850, when, according to his biographer:

'for the first time for centuries in England, a Bishop has been seen giving to the earnest parochial clergy of his diocese active personal assistance in railing the lukewarm or reclaiming the erring children of her church'.

The mission began at Wantage, and moved through Farringdon to Banbury, where Wilberforce arrived on Saturday 23 February to address 200 communicants in the National School. On the following Sunday morning there was a sumptuous display of ecclesiastical pomp at a five hour ordination service, with a procession to the church of the bishop, 12 officiating clergy, and 16 ordinands. All 2,700 seats in St Mary's were filled. Later Wilberforce returned to the church to confirm 120 young people. At evensong 3,000 heard him preach on 'Death and Judgement'. The next day the Revd. William Wilson, Senr. addressed schoolchildren on 'Sanctity in Childhood', and the mission concluded with a ritualistic flourish on Wednesday 27 February at a service attended by 26 clergy and a congregation of 2,500. The townspeople were said to have been deeply impressed by 'the long and ordered stream of surpliced clergy which passed continually during each day in reverent and earnest silence to and from the church'. An observer remarked:

'the counsel and example of the Bishop and the sympathy of many brethren must have left the earnest vicar of the parish strengthened and encouraged to carry out the work begun with increased energy, and with enlarged prospect of success'.[4]

Wilberforce regarded Wilson with favour and described him in 1855 as 'Good Wilson'. His energy and capacity for organisation closely matched the bishop's own abilities.[5]

In August 1850 Wilson organised a sophisticated social survey of the township of Neithrop. Sketch maps were drawn on which every house was numbered. The names and occupations of householders were recorded, and their religious affiliations indicated by a code of coloured circles. Their children, and the schools they attended, were also listed. Wilson was an energetic visitor of the poor, and his influence was extended by his 15 district visitors who assembled on the firest Wednesday of each month, when alms books were examined, tracts exchanged and the problems of the poor discussed. A ragged Sunday School was established, and the school at St Mary's re-organised, with meetings for teachers two evenings a week. Wilson was active in many organisations and was welcomed as the first Anglican clergyman resident in the town to support the Mechanics' Institute.[6]

Wilson donated the site for the new church of St Paul in Neithrop of which the foundation stone was laid on 24 May 1852. He declared that it was 'for the spiritual good of the poor, to bring to them, where they lie closely congregated, the pure Gospel'. He suggested that the poor had been denied access to the Gospel because the previous generation had thrown them out of the church. The new church was consecrated in February 1853, and in 1854 had an average congregation of 360.[7]

The long-planned church of South Banbury was also built in the early years of Wilson's ministry. In 1846 the parish had been formally constituted, with the Revd. Charles Forbes as its incumbent. A lithograph of the proposed building, known as Christ Church, was published in 1850, when Forbes called for money for the church in order to combat papal aggression. Wilberforce described Forbes as 'a good man (very)', but the bishop and William Wilson disagreed with him during 1851 over the boundaries of the new parish.[8] A site was obtained for the church in Newland, where Wilberforce laid the foundation stone on 18 November 1851, preaching on the Gorham Judgement and papal aggression. The boundaries of the parish were formally defined on 2 February 1852, and in September of that year, 'after long and anxious preparations', a bazaar in aid of the building fund was held at the LNWR station. Wilberforce consecrated the church on 19 February 1853, but there was insufficient money to build the proposed spire. An extra 60 ft. of tower was added through the exertions of the Revd. T. J. Henderson in 1880, but the design was never completed.[9] In 1854 Forbes said that his congregation was 'chiefly composed of mechanics and the lower classes who have not been much accustomed to church'. There were usually about 40 communicants and about 55 for the major feasts. By 1860 the congregation numbered about 600, and Forbes had been joined by two curates.[10]

The lack of accurate information about Anglican congregations in Banbury in the 1830s and '40s makes it difficult to measure the impact which Wilson made upon the town, but it is clear that he greatly increased attendances. By 1854 there were average congregations of 1,000 at St Mary's and 360 at St Paul's, and it was observed that the opening of two new churches had not diminished attendances at St Mary's. Wilson died in 1860, and nine years later an article in the *Church Times* dated the recovery of the fortunes of the Established Church in Banbury from the time of his appointment. By preferring him to the vicarage, Samuel Wilberforce helped to turn the tide of Dissent which had been rising in Banbury since the 1770s.[11]

Wilson's energy aroused resentment as well as admiration. Only five months after his arrival in Banbury he inspired an agitation in support of a Lord's Day Observance Society campaign to end Post Office work on Sundays. His name appeared at the head of a petition to the mayor calling for a public meeting on 18 December. He opened the discussion by asking if citizens could demand that postmen, their servants, should break the law which God had given, reminding his audience that God could chastise nations as well as individuals. Edward Cobb quietly argued in reply that the ultimate object of the petition was the familiar Exeter Hall aim of creating gloom. The cholera, he maintained, was not a chastisement upon the nation, as Wilson had suggested, but the consequence of dirty sewers which could be cleansed. He raised cheers from the meeting by observing that he had seen a carriage at the Vicar's door on a Sunday, and provoked an interruption from Charles Forbes to which he addressed a devastating reply. The debate continued, but the issue was decided by Cobb's dazzling speech, which embarrassed some of those who had petitioned for the meeting, one of whom said 'I deeply regret this evening's proceedings: I do not know when I have spent an evening so miserably'. William Pritchard, a Chartist, argued that the motion was meant to prevent the delivery of radical newspapers. Wilson's proposition was lost in humiliating fashion, only about 20 hands being held up in his support. It seems that the meeting had enabled the bawdy and riotous to display their dislike of the town's respectability, and the mayor concluded with a warning: 'I hope that what has transpired tonight will be a lesson to people who have their own whims and fancies to be careful how they get up a requisition to the Mayor to call a public meeting'.[12]

Samuel Wilbeforce maintained a lively hostility to Dissent. William Wilson followed the lead of his episcopal superior, and in so doing antagonised many Banburians. The first major cause of discord concerned the town's two long-established charitable societies. In 1850, on Wilberforce's instructions, he refused to preach a sermon in the church for the Old Charitable Society. The *Banbury Guardian* commented:

> 'The Bishop of Oxford, not intentionally of course, but not understanding Banbury ... has caused people to fly from the Church ... of all the charities in the town there is not one that stands so high in the favour of all sects as does the Old Charitable Society, and many churchmen, annoyed at the Vicar's determination on Sunday last, flew from the Parish Church, and betook themselves to various other places of worship, where the claims of the charity were to be pleaded'.[13]

Wilson also proposed that the Visiting Charitable Society should be managed entirely by Anglicans, and that applicants for relief who were members of the Establishment should have preference over those who were not. He again refused to preach for the Old Charitable Society in 1851 because Nonconformist ministers were *ex officio* members of its committee. In January 1854 there were sectarian clashes at a meeting called to raise money for the poor during a hard winter.[14] In 1858 Samuel Wilberforce was so unpopular that his health was not proposed at the annual dinner of the Banbury Agricultural Association, an unprecedented slight.[15] While the energies of Wilson and Wilberforce strengthened the Church in Banbury, they also exacerbated the tensions between the Establishment and Dissent.

Wilson's successor was Henry Back who remained Vicar from 1860 until 1881. In 1864 he was responsible for the re-painting of the church to the designs of Arthur Blomfield, who planned the re-building of the chancel.[16] Back was a Tractarian and after seven years in Banbury he introduced vestments and the ceremonies. In December 1866 he preached in a white surplice, and some of the responses in the liturgy were sung. On the same day his curate at St Paul's wore a stall and hood. Opposition to the innovations was led by Dr. John Griffin. A petition signed by 121 people, representing about 500 members of the congregation, condemned the new modes of worship. William Munton proclaimed that he had used the parish church for many years, but could do so no longer. On 19 May 1867 the two churchwardens walked out of the service to show their disapproval of the new practices.[17] At a vestry meeting in April 1868 Dr. Griffin accused Back of being afraid to meet the people, and declared: 'It is very painful for many of us to have been driven from our parish church by alterations and changes which have caused a great amount of excitement in the town', James Stockton complained about young preachers continually turning east, south and north, and said that he expected soon to see them standing on their hands. In 1869 there were more stormy meetings after Back obtained a faculty to go ahead with Blomfield's planned alterations to the chancel, which were eventually completed in 1873-74.[18] In 1873 there was a prolonged dispute about Ascension Day, and in 1875 five choirmen were expelled from St Paul's because they 'refused to twist and turn about after the example of their spiritual pastors and masters'.[19] When Bishop Mackarness visited the parish in 1878 he called for an end to contention, but the controversy flared later in the year after a 'Popish' speech was made at the institution of a High Churchman, the Rev. T. J. Henderson as vicar of Christ Church. Shortly before Christmas 1880 a curate at Christ Church was asked to resign after making remarks in support of two High Churchmen imprisoned at Penzance which caused two churchwardens and a sidesman to walk out of a service.[20] Many of those who opposed ritualistic innovations went for a time to Evangelical village churches, but then returned to St Mary's. There was no substantial exodus from the Establishment to Dissent. In 1873 the average congregation at St Mary's remained 1,000, while that at Christ Church was 500, and in 1880 the Anglicans contributed over 1,000 children to the Sunday School Centenary procession.[21] Nevertheless the introduction of ritualistic practices solidified the divisions between Church and Dissent.

William Wilson's career in Banbury had curious parallels with that of his principal clerical antagonist, the Baptist minister W. T. Henderson. Both were energetic, and both were young during their time at Banbury. Wilson was 27 when he became vicar in 1849, and Henderson was 25 when he was recognised as ministe: of Bridge Street chapel on Good Friday 1851. Following the death of the minister of the Bridge Street chapel in 1849, Henderson had spent three vacations from Stepney College filling the pulpit. He was a native of north London who attended Providence Chapel, Shoreditch, where one of the deacons was William Cubitt, a traveller in the plush trade for Gilletts of Banbury. Henderson entered Stepney College in 1847, and it was on the suggestion of Cubitt, who had gone to live in Banbury in 1849, that he was invited to Bridge Street.[22] Henderson worked to reduce the debts of the congregation, using his contacts as a 'London Dissenter' to approach such philanthropists as Sir S. M. Peto. Like the deacons in Margaret Oliphant's *Salem Chapel*, he favoured series of Sunday evening 'lectures' as a means of increasing church attendances. He began with 'The Mountains of the Bible' in 1854, and followed it with 'Bible Heroes and Heroines' in 1855.[23] He lectured on literary subjects at the Mechanics' Institute and in neighbouring towns. In March 1857 and July 1862 he brought Charles Haddon Spurgeon to preach in the chapel. In October 1863, Henry Vincent, 'as popular in the pulpit as on the platform' drew vast crowds to the chapel anniversary.[24] In the early 1860s Henderson introduced the 'Penny Reading' to Banbury, 'with the object of acquainting the working-class with books they had neither the time nor the opportunity to read'. He preached in the open air, and maintained close relations with other Dissenters. An assertion by a Primitive Methodist that Henderson was 'as like a Primitive Methodist as any man he knew' was scarcely accurate, but was intended as a deeply-felt compliment.[25] Henderson transformed the Bridge Street church into the most influential Dissenting congregation in the town in the late 1850s and early '60s. He was strongly disestablishmentarian, and took the lead in opposing church rates, asserting Dissenters' rights in the town cemetery, and, ultimately, in putting forward radical parliamentary candidates. He was for a time the editor of the *Banbury Advertiser*. In 1864 when he left Bridge Street for the prestigious Devonshire Square Church in London, he claimed that 'they had won a character as a church. They held the balance in the town in their hand, and had their influence felt'.[26]

More celebrated than either Wilson or Henderson was Joseph Parker who first preached in Banbury in the summer of 1853 and was ordained as minister of the Independent Chapel the following November. 'From the first Sunday', wrote W. T. Henderson, 'Parker was a sensation. His eccentricities were marvellous, and at the same time not at all under control'. Later Parker became minister of the City Temple, and the guest of Gladstone in Downing Street. In 1853 he was a 23-year-old, ill-qualified Northumbrian, who had spent just one year at University College, London.[27] Immediately after his arrival in Banbury he began a series of lectures on atheism which provoked a local secularist to enter into public debate. Parker crushed his opponent, referring disparagingly to his beard, and drew applause from the audience, who hissed his opponent. He resumed the debate in May 1854 when G. J. Holyoake gave a series of lectures on Secularism in Banbury, following the example of the eminent Congregationalist Henry Townley, who debated with Holyoake in London in 1852. Parker won Holyoake's respect, but some were disgusted by his vituperative tones. He declined a further debate when Holyoake visited Banbury in 1855.[28]

Parker revived the Independent meeting in Church Passage. At a tea party in August 1854 he boasted of a three-fold increase in the congregation and of 34 new members. There were 55 members when he arrived in Banbury in 1853, and 89 were added during the four years of his ministry. He preached in the open air in the summer, and in secular buildings in winter, and organised educational classes for young men.[29] In January 1856 he suggested the building of a new chapel. Land in South Bar was acquired soon afterwards, and the foundation stone of a new building laid in September 1856. The chapel was opened on 3 April 1857, when Parker claimed that:

'the cause of Congregationalism was never in such a flourishing condition in Banbury. Attendance in the Sunday School is larger than has been known for many years, and the number of members in church fellowship is higher than any found in the records of the church'.

He wrote in his biography:

'After about four years' residence in Banbury, I could boast of a chapel, a vestry and a commodious schoolroom'.[30]

The new church, designed by W. M. Eyles, was a Doric oratory, with galleries on all four sides, lit principally by a clerestory. It was criticised as 'Independent of all architectural grammar or rules' even before the foundation stone was laid.[31]

Parker, like William Wilson, discovered that the Sabbath Question aroused uncontrollable passions in Banbury. In the autumn of 1855 he wrote in a tract on Sunday excursion trains that:

'If we thoroughly knew the history of the Sunday excursionists, we should find amongst them the dirtiest, silliest, laziest and poorest of the toiling population'.[32]

He spoke in similar vein in a sermon, provoking a fierce controversy. Walls and shop windows were plastered with posters and squibs, many of them highly embarrassing to other clergy. Since Parker lived 'on the religious dodge' claimed one of them, he must make a noise, but he was always willing to accept the working man's money. Another squib declared:

'Hail Thumper of the Sabbatarian gong,
Bell wether of sour Calvin's maudlin flock
Of Banbury's saints, continue still to mock
The sons of toil, vile lie, with thy tongue'. [33]

The secularist William Bunton asked in a pamphlet if keeping the Sabbath holy was:

'to go like a poor, weeping, wailing, woeful being to the crowded chapel, to join in doggerel rhymes and bellow forth what you know nothing of, or listen to some unintelligible jargon about your being a child of sin, shaped in iniquity'.[34]

On 18 and 19 April there was a mock trial at the *Wheatsheaf Inn* at which the 'dirtiest, silliest, laziest and poorest' were given an opportunity of 'testing the sincerity of Old Joe's motives'. Witnesses included Miss Sarsanet Satinstitch, 'a nice young person, favourable to Sunday trading', Mr. Godfrey Gothepace, 'a realisation of modern speed, a gentleman doing his half-hour in five minutes', and the Rev. Mr. Dismal Horrow, 'Shepherd of the Sabbath . . . a Missionary for the propagation of moral pocket handkerchiefs amongst niggers, a victim of sneezing, snuff, sorrow and gin spasms'. It appears that the proceedings were thoroughly bawdy, and much embarrassment was caused when a list of those present was published.[35] Crude pictures of Parker were displayed on pieces of calico in the streets, and one Sunday afternoon they were waved around the windows of his house.[36] His language had provided a licence for obscene invective well outside the normal conventions of local society. He had inadvertently blown a gaping hole in the walls of Banbury's respectability, and the church-going classes were deeply embarrassed as the armies of profanity poured through it. Like the skimmity-ride in Hardy's *Casterbridge*, it proved 'too rough a joke and apt to make riots in towns'.[37] Like the skimmity-ride, it was not so much an expression of class warfare but a skirmish across the boundary which divided those who were respectable from those who were not. Parker became unpopular among both groups, the corporation refusing him the use of the town hall for Sunday afternoon services, and the newspapers consciously avoiding discussion of the issue.[38] Apart from secularists and bawdy public house comedians, Parker's opponents included some Unitarians who called themselves the Parson's Street Infidels, and followed the teachings of the American Unitarian Theodore Parker. In May 1856 Parker invited to Banbury the Italian ex-monk Alessandro Gavazzi, who lectured on the evils of the Church of Rome, putting on an astonishing theatrical display which seems to have been as bawdy as it was dramatic. Catholics hooted and whistled during one of his performances, and Protestants alleged that Parker misled the Italian into lecturing for his building fund by leading him to believe that an 'Independent' school was non-sectarian.[39]

In June 1838 Parker accepted an invitation to Cavendish Street Chapel, Manchester, one of the leading Congregationalist causes in the north, on the understanding that the debts on the new chapel in Banbury would be paid off. He was presented with a silver tea service and a clock modelled on York Minster, and his departure aroused feelings of relief among his ministerial colleagues.[40]

Henry Hunt Piper was 62 when he moved from Derbyshire to be minister of the Unitarian Old Meeting in Banbury in 1844 but his effects on the history of religion in Banbury proved to be as profound as those of the younger clergy like Wilson, Henderson and Parker. His daughter, Octavia, married Edward Cobb, who came to share many of his father-in-law's sentiments. Piper's most considerable achievement was to replace the gaunt converted barn, which had served the Great Meeting since the early 18th century, with a neat Gothic chapel in Bletchingdon stone to the design of H. J. Underwood. The foundation stone was laid in September 1849. The last service was held in the old meeting house in June 1852 and the church was dedicated the following August, the opening services including chants, a Mozart anthem and a Purcell *Te Deum*. Much of the cost of the new building, which was named Christ Church Chapel, was borne by Edward Cobb.[41] In 1852 Piper published a Unitarian liturgy, *The Book of Common Prayer of the Church of England adapted for general use in other Protestant Churches*, which was introduced at Christ Church Chapel in the autumn of that year, against the wishes of 39 members of the congregation who called it a violation of the right of private judgement. Piper's chief opponent was the chemist J. B. Austin, an adherent of Theodore Parker. A pamphlet alleged that 'the idea of a liturgical service and Episcopal conformity rose with the Gothic structure in which they now most unseasonably develop themselves'. At a meeting in August 1853 Piper was openly jeered by a cabinet maker, and in October he left the town with his daughter and son-in-law.[42] The Unitarian congregation lapsed into decline. The church was threatened with closure in 1861 and its Sunday School, the oldest in the town, was suspended in 1863. The congregation was sustained only by its endowments. Under Charles Case Nutter, who became minister in 1865, the decline was stemmed for a time, but the church never prospered again.[43] The effect of Edward Cobb's departure on public life in Banbury was severe, for few townsmen could match his eloquence or his intellectual capacity. He remained in touch with the town as a property owner and as a trustee of the church, and his shrewd, perceptive, humane letters to his friends from London, Bath and Lewes are a source of many insights into Banbury society, as well as an indication of the qualities of leadership which were lost to the community.

In 1852 the Austin family's Calvinistic Baptist chapel in South Bar closed, and in 1854 the building was offered for sale.[44] Meanwhile the Calvinistic Baptist congregation meeting in West Bar continued to prosper, and built a new Gothic chapel in Dashwood Road in 1877.[45] By 1851 the brothers Ebenezer, John and Thomas Wall, the ropemakers, were leading the local Disciples of Christ, who met in the Infants School. In 1866 they built a chapel in Gatteridge Street, at which Ebenezer Wall conducted the first service. About 1860 there was a schism between Ebenezer and Thomas Wall during which the latter built a chapel on land adjoining his house at 7 South Street, Grimsbury, where he acted as pastor and administered the sacraments. In 1864 the brothers split their business interests, possibly because of a dispute involving Elizabeth Redford, the 'Banbury Female Martyr'.[46] The Plymouth Brethren had established a meeting in Banbury by 1857, when they were assembling in the Temperance Hall. John Poulton, a cabinet maker, left the Congregationalists to join them some time after 1853. By the early 1860s they were meeting in the former Congregationalist chapel in Church Passage.[47] Most Banburians who joined the Mormons chose to go to America rather than stay to form a meeting in the town. In December 1850 three daughters of Thomas Lee, driver of the Wolverton mail coach who had been made redundant by the Buckinghamshire Railway, were married on the same day. Within a fortnight the entire family with about 20 other Banburians left for California by way of Liverpool and New Orleans.[48]

The Quaker meeting remained a small but influential body, its proceedings rarely being marked by any event more dramatic than the entertainment of an American Friend or the occasional dismissal of a member for drinking. There was a steady exodus of poorer Friends to Australia.[49] Banbury Quakerism was epitomised by James Cadbury, a tireless campaigner on many issues, including peace, temperance, the British Schools, emigration, the Bible Society, the Mutual Aid Society, the Freehold Land Society, allotments and the Board of Health.

Dr. Tandy, the Roman Catholic priest who had opened St John's Church, remained in Banbury until 1864, when he was replaced by Dr. Joseph Souter. The Catholic congregation increased, although its growth owed very little to Irish immigration since the number of Irish-born residents in Banbury fell from 78 (0.89 per cent) in 1851 to 68 (0.58 per cent) in 1871.[50] There were 353 in the congregation at St John's in 1864, 455 in 1873, and 512 in 1876, when 267 Easter communicants were recorded. The chief Catholic lay organisation was the St Vincent de Paul Society, established in 1853.[51] Catholic employers like P. J. Perry, the nurseryman, tended to employ fellow Catholic workmen, but most Catholics worked alongside Protestants, and some like Henry Neville a borough policeman who died in 1860, held public positions.[52] The very ordinaryness of the congregation was a standing reproach to those who tried to simulate anti-Catholic feeling. Protestant Banburians might listen with enjoyment to Alessandro Gavazzi's bawdy descriptions of nunneries, or grunt approval when a Wesleyan minister contrasted the prosperity of the Protestant areas of Switzerland with the poverty of the Catholic cantons,[53] but the Catholic congregation in Banbury was not very different from other Dissenting groups, and anti-Catholicism in the town was a necessary obeisance to a Protestant orthodoxy rather than an expression of social realities.

During the 1860s the Wesleyans emerged as the most influential denomination in public life in Banbury. By 1851 they already had the largest of the town's Nonconformist congregations, but it included few men of influence. In 1848 the church was in 'a peculiar and embarrassed condition', pressurised by mortgagees. Debts in 1849 amounted to £1,800.[54] During the following decades the church moved steadily towards a position of dominance.

The Wesleyans faced no significant challenge from other Methodist bodies. The Primitive Methodists continued to accept a particular role in missioning among the working classes, and in consequence were accepted, patronised and supported by other denominations. Membership grew from 64 in 1851 to 94 in 1871. Outdoor meetings attracted attention every summer. In July 1857 a camp meeting on a Sunday afternoon in the meadows by the railway stations was attended by between 3,000 and 4,000 people, after which the Primitives were praised for 'their characteristic ardour, sincerity and simplicity'.[55] The Primitives always gave prominence to women preachers. In 1858 a Miss Buck of Leicester preached anniversary sermons in the chapel vacated by the Congregationalists, many of whom returned to their former place of worship for the occasion and sat in their old pews. In the 1870s Annie, daughter of Joseph Arch, preached to crowded congregations on several occasions.[56] The Primitives placed more emphasis than any other denomination on temperance, and held special temperance meetings whenever their Brinkworth District assembled in Banbury. In September 1866 the Primitives moved to the chapel in Church Lane vacated by the Wesleyans. Baptists, Independents and Wesleyans were present at the opening service, and it is clear that they did not regard the Primitives as rivals for the support of the middle classes.[57]

The challenge of the Reform movement which gravely weakened the Wesleyan Connexion in the 1850s spluttered weakly in Banbury. In December 1851 the Revd. James Bromley of Bath preached in the town, and in January 1852 'the seceders ejected from the Wesleyan establishment' began to worship regularly in the Temperance Rooms.[58] The speeches made at Reform meetings were as much political as religious. R. J. Langridge in May 1852 declared that the House of Commons should be reformed so that more men like Cobden, Bright and Hume could be elected, and that working men, the producers, should have the vote. The Revd. W. Griffiths asserted that 'if "God hath made of one blood all nations" is Chartism, I am a Chartist. The Bible is full of Chartism', and that the Methodist Conference should not be restricted to ministers. A Wesleyan Reformers' circuit based on Deddington was formed by 1853, and the movement took root in Brackley and Buckingham, but while the Reformers in Banbury were numerous enough to entertain a circuit meeting in 1854, they never drew significant numbers away from the Wesleyan society.[59] A minister remarked defensively in March 1853 that 'because only a few are connected with the work in Banbury, that does not prove it is not right'. At the beginning of 1855 the Reformers were worshipping in South Bar, probably at the former Calvinistic Baptist Chapel, but they ceased to meet during that year.[60]

In 1850 the Banbury Wesleyan society had 195 members, 35.7 per cent of the membership of the Banbury Circuit. Surviving statistics do not enable fluctuations in membership to be traced year by year, although figures for the circuit are available. From a peak of 642 in 1851, circuit membership declined to 500 in 1857, then rose to 790 during the religious revival of 1862-63, and remained above 700 in 1870. In 1862-63 there were 248 members in Banbury, 31 per cent of the membership of the circuit. By 1883 membership of the Banbury society had fallen to 181, but there were 180 members in the society at Grimsbury, so that the general trend of Wesleyan membership throughout the 1860s and '70s was upwards.[61] In the mid-19th century it was widely believed that the founding of new congregations increased the overall level of church membership and attendance. In September 1851 the Wesleyans opened a Sunday School in Windsor Terrace, and soon afterwards initiated services for adults in the building. On opening, the school attracted 72 children, and there were 103 on the register during 1852, but in January 1854 when it closed, only 13 children were attending.[62] The Wesleyans expanded more successfully in the middle-class suburb of Grimsbury. There had been services in the agricultural hamlet of Old Grimsbury since 1812, and after the development of the Freehold Land Society's estate a chapel holding 200 was opened in North Street in January 1858.[63] By 1862 there were 48 members, more than in all but one of the village societies in the circuit. The building was expanded in 1868 and a new chapel in West Street opened in 1871. It was greatly enlarged in 1876, and it was anticipated that the Grimsbury society would become the centre of a separate circuit.[64]

The financial position of the Banbury Wesleyan society steadily improved during the 1850s. In March 1863 it was proposed to build a new chapel on the road being laid out on the Calthorpe estate by Dr. Stanton Wise, later to be called Marlborough Road.[65] The foundation stone of the new chapel was laid on Whit Monday 1864, and it was opened on 9 May 1865. The church cost £6,800 and had 1,162 sittings. It was in the Gothic style, with a spire which so troubled some tender consciences that it was paid for from a separate fund, so that those with scruples could avoid contributing to it.[66] The new church was the largest Nonconformist place of worship in Banbury and architecturally the most fashionable. It fulfilled the aspirations of the middle classes for a chapel which was ecclesiastical in appearance, and provided accommodation for more of the poor than could be accommodated in any other Dissenting church in Banbury. Nevertheless there was a gulf between fashionable Wesleyanism and the poor, which was made obvious by the founding of two missions, one in Neithrop, where in the 1870s a mothers' meeting was regularly patronised by leading members of the congregation, and one in Calthorpe Street, where services began in 1880 in a pair of cottages within a few yards of the Marlborough Road chapel premises.[67]

The stonelaying of the Marlborough Road chapel in 1864 was attended by William Mewburn, a railway stockbroker, who came to dominate local Wesleyanism. In 1865 he leased the Wykham Park estate, and purchased it two years later.[68] He was born in Cleveland in 1817, became a solicitor's clerk, and subsequently worked in Halifax where he set up an agency for railway shares. He subsequently transferred his office to Manchester and became chairman of the South Eastern Railway and the Star Life Assurance Company, and a director of the Manchester, Sheffield and Lincoln Railway and of a Shropshire ironworks. He attended the Banbury Circuit Quarterly Meeting in September 1865, and became circuit steward in 1866. He contributed substantially to the costs of both the Marlborough Road and Grimsbury chapels.[69] He was active in Wesleyan connexional committees from 1858 and brought the Banbury circuit into the mainstream of the denomination. He may have become associated with Banbury through the Star Life Assurance Company, which was the principal mortgagee of the Church Lane chapel in the 1850s. Mewburn made the Wesleyan congregation an object of compelling interest to the community at large. When his daughter married Mark Olroyd in 1871 arches were erected outside the church and at the end of Marlborough Road, the streets were adorned with flags and bunting, and every free seat in the chapel was taken hours before the ceremony. Large crowds watched the arrival of the family coaches drawn by nine pairs of specially hired greys. The wedding was performed by leading Wesleyan ministers who took part in the stone-laying ceremony at the Grimsbury chapel the following day. Seven years later when Mewburn's fourth daughter was married to Robert Perks, a solicitor, son of an ex-President of the Methodist Conference, and later Liberal chief whip, the *Banbury Guardian* remarked that 'scarcely has any marriage in Banbury excited so much interest'.[70] Mewburn paid off debts for the Bridge Street Baptists, the Congregationalists and the Primitive Methodists in the early 1870s, and contributed to the new Calvinistic Baptist Chapel in 1876, and it was due largely to him that in 1873 there was not a chapel in debt in Banbury.[71]

By 1870 the pre-eminence of the Wesleyans was widely acknowledged in Banbury. In 1874 the vicar of Christ Church said:

'The Wesleyans were a wealthy body, and their liberality had passed into a proverb, for it was said that if you wanted money you must go to the Wesleyans'.[72]

As the Wesleyans prospered, the other Dissenting congregations suffered a relative decline. W. T. Henderson was succeeded at Bridge Street by George St Clair who resigned after differences within the church in 1869, and became a lecturer for the Palestine Exploration Society, and subsequently minister at George Dawson's former church in Birmingham. He told Bernhard Samuelson during the 1868 election that he considered it best as a Christian man to abstain from active participation in politics, remarking, 'I understood that my predecessor damaged his ministerial position by a contrary course'. He was followed by a succession of ministers who stayed only for short spells.[73] The Congregationalists maintained a membership of over 100 in the 1860s and '70s, but had five ministers in the two decades after Joseph Parker's departure, at least two of whom departed after discord within the church.[74]

The Wesleyans' prosperity was not due entirely to William Mewburn's money. Indeed, a cynical interpretation of Mewburn's move to Banbury might be that he saw in the flourishing Wesleyan society a promising base for his connexional and political ambitions. One reason for the Wesleyan success was the way in which the circuit organisation mirrored the economic reality of the market town and its hinterland. There can have been few more effective ways of becoming well-known in the countryside around Banbury than by becoming a Wesleyan local preacher. Many leading Wesleyans were concerned in trades like grocery and ironmongery which involved many contacts with the countryside. When Joseph Ashby first visited Banbury about 1870, he was advised to go to a certain bookseller, because 'He preaches for the Wesleyans; he'll not let you buy any harm'.[75] It would be absurd to suggest that men became Wesleyans rather than Baptists or Unitarians to advertise their wares, but the strength of the denomination in the 1860s and '70s does seem to owe something to the way in which it reflected economic patterns. The Baptists and Congregationalists moved towards a similar form of organisation. W. T. Henderson regretted that his preaching was not acceptable in what he called the 'circuit' of small, Calvinistic Baptist chapels around Banbury. The Congregationalist minister in 1859 called for a 'domestic mission' to the villages. In 1869 a Nonconformist Preachers' Association was formed to supply village chapels, and links between the Banbury Congregationalists and those at North Newington and Adderbury were formalised in the 1870s.[76] Such imitation of Wesleyan practices was an acknowledgement of that denomination's pre-eminence.

By the 1870s Dissenters had retreated from the intellectual frontiers which they had at least kept in sight in the 1850s into a narrow Evangelicalism, which rejected modernist Christianity and discouraged debate. As early as 1860 the Wesleyans had welcomed the American revivalists Dr. and Mrs. Palmer. In 1877 the Baptist minister John Davies called, at a Primitive Methodist gathering, for revival as an antidote to 'a good deal of intellectual conceit'. It was Davies who introduced the hymns and forms of service of Moody and Sankey to his church in 1875, an example which was quickly followed by Methodists and Congregationalists.[77]

During the 1860s and '70s the Banbury Dissenters increasingly co-operated in missions to the working class. Even in the '50s, Henderson, Parker and the Primitive Methodist ministers had preached in the open air on Sunday afternoons to an informally organised rota. In 1860 revival meetings were organised in various chapels on Sunday afternoons. Attendances were said to be so great that the buildings overflowed, and it was suggested that they might continue in one of the Corn Exchanges, or in 'any other building to which those who will not enter a chapel might go'.[78] In 1864 the Banbury Town Mission was formally constituted. It sustained the work of Kenrick Kench, a full-time missioner, who was praised in 1870 as one who 'reached a class of people that neither the ministers of the churches nor the chapels reached'. Two thousand attended his funeral in 1874. In 1868 interdenominational services were begun in a cottage in Neithrop which five years later led to the erection by the Banbury Sunday School Union of a mission hall, which was subsequently run by Quakers.[79] In the early 1880s two new groups drew attention to the rift between Banbury's respectable church- and chapel-goers and the poor. In May 1880 the Salvation Army officers began to hold services in the Central

Corn Exchange. They accused Christians in Banbury of wanting 'order, eloquence and respectability' in their chapels rather than souls, asserting that half the town's population never went to a place of worship, and that three quarters had one foot in hell. As in other towns the Army provoked disorder. There was 'indescribable uproar' outside one meeting, and the officers left the town. The Army established a permanent presence in 1888, but not before further turmoil.[80] In 1882 a group called the Apostolic Band began to mission from a room in Butcher Row and from the Neithrop Mission Hall. They were attacked by hooting mobs and throwers of missiles, and when a labourer imprisoned for assaulting them was released from gaol 300 sympathisers welcomed him at the station. The Band was determinedly proletarian in outlook and composition. A member proclaimed 'there was not a respectable person in the band — they were all poor people'.[81]

The alienation of the poor from the chapels was as much a cultural as a religious phenomenon. Respectable society in Banbury developed a range of social activities which during the 1860s and '70s became increasingly self-contained within individual congregations. All of the Dissenting chapels had rooms for purposes other than worship, which were used by Young Mens' Associations, Literary Institutes and Mutual Improvement Societies.[82] Such developments had important repercussions for interdenominational groups, which tended to cater spasmodically for mass audiences, by bringing well-known speakers to Banbury, or to become increasingly uncompromising cadres, totally committed to particular causes. The Baptist or Wesleyan, who might have been active for social reasons in the Temperance Society in the early 1850s, by the late 1860s had his needs met within his own denomination. The growth of chapel-based culture also sapped the evangelical energy of the Dissenters. The young men of talent, who in the 1820s or '30s might have displayed his abilities and courage by seeking martyrdom preaching in the open in a disorderly village, now had the opportunity to shine in a debate at the YMCA.

All of the churches placed increasing emphasis on Sunday Schools in the 1860s and '70s. The Sunday School centenary celebrations on 29 June 1880 proved one of the largest, though not one of the most harmonious, religious demonstrations ever held in Banbury. Hopes of an interdenominational celebration had been disappointed, as a result of which the Anglicans, who had met at the National School, marched into the Horsefair en route to St Mary's at just the time when the Nonconformist schools were assembling there. Much confusion resulted. The Anglicans mustered 2,058 children with 300 teachers, and the Nonconformists had 3,209, with 500 teachers. After the Nonconformist service the Wesleyans separated from the rest to organise their own tea and games. Both processions included children from the countryside. The totals of the individual Banbury schools give an indication of the relative strengths of the congregations in 1880.[83]

Sectarian conflict reached its height in Banbury during the 1850s. Conflict over Church Rates, which had died away in the 1840s, resumed in 1853, when at a vestry meeting, where Dissenters 'mustered in strong force', W. T. Henderson demanded that a rate of a farthing should be granted rather than the 3d. rate proposed. A poll took place on 11 April, when the farthing rate, which would have yielded less than the costs of collection, was supported by 530 voters and the 3d. rate by 297. The decision effectively brought about the end of Church Rates in Banbury, although it was not until 1868 that they were formally abolished. The language of the campaign was vivid and embittered. 'Show your disgust', urged one Dissenting poster, 'at the shame of mendicancy'. Henderson saw the contest as a means to an end, and urged Dissenters elsewhere to attack the rate through vestry contests rather than by demanding legislation, since such campaigns could 'sharpen the feelings for the battle to abolish the state church'.[84]

A branch of the Liberation Society was formed in January 1855 at a meeting called at Henderson's initiative and addressed by the national secretary of the Society. Further meetings were held, but the movement failed to attract a large formal membership in Banbury, although its ideas were supported with enthusiasm.[85]

The controversies over the new cemetery in Banbury took denominational issues into the arena of party politics, and had important long-term consequences. The denominational graveyards in the town centre were closed by the Board of Health in December 1853, and land was acquired for a new cemetery, where the first burial took place in October 1853. The abolition of the church rate earlier in the year made it impossible to raise money for the Anglican portion, which had been purchased with £1,000 borrowed from the Liberal miller, Robert Field. In May 1854, a conflict was anticipated and Nonconformists were urged to show their strength, and the following year several Dissenters were found guilty of refusing to pay a cemetery rate by a bench of which Field was a member. The *Banbury Guardian* accused the magistrates of partiality, and an action 'Queen versus Walford' was commenced against the newspaper's proprietors.[86] It was withdrawn on 11 December 1855 as a violent controversy was brewing. In January 1856 it was remarked that the case was quietly being disposed of, but the *Advertiser* proclaimed that it would have significant political consequences:

'. . . the future will bring to light a new Liberal party in Banbury that will educate its own leaders, adopt its own tactics, and time may show that it is strong enough in the event of any change in in our representation to carry its own candidate'.[87]

The cemetery problem remained until lobbying by Henry Tancred secured the insertion of a 'Banbury clause' in the Burial Law Amendment Act of 1851. A Burial Board was formed in 1857 which soon became a forum for sectarian agitation. In November 1858 it insisted that the iron railings separating the Anglican and Dissenting portions of the cemetery should be removed. In 1859 the foundation stones of separate Anglican and Nonconformist cemetery chapels were laid.[88]

Religion in Banbury in the mid-19th century presents a kaleidoscope of bewildering patterns. Congregations flourished and declined, controversies arose and subsided, new chapels were built, small sects proliferated. The divide between Anglicans and Dissenters tended to deepen in the period up to 1880, and was one of the most obvious features of local society. The burial question and hostile Anglican attitudes to Nonconformity had increased the numerical strength of Dissent by completely detaching the Wesleyans from their Anglican roots. The Wesleyans were a powerful body, but their ambitions tended to be self-contained. In the long term they tempered the political militancy of Dissenter since they expected to expand and saw little advantage in directing their energies to bringing down the Establishment. At the same time the great range of social activities which the provided for their members, which was copied by other Nonconformist congregations, meant that their contacts with Anglicans were diminished. Within the town there were no longer substantial Nonconformist disabilities or recognisable class distinctions between Churchmen and Dissenters, although feelings of separateness were intensified by what happened in the countryside where Dissenting disabilities were still real. Religious militancy by 1870 was more and more the province of inter-denominational reforming agencies, whose energies were directed not so much against the Church of England, but at the whole apparatus of established authority, which they saw as corrupt and un-Godly. No Banburian would have denied the importance of religion within the community. The relative strengths of congregations fluctuated, but such changes were of less moment that the continued dominance of religion within the town. 'Away for an hour with Theology and Politics'[89] wrote the *Banbury Advertiser* in 1868 at the approach of the Michaelmas Fair, which coincided with the General Election. Religion was a continuing pre-occupation, as divisive as politics, and to be forgotten for only a few hours in the year.

JUDGE & JURY,
From the Coal Hole, London.

AN announcement having been made that "An opportunity would be given to the Dirtiest, the Silliest, the Laziest, and the Poorest, in Banbury, of testing the sincerity of Old Joe's motives," the following *Gentlemen*, supposed to represent the above class, met last evening, at the Wheat Sheaf Inn, Fish Street, when the prisoner was duly arraigned, and by the Jury found guilty.

Mr. Thos. Carpenter, Black Swan (Juryman)
„   Cubitt, at Mr. Coleman's   (ditto)
„   Daniel Sutton, Sun Inn   (ditto)
„   Thomas Grimes, West Street   (ditto)
„   William Hayward, White Horse Inn
„   Charles Hayward, ditto
„   J. H. Bates, Buck and Bell Inn, Parson's Street
„   Charles Bates, ditto
„   Thomas Jarvis, Printer, Church Lane
„   John Reiley, Fruiterer, High Street
„   Charles Collins, Hatter, ditto
„   Henry Busby, Tobacconist, Cow Fair
„   William Bolton, Neithrop
„   William Edwards, Elephant and Castle Inn
„   Craddock, junr., Shoe Maker, Parson's Street
„   George Webb, Shoe Maker, High Street
„   John Barton, junr., Calthorpe Road
„   Ern. Merry, Butcher, Pepper Alley
„   J. J. Willis, Upholsterer, High Street
„   Joseph Carpenter, Back Lane
„   William Jenkins, Wheat Sheaf Inn, Fish Street
„   Beseley, Shag Weaver

An eye witness describes the proceedings as totally unfit for publication.

Banbury, April 19th, 1856.

G. WALFORD, PRINTER, "ADVERTISER" OFFICE, BANBURY.

Figure 17. A list of those who attended the mock trial of the Rev. Joseph Parker.

X

A BOROUGH OF GREAT INDEPENDENCE OF ACTION:[1]
BANBURY POLITICS 1850-1868

'There is scarcely a prospect in the world more curious than that of England during a general election. The congregations of people; the interests called into operation; the passions roused; the principles appealed to; the printed and spoken addresses; the eminent men who appear; the guarantees demanded and given; the fluctuations of the poll; the exultation of the victorious party − it is a scene in which there is much to attract the eyes and ears but more to fix the mind'.[2]

IN 1850 HENRY TANCRED was securely established as MP for Banbury and he remained the town's representative until ill-health forced his resignation in 1858. The by-election which followed his retirement was narrowly won by Bernhard Samuelson, but he held the seat for only 11 weeks before it was wrested from him by Sir Charles Douglas, backed by a curious coalition of radicals and Conservatives. Six years later Samuelson began an uninterrupted spell as MP for Banbury which lasted for the 20 remaining years of the town's existence as a parliamentary borough. These changes might seem a logical reflection of the passing of influence from the professional classes to manufacturing interests. Manufacturers represented numerous boroughs in which their works were situated. The lacemaker John Heathcoat sat for Tiverton, and the ironfounder E. H. Bentall for Maldon.[3] But politics was more than the choice of a representative to the House of Commons and the politics of Banbury in the 1850s and '60s reveal much about the town as a community, and about national political moods. Banburians relished their independence, and the feeling that they were playing a significant role in national affairs. Liberals still felt that independence meant the exclusion from the town of aristocratic influence. Conservatives and radicals were concerned to see Banbury independent of the power of its leading employer. Political activity in Banbury was an expression of identity, of the identity of the borough itself, and of the groups within it.

While some aspects of the politics of Banbury in the 1850s and '60s are well documented, certain areas remain obscure. In particular, it is difficult to assess the influence of working-class non-electors upon shopkeepers' votes. Many contemporaries considered that it was a decisive element in local politics. The radical William Bunton told the Non-Electors League in 1858 that they should consider whether they might not be better off without the vote. Local Chartists were told in 1852:

'an elector is bound to listen to whatever you have to say to him upon the subject of his vote, and is liable to be called to account by you if he either sells it, or gives or withholds it improperly and without sufficient reason'.

A member of the Non-Electors' League boasted in 1858 that non-voters had more power and influence than electors, and a Reform Association official sadly admitted 'That is just it'.[4]

Tancred continued to cultivate goodwill in the constituency in the early 1850s. He cheerfully subscribed to such Liberal projects as the Freehold Land Society and the Central Corn Exchange, dutifully supported funds for celebrating peace in the Crimea and relieving the victims of the Indian Mutiny, and left to his agents decisions about the National Schools and the town band. He appointed Post Office messengers according to the advice of his agents, and occasionally arranged for the sons of his supporters to be made excisemen. He was closely identified with the building of the new town hall in 1854, subscribed £500 towards it, and referred to it as 'our hall'.[5] His most time-consuming service to his supporters was his part in the Banbury cemetery affair. He spent much time in 1856 and 1857 securing clauses in the Burial Law Amendment Act to enable Robert Field's loan to the Banbury Board of Health to be repaid.[6]

The general election of 1852 was not contested at the polls in Banbury. Tancred saw it as an opportunity for voters to confirm their adherence to Free Trade, but insisted that he would not be bound to universal suffrage as he had been in 1847. Thomas Sidney, a City of London alderman, spent some days canvassing, but did not go to the poll.[7]

In the four parliamentary elections which followed that of 1852, the Liberal Party in Banbury was split. The schism arose initially from the cemetery controversy. The *Banbury Advertiser* forecast in the aftermath of the affair that the future would bring into being a new Liberal party, which would field its own candidate when Tancred retired.[8] The group adopted radical stances on matters beyond the immediate concerns of Dissenters. In 1856 W. T. Henderson and others led working-class protests against high bread prices and the adulteration of flour. Magistrates were criticised for failing to enforce the law, and a new bread company was formed.[9]

Tancred was opposed in the general election of 1857 by Edward Yates, a 28-year-old lawyer and writer, who owned property in Banbury and was the principal mortgagee of Austin's brewery. Yates was supported by W. T. Henderson and other dissenters, and by the *Banbury Advertiser*. He proved an ineffective candidate, winning only 57 votes against Tancred's 216, but Henderson forecast:

'Under different auspices, with more preparation, assisted by better embodiments of the same sterling principles, the battle of last week will before long be fought over again'.

Yates had expressed bitter opposition to the aristocracy, and to Palmerstonian foreign policy. Henderson saw the radicals who nominated him as the embodiment of Banbury's dissenting traditions:

'He had worked with them for the abolition of church rates, and was he not confident that Mr. Yates was the man for the people, he should not commend him to their suffrages. Mr. Yates was an admirer of the great Cromwell ... they did not intend to take any man's banker to him to tell him how to vote. Let them show to the country that they were not Palmerstonians by following out with heart and hand those mighty principles for which Milton sung and Cromwell fought'.[10]

Yates's late nomination lost him the support of some voters already pledged to Tancred. Twenty-four of his voters can be identified as dissenters, as can 30 of those who voted for Tancred. The *Banbury Advertiser* complained that Tancred's majority was swelled by 'the rankest Tory votes', but only 11 of Tancred's supporters had favoured MacGregor in 1847. Yates gained 18 votes from those who favoured Tancred in 1847, and had the support of five ex-Chartists against Tancred's seven.[11]

After the election, rumours about the succession multiplied, particularly during the dissolution scare in March 1858.[12] In the autumn of 1858 Tancred's health deteriorated, and the solicitor to the Reform Club arranged for him to apply for the stewardship of the Chiltern Hundreds on 1 November 1858.[13] In the weeks that followed, a Conservative, John Hardy of Dunstall, Burton-on-Trent, and three Liberals, Bernhard Samuelson, Gillery Pigott, the barrister, and Edward Miall, editor of the *Nonconformist*, emerged as contestants in the impending by-election. Pigott withdrew on the eve of nomination day, and Miall, who was supported by the group who had favoured Yates in 1857, went to the poll with great reluctance. Ten minutes before the close of poll on 9 February 1859 Samuelson and Hardy each had 176 votes, Miall being well behind with 117. William Thompson, Superintendent of the Borough Police, who had a doubtful claim to the franchise, settled the issue by voting for Samuelson. According to W. T. Henderson he was sent from Miall's committee room to save the seat from the Tory. A Conservative described the polling of the policeman as 'one of the most despicable tricks that ever was heard of in the annals of electioneering'.[14] Nearly 20 years later, when Thompson retired, Samuelson admitted with evident embarrassment that:

> 'I don't know any individual whom I have reason to regard, more particularly when I remember what occurred on a rather "warm" day in February in 1859, for which, gentlemen, whatever you may think, I feel extremely grateful to my friend Mr. Thompson'.[15]

The nature of Samuelson's support indicates a substantial degree of continuity with Tancred's party. He received the votes of 99 who had voted for Tancred in 1857, of two electors who had previously voted Conservative, of seven who favoured Yates, and of 63 new voters. Miall gained the support of 34 who voted for Tancred in 1857, of 35 who had favoured Yates, and of 39 new voters. Hardy attracted 52 who had previously voted Conservative, 27 who voted for Tancred in 1857, and 85 new voters.[16] The *Times* was angry that Banbury had preferred Samuelson, a 'pursy manufacturer hurraed by a crowd of squalid artisans', to either of the professed politicians in the election, and concluded that they were:

> 'too many Banburys, too many family men addicted to eating and drinking and fond of their wives and children, too many men sapping the independence of the £10 householders with constant employment at good wages. These, and not the ·boroughmongers are the real dangers to our parliamentary system'.[17]

Eleven weeks after Superintendent Thompson's dramatic appearance on the hustings, the voters went to the poll in the general election of 1859. Parliamentary Reform caused Lord Derby's defeat and the dissolution, and the campaign took place against the background of Napoleon III's campaign in Italy, which was extensively reported in the local press, but Banbury remained preoccupied with its internal quarrels. Samuelson was opposed by William Ferneley Allen, a City of London alderman, who withdrew before nomination day, and by Sir Charles Douglas, illegitimate son of the first Earl of Ripon, who was initially the candidate of the dissenting radicals, but after Allen's withdrawal, gained the support of the Conservatives. Both candidates favoured the ballot, an extension of the franchise, the abolition of church rates, and a non-interventionist foreign policy. Polling day, 30 April 1859, saw some of the most violent electoral disorders in

Banbury's history. From about 2 p.m. there was fighting around the hustings in the Market Place. Douglas gained 235 votes and Samuelson 199, but neither candidate dared go to the declaration. Douglas hid in the *Red Lion*, eventually escaping through a back window to catch a train to London from Aynho station, while his effigy was burned in the High Street. The windows of Conservatives and of Radicals who supported Douglas were smashed, as a result of which 32 individuals, 24 of whom were employed at the Britannia Works, were charged with various offences. The younger William Potts, son of the owner of the *Banbury Guardian*, and the chief clerk at the foundry were charged with incitement. Samuelson's dejection was encapsulated by one of his literary opponents:

'O that this too, too stupid body had
Made its exit, and ne'er come back again!
O that the Superintendent had not fixed
His name, against the law! and thereby
Elected me his representative! Cob! O Cob!
How worthless, senseless and unprofitable
Seem to me all the uses of thy borough'. [18]

One commentator reckoned that Douglas had the support of 125 Liberals and 110 110 Hardyites. Another estimated that Samuelson lost only one of his supporters of February to Douglas, and calculated that Douglas received support from 89 Miallites, 116 who supported Hardy, one who voted for Samuelson, and 29 who had been neutral in February. Analysis of the poll books suggests that these figures were substantially correct. 115 who voted for Douglas had supported Hardy, of whom 100 were reckoned to be Conservatives and 15 Liberals. 30 had previously been neutral, and 82 had voted for Miall. Samuelson had the support of 12 who had voted for Hardy. The relatively slight swing was mostly among voters who were traditionally volatile. It is clear that the Liberal, Conservative and Radical blocs remained largely intact between February and April, and that the two latter acted in concert, the Conservatives being so disgusted with the polling of Superintendent Thompson that they were prepared to vote for almost anyone who would deny Samuelson the seat.[19]

Within the Liberal Party the new MP and Bernhard Samuelson co-existed uneasily. At some public meetings both were called upon to speak. Samuelson was accused of calling a Reform Association dinner in 1861 without inviting Douglas. The latter became parliamentary agent for the Liberation Society in 1864, acting as a whip for bills concerned with religious equality, an action ill-calculated to retain him the support of Conservatives.[20] The demonstration of the power of the Conservative Party in the 1859 election seems to have brought it a surge of support in local elections. Four Conservatives swept the board in the borough council election in 1860, and by 1862 there was a situation of parity, with eight members of each party comprising the corporation. In the next two years the Liberals regained their dominance but it is significant that this was the peak of Conservative strength on the council between 1835 and 1880.

The demise of the parliament of 1859 was foreseen long before its eventual dissolution on 6 July 1865. Samuelson's conduct between 1859 and 1864 left no room for doubt that he would again contest Banbury, and the prospect of his opposing Douglas made the seat attractive to Conservatives. Douglas was reluctant to stand: His supporters annotated a register, showing that he could expect to be re-elected, and W. T. Henderson, by then resident in London, took it to him, but Douglas declined to stand, probably because he was about to enter the Church of Rome. Samuelson declared that he would again contest Banbury in May 1865 as it became evident that an election was imminent. Charles Bell, a Conservative, declared his candidature, and on 23 May Douglas was persuaded to stand. On 29 June he withdrew, probably under pressure from the government whip, although his supporters insisted on nominating him.[21] The situation on polling day was very confused. Douglas's supporters voted early, giving him a temporary lead, but it soon became evident that Samuelson would head the poll. Between 1 and 2 p.m. the town was plastered with posters, declaring that as an alien he was ineligible. Liberals began to tear them down and substitute their own placards. At the close of poll Samuelson had 206 votes, Bell 165 and Douglas 160. Conservative posters proclaimed Bell's victory, and he was greeted on the hustings with volleys of eggs as he jeered that Samuelson could not take his defeat like an Englishman.[22]

Samuelson drew his 206 votes from 102 electors who had supported him in April 1859, from two who had voted for Douglas, 14 who were neutral and from 86 new voters. Bell drew the support of 62 who had voted Conservative in 1859, six who voted Liberal, four who were radicals, 28 who were neutral and 65 new voters. Douglas gained the votes of 71 Liberals and 9 Conservatives who had supported him in 1859, four who had voted for Samuelson, 11 neutrals and 65 new voters. Support for the three factions had remained remarkably stable during the parliament of 1859. The radical share of the vote was 29.49 per cent in 1865 and 30.13 per cent in 1859. The Conservative share increased from 24.66 per cent to 31.07 per cent, while Samuelson's fell from 45.85 to 38.80 per cent, but with a divided opposition such a share was sufficient for victory. The three shared the support of new voters in almost exact proportion to their share of the total poll:

	Share of new votes	Share of total poll
Samuelson	38.80	39.82
Bell	31.07	30.09
Douglas	30.13	30.09

From Samuelson's papers for the 1865 election it is possible to observe how a campaign was conducted more closely than in any other parliamentary contest in Banbury. His two agents were each paid £150. Three inspectors were paid two guineas each to observe voting on the hustings. Three check clerks were each paid £1 10s. 0d. to mark the names of electors in a book as they voted. Three slip clerks were paid the same amount to despatch returns at 15-minute intervals to the committee rooms where nine clerks were paid between £1 and £2 2s. 0d. each. Most of those involved were traders or professional men, several of them schoolteachers. Twenty messengers, four of whom were illiterate, were paid up to 15s. for two days' work. Over £30 was spent by canvassers travelling as far afield as Birmingham, Bewdley and London to see voters who had left the town, and on railway tickets to enable such electors to travel to Banbury on polling day. One elector in Birmingham sought capital from Samuelson to set up as a hairdresser. Another enquired whether the candidate would be interested in buying an oil painting and a vase. The Liberals collected evidence of two Conservative attempts to buy votes. Canvassing returns show that some electors were inclined to support the strongest Liberal, and others promised to vote tactically to keep out the Tory. The names of employers or the word 'foundry' written against some names were considered sufficient to show how they would vote. 'Band of Hope' indicated a voter sensitive on Temperance issues, and 'DRINK' was written by the names of two publicans. One elector told the canvassers of his past role in fighting for Reform, while one zealous Protestant was still, some 20 years after it had been a matter of public debate, 'mad upon the Maynooth Grant'.[23]

On the day after the 1865 election Samuelson's solicitors opened what grew to be a vast file refuting Bell's claim that he was an alien. The matter was judged at a hearing which began in London on 20 February 1866, and Samuelson's victory was announced on 28 April 1866, when the church bells were rung in Banbury. The MP returned home a week later to be drawn through the streets on a waggonette by his workmen, using a blue and white rope specially made by Ebenezer Wall. Four days later 300 people were entertained to lunch at the Central Corn Exchange, sports were organised, and there were balloon ascents. Sir Charles Douglas's supporters condemned the festivities and accused Samuelson of obtaining votes by corruption.[24]

Reformers in Banbury were closely involved with the campaign for the extension of the franchise in 1866-67. A branch of the Reform League was active in the town, and on 19 November 1866 between 4,000 and 6,000 people gathered in the Cowfair for a torch-light demonstration. From Grimsbury came the Ancient Order of Foresters and Reformers from Grimsbury and Northamptonshire. From Banbury Cross came plush weavers. Reformers from Cherwell marched from Britannia Road, and the Neithrop Reformers from the Vulcan Foundry. The whole assembly marched behind the Reform Banner of 1832 around Banbury Cross and back to the Town Hall, where they were addressed by Professor Thorold Rogers, Ernest Jones and Arthur O'Neill. Another huge meeting assembled in the Town Hall on 29 April 1867, a week before the Reform League's demonstration in Hyde Park forced the resignation of the Home Secretary. The official Liberal Party leadership was more in evidence than at the meeting in November 1866, and many allusions were made to the Chartist period, the spirit of the years 1838-42 being credited with the beneficient legislation of succeeding decades.[25]

The Second Reform Act of 1867 more than doubled the electorate in Banbury, and the election of 1868 was less predictable than any since 1832, and, as in 1832, the campaign was lengthy. Parliament was dissolved on 31 July 1868, but the election did not take place until November. At the end of September the former supporters of Sir Charles Douglas, abetted by leading Wesleyans, brought forward William Mewburn as a rival Liberal candidate. Both Mewburn and Samuelson strove to gain endorsement from Gladstone, and to identify themselves with the man they called 'that brilliant orator and statesman' and 'the first financier of the age'. Mewburn retired on 10 November, less than a week before polling day, and two days later a Conservative landowner from Market Harborough, George Stratton, declared himself a candidate. Both Stratton and Samuelson sought the support of the Wesleyans in their nomination speeches, the former even expressing his approval of an Established Church, 'whether it took the form of the present Establishment or the Wesleyan model'. Samuelson was elected by 772 votes to 397, and attributed his success to his Working Mens' Committee. A surviving list of his active supporters street by street, the care which his agent took to arrange for a Wesleyan to speak at a public meeting against Mewburn's candidature, and the ease with which information was obtained from Leicestershire about Stratton all suggest a meticulous standard of organisation.[26]

The *Banbury Advertiser* concluded that some of Mewburn's supporters voted for Samuelson, some for the Conservative and many abstained. Analysis of the poll shows that the newspaper was substantially wrong. Of 65 who sat on Mewburn's platforms, only two voted for Samuelson, 26 abstained, and 37, many of them with long records of support for Liberal or Radical candidates, voted for the Conservative. Samuelson retained the votes of 126 of the 206 who had voted for him in 1865, and gained seven of Bell's supporters, and 35 who had voted for Douglas, including some of the leaders of the Radical group. The rate of abstention was exceptionally high, particularly among experienced voters. Only 76.71 per cent of the electorate went to the poll. Twenty-one of those who voted for Samuelson in 1865 and were still on the register abstained in 1868, together with 22 who had voted for Bell, and 44 of those who favoured Douglas. Of those who voted in 1865 and were still qualified in 1868, 38 per cent chose not to vote. The 880 new voters behaved in much the same manner as the established electorate. Samuelson gained 604 or 68.64 per cent of their votes, compared with his 66.04 per cent share of the total poll.[27]

Temperance was a powerful though not a widely discussed issue in the election. Two important temperance meetings took place during the campaign, at one of which F. R. Lees, the prohibitionist, pointed out that while Samuelson would support the Permissive Bill only with heavy qualifications, Mewburn was willing to give it fair consideration. John Butcher, secretary of the Temperance Society, forecast that the contest would be close, and that the votes of a dozen teetotallers might decide it. He looked forward to a *more* moral future, suggesting that after the Permissive Bill was obtained, 'they could get a good deal more in other matters for the good of the borough'. In the event Samuelson totally lost the support of the teetotallers, many of whom voted Conservative.[28]

Banbury in the 1850s and '60s might seem typical of the 'bigotry-ridden small boroughs' to which a Conservative newspaper attributed Gladstone's victory in the 1868 election,[29] but it is possible to see amidst the labyrinthine parochial rivalries some indications of the wider state of political and social consciousness of the time. The significant divisions in politics were among the Liberals. The local Conservatives were little more than standard bearers, still deserted by the Conservative gentry of Oxfordshire, who could do no more than prey upon divisions among their opponents. The immediate causes of the Liberal division had local origins. The radical group which emerged during the Cemetery controversy in 1855–56 gained momentum and a distinct identity in the elections of 1857 and 1859. By the mid-1860s it was an established part of political life in Banbury, a party, informally constituted, but with a solid core of electoral support. Seventy-one people who voted for Douglas in 1859 still supported him in 1865.[30]

Yet the division was more than the accidental outcome of a denominational quarrel in 1855–56. It was in part a class division, even if the leaders of the radicals were socially scarcely distinguishable from Samuelson's principal supporters. The motive force of the radicals was the energy of the old working-class, the shoemakers, tailors and other craftsmen. Edward Yates in 1857 had the support of 35 per cent of the craftsmen who voted, yet gained only 21.17 per cent of the total poll. In both elections of 1859 the radicals polled more than 45 per cent of the craftsmens' votes. Mewburn's sponsors claimed that he was the candidate of the working man, and he received the support of most of the working-class leaders of the temperance and co-operative movements, even those who might have regarded his Wesleyanism with hostility. By contrast the core of Samuelson's popular support was amongst his own employees, the new working-class.

The Banbury foundryman was obviously very willing to cheer at his master's meetings and to disrupt those of his opponents. At every election he contested, Samuelson won the votes of more than 75 per cent of those engaged in engineering.[31]

Religious differences also underlay the divisions within the Liberal Party. In the 1850s the radical faction was led by Baptists. By 1868 the Wesleyan congregation was taking the initiative, but the group which it led was essentially the same. For many of the working- and lower-middle classes denominational affiliation was as important a means of self-identification as employment. While those who saw themselves principally as foundrymen enthusiastically supported Samuelson, those who regarded themselves first and foremost as dissenters voted for Miall and Douglas, and supported Mewburn. The denominational division in Banbury politics was never clear-cut, but the care taken by Samuelson's agents to secure speakers of appropriate denominations for particular occasions is evidence of the importance of religion as a means of identification in local politics.

The Liberal division can also be interpreted as a cultural difference. Samuelson's life-style detached him from Banbury's professional and trading classes. An MP who sailed a yacht in the Mediterranean, was a Fellow of the Royal Society and President of the Iron and Steel Institute, could not have the same easy relationship with solicitors and shopkeepers that the unambitious Tancred had enjoyed, although he could appeal over the heads of the middle classes to his own employees and the working class generally, many of whom saw him as a champion of their interests, a provider of high wages and of cheerful, uninhibited recreation. It was this ability which led others to regard him as a source of moral danger, as a patron of all that Banbury's dissenters wished to change in local society. Opposition to Samuelson could seem, however illogically, a declaration of a godlier dissenting identity. Henry Walford proclaimed in 1868 that the return of Mewburn would 'tend socially, morally, religiously and politically to the elevation of the town' and it was suggested that Mewburn's candidature was an inspiration for working men swimming against a sea of temptation. Samuelson's celebration of his legal victory in May 1866 was criticised because he enabled many people to get drunk and to enjoy vulgar sports like bobbing for oranges. There was no more ardent patron of sober, rational recreation than Bernhard Samuelson, yet it was possible to interpret his easy relationship with his foundrymen and with the working class in general as an endorsement of the drunkenness and vice which formed the backcloth against which respectable life in Banbury was lived.[32]

In the 1850s the radicals were trying to assert their dissenting identity, assuming that victory was more important than what was done with it, that the success of the better men would bring about a better society. By the late 1860s they were increasingly identifying themselves with specific issues. In 1865 Sir Charles Douglas still had the support of 17 per cent of the drink traders, but by 1868 the Permissive Bill was a major item of discussion, and was alienating the trade from radicalism. John Butcher said that the bill for him over-rode every other political question, and there were others who were similarly single-minded, not just about temperance but about vaccination, disestablishment and other 'crotchets'. Radicals were increasingly seeking power for what they could do with it, but their ambitions were tending to become narrower and narrower.

Many of the radicals of the 1860s saw themselves as members of the working class, and felt a need to identify themselves as morally superior beings to the bourgeoisie.

Joseph Maycock, radical, teetotaller and co-operator, urged Samuelson's canvassers not to use soft soap in approaching the wives of working men, for if they wanted flattery to succeed they should go higher in the social scale.[33] Many of the distinguishing marks of this superiority separated the artisan élite as effectively from the fellow workers as from the middle class. In one sense the artisan radicals of the '60s can be seen as members of a working class not yet completely conscious of its own identity, still conforming to bourgeois concepts of morality, still seeking bourgeois champions like Mewburn, and still dependent on political organisations run by the middle class. They can also be seen as Liberal deviants, without any solid base in the class structure, isolated from the middle class by the lack of common economic interests, and from their fellow workers by cultural differences, noisily storming up culs-de-sac, slowing the whole process of social change by subtracting their own strength from the mainstream of the Liberal Party, and depriving it of wider support by identifying it with a particular culture which could alienate the working class at large. There was much in the politics of Banbury in the 1850s and '60s which was parochial, petty and spiteful. It is possible nevertheless to see in the tangled manoeuvrings of the period two classic political situations; that of an immature working class striving to establish its own political and social identity, and that of radicals, uncertain whether to compromise their principles by allying with a party of limited reform, or whether, by asserting their identity, to risk aiding the forces of reaction.

A MARKET TOWN CULTURE: 1850-1870

'Future history must relate the progress of the people and the rapid development of popular improvement'.[1]

THERE WAS WIDESPREAD AGREEMENT that dramatic changes in popular recreation occurred in England during the 19th century. The Shropshire historian John Randall observed in 1879 that fifty years previously animal cruelty sports were still practised in the mining district, partly because 'social tea parties, entertainments, lectures and reading rooms were things unknown at the time'.[2] At the end of the century T. W. Boss, who had spent a lifetime in Banbury, observed:

'the blessings of sobriety have vastly increased in our midst. In my younger days I have seen many drunken brawls and much fighting in the streets, women as well as men being combatants . . . The recreation and pastimes of the people have undergone an agreeable change since I was a youth, when bull-baiting, prize-fighting, cock-fighting and dog-fighting and many other cruel amusements were permitted and freely indulged in'.[3]

Changes in recreation accompanied the political changes in Banbury in the 1830s, and recreation-providing agencies were prominent among the voluntary associations founded between 1830 and 1850. The subsequent history of recreation could be interpreted as a continuation of established trends, an expanding provision of rational activities. It can alternatively be seen as a counterpart of Banbury's economic prosperity in the 1850s and '60s, the flourishing, for a limited period, of a lively and wide-ranging culture.

Banburians were judged as much by their leisure activities as by their occupations or the churches they attended. Liberals referred with derision to the drunkenness and gluttony of members of the Old Corporation. Professor Vincent has suggested that when most working units were small, 'the manual working class was more likely to be united by the leisure activities which it had in common than by its infinitely various occupational industrial experience'.[4] The prosperity of the Liberal Party in Banbury rested on a broad common culture, and when there were divisions among the Liberals they arose in part from cultural differences. One reason for the emergence of a radical faction in 1857 was that:

'the tone of general society in Banbury was but low . . . the very sports promoted by leading men were of a vicious character, and public houses and breweries were of all concerns the most profitable'.[5]

Respectability was one of the essences of market town culture, and just as a flourishing temperance movement was dependent upon a perceived problem of public drunkenness, so a culture based on respectability was sustained by the obtrusive presence of a non-respectable sub-culture. Disorder on the streets of Banbury continued as a constant reminder of the presence in the community of the non-respectable. In August 1857 the police were pelted with stones during a drunken brawl in Cherwell Street. Defendants at the borough court in 1858 included John Spencer, 'an individual noted for his attachment to Bacchanalian enjoyments', who was found wanting to fight at 2 a.m. on a Sunday morning, and Charles Walker, 'a disciple of the same school', who had been shouting obscenely in Bridge Street. In January 1858 when James Sanders, a coal heaver, was charged with being drunk and riotous and assaulting the police, he was described as 'an old incorrigible'. In 1851 he had been living with one Elizabeth Hall in Gould's Buildings in Neithrop, one of five co-habiting couples in the terrace. By 1863 he was residing in the same house and living on the earnings of Mary Brain *alias* Poll Curl, whom he attacked and stabbed when he was drunk.[6] Squalid saturnalia continued in Mill Lane and the yards. A topical disturbance in 1868 was headlined by a local newspaper as 'Christmas Eve in Crown Yard'. There was a debate amongst the inhabitants about Fenianism, and fighting began when someone remarked that a Mrs. Taylor looked like a Fenian bitch. One participant said 'I don't know nothing about it. We was all drunk together'.[7] Prostitution was very evident on Banbury's streets and, as in York, it was closely associated with poverty and crime. In 1855 fighting broke out amongst a group of prostitutes assembled in the *Saracen's Head*, including Emma Gray, whose face 'bore incontrovertible evidence of a severe bellicose encounter', 'Big Liz', otherwise Rebecca Lapper, and Susan Owen. The latter was killed in October 1858 by William 'Badger' Wilson, who had lived on her earnings for 16 years. She had been drinking with a man in the *Rose and Crown*, a notorious beerhouse in Calthorpe Street, when Wilson pulled her to the room where they lived and beat her insensible. He was discharged when tried for her murder because forensic evidence showed that she had a thin skull.[8] In 1859 two prostitutes from Blue Pig Yard were imprisoned for an assault on their landlord who received threepence in the shilling of their earnings.[9]

The principle centre of prostitution was the *Jolly Waterman* beerhouse in Mill Lane, kept by Thomas Matthews. The 1861 and 1871 censuses both show that prostitutes whose occupations were given as 'domestic servant', 'staymaker', 'sempstress' and 'washerwoman' were living in the rooms adjacent to the beerhouse. In 1861 a correspondent of the *Banbury Herald* complained that in other towns brothel keepers were punished but that 'the Bawd of Mill Lane in the heart of Banbury' was tenderly protected. The same year a farmer from Chipping Warden accused a prostitute of stealing his watch while he was upstairs with another woman in the rooms next to the *Jolly Waterman* and one Elizabeth Goodwin was accused of luring a labourer from Fewcott who had just finished working at Bourton, to her room next to the *Jolly Waterman* and robbing him of his wages.[10] In 1863 the *Banbury Advertiser* called for the enforcement of the law against the Mill Lane brothel:

'one of the principal places of residence within the borough for those ladies of easy virtue who are occasionally denominated "Nymphs of the Pave" '.

Action was not forthcoming and three years after robbing the man from Fewcott, Elizabeth Goodwin, known as 'Banbury Cross' on account of her great height, stole a labourer's threshing money. In 1868 Thomas Matthews and Daniel Thomas, landlord of the *Steam Packet*, were charged with allowing women with bad characters to assemble on their premises. Both were found guilty but given trivial fines.[11]

Traditional recreation was a constant reminder that irrational pleasures could lead to disorder. Most traditional festivities were based on occasions rather than organisations and some continued to flourish. The Michaelmas Fair remained the climax of Banbury's recreational year. Each January the gentry still held their annual ball. May Day was still widely observed. In 1861 the streets were 'liberally infested with bedaubed and decorated ragamuffins begging', and in the 1870s many boys from the National Schools absented themselves on 30 April to gather flowers, and on 1 May to display their garlands. Children continued to devote much energy to traditional 'fooling' on 1 April, and village feasts still drew many holiday makers from Banbury in the summer months.[12]

Banbury's suburban wakes disappeared into oblivion in the 1860s. The Grimsbury Wake, held on the fourth Monday in July, gained some new life as the suburb expanded. In 1855 the landlord of the newly-built *Prince of Wales* organised a sheep roasting, a prize fight and a donkey race, which was stopped by a policeman after one animal's side was cut open by its rider's spur. The *Banbury Advertiser* reported that about 100 attended, 'principally of the lower orders', and they drank heavily. By 1864 the wake was confined to the consumption of 'much beer and 'bacco' on the Monday evening, with a few merrygorounds, cake stalls and fiddlers in attendance.[13] The Newland Wake held a week earlier enjoyed no such final flourish. No mock mayor was chosen in 1861, although some races took place. In 1862 'only a few remembered, and they did no more than drink'. There were cake stalls and fiddlers in 1863 and a few races in 1864, but if either wake continued afterwards it was of no consequence.[14]

The celebrations of Guy Fawkes Night also declined. By tradition crowds gathered in the Market Place to watch a bonfire and let off fireworks. In 1866 there was sufficient disorder in the town centre for the ear of the Superintendent of Police to be singed by a squib, but the previous year fireworks were reported 'throughout the town'. In 1875 there was 'only a faint observance of Guy Fawkes'. What had once been a communal celebration in the town centre had become an occasion for optional private festivities.[15]

Prize-fighting retained a considerable following. In April 1860 Banbury was regarded as a possible venue for the notorious fight between Sayers and Heenan, which eventually took place near Aldershot. Both fighters subsequently appeared in Banbury with circuses.[16] Banburians also enjoyed fox-hunting. When the Warwickshire Hunt met in the town in 1876 it was remarked:

'no town in England of its size and character contains so many staunch foxhunters, nor sympathises more with the love of sport'.[17]

The structure of the new culture in mid-19th-century Banbury needs to be analysed separately from its content. There were several 'agencies' in the town whose function was to promote and sponsor performances given by local people or by professionals. Local amateurs whether glee singers, lecturers on literature or readers of Shakespeare, often modelled their presentation on those of itinerant professionals. For some 'agencies' the provision of lectures and concerts was a manifest function, explicit in their constitutions. For others, it was a latent function, a by-product of activities designed to achieve other ends.

More than any other organisation in Banbury, the Temperance Society was sustained by the evils it sought to remedy. It continued to attract sympathy from a wide range of society, but its active membership was drawn from a more restricted group than its subscribers. The society had become an institution within the town which, it was generally assumed, would provide a programme of lectures, concerts and similar activities. Yet its manifest purpose was to do none of these things but to bring about changes in drinking habits. Its inability to effect such changes led the society to demand legislation to enforce its wishes. In April 1852 James Cadbury published a pamphlet on the 'Maine Law', and delivered a lecture on prohibition in the United States. In 1854 the Banbury Temperance Society passed a motion sympathising with the United Kingdom Alliance, formed the previous year to promote prohibition.[18] In 1855 Dr. Dawson Burns, one of the Alliance's leading speakers, addressed a meeting of prohibitionism, and Dr. F. R. Lees, the Yorkshire prohibitionist spoke in Banbury in 1856. The 'Permissive Bill', which would have enabled a two-thirds majority of the ratepayers to ban the liquor trade from their locality, was adopted as the policy of the Alliance in 1857, and became a familiar term in Banbury. In 1867 a meeting was addressed by the Civil War hero General Neal Dow, who, as mayor of Portland, Maine, in 1850, had inaugurated the Maine Liquor Law on which the bill was based.[19]

The Temperance Society was responsible for the foundation of Banbury's first youth movement, a Band of Hope. Inaugural meetings held in 1855 came to nothing, but the movement was re-formed in 1861.[20] The Band of Hope Festival in July became one of the principal events in Banbury's recreational calendar. In 1865 the festival coincided with nomination day in the election, a means of removing the young from temptation which had a long Evangelical pedigree. In 1866 the Rifle Corps Band led 500 children to the fields around Wood Green where 900 had tea and played 'Kiss in the Ring'. In 1870 tea was provided for 750 children and 600 adults. The winter equivalent of the picnic was a festival in January which incorporated the organisation's annual meeting.[21]

The Temperance Society was also a recreational agency. In 1866 it sponsored a railway excursion to Woburn.[22] Its lectures were regularly reviewed by the press as entertainments. The zenith of temperance entertainment was the visit of the American, John B. Gough, who in 1858 addressed the largest temperance meeting ever held in Banbury. The *Banbury Guardian* was impressed by his activity on the stage, 'he is never for a moment at rest, and seems to love ample space, darting hither and thither across the platform and exhausting every tone and attitude', and went on to discuss his abilities as an actor. The *Advertiser* reported:

'The little man advances to the front of the platform; he commences speaking in a low tone of of voice, presently a little louder, and then comes thunder, pealing through the building, accompanied with real flashes of lightning eloquence, striking and lighting up the myriad human countenances before him. On he goes, depicting the horrors of drunkenness, till sights and groans and tears begin to flow ... The "Ohs" and "Oh dears" seem to battle with his own voice for the mastery, when, in an instance, the magician changes his manner, waves his wand, and those eyes just filled with tears become full of laughter: seriousness has given place to ludicrousness, and the meeting is once more happy'.

Gough spoke again in Banbury in 1859, and was praised because, unlike some temperance lecturers, he did not abuse those who were not teetotallers.[23] T. I. White, another temperance lecturer, was found less of an actor than Gough, but more convincing, while John Ripley in 1856 was compared unfavourably with him, and a speaker in 1861 was said to be in the same class as Gough.[24] Many lectures on the theme of self-help were given by teetotal speakers, and the topically named Garibaldi Life Boat Crew who entertained in 1864 were a teetotal concert party from

Leamington Spa. By 1869 a Temperance Choral Society had been established, and the previous year a temperance hotel was opened in High Street by the confectioner Levi Tearle.[25]

The increasingly working-class nature of the temperance movement was shown by occasional testimony meetings. In 1865 and 1867 there were Teetotal Working Mens' Demonstrations, and in July 1867 a large crowd at a Temperance Camp Meeting heard testimonies by working men. In May 1868 a revivalist from Birmingham addressed an open air temperance meeting in Cornhill. A man climbed on to the waggon used as a platform and asserted that a man was better for his beer. Disorder ensued, and the corporation instructed the police to prevent further open air meetings, but in July the teetotallers continued their assemblies outside the Town Hall.[26] Increasingly temperance speakers vilified brewers and publicans. At a meeting in 1867 calling for the closure of public houses on Sundays, a landlord politely protested against insults to publicans, but was jeered off the platform. A speaker of 1870 insisted that the public house was the half-way house to Norfolk Island or the hulks, and that it should have a red flag outside. Little sympathy was shown by the temperance society for pleas like that of a man who insisted at a meeting in 1870 that 'When a working man was on the road, the public house was his home', and that temperance hotels could not fill the place of the pub.[27] By the late '60s the Temperance Society was more confident of its ultimate success and less and less tolerant of its opponents. It continued to be one of Banbury's principal providers of organised entertainment, and to play an important role in local culture.

Other societies for the reformation of manners were of less significance. Anti-tobacco meetings were held in 1854 and 1855 but no lasting association was established.[28] The Banbury Pure Literature Society enjoyed a brief flurry of activity in 1865-66, commending the *Children's Friend*, the *British Workman* and the *Gospel Trumpet*, and hoping to wean away the working-class from *Claude Duval, Tales of the Pirates* and *Jack Shepherd*, but it proved no more than a passing enthusiasm of James Cadbury and the Congregationalist minister.[29]

In the Mechanics' Institute as in the Temperance Society there was confusion of manifest and latent functions. For those who saw the task of the Institute as bringing formal and vocationally-orientated educational opportunities to the working class, its history was one of almost unbroken failure. For those who saw it as an animating agency, with a broad mission to enliven provincial culture, it could have appeared a significant and successful body. The Institute's vision of itself altered frequently. In the spring of 1850 pessimists were in the ascendance. The prospect was 'not a very encouraging one', and the committee regretted:

> 'that there is not a progressive increase in the number of members corresponding to the larger number of the class for and by whom it was originally supported now resident in Banbury'.

In March 1851 the Institute was in debt, and its activities were being curtailed.[30] Fifteen months later membership stood at 230, the highest to that date, and in 1854 it was concluded that 'the purposes for which the Institute was established were never more fully attained than at present. In 1857 there was again pessimism, but morale rose following the appointment of Thomas Ward Boss as librarian, and the half-yearly report in September 1858 had a jubilant tone.[31] In 1865-66 the Institute was very prosperous, but by 1867 the committee was again worried about the lack of artisans among the 284 members. The composition of the membership was:

Clerks & assistants in places of business	77
Tradesmen & manufacturers	54
Mechanics & apprentices	48
School teachers	14
Farmers	11
Solicitors	8
Bankers	6
Surgeons	3
Ministers of religion	4
Ladies	18
Youths under 16	15
Peers	1
MPs	2
Gentlemen without occupation	23 (32)

It seems likely that such inconsistent views on the Institute's success do not reflect real changes in levels of activity, but differing concepts of what it should have been doing.

For more than ten years the Institute was the only link between Banbury and the national agencies for post-elementary education. In June 1854 it made contact with the Society of Arts through its president Lord Saye and Sele. J. H. Beale, headmaster of the British Schools, was responsible through the Institute for setting up a local board to administer the Society's examinations in the winter of 1857-58.[33] The scheme was extended, and in October 1864 classes in more than a dozen subjects were planned. A proposal to found a School of Art was abandoned in 1867 because those involved 'could not agree'.[34] Progress in creating a post-elementary system of education in Banbury was slow, and owed more to Beale than to the Institute as such, but development of any sort was only possible because the Institute existed as a stake to which a sapling system of classes could be tied.

The Institute's role in providing other cultural facilities was vital. It maintained the only public library and reading room in Banbury, which was used by an average of 45 members a night in the winter of 1857-58. It was one of the principal sponsors of public lectures, and of performances by such bodies as the Banbury Shakespearean Amateur Society and the Glee and Choral Union. It pioneered innovations in entertainment like the promenade concerts held at the GWR and LNWR stations in 1851 and 1852.[35] In 1876 it introduced the American craze for spelling bees, although within a few months the enthusiasm had diminished to 'a distant hum in the villages'.[36] Debates and discussion classes were sometimes well supported. Meetings in 1854-55 were 'sustained with a great deal of spirit', and in 1861-62 there were debates on such subjects as whether machinery was beneficial to the working class, and the character of Cromwell.[37] The Banbury Mutual Improvement Society, formed in 1862, amalgamated with the Institute in 1864 when it was agreed that the united societies should arrange a programme of readings and recitations.[38] By 1854 a Chess Club had been formed, and 10 years later that 'skillful and intellectual pastime' was said to be flourishing.[39] The Institute demonstrated that the railway excursion could be a pleasant, educational and respectable activity. In 1854, 400 travelled on the Institute's first excursion to Kenilworth, which was preceded by a lecture on the Castle by J. H. Beale. Outings were then organised every year until 1866 to such places as Nuneham Courtenay, Warwick, Woburn, Windsor, Malvern and Ashridge.[40] Subsequently the railways' quotations were regarded as too high, and from 1868 picnics were organised at such places as Wroxton and Broughton Castle.

The Institute was frequently the subject of ridicule. A skit in 1860 drew attention to the coming programme, a drama, 'Squabble in the Committee Room', and a lecture on Nothing by Nobody, which would probably be postponed.[41] The Institute failed to provide a framework of formal adult education, and failed to reach many of the artisan class, yet its record of innovation was impressive, and the Institute was an essential member of the framework which sustained the town's culture in the 1850s and '60s.

In the 1870s the Mechanics' Institute was faced with competition from a Literary and Philosophical Society, formed in 1875 at the instigation of the Revd. J. Spittal, vicar of Christ Church, after he had remarked, somewhat tactlessly, that it was a disgrace that Banbury had 'nothing better than a Mechanics' Institute'. Most of the Society's early speakers had also appeared at the Institute, but from 1877 it sponsored lectures by the historian, the Revd. G. W. Kitchen, Censor of Non-Collegiate Students at Oxford, which marked the beginning of university adult education in the town.[42]

Many artisans in Banbury found their recreation through their places of work. Bernhard Samuelson set an example in the provision of facilities. In the early 1850s dinners, picnics and cricket matches were organised for his foundry workers, and in October 1856 the Britannia Works Mutual Instruction and Recreation Society was founded, and soon became one of the town's principal recreational agencies. In 1857 there were 130 members, and the average nightly attendance at the reading room and library was between 70 and 90. Officials and the more educated men gave instruction in reading, writing and arithmetic to those of their fellow workmen who required it.[43] In the summer cricket was organised, and in April 1858 Samuelson hired part of the former racecourse for use as a sports ground. Workers were given half-holidays on Wednesdays and Saturdays during the summer, and cricket matches were played between different departments. The field became the venue for an annual works fête, in which the works brass band, founded in 1857, always took part.[44] In 1869 new playing fields were acquired near the Great Western Railway, and the old ground was made available for wider use by the landlord of the *Cricketers* public house on its perimeter.[45] In 1866 the Recreation Society organised the public celebrations of the coming-of-age of Samuelson's eldest son.[46] In the 1870s the Society promoted annual railway excursions. In 1877 some 700 went to Portsmouth, some of whom had never previously seen the sea. There was astonishment in 1878 that, after leaving Banbury at 6.40 a.m., 800 people could be afloat off the Needles by lunchtime. In 1880, 1,200 set out for Weymouth, where they inspected Samuelson's yacht, and cheered while passing through H. B. Samuelson's constituency at Frome.[47]

Other employers imitated Samuelson's provision of recreational activities but none had the resources to match his achievements. In 1870 the Royal Show in Oxford was visited by 600 from the Britannia Works, 200 from Barrow's foundry, and parties from Harman and Bryden's and Hunt Edmunds breweries, and the gasworks.[48] Some workers doubtless preferred to take their recreation in public houses or chapels, and many were employed by concerns too small to organise even a cricket team, yet the role of the workplace as a recreational agency was significant. Such activities might ease class tensions within the workplace, but, by separating occupational groups, they could have sharpened class differences in the community at large.

The friendly societies were long-established recreational agencies. The older and smaller societies participated in the Club Day celebrations which gradually declined. In 1867 only two clubs took part in the church parade, which had been abandoned by 1870. Nevertheless the first week in July remained a time for general festivities. In 1867, 1868 and 1869 the headmaster of the National School remarked that few children had attended throughout the week.[49] Societies which had never paraded to church also celebrated in Club Week, among them the Tradesmen's Benefit Society, an almost secret body which was reputedly the richest society in the town,[50] the United Britons, founded in 1850, who did not meet in public houses and had 134 members in 1866, and the Mutual Aid Society, which also eschewed licensed premises and had over 400 members in the mid-1870s.[51]

The most flamboyant friendly societies were the affiliated orders. The first Foresters Lodge in Banbury was formed at the *Prince of Wales*, Grimsbury, in 1856. In 1859 its members processed in costume on Club Day and then held an archery competition. In 1861 members dressed in Lincoln Green accompanied Will Scarlet, Friar Tuck, Little John and a Lady on a White Horse to Banbury Cross where Banbury Cakes were distributed. At their dinner on Club Day in 1865 members wearing green scarves were regaled by the band of the Rifle Corps.[52] The Oddfellows, by tradition, did not celebrate on Club Day but held their annual festivals at Michaelmas, until in 1866 it was announced that they would dine on the first Tuesday in July. In 1869 the Oddfellows and Foresters jointly organised a fête.[53] While the older friendly societies played a diminishing role in the community, the affiliated orders became important recreational agencies. In 1858 the Oddfellows had a cricket team, and in 1860 they organised a railway excursion to a Grand Gala for the Order at Berkhampsted and promoted a ball. In 1868 the Foresters went by train to a national fête at the Crystal Palace.[54]

The Co-operative Society was also a recreational agency. Formed in 1866, it held its first annual soirée in December of that year. Various lectures and a library were provided, and in the 1870s the movement became one of the most lively cultural bodies in Banbury.[55]

The Volunteer movement was also a provider of recreation. A local Rifle Corps was founded in 1859, drawing support from Liberals like the Cobbs, the Pottses and William Munton, as well as landed gentlemen. This was a time when the Volunteer movement benefited from the coincidence of wealth, youth and middle class enthusiasm, 66.5 per cent of the force being recruited from the professional and trading classes. A second company was formed from 91 men from the Britannia Works whose services were offered by Bernhard Samuelson in May 1860, while local farmers' sons formed the 1st Oxfordshire Light Horse Volunteers. The Rifle Corps organised a ball in 1866, its band gave concerts, and it had a football team. In 1863, 1,200 Banburians travelled to Oxford to see its members take part in a review. In 1865 the band travelled on the Mechanics' Institute excursion train to Malvern, and serenaded dining Foresters on Club Day. In 1866 the band took part in the Band of Hope Festival.[56] The volunteer movement was an integral part of the town community and an important contributor to its culture.

The new town hall, opened in 1854, was one of several new meeting places in Banbury. Conservatives opposed the project because, they argued, the town could not afford premises unconnected with business. When it was opened, Henry Tancred commended it as 'typical of the progress, prosperity and independence of the town', and because he favoured 'scientific pursuits, rational amusements and recreation'.[57] Both of the Corn Exchanges opened in 1857 were intended for recreational purposes, the specifications for the Cornhill Exchange demanding that 'it must be so constructed as to be adopted to the use of a concert or lecture room, for dinner parties or balls'.[58] These three buildings, with various chapel schoolrooms and the Vicarage Hall, freed recreation in Banbury from its previous dependence upon public houses.

Organisations like the Mechanics' Institute and the Rifle Corps were 'agencies' for the provision of culture. The new buildings were the venues where new activities could take place. It now remains to analyse the content of market town culture.

An essential element within it was the public lecture. In 1859 the *Banbury Advertiser* observed:

'the working classes now enjoy opportunities of hearing lectures, amusing or instructive as the case may be, of which their grandfathers never dreamed'.

Previously, said the editor, lectures were given only to students or to those already learned, but now they were available for all.[59] In the 1850s and '60s the popular press enabled lecturers to gain national reputations, and the railway system took them to all parts of the country. 'There were giants in the earth in those days' wrote one organiser of lectures.[60] By 1860 there was usually at least one public lecture a week in Banbury except at the height of summer. One of the most popular speakers was Henry Vincent, Chartist candidate in 1841, and subsequently a 'lecturer on Civil and Religious Liberty, the Commonwealth and other subjects'. His biographer remarked that at the start of Vincent's career 'lectures were only just gaining popularity in the sense of instructive addresses'. Vincent was a speaker of unusual ability:

'... with a fine mellow, flexible voice, a florid complexion, and, excepting in intervals of passion, a most winning expression, he had only to present himself in order to win all hearts over to his side. His attitude was perhaps the most easy and graceful of any popular orator of the time. For fluency of speech he rivalled all his contemporaries ... His rare powers of imitation irresistibly drew peals of laughter from the gravest audience'.[61]

Vincent lectured at Banbury on at least eight different occasions between 1856 and 1866, and often called the town his 'first love'.[62]

George Dawson, minister of the Unitarian Church of the Saviour in Birmingham, described by Charles Kingsley as 'the greatest talker in England', lectured in Banbury on at least nine occasions between 1856 and 1869. In 1858 a newspaper commented that a poster with the message 'George Dawson at the Town Hall this evening' was sufficient to bring in a large audience, 'such was his reputation'.[63] Many other nationally famous lecturers appeared in Banbury. In February 1851 Albert Smith gave his lantern lecture on the Overland Mail, first delivered in London in May 1850, which included an imitation of a conversation at the pyramids between an Englishman and an Arab.[64] Henry Russell who presented a musical lantern lecture, 'The Far West or the Emigrant's Progress from the Old World to the New' in 1854, was a singer who had spent eight years in America, and was the author of 'There's a Good Time coming boys', a song particularly popular among Banbury's Liberals.[65] The former Chartist Arthur O'Neill, minister of the Zion Baptist Church in Birmingham, lectured in Banbury in 1858 and 1869, and another ex-Chartist, Thomas Cooper, lectured and preached in the town in 1867 and

1868.[66] George Grossmith, the *Times* journalist who became one of the most celebrated speakers in England, lectured in Banbury in 1858 on 'Pickings from Pickwick', and when he gave more talks in 1859, his mimicry was commended.[67] Many distinguished Americans spoke in Banbury, among them John B. Gough, Neal Dow, Elihu Burrit, the 'learned blacksmith' from Bristol, Connecticut, who lectured in 1852 and 1865, and Phineas T. Barnum, promoter of Tom Thumb and Jenny Lind, who spoke on 'Money-Making' in 1859.[68] It is some indication of the cultural vitality of market towns in this period that Banbury was able to attract the most celebrated lecturers of the time.

The successful lecture was not just an academic discourse. Its purpose might be to instruct. It was certainly to amuse and to provide a talking point. In 1859 Gough's lecture, along with an agricultural exhibition and an excursion to Weymouth, was considered a subject on which magistrates might gossip if there were no cases.[69] The successful lecturer was a dramatic actor, like Gavazzi, a mimic, like Gough, Grossmith, Vincent or Albert Smith, and he might sing or lead his audience in singing. Some depended on slides or 'dissolving views'. In 1855 and 1858 Ephraim Hutchings, a Banburian who was secretary of the Manchester Mechanics' Institute, organised displays on English Cathedrals, Swiss Scenery and the Holy Land. 'No exhibition ever shown in Banbury before can at all compare with this, combining as it does, much instruction with a great deal of pleasure', remarked one spectator.[70] Lectures were critically reviewed. In 1853 a Dr. Walsh spoke on American Slavery, but merely took advantage of the popular interest in Harriet Beecher Stowe's *Uncle Tom's Cabin*. A newspaper commented:

'it is quite probable that the same person has, within no long space of time, exerted his talents upon Chartism, Peace, Temperance, Mesmerism, Bloomerism, or any other subject that might happen to be uppermost in the public mind . . . unprincipled adventurers are Uncle Toming it in all directions, both from the Press and the Platform'.[71]

The lecture might teach the citizen of the market town something of India, the Holy Land or Australia, and in particular of America. Many Banburians must have considered emigrating on the basis of what they learned from lectures. America symbolised ambition and enterprise. 'Do you intend Tambourlain to represent earthquakes and volcanoes?' asked Dorothea in George Eliot's *Middlemarch*. 'O yes', replied Will Ladislaw, 'and migrations of races and clearings of forests — and America and the steam engine'.[72] Matthew Gompertz's 'Panorama of the Eastern Wars' displayed views of the Crimean War in 1855.[73] The American Civil War was illustrated in his 'Panorama of the Great War of the Western World' in 1863.[74] In 1860 Barker's 'Panorama of Southern Africa' displayed the discoveries of Dr. Livingstone.[75] Many people knew Dickens through George Grossmith, Defoe through George Dawson, or Charlotte Brontë through Gerald Massy, just as in the 20th century they may be acquainted with literature only through television. Popular lecturers propounded a broadly accepted view of self-help. Many historical lectures were essentially on this theme. A Dr. Brindley who lectured on Benjamin Franklin and Lord Chancellor Campbell in 1857, offered to the working class 'direction and guidance in self-culture and self-advancement, or Gold Mines at Home that everyone may dig in'.[76] Vincent in 1859 drew attention to 'the nobby young man in a draper's or a grocer's or a bank, with £50 a year and the chance of a roise', who might be a future employer. 'God always blessed industry and economy' he declared, 'and the laws of nature would not be suspended to suit dandies, idlers, profligates or even "nice young men" '.[77] If small towns were influenced by famous lecturers, they also influenced what such speakers said. The message of the majority was much the same, that individual enterprise was to be commended, that virtue resided in the provinces, among the middle and the respectable working classes, but not among the idle, the rich and the disreputable, and that beyond the shores of England were territories, less hidebound by aristocratic vice, where townspeople might find outlets for their talents. By the 1870s the public lecture was in decline. Only a small and elderly audience heard Vincent quote Cromwell's warning, that English cannon might be heard in the Vatican during his last lecture in Banbury in 1874.[78] While a few lectures did attract large audiences in the '70s, Banbury's intellectual entertainment was increasingly provided in a denominational context.

Music was another element in market town culture, which was provided both by local talent and by professionals. Musical societies in Banbury were essentially performing associations, usually giving concerts under the patronage of the recreational 'agencies'. William Wilson's Vicarage Hall was the meeting place of the Glee and Madrigal Union, which later amalgamated with a group of church choir members to form the Glee and Choral Union, with one director for sacred and another for secular music. It gave concerts sponsored by the Mechanics' Institute, and performed before 1,700 people in celebration of the Royal Wedding in 1858. In the 1860s the Minstrels fashion affected Banbury and a group called the Banbury Christie's Minstrels was formed, named after Frederick Burgess's Christy Minstrels in London. There were four brass bands, the town band and those sponsored by the Temperance Society, the Britannia Works and the Rifle Corps.[79] Among the musicians who appeared in Banbury were Sam Cowell, the 'king of English comic vocalists', who visited the town on at least three occasions between 1857 and 1862. 'Who has not heard of Sam Cowell?' asked the *Banbury Advertiser*.[80] W. S. Woodin performed his 'Carpet Bag and Sketch Book' in 1858, his 'Cabinet of Curiosities' in 1862, and his 'Elopement Extraordinary' in 1864.[81] Dr. Mark and his Little Men performed in Banbury at least four times between 1858 and 1864. Bertram von Mark was a German who had run a music school in Bristol until 1851 when he began to take 'apprentices' on tours, during which performances were combined with musical training and general education. He was a teetotaller who enforced abstinence upon his pupils. Others who performed in the town included the Brousil Family, Sime Reeves and George Buckland.[82] In the late 1860s and early '70s several itinerant operatic companies visited Banbury. Stanley Betjeman's English (or London) Opera Company performed several times, staging *Faust* and *Die Freischütz* in 1869.[83] In 1858 Pell's American Opera Company appeared, but they offered 'burlesques, songs, dances and acrobatics delineating the Negro character', and seem to have been no more than a minstrels' company.[84]

The best-known circuses all visited Banbury, often at the time of the Michaelmas Fair. Wombwell's menagerie was in the town on at least eight occasions between 1850 and 1870.[85] Howe and Cushing's American circus performed at least four times between 1858 and 1863.[86] Lord George Sanger's circus made at least five visits.[87] Another entertainer of national repute was Gyngel of Vauxhall, who gave firework displays in 1850 and 1857, the latter including a representation of the ascent of Mont Blanc.[88]

Recreational activities like circuses and fairs provided Banburians with a considerable amount of information. Ginnett's Monstre Cirque de Paris in 1855 presented an embarrassingly bad representation of the Battle of Alma. Hengler's Circus in 1858 included scenes from the Indian Mutiny. In 1855 engravings of the storming of Sebastopol were sold at two for a penny at the Michaelmas Fair, and a newspaper remarked 'it was the martial and patriotic spirit which seemed to pervade everyone'. Another topical theme was represented by a cheap John selling pictures from *Uncle Toms's Cabin* engraved from originals by Michaelangelo.[89] In 1856 peep shows offered 'all the Russian battles', as well as William Palmer, the Rugeley poisoner. In 1861 'every important engagement in the present American war was truthfully represented by scenery which has performed the same good office for the Battle of Waterloo, the Crimean, Indian and Chinese Wars'. In 1862 there was an exhibition of the battles of Garibaldi. By 1868 'stereoramas' were depicting events from the death of Abel to the Abergele railway disaster.[90]

There were no well-established theatrical societies comparable with the Glee and Choral Union, although the Banbury Shakespearean Amateur Society performed *The Misteltoe Bough* in 1851, the 'gentleman amateur actors' put on two plays in 1860, and Shakespeare's Tercentenary was celebrated with music and readings in 1864.[91] Henry Jackman died in 1852, but his company continued under the direction of his son and son-in-law, who visited Banbury for a spring season every year until 1863 when the company was wound up.[92] Travelling companies like Holloway's Theatre occasionally visited Banbury in the '60s, and in the '70s Sarah Thorne paid regular visits with her pantomime company. Dramatic readings, particularly from Shakespeare were popular. Among the professional readers who appeared in Banbury were Mrs. Ormonde, R. K. Lucas and Barrow Blake.[93] The theatre depended upon patronage by recreational agencies like the Mechanics' Institute, the Rifle Corps and the Cricket Club, and like other forms of entertainment, it provided topical information. In 1854 Jackman's company presented *Uncle Tom's Cabin*, and in 1861 they staged *Garibaldi, the Hero of Italy* or *A Struggle for Freedom.*[94]

The flower show, first organised in 1847, drew steadily greater crowds, and was described in 1866 as 'one of our greatest holidays'. 'Why?', as the *Banbury Guardian* in 1856:

> 'do we thus rejoice and give all the support in our power to Flower Shows? Simply because Floriculture and Horticulture, while being a health-giving, is also a pure and harmless recreation, which may be engaged in by individuals of either sex and of all stations in life — the peasant as well as the peer, the over-toiled man of business, and the industrious artisan, on every imaginable scale, from a single flower pot to a princely conservatory; and which, by leading to the tranquil contemplation of natural beauty, and diverting the mind from grave worldly occasions, has a positively moral and therefore highly beneficial tendency. Even our Sovereign, with her Royal Consort, may be seen at Osborne, with garden implements, tending and cultivating the flowers upon which she looks down from her palace windows and terraces'.

In 1863 the *Advertiser* called the show:

> 'one of those happy occasions when rich and poor mingle freely together and when young and old drink deep draughts of delight from the common spring'.[95]

The event always took place in the grounds of a large suburban house, and was above all an occasion for class-mixing. It was admitted that people went for the company rather than the flowers. It was a time when it was possible to imagine that class differences did not exist, although ironically, there were few occasions on which they were more sharply defined. It was noted in 1858 that 'the principal families of the town' attended. Agricultural shows were of less importance. The Banbury Agricultural Association merged with the Oxfordshire society in 1854-55. Occasionally shows took place in Banbury, the most notable occasion being in 1877 when the Oxfordshire Show was combined with the Banbury Flower Show.[96]

Within two months of the opening of the Buckinghamshire Railway in 1850, an excursion train took 130 Banburians to London, and in the first three months of the Great Exhibition in 1851 the railway carried over 2,600 passengers to the capital.[97] The railway excursion became one of the staple recreational activities in Banbury. A newspaper commented in 1857:

> 'In the "good old times" and even within a few years, boys and girls were shut up in the little towns and villages in which they were born till they were close upon twenty years of age, but now excursion trips are announced and we see them preparing for jaunts to London, Portsmouth, Manchester or Warwick, without timidity or unnecessary excitement'.[98]

Excursions offered by the railway companies and their agents ran to almost every resort on the south coast from Margate to Weymouth, to Bath, Bristol, Malvern, Birmingham, Manchester and Liverpool. London excursions enabled members of voluntary bodies to take part in national events like the Oddfellows' Fête at the Crystal Palace in 1858, the Foresters' Fête in 1868, or the Rifle Contest on Wimbledon Common in 1861.[99] Often tickets enabled passengers to stay at their destinations for several days, thus introducing to Banburians the concept of the annual holiday. In 1861 some working men were taking lessons from a French teacher to enable them to converse with working men during a railway trip to Paris.[100] The excursion was a medium, like the lecture or the concert, and was discussed in similar critical terms. There were complaints in 1855 about the slow and uncomfortable excursion trains on the LNWR, and warnings that the Mechanics' Institute excursion to Malvern in 1865 would be in narrow gauge stock with hard seats.[101]

There was a substantial expansion of sporting activities in Banbury between 1850 and 1880. The Cricket Club, established in 1836, was one of the pillars of local respectability. Some matches with teams of unconventional size were still played, but as such regular fixtures as that with Christ Church, Oxford, became established, adherence to accepted rules prevailed. The Club generally encouraged cricket in the town, and matches were organised by most of the recreational 'agencies'.[102] Football became popular in the 1860s. In 1863 a club began to organise games on Saturday afternoons, and it was observed in 1864:

> 'This ancient game appears to be reviving among the young men of this district, and bids to be in the winter what cricket is in the summer. Indeed, it is a much more exciting game than cricket, as all the players are more actively engaged, and the fortunes of the field are constantly varying. It is a thoroughly English game, admirably adapted to our winter climate, and well calculated to develop the thews and sinews of our youth. It is moreover remarkably well-suited for counteracting the effects of sedentary occupations and throwing off the drowsy influences of the desk or the office. Everyone is supposed to know what football is, yet few have seen it played according to rule'.[103]

Like all early football clubs, the Banbury team found it difficult to find rules acceptable to opponents. In March 1864 a match was played against a team of 12 from the University of Oxford. A game between the Treasurer's and the Secretary's teams on Boxing Day 1864 was played with 20 a side. Gradually the club adopted rules similar to those recognised by the English Rugby Union in 1871. The club stimulated the game amongst the recreational 'agencies', and played a game in 1866 against the Rifle Corps.[104] An Association Football club, the Banbury Rovers, was formed in 1879.[105] Swimming was organised on a respectable basis when Thomas Draper built a public baths near the canal in 1855 which attracted 500 bathers a week. In the late 1860s the site was taken over by the Britannia Works, and nude bathing in the canal within the sight of respectable females brought demands for a new pool, which was provided by a private company in the meadows north of the station in 1868.[106] Bowls, quoits and archery were played in Banbury, but it was observed in 1864 that the town played second fiddle to Brackley for horse-racing. Cycling became fashionable in 1869, when races were organised at the Flower Show and the Mechanics' Institute fête, and a Cycling Club was established in 1877.[107] Attempts to found a regular Whit- or August Monday Athletics meeting in the 1870s met with only limited success, but the Banbury Harriers Athletics Club was formed in 1879, and opened a gymnasium in 1880.[108]

A complaint in 1863 that there was 'not an inch of recreation ground in Banbury'[109] was scarcely justified, since the cricket field on the Oxford Road and the Britannia Works recreation ground were in use, and there was space used by the football club on the Hardwick Road, and a cricket ground at the *Bowling Green*, Nethercote, a suburban public house much used for works outings. Nevertheless the complaint does highlight the role of sporting clubs in the town, which, by bringing together individuals of limited means, were able to secure for them facilities previously available only to landowners. They could adopt codes of rules which enabled matches to be played with teams from elsewhere. While the specifically sporting clubs in Banbury were almost entirely middle class, the stimulus they gave to the playing of games between others groups brought sporting activities to a wide range of the population.

The churches' role in recreation steadily increased. Most dissenting congregations built new schoolrooms in the 1850s and '60s, and their recreational activities expanded to fill them. Sunday Schools grew in size, and the scale of their annual treats increased. While town-based societies could organise lively and informed discussions, and promote visits by national figures, denominationally-based bodies could rarely do so. In May 1861 a Wesleyan YMCA was formed, one of its first meetings being a discussion on the immortality of the soul. The group of 'beardless pretenders' soon ceased to meet, because its members lacked the education to discuss theology.[110]

The period between 1850 and 1870 was a plateau in the history of recreation in Banbury. A variety of institutions and activities which had their origins in an earlier period flourished, and then began to show the first signs of decline. Many of the recreational activities of the period can be interpreted as attempts by the middle class to build bridges between themselves and the respectable artisans. Like the Lincolnshire farmers of the period who organised harvest suppers, they were aware of a rift between themselves and the working-class and were anxious to bridge it.[111] By the 1870s there were increasing indications of working-class independence, expressed particularly in the co-operative movement, and in the strident, class-aware propaganda of the teetotallers and the anti-vaccinators. The strength of community-based organisations like the Mechanics' Institute was being undermined by the growth of denominational agencies, which offered blander, less potentially offensive, and ultimately less attractive activities. The cult of domesticity, a prominent part of the ideology of self-help, also threatened the whole framework of recreation in Banbury. The working man's love of his home was described in deeply sentimental terms by radicals, and by the 1870s home ownership was becoming one of the objectives of the artisan élite. Thomas Proverbs, a teetotaller and co-operator, declared in 1869 that he was 'determined to have a house, a castle of his own'.[112] Such sentiments could be destructive, not just of a recreational pattern which involved going to public houses, watching prize fights and gambling, but also of one which comprised visits to reading rooms, attendance at public lectures and participation in temperance railway excursions. The recreational pattern of the 1850s and '60s was also undermined by the very respectability it fostered. While some drunkenness and disorder persisted, it was agreed by 1900 that there had been a vast improvement in public order during the previous half century. If there was less disreputable behaviour on the streets, there was less incentive for the respectable to display their solidarity by supporting alternative recreations.

The cultural pattern of the mid-19th century was a feature of a particular phase in educational development. Literacy was almost universal among the respectable, but newspapers were expensive, and the lecture, the peep shows and the panorama were still effective means of disseminating information about current affairs. Newspapers became cheaper after 1855. The local press's coverage of national and international affairs improved, and national newspapers were distributed by train. 'The *Morning Star*', wrote W. T. Henderson, 'was our sheet anchor'.[113] Doubtless other groups were held at their moorings by different anchors, but each had begun to look to London for its information, and the itinerant lecturer on current affairs gradually became redundant. Mark Rutherford wrote of;

'the clubs and parties which, since the days of penny newspapers, now discuss in Cowfold the designs of Russia, the graduation of the Income Tax, or the merits and demerits of the adminis-tration. The Cowfold horizon has now been widened . . . '[114]

The mid-19th century as a 'liberal hour' in the history of some English market towns, a period of self-rule, when townspeople devised new organisations, created opportunities to display their own and imported talents, and used the railways to broaden their horizons. There was sufficient that was distinctive in the pattern of lectures, music, sport and excusions which flourished in Banbury between 1850 and 1870 and began to decline in the 1870s to describe it as a market town culture. It was the blossoming of a particular way of life which was to wither with the decay of the economic and political stems which sustained it.

XII

GOING DOWNHILL:

MARKET TOWN SOCIETY IN THE 1870s

'While the reaper yonder slashes at the straw, huge ships are on the ocean rushing through the foam to bring grain to the great cities'.[1]

IN HIS POIGNANT DESCRIPTION of a declining farmer in the 1870s, Richard Jefferies remarked that the fall of a farmer was so gradual that he might be excused for thinking it would never come, but that blind work was of no avail against the ocean steamer with cargoes of wheat and meat, a general fall of prices, and successive low yields consequent upon a run of bad seasons.[2] Banbury declined in a similar manner in the 1870s. Every indicator of the state of the local economy suggests a lowering of the rate of activity, and an undermining of the foundations of the prosperity which the town had enjoyed during the age of high farming. Yet institutions did not collapse in the '70s, and the facade of local society was remarkable little changed by the onset of the agricultural depression.

Banbury's prosperity depended upon the state of agriculture in the hinterland. Farming in the region suffered a series of disasters in the second half of the 1870s which culminated in a rapid succession of calamities in the years 1879-82, and in the long term this proved to be the beginning of a protracted period of agricultural decline. Grain production had been increasing in Oxfordshire in the last years of the era of high farming. The area devoted to wheat increased by 8,000 acres in the four years between 1868 and 1872, and a peak of barley production was reached in 1879. Between 1874 and 1900 the wheat acreage in the county fell by 45 per cent, and the number of sheep, an integral part of the arable economy of the mid-19th century, fell from 350,000 to 232,000. While in the long term the loss of grain production was to some extent matched by an increased concentration on cattle, whose numbers in Oxfordshire rose from 4.7 million in the early 1870s to 5.8 million in 1906-10,[3] in the late '70s and early '80s stock farmers were afflicted by a succession of plagues. There was foot-and-mouth disease in the Banbury district in 1872 and 1875. Epidemics in 1877 and 1882 closed the market, and another in 1881 closed the railway stations, which were both within the afflicted county of Northamptonshire, to livestock traffic.[4] During 1880 there were severe losses of sheep from liver fluke, and the sheep population of Northamptonshire fell by a quarter between 1875 and 1882.[5] The late '70s and early '80s were also marked by adverse weather conditions of unusual severity. The harvest of 1874 was the last for many years to be gathered in favourable conditions. Damaging winds and floods added considerably to agricultural distress in 1880-82.[6] Rising rates, the alienation of farmworkers from farmers brought about by the agricultural trades unions, and the effects of the 1870

Education Act were among other causes seen as contributing to the distress of agriculture in the region,[7] but above all imported food was blamed for the situation, which by 1881 was being interpreted as a catastrophic break in the normal cycle of good and bad years. The years 1879-82 were a time of exceptional misfortune for farmers in the Banbury area, and the parliamentary enquiries of the early '80s gave them opportunities to blame a variety of causes for their distress. It was the beginning of a massive swing from arable to cattle farming, which by the beginning of the 20th century had restored a measure of optimism within the agricultural community. There was much rationalisation of holdings in the last two decades of the century, and an increased emphasis on the production of milk for the London market.[8]

This was also a period when the decline in the population of Banbury's hinterland was accelerated. The population of the rural parishes in the Poor Law Union stood at 19,440 in 1871, then fell by 7.4 per cent in the 1870s and '80s, and by 6.9 per cent in the '90s to reach 15,527 in 1901, a lower figure than a century earlier.[9] After the mid-1870s, farmworkers' wages fell below the levels of the previous decade, until in 1879 strong lads were being offered only £10 p.a., and some adult labourers as little as 9s. per week.[10] While the worst panic-inspired predictions made around 1880 were not realised, it was true that the 1870s had marked the beginning of a long-term decline in agricultural prosperity. In many parts of the region it was reckoned in the second decade of the 20th century that while conditions were slowly improving, the state of farming had once been much better, and it was still possible to clain in 1944 that active development of agriculture in the region had practically come to an end in 1880.[11] Not until after the Second World War was there a revival of the confidence in agriculture which had been a feature of the era of high farming.

There was a rising tide of migration from Banbury and its hinterland in the 1870s. Over 30 Banburians were among a party who left in 1872 for Cananea in Brazil, an ill-fated settlement where many Europeans died, the failure of which was blamed on Joseph Arch and the labourers' union which had sponsored the migration. In 1873 a local newspaper published letters from Banburians extolling the working conditions at Lake Rosseau, Canada, and in Wayne County, Pennsylvania, while the Burlington and Missouri River Railroad reminded intending migrants that its services put Iowa and Nebraska within fifteen days of Liverpool. Three hundred labourers from the Banbury area left for New Zealand in May 1875. In the late 1870s the press constantly drew attention to local people who had prospered after emigration, among them George Reynolds, who by 1877 owned 9,000 sheep at Palo Vantana, Texas, Frederick Goffe of Coperstown, Otego, New York, and George Bolton of Minneapolis.[12]

Slowly the shadow of the depression crept over the town of Banbury. While the town's population increased during the '70s, it did so more slowly than in any previous decade of the century, and at a lower rate than the national average.[13] The numbers of retailers remained stable, but newspaper advertisements suggest that increasing numbers of products like Burton ales and seeds from Webbs of Wordsley were being brought into the town to compete with those of local manufacturers. The carrying trade actually expanded in the 1870s. By 1881, 191 individual carriers were making 438 journeys per week into Banbury, and the area they served was marginally enlarged to include villages like Ascott-under-Wychwood and Chesterton near Bicester. Banbury may well have been gaining some trade from small declining towns like Buckingham, Chipping Norton and Deddington.[14]

In January 1881 the *Banbury Advertiser* noted that 'distress in the town at the present time is more general than has been known for many years past'. In part this was the result of severe snow storms, but it was no more than the intensification of a trend which had been evident in previous winters.[15] In the early months of 1879 relief for the poor was organised on an unprecedented scale. The two principal charitable societies set up a joint coal fund, while two soup kitchens were established, one at the Grimsbury Wesleyan Chapel and one in North Bar.[16] The following winter kitchens in Grimsbury and Calthorpe Street were open from early December until after Easter, and distress at Christmas 1879 was said to be 'very severe'. The opening of the soup kitchens each autumn became in the 1880s as regular a feature of life in Banbury as the Michaelmas Fair.[17]

There was no appreciable expansion of manufacturing industry in Banbury in the 1870s. The Britannia Works was subject to periodic slumps in demand. The Eastern Crisis of 1876–78 closed markets in Russia, but following the Congress of Berlin a 23-waggon train loaded with reaping machines for Odessa was despatched from Banbury to Hull. Bernhard Samuelson attempted to maintain his skilled labour force, and explained his policy in detail during the election of 1880 when accused of creating jobs to buy votes.[18] The foundry suffered from being part of a very large concern whose primary purpose was to make iron rather than iron products, and its furnaces and forges in Cleveland encountered severe difficulties in the 1870s. It was also a relatively small concern in the context of the agricultural engineering industry. Samuelson employed only about 500 men at Banbury, but Marshalls of Gainsborough employed 2,000 in 1892, Ransomes of Ipswich 1,500 in 1885, Clayton & Shuttleworth of Lincoln 1,400 in 1855, and Garretts of Leiston over 800 in 1861. The Britannia Works was specialised in reapers and mowing machines which were notoriously the most difficult machines to make and to market. Nor were its attempts to diversify its products as successful as those of the East Anglian foundries, which, having begun as makers of farm implements, by 1900 were manufacturing such diverse products as tortoise stoves, piano frames and mining equipment. The Britannia Works became a limited company in 1887, but the peak of its prosperity was passed.[19] None of the other engineering firms in Banbury adopted new products or significantly increased its labour force, and while Hunt Edmunds brewery expanded, this was only at the expense of the smaller brewing concerns in the town which Hunt Edmunds acquired for the sake of their public houses.[20] The former girth mill on the canal bank was opened as a tweed factory in 1871, was damaged by fire in 1876, but re-opened with the backing of a consortium of shopkeepers in 1879.[21] Plush-making and girth weaving continued but only on a workshop scale.

Changes in the local transport system did little to alter the economy of the region. In 1872 the Northampton and Banbury Junction Railway reached Banbury from Blisworth, and in 1875 the first sod of the long-awaited line to the west, the Banbury and Cheltenham Direct Railway was cut. Goods traffic was being handled at Adderbury and Bloxham by 1877, but it was not until 1887 that the whole line was opened. The importance of the railways as carriers of freight was acknowledged by a dinner given by the town traders for GWR employees in 1880, but Banbury was not a major railway centre, nor did the new railways of the 1870s bring it significant benefits. The most notable railway events of the period were the annual rituals each August at which Queen Victoria was presented with Banbury Cakes on her journeys from Osborne to Balmoral.[22]

On the surface society in Banbury changed little in the 1870s. The institutions of the town, its forms of government, its main economic activities were still what they had been in earlier decades. Real decline came with a succession of bankruptcies and an acceleration of the migration from the town of people of talent during the 1880s. In 1881 two solicitors' partnerships, two substantial innkeepers and a prominent draper all went bankrupt, while the profits of Gilletts Bank fell by almost two thirds between 1878 and 1884, and remained low thereafter.[23] Just as the business enterprises which had risen to prosperity in the 1830s and '40s were facing difficulties, so the social institutions which dated from the aftermath of the Reform Bill had reached a state of near-ossification. There was an element of complacency about bourgeois society, about which the Literary and Philosophical Society, set up to challenge the Mechanics' Institute, and the Apostolic Band, which alleged that the existing church and chapel congregations lacked zeal, were two very different expressions of concern. A more coherent critique of the established order was expressed by a range of increasingly influential radical groups which dominated the political debate in the town.

The Banbury Co-operative Society established its own premises in Broad Street in 1868, and subsequently opened departments for boots and shoes in 1869, butchery in 1871 and drapery in 1872, and went on to manufacture its own flour, bread and clothing. In 1869 the committee decided to devote 2½ per cent of its net profits to educational purposes and a library was formed the following year. The early '70s were remembered as a period when:

> 'men were obsessed with principles by which they thought the world would be "turned upside down in a generation or so". A new idealism propagated with the passion of a religion sought a new earth'.

Its educational activities brought the Banbury society to national prominence. It published a series of tracts of which 30,000 were printed in 1870 alone. In 1871 it instituted the *Co-operative Record*, the first widely circulated journal in the movement, which from 1871 until 1875 provided an eloquent commentary from below upon Banbury society. In the first issue Thomas Proverbs, a clerk, proclaimed:

> 'We believe we have got hold of a principle which is destined to work wonderful changes for the better in the social and moral conditions of the English working class ... we may hope for the time when the wretched cut-throat, barbarous system of society which now prevails shall be replaced by one of peace and brotherhood, when a few shall no longer grow immensely rich while the many are extremely poor, but when plenty and happiness shall be the common lot of all'.

William Bunton, the former Chartist, wrote in the same issue:

> '... It will not always be as it has been in the past, nor even as it is at present. Labour will not always be the slave of capital, nor purposely kept in ignorance that idleness may live on it. The working man need not toil double length of time to keep another man doing nothing. Hard work and privation will not always be associated together. Wrong and misrule will not always endure, nor folly and vice last for ever'.[24]

John Butcher, secretary of the Society, urged in 1872 that co-operators should elect their own representatives to the Board of Health and the corporation. The *Record* supported the cause of the agricultural labourers, and drew attention to national trades union issues. It greeted the result of the 1874 general election with abhorrence.

Co-operative congresses in Banbury addressed by such speakers as George Odger of the London Trades Council, Professor Thorold Rogers and G. J. Holyoake, drew audiences from all over England.[25] The Society provided varied social activities for its members, soirées in the winter months and fêtes and picnics in the summer.

The dramatic meeting on 7 February 1872 at which Joseph Arch spoke under a chestnut tree to an audience of farm labourers dimly illuminated by lanterns hung from bean poles, from which developed the National Agricultural Labourers' Union, took place on the village green at Wellesbourne, only 14 miles from Banbury. The union was formally constituted at a conference in Leamington in May 1872.[26] It provided opportunities for sympathetic action by Banbury radicals, and its early successes were an inspiration for other causes. Banbury was the focus of many union activities, and the scene of several notable incidents in its history. On 25 April 1872 Joseph Arch spoke in the Corn Exchange to a crowded audience which included foundrymen and members of the middle class, as well as labourers from many miles around. On 10 May 1872 the Banbury branch of the union was formed, and within three weeks it had 42 members.[27] Banburians could not have failed to be aware of the struggles of the union during 1872 and 1873. In June 1872 the notorious Bodfish case was heard at the magistrates' court at the Neithrop police station in Newland. A Tadmarton farmer, Charles Garrett, was acquitted of savagely beating a weakly labourer, Isaac Bodfish, to prevent him from joining the union.[28] On 13 August 1872, 64 striking labourers from Middleton Cheney paraded through Banbury behind a drum and fife band, and in April 1873 Wiggington men came seeking advice on emigration, and marched through the streets singing union songs.[29] After the disastrous migration of labourers to Cananea in Brazil in 1872, one William Stanton of Great Bourton who had safely returned attempted to discredit the union. When he interrupted a meeting in Banbury in March 1873 he was chased through the streets by angry labourers.[30] Later in 1873, one James Phillips, secretary of the 'National Association for the Prevention and Repression of Strikes', held meetings and interrupted NALU gatherings. He was subsequently prosecuted for gaining money by false pretences.[31] As the union faltered in the mid-1870s, its role was increasingly that of an emigration agency. By 1879 its membership in the Banbury district was no more than 1,000 compared with over 2,500 in 1874, but it maintained an office in the town, and Joseph Arch spoke regularly at local meetings.[32]

Vaccination within the first three months of a child's life was made compulsory by the Vaccination Act of 1867.[33] It first became a cause of controversy in Banbury in August 1871 when a lecture was given by a doctor from London, who was introduced by a Conservative physician, but resistance to vaccination subsequently developed into a radical and dissenting cause.[34] In the summer of 1872 distress warrants were issued against several Banburians who had refused to pay fines imposed for refusing vaccination for their children.[35] In November 1873 the Board of Guardians, which was responsible for vaccination, decided not to prosecute objectors. There was a serious outbreak of smallpox in the town the following spring, and the Guardians were reminded of their duty by the Local Government Board. By 1874 a Banbury branch of the Anti-Vaccination League had been formally constituted.[36] During 1875 membership grew to more than 200, and many columns of the local press were occupied with the subject. The first local man to be imprisoned for not having his child vaccinated was a labourer from Middleton Cheney who was greeted by bands, flags and a purse of sovereigns when he reached Banbury after his release in June 1875.[37] When two Deddington men left gaol in June 1876 they returned home in a procession marshalled by J. G. Freeman, secretary of the Banbury branch of the League. The first Banburian to be imprisoned was one Solomon Busby, who was released in February 1877 to be greeted by a torchlight procession, whose members hooted outside the houses of doctors, and burned an effigy of Dr. Jenner on Grimsbury Green.[38] In September 1876 an anonymous letter was sent to the vaccination officer whose duty it was to enforce the law. The *Banbury Guardian* remarked that it was modelled on current Irish practice, although such letters had a long pedigree in the history of English agitation.[39] During 1876 and 1877 the movement developed a broader critique of society. In March 1876 it affirmed that the vaccination law was of more interest to the working classes than to those from high places. One of the national leaders of the movement, W. Hume Rothery, speaking in Banbury in June 1876, compared those imprisoned with Cranmer, Ridley and Latimer, and declared:

'Political parties, both Whig and Tory, are utterly unfit to rule; they have proved themselves fit for nothing but misrule'.

He suggested that the Established Church through its parson magistrates was aiding rampant wickedness by supporting compulsory vaccination.[40] In 1878 and 1879 the movement passed to other stages of agitation, and began to seek redress by political means. Frederick Lamb, secretary of the Co-operative Society, urged that the Working Mens' Liberal Association should oppose vaccination.[41] In April 1878 Charles Gillett was elected a Guardian for Neithrop, pledged to oppose prosecutions for refusal of vaccination. In the borough election of 1879 anti-vaccinators were urged to vote for two Liberals and two Conservatives who favoured their views, and when three of the four were elected the movement was congratulated on its success.[42] A campaign of direct action developed. An anti-vaccination station was opened near the vaccination station, displaying banners with such slogans as 'Mothers Beware!', and supplying borax with which vaccine could be washed from the arms of children who had been injected.[43] The League arranged its own social functions. In June 1878 a fête was held at Wood Green at which blue silk favours were worn by unvaccinated children.[44] By the beginning of 1880 the magistrates were desperately trying to calm the feelings which had arisen on the vaccination issue by fining those who came before them a nominal sixpence. Some defendants had as many as six previous convictions. The Board of Health found considerable difficulty in persuading anyone to take up the post of vaccination officer.[45]

At the head of the Anti-Vaccination League in Banbury were members of the middle class, notably Charles Gillett the Quaker banker, who was reckoned among the national leaders of the movement. Yet most of its supporters were working men. Those who were fined and imprisoned in October 1876 included a carpenter from Neithrop, an iron moulder from Bath Road, a carpenter from Queen Street and a brickmaker from Cherwell. Most of those sent to gaol by magistrates in the countryside were farm labourers.[46] The movement was strong in other towns like Leicester and Keighley, but Banbury had the reputation of being 'the home and headquarters of the anti-vaccination agitation'.[47]

The Temperance movement in Banbury enjoyed many successes in the 1870s. In January 1876 a temperance coffee cart began to provide non-alcoholic refreshments in the streets.[48] In 1871 the building in Parson's Street used as a temperance hall since 1842 was sold by its owners, but in August 1875 the Temperance Society announced that it would build a new hall at the junction of Mill Lane and Bridge Street. The foundation stone was laid in October, when a visitor called Banbury 'a hot bed of Teetotallism'. It was opened in 1876 and soon accommodated a 'British Workman' alcohol-free public house, a library and reading room, an Anglican Sunday School, a club for young men, a YMCA, a YWCA, and several specifically temperance organisations.[49] Francis Litchfield, high Tory rector of Farthinghoe supported the Permissive Bill by the 1870s, and helped to construct the doorway of the hall.[50] In 1875 a branch of the Church of England Temperance Society was formed at Christ Church, whose vicar, the Revd. John Spitall, was active in the Temperance movement throughout his incumbency,[51] and in 1873 the Wesleyans in Banbury held their first temperance meeting.[52] The Good Templars, a teetotal friendly society, established two lodges in Banbury in 1872, while the Band of Hope, a drum and fife band, and a temperance choral society were all active. The Alliance held regular meetings, and there were still traditional temperance lectures by speakers like T. Horrocks of Darwen, the 'converted clown', and B. W. Blades of Birmingham, 'who had been raised by teetotallism from a drunkard's hut to a palace'.[53]

Teetotallers became increasingly abusive towards the drink trade, speaking of publicans with the kind of language that anti-vaccinators used about doctors. Magistrates were accused of forcing liquor traffic on communities which did not want it.[54] Temperance arguments were refuted at public meetings by Thomas Orson (or Hawson) who maintained that the public house was the resting place of the itinerant artisan, and the meeting place of the poor man's parliament, and of trade clubs, which kept up wages. At one meeting John Butcher, the teetotaller, observed that both he and Orson were shoemakers, and that shoemakers were generally radicals.[55] Temperance meetings were increasingly occasions of disorder. On 1 October 1872 as the drum and fife band marched to play outside the homes of leading teetotallers, they were surrounded by roughs shouting 'Bring out the beer'.[56] On 21 June 1873 James Phillips, the opponent of the NALU, climbed on to a waggon used as a platform at a temperance meeting in the Cowfair and declared his opposition to total abstinence. There was uproar when he was recognised. The following day a party of 300 followed and jeered teetotallers after a meeting in the fields off Bath Road. Dr. Griffin, a Liberal magistrate, deplored the language used by temperance reformers, who in his hearing had called publicans 'murderers'. The magistrates declared a ban on open air meetings, to which the *Banbury Advertiser* retorted that public houses were never closed when they were the scenes of disorder.[57] In July the Primitive Methodists held an open air meeting to test the ban, and James Cadbury established that the magistrates had no authority to prohibit such gatherings. On 18 August when a rally was held at Banbury Cross, temperance speakers were booed and attacked as they went home by 'young, half-grown lads, smoking dirty pipes'.[58] The temperance movement was increasingly politicised during the '70s. A Liberal declared in 1871 that he could not vote for another parliamentary candidate who did not favour the Permissive Bill, and in 1873 James Cadbury declared that the first question was the temperance question and other matters were of no consequence. Other Liberals feared the effects of such single-mindedness, and Dr. Griffin said in 1874 that he hoped Liberals would not begin to vote according to whether they drank water or beer.[59]

Other radical causes attracted the attention of Banburians in the 1870s. Jessie Craighen, Mrs. Fawcett and Mrs. Ronniger were among speakers at meetings on the rights of women, which were chaired by such radicals as William Bunton and John Butcher, and were sometimes occasions for disturbances of a similar nature to those at temperance meetings.[60] Several meetings protesting against the Contagious Diseases Act were held, which gave opportunities for criticisms of doctors similar to those made by anti-vaccinators.[61] Disestablishment was demanded at several Liberation Society meetings.[62] In 1879 there was disorder when the Northampton radical Charles Bradlaugh lectured on Christianity. The mayor forbade further use of the town hall by Bradlaugh, but the matter was raised during the town council election, and he was able to give further lectures in 1880.[63]

There were many similarities and many intricate connections among the radical movements. All saw Banbury as a centre of enlightenment which had a mission to the countryside. The moving spirits behind the NALU branch were not farm labourers but radicals like John Butcher and William Johnson.[64] The Co-operative Society established branches in eight villages between 1868 and 1874, a development which was interpreted as a consequence of the labourers' movement:

'The labour of the countryside became alive to its unjust conditions. Joseph Arch roused the villages in this respect as perhaps no one else had, and his call to union met with loyal response. Labourers locally . . . through the agitation, got intimate knowledge of town life and conditions, and among other things discovered the help that lay in Co-operation. In return the principles of the movement got disseminated more and more in the locality'.[65]

In 1879 the Temperance Society renewed its commitment to evangelise in the country-side, while the Anti-Vaccination League also despatched 'missionaries' to the villages and staunchly supported farm labourers prosecuted by parson magistrates.[66]

The four radical movements shared to a considerable extent a common ideology, one in which there was a strong element of pragmatic pessimism, as well as an occasional sense of utopian fervour. The adoption of Prohibition by the Temperance movement was an admission of its failure to convince the population at large of the rightness of its beliefs. The exhilaration which the movement experienced from time to time in the 1870s came because it saw the Permissive Bill as a practical possibility, not because large numbers of people were turning to total abstinence. Even before the NALU went into decline after 1874, Joseph Arch saw emigration as the only way in which to improve the condition of the farm labourer. Co-operation was seen as a means of securing a limited but real improvement in an economic system in which working men could expect no justice. Thomas Proverbs described it in 1871 as 'one of the means by which they might raise themselves . . . if they waited till Parliament or their neighbours would do it for them, it would never be done'.[67] All four movements assumed an air of moral superiority over the upper and middle classes. All but the NALU organised social activities which drew their members away from established institutions. All propagated a philo-sophy of the simple life, of gaining satisfaction by the suppression of aspirations. Bunton urged co-operators in 1873:

'Dress yourself in garments plain and good of your own manufacture, and let those who know no better have all the fal-lals and feathers. Strive to make your own bricks; build your own houses and take your own rents: do this, and get wisdom and happiness and comfort, and peace shall dwell amongst you'.[68]

All of the movements had an element of middle-class leadership. The Anti-Vaccination League enjoyed the patronage of the banker Charles Gillett. The Temperance Society was supported by James Cadbury, and by William Johnson, a currier employing four men, who was a town councillor, treasurer of the Banbury branch of the NALU, and a proponent of disestablishment. It was while the temperance band was playing outside his house that disorder broke out on 1 October 1871.

Some radical leaders were working men. John Butcher, teetotaller, chairman of the first labourers' meeting in Banbury and of meetings on womens' suffrage, was a journeyman shoemaker before he became manager of the Co-operative shop. He delivered what Joseph Arch called 'a capital paper' at the founding conference of the NALU in May 1872. William Tustain, chairman of the Co-operative Society, and a teetotaller, was a railway guard. Thomas Proverbs, editor of the *Co-operative Record* and secretary of the Band of Hope and the Anti-Vaccination League, was a clerk. William Bunton, a mechanic who kept a newsagent's shop, was an atheist, former Chartist, an editor of the *Co-operative Record*, and chairman of meetings addressed by Mrs. Fawcett and Charles Bradlaugh.[69] Even working-class radical leaders saw their task in almost paternalistic terms, and were obviously conscious that their view of society isolated them from many of those they were trying to lead. Bunton wrote in 1871 that:

> 'Co-operation appeals only to the thoughtful and wise, it has nothing whatever to say to the profligate, the foolish or the vicious. It says to him who desires to better his condition "Help yourself, and I will help you", "Look, and I will show you the way", but it says nothing to him who, being in the gutter, is content to lay there'.[70]

The radical causes were increasingly intermixed. The first issue of the *Co-operative Record* drew attention to the Anti-Vaccination League and a temperance insurance society.[71] When Thomas Fountain, an anti-vaccinator, was released from prison in 1876 he boasted that he assured his warders that he would miss neither beer nor tobacco, since he had been a teetotaller for nine years. Frederick Lamb, secretary of the Co-operative Society, was an active anti-vaccinator. W. Hume Rothery, a national leader of the Anti-Vaccination League, often lectured in Banbury, on one occasion on the Permissive Bill. James Phillips, scourge of the NALU, provoked disorder at a temperance meeting.[72] Both the temperance movement and the Anti-Vaccination League came into conflict with the law, and developed an almost paranoiac view of government, magistrates, doctors and publicans. A writer in 1877 said the vaccination law was passed by the House of Lords, which had been led by the nose by the medical professions, just as the upper classes were being led by the Jesuits to Popery. He boasted of the 'revolution that has already been accomplished by the Labourers' Union', and warned 'our cruel persecutors' that a government based on publican votes could not last for ever.[73]

The radical movements in Banbury were undermined by the slow depression of trade, and the increasing pressures on men with talents to leave the town. In 1873 both Thomas Proverbs and John Butcher left Banbury, the latter to manage a co-operative footware factory in Leicester.[74] By the end of the '70s the creativity though not the stridency of radicalism had declined. The NALU was in demise, and the Co-operative Society had temporarily lost some of its entrepreneurial zeal. Radical energies were increasingly concentrated on the essentially negative causes of prohibition and resistance to the vaccination laws. Radicalism was increasingly class-orientated, directed against magistrates, publicans, doctors and parson magistrates, and proud of its moral superiority to the wealthier classes. It was a way of life, different both from that of the majority of the working class and from that of the Liberal, dissenting middle class from which it was derived. Both its lack of solid foundation in the working class and its umbilical connection to the chapels were in due course to weaken it, but in the '70s the four movements had all drawn national attention to Banbury, and radicalism as a whole profoundly influenced the pattern of conventional politics in the town.

Walter Bagehot wrote that 'constituency government' was:

'the precise opposite of Parliamentary government. It is the government of immoderate persons far from the scene of action, instead of the government of moderate persons close to the scene of action; it is the judgement of persons judging in the last resort and without a penalty, in lieu of persons judging in fear of a dissolution, and ever conscious that they are subject to an appeal'.[75]

Throughout the 1870s the Liberal ascendency in Banbury was threatened by some of the town's radicals, by immoderate persons zealous about particular issues, by exactly the forces which Bagehot feared might gain an undue influence in the workings of the constitution. The radicals seemed at times to be concerned as much to demonstrate their destructive power, by dividing the Liberal Party and aiding the Conservatives, as to see the realisation of their particular objectives.

Leading Liberals were aware during Gladstone's first ministry that the unity of their party was endangered by issues which Dissenters regarded as particularly important. There was contention in Banbury about the 1870 Education Act, and during the election campaign of 1874 Dr. Griffin admitted that his view of it differed from Bernhard Samuelson's but that he would nevertheless vote for the ironmaster. 'Little crotchets or fancies', he declared, 'should not step in and cause splits in their party'.[76]

When Gladstone announced his decision to go to the country on 24 January 1874, Bernhard Samuelson was on his yacht in the Mediterranean. Notices confirming that he would be contesting the election were despatched from Rome, Dijon and London as he travelled home. He was adopted as the Liberal candidate on Wednesday 28 January, but did not arrive in Banbury until the next day, and addressed the electors for the first time at the nomination the following morning. Polling took place on Monday 2 February.[77] Two and a half hours before Samuelson reached Banbury, Josiah Wilkinson of Highgate, a Conservative candidate, a lawyer and volunteer colonel, arrived at the station. He claimed to be a 'Liberal Conservative' anxious to preserve the country from the 'ruin, communism and confusion' threatened by Gladstone's tail. He accused the Liberal government of coercive policies on licensing and education, and opposed further extension of the franchise.[78] His meeting in the Town Hall on Saturday 31 January was one of the critical events of the short campaign. There were shouts of 'Samuelson for ever', and fighting developed into what one newspaper called 'one and a half hours of indescribable confusion and uproar'. A Conservative alleged that the disorder was caused by an organised group from the foundry, and urged small traders and working men to show that they were not 'in bondage to any local nabob, Christian or Jew'.[79] Meanwhile, at his own public meeting, Samuelson was assailed by disgruntled Liberals about vaccination, the effects of the Criminal Law Amendment Act on trade unions, the Contagious Diseases Act, the Education question and the Permissive Bill.[80] Samuelson won the election by 760 votes to 676, a margin which by Banbury's standards was slender. He gained 12 votes fewer than in 1868, while the Conservative vote increased by 179, and had only 52.93 per cent of the poll, compared with 66.04 per cent in 1868.[81] His loss of support was part of a national swing towards the Conservatives, but locally it was ascribed to Liberal disunity, the defection to the Conservatives of Sir Charles Douglas's supporters, the influence of publicans and the disorder at Wilkinson's public meeting. Some blame was placed on inadequate organisation, and a Working Men's Liberal Association was established, although its meetings served only to ventilate those questions on which Liberals were divided. At one meeting on 19 October 1874 the time was taken up with the discussion of vaccination and the opening of museums on Sundays. Samuelson confronted his critics with considerable courage. He was always ready to propound capitalism among co-operators, to argue that compulsory vaccination helped to eradicate smallpox, or that public sobriety could not be achieved by compulsion.[82]

The Conservative government's foreign policy finally overcame the fissiparous tendencies among the Banbury Liberals, but until the eve of polling in the general election of 1880 the party was threatened by the withdrawal of support of groups campaigning on single issues. Expressions of disgust at the Turkish suppressing of the rising in Bulgaria appeared in Banbury newspapers in June 1876, and on 12 September Bernhard Samuelson spoke at a meeting protesting against the atrocities, when it was remarked that party political feeling was notably absent.[83] Public feelings intensified during the autumn and throughout 1877. The Eastern Question was the subject of sermons, YMCA discussion and Mechanics' Institute lectures.[84]

As the time for an election in 1880 approached other issues were raised. When Samuelson spoke about the Eastern Question in October 1878 there were shouts of 'We want plenty of trade and not so many parsons'. The Electoral Permissive Bill Association was formed in 1878 to lobby him about prohibition and the teetotallers began to link the drink question with the depression, pointing out that drinksellers were prospering while other traders' tills were loaded with debts.[85] There was a proposal in 1878 that W. Gibson Watt might stand for Banbury as candidate of the anti-vaccinators, opposing the publicans on the drink question, supporting Gladstone's foreign policy, and seeking land reform. In February 1879, 120 people declared that they would not vote for any parliamentary candidate who was not pledged to end compulsory vaccination.[86] Although three quarters of the 120 were committed Liberals, they re-affirmed on the eve of the election in March 1880 that they were bound to vote for a Conservative who had yielded on Vaccination against a Liberal who had not.[87]

In February 1880 the Conservatives in Banbury adopted as their candidate Thomas Gibson Bowles, founder of the journal *Vanity Fair*, the 38 year old illegitimate son of Thomas Milner Gibson. He declared in his first speech in Banbury that there were too many laws, and that the one on vaccination could be done without.[88] He proved the most flamboyant of Banbury's parliamentary candidates on the 19th century. He was an unabashed imperialist, asserting that a vigorous foreign policy was essential for the protection of India, and proclaiming 'I am a Jingo and proud of it'.[89] He openly appealed to anti-Semite and anti-German feelings, suggesting that Samuelson was 'a man from Hamburg, a sham Englishman'. Although he agreed to vote against compulsory vaccination, he made no concessions to the temperance movement, accusing Gladstone of attacking the legitimate rights of publicans, and conspicuously drinking jugs of ale at his open air meetings.[90]

Samuelson was clearly concerned about vaccination and announced that he would seek an end to compulsion for those who conscientiously objected. Gradually the single-issue opposition dissolved. At a meeting on 19 March a succession of anti-vaccinators declared that they would sink their cause to return the Liberal. The Alliance determined to support Samuelson against Bowles. Two issues overrode Banbury's many crotchets. One was foreign policy, in this election a question of morality on which any dissenter found it difficult to oppose Gladstone. The other was the depression. Speaker after speaker at Liberal meetings referred to bad trade and the need to restore to office, 'the greatest financier in this or any other country'.[91] Samuelson's most important convert was William Mewburn who wrote a letter saying that minor differences must be sunk for the general good of the party, and that he regretted 'the dreadful feeling of war and bloodshed which has demoralised and degraded old England'.[92]

Samuelson was elected with 1,018 votes against 583 cast for Bowles, a 63.59 per cent share of the poll.[93] The *Banbury Advertiser* noted:

> 'a singular unanimity existed among the Liberal Party. The teetotallers and Nonconformists supported him (Samuelson) almost to a man, and many of the anti-vaccinators who had pledged themselves not to vote for him . . . gave him their support'.[94]

Bowles had appealed with success to Jingoists and drinkers, and on the night of the election a group of between 100 and 150 left the *Old George* at 8.30 p.m. led by Henry Bolton, a woolstapler, and attacked the homes of Liberals in Oxford Road, leaving several completely wrecked.[95]

The national issues of foreign policy and the economy, often encapsulated in the personality of William Ewart Gladstone, overshadowed every local schism. The radicals were for the most part men whose beliefs were as much derived from Dissent as those of the leaders of the local Liberal Party. When it was possible to state issues in clear-cut moral terms, it was difficult for them merely to demonstrate their power and return the Conservative. Moreover radicalism was a way of life which was indivisible. When Bowles appealed to anti-vaccinators, the same individuals were often teetotallers who could hardly applaud his public beer-swigging. The Bulgarian Atrocities and the agricultural depression brought an end to the 'age of the crotchet', but politics as well as the local economy was on the verge of transformation. Parliamentary Reform, the extension of the franchise to farm labourers and the re-distribution of seats, was a part of the radical programme and, when it was realised in the Third Reform Act, it brought to an end the parliamentary borough of Banbury, and the political division between town and countryside which had existed since the reign of Mary I. The game of politics was played thereafter to a very different set of rules from that which had obtained between 1832 and 1880.

And there was a change in the character of the players as well as in the rules. In 1882 the Liberals celebrated the Jubilee of Reform at a dinner at which the Reform Banner of 1832 was hung in triumph. Old men recalled the excitement of the 1830s, and congratulated themselves on the improvements and increased wealth which had followed their success. Significantly the principal speakers were all non-townsmen, yet the Reformers' Committee of 1831–32 could have provided a feast of home-bred eloquence. By the 1880s the Liberal Party in Banbury lacked dynamic roots, and its increasing identification with teetotallism was diminishing its social appeal. Six months before the Jubilee, the Conservative Club opened, ironically in James Wake Golby's old house in High Street,[96] providing the party with a centre for social cohesion which it had lacked since the demise of the Old Corporation. The Liberals won every parliamentary election in the borough between the First and the Third Reform Acts, but only five of the 13 contests in the Banbury division of Oxfordshire between 1885 and 1931. The political era which began in 1831 came to an end in the 1880s.

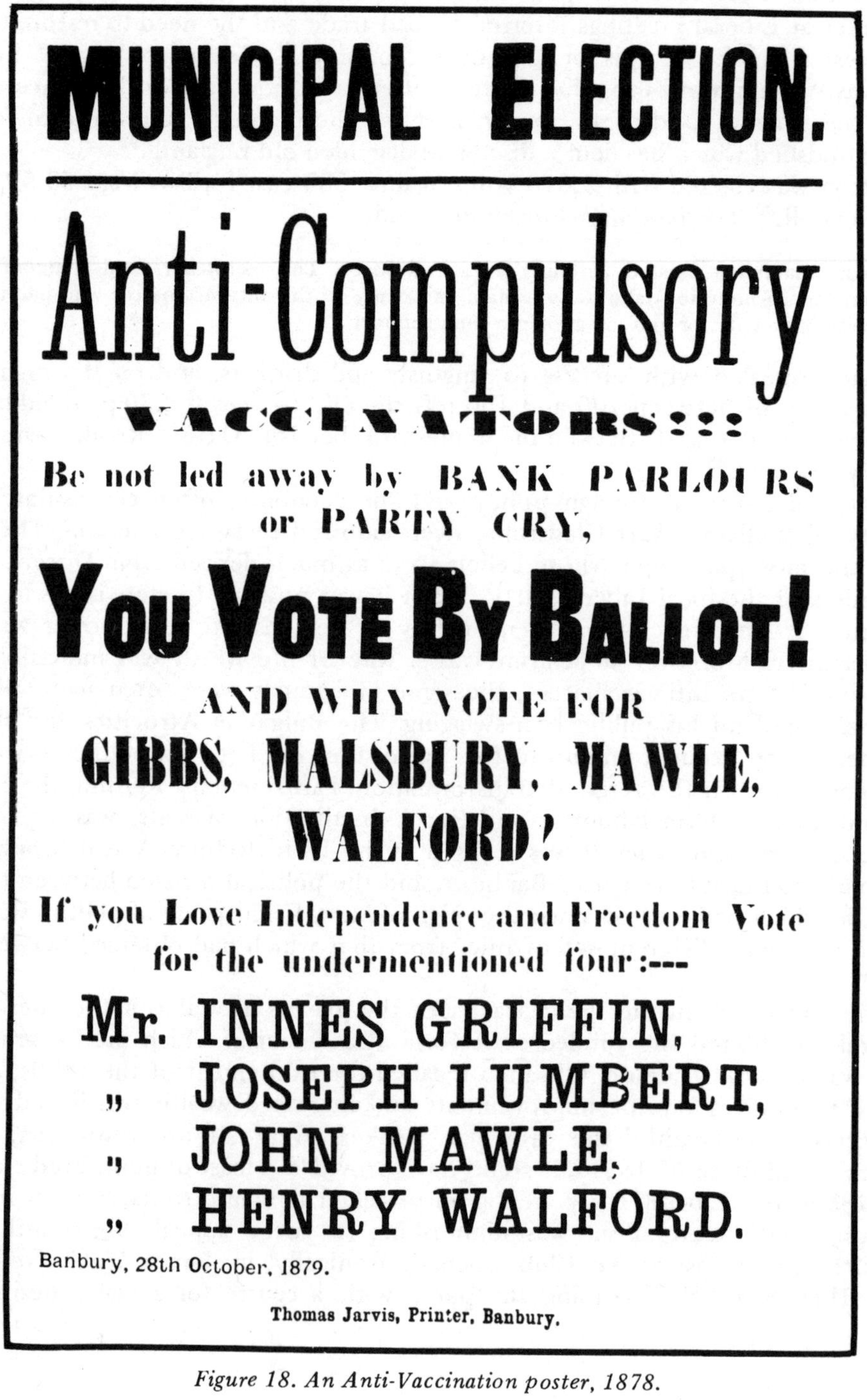

MUNICIPAL ELECTION.

Anti-Compulsory

VACCINATORS!!!

Be not led away by BANK PARLOURS
or PARTY CRY,

YOU VOTE BY BALLOT!

AND WHY VOTE FOR

GIBBS, MALSBURY, MAWLE, WALFORD!

If you Love Independence and Freedom Vote
for the undermentioned four:---

Mr. INNES GRIFFIN,
  „   JOSEPH LUMBERT,
  „   JOHN MAWLE,
  „   HENRY WALFORD.

Banbury, 28th October, 1879.

Thomas Jarvis, Printer, Banbury.

Figure 18. An Anti-Vaccination poster, 1878.

XIII

RECONSIDERATIONS

An agricultural district, like a little kingdom, has its own capital city.[1]

THE PERIOD BETWEEN 1830 and 1880 was a distinct phase in the history of Banbury. In economic terms it had begun slightly earlier in the 19th century, with a quickening in the growth of population, and ended about 1870 as the rate of increase slackened. Between 1831 and 1871 the population of the town rose by 83.10 per cent, but between 1871 and 1931 it increased by only 18.56 per cent. In political and social terms the period began when the town secured control of its own affairs through the Reform Act, the Municipal Corporations Act and the founding of publicly accountable voluntary societies. That control was gradually relinquished after 1880. Banbury lost its separate parliamentary representation in the Third Reform Act, and its powers over its own affairs have dwindled in the present century until the town is now controlled by a district council which governs all of north Oxfordshire. The mid-19th century was marked by a passion for innovation which had certainly ended by the 1880s. The cultural societies founded in the 1830s brought the town together as a community, attracted the best talents to Banbury and encouraged local performers. This vitality had ended by 1880, undermined by chapel-based activities, and by such general cultural changes as the spread of musical activities in middle-class households and the growth of national newspapers. The predominant memories of cultural activities in Banbury about 1900 are of informally organised performances by local people.[2]

In her classic social survey of Banbury in the late 1940s, Margaret Stacey convincingly delineated a 'traditional' town community, whose ways of life and assumptions were abruptly challenged by the building in 1931–33 of an aluminium factory, which brought to the town professional managers, migrant workers from Lancashire, South Wales and Nottinghamshire, and effective trades unions.[3] The early '30s certainly mark the end of another distinct phase in the history of Banbury as clearly as the years around 1880 mark its beginning.[4] Since the '30s Banbury has increasingly been part of the light industry dominated, semi-urban south east. Its economy is now based on several large concerns which belong to multi-national groups, and a great variety of small-scale manu-facturing and service industries. Its flourishing livestock market now looks to Europe rather than to surrounding counties as its hinterland. The motor car and the restoration of cottages and farmhouses have stimulated commuting thus eroding the historic distinction between town and countryside.

As history, Margaret Stacey's penetrating analysis of a 'traditional' community requires some qualification. Memoirs of the 1890s and the Edwardian period confirm most of her conclusions, yet examination of society in Banbury in the mid-19th century reveals a very different kind of community. The 'traditional' society which was undermined in the 1930s was that which had grown up in the years of Banbury's stagnation, not one which had existed since time immemorial. The division of society in Banbury into two 'sets', one Free Church, Liberal and teetotal, the other Anglican, Conservative and partial to drinking,[5] obviously had its origins in the social and political polarisation of the mid-19th century but there were certain clear differences. The Liberal Party of the period between 1830 and 1880 included many Anglicans. The issues between Dissenters and the Establishment in that period were real ones, and the protagonists were often in direct conflict. The divisions of the period after 1880 were social rather than economic or political, the result of suspicion and of ever-decreasing contacts, the consequence above all of the emergence of teetotallism as almost a condition of chapel membership in the 1870s. Professor Stacey concluded that before the 1930s Banbury was a place with a rigid social hierarchy, 'where you knew where you were'.[6] It is only with considerable qualification that this description could be applied to Banbury in the mid-19th century. There was a broad division between respectable and non-respectable, but above that line the boundaries of social intercourse seem to have been less rigid than they were about 1900. In the 1940s the 'traditional' businessman was 'concerned less with making as much money as possible . . . than with living comfortably and maintaining his social status and position'.[7] This was emphatically not true between 1830 and 1870 when Banbury abounded in zeal for innovation. Another characteristic of 'traditional' society was the avoidance of serious discussion of political and religious issues,[8] something where the contrast with the 19th century is very marked. Banbury was then an unusually disputatious society, capable of debating issues in its newspapers, with pamphlets and handbills, or at public meetings. Mid-19th century Banbury was very different from the stagnant, conformist community of 1880–1930, and from the 'sleepy hollow' stereotype of the Victorian small market town. It remains to examine the ways in which its history illuminates Victorian society at large.

Nineteenth-century England was divided into several hundred centripetal economic networks centred on market towns, their limits being defined by the extent of country carriers' journeys. Taken together the market towns were the homes of a considerable proportion of Englishmen, and as centres for countrymen they were of importance to millions more. Variations in terrain and in the spacing of towns ensured that hinterlands were uneven both in size and shape. Each market town, like Hardy's Casterbridge, was 'the pole, focus or nerve knot of the surrounding country life'.[9] Each network had its frontiers:

'the fields roll on and rise into the hills, the hills sink again into a plain, just the same as elsewhere; there are cornfields and meadows; villages and farmsteads, and no visible boundary. Nor is it recognised upon the map. It does not fit into any political or legal limit; it is neither a county, half a county, a hundred or police division. But to the farmer it is a distinct land. If he comes from a distance he will at once notice little peculiarities in the fields, the crops, the stock or customs. . . . The district, with its capital city . . . really is distinct, well-marked and defined. The very soil and substrata are characteristic. The products are wheat and cattle and sheep, the same as elsewhere, but the proportions of each, the kind of sheep, the traditionary methods and farm customs are separate and marked. The rotation of crops is different, the agreements are on a different basis, the very gates to the fields, perhaps, are not used in other places'.[10]

Some of the towns at the centres of such networks were places with many functions like Nottingham, Cheltenham or Cambridge. Some had a volume of market trade out of all proportion to the size of their resident populations. Cirencester, with a population of just over 6,000, had 160 carrier journeys per week, more than Wolverhampton, Shrewsbury or Stafford. Jefferies wrote of it:

> 'The place is a little market town, the total of whose population in the census sounds absurdly small; yet it is a complete world in itself; a capital city, with its kingdom'.[11]

Newark with 120 carrier journeys a week, Newbury with 106, Daventry with 96 and Chesterfield with 90, were all places which seem to have been primarily market towns, with as much market trade as some county towns.[12] In this group Banbury stands predominant, its trade being comparable with that of all but the largest market centres in the Midlands.

Banbury had many natural advantages. It stood at a focal point of transport routes. There was no rival town within carrying distance. Its whole hinterland within a 15-mile radius consisted of highly productive farmland. Yet the character of a town was shaped not merely by its geographical locations but by the philosophy of its citizens and by its history. Joseph Ashby's remarks on the varying characteristics of neighbouring villages could apply equally well to market towns.[13] Cirencester, like Banbury, was a place whose trade was larger than might be expected from the size of its population, but, unlike Banbury, it was wholly under the influence of a great estate. Its landscape was dominated by the 'immensely high and endless wall' of the Duke of Beaufort's park, and the dominant topic of conversation in the inns was 'What will *he* do?' and 'What will *he* say to it?'.[14] It was a very different community from Banbury which prided itself on its freedom from aristocratic interference. Some market towns had long traditions of political radicalism. In Coventry this dated from long before the Reform Act, and arose from the wide franchise, under which a large body of artisans, the freemen of the city, were able to vote,[15] but in Banbury the rise of Liberalism was relatively sudden. Throughout the 18th century the town had rendered almost unquestioned fealty to aristocrats, but in the 1830s the townspeople quite deliberately and consciously took the opportunities provided by national political developments to seize power for themselves.

This development had several roots. One of the most important seems to have been a passion for honest, efficient government, which arose from Evangelicalism, both Dissenting and Anglican, and which inspired men like William Spurrett, Thomas Tims and T. R. Cobb to sweep from power those who for generations had paid homage to Wroxton. Tribute was paid to William Spurrett on his death in 1833 as 'One of the most early, active and constant of our townsmen in contributing to the overthrow of political corruption in Banbury'.[16] The growth of a Reform party was aided by the roles which men of Liberal views were able to play in the 1820s in the Church Trustees and the Paving and Lighting Commission which gave them experience of public administration without being corrupted by the hospitality of Wroxton. The morale of Reformers in Banbury was strengthened by the repeal of the Test and Corporation Acts, always seen in the town as the beginning of an age of enlightenment, and by Roman Catholic Emancipation, which in Banbury, as in George Eliot's *Treby Magna*, was the first of a series of issues which polarised public opinion.[17] There was a sense in which the town felt itself to be recovering its Puritan past, to be dismissing the subservience to Wroxton in the 18th century as an abberation. It was remarked in 1833 that:

'the same zealous, independent way of thinking her ancients followed in religion, her native and adopted children, without abandoning religion, pursue in politics'.[18]

Liberalism became Banbury's dominant political creed and Conservatives were largely excluded from office, the main challenge to established authority in the mid-19th century coming from radicals.

Banbury's wide range of shops and small-scale manufactures marked the town as a market centre of consequence. A characteristic of the 'sleepy hollow' type of town was that most shops tended to 'general' trade, with drapers selling footware and grocers offering stationery and animal medicines, as in Rutherford's Cowfold, or in Rugby, where the three ironmongers in 1835 were all grocers.[19] This was emphatically not the case in Banbury, but the town lacked the law stationers, equity draughtsmen and architects to be found in county towns, the professors of dancing and share-brokers who flourished in places of resort like Ludlow or Leamington, or the booksellers, cricket bat dealers and billiards table proprietors who prospered in Oxford. The fortunes of manufacturing industry contributed substantially to Banbury's prosperity in the mid-19th century and to the town's subsequent decline. The rise of iron-founding was an experience which Banbury shared with almost every market town of consequence in western Europe. A recent study of East Anglia shows that there are remains of iron foundries in 38 towns, most of which began by making agricultural implements.[20] The crowded condition of Basingstoke in 1865 was said to be due to the foundries.[21] There were foundries called the Britannia Ironworks not just in Banbury but in Bedford, Birmingham, Derby and Nottingham. Even much smaller towns had their ironworks. Wantage was famous for the White Horse Ironworks, manufacturers of steam threshing machines, and in 1854 a Daventry ironfounder sold up his stock which included a 6 h.p. steam engine, and patterns for grates, door scrapers, pig troughs and stoves.[22] A foundry became almost a *sine qua non* of a market town, a facility to be sought by aspiring communities. In 1855 a meeting of influential citizens of Buckingham decided to form the Buckingham Castle Ironworks, after a resolution that a foundry 'was required' in the town.[23] In the 1850s the mass production methods, the overseas connections and the paternalism of the Britannia Works made it an altogether exceptional enterprise, but by 1880 it was such a foundry as was to be found in many other towns, much smaller than many of its competitors, and part of a concern whose chief interests were elsewhere. At the same time Banbury's traditional industry of plush weaving, unlike shoemaking in Northampton, hosiery in Leicester or biscuit-baking in Reading, had shrunk almost to vanishing point. Nor had any of Banbury's traditional craft-manufactures expanded to employ significant numbers of people. The stagnation of market trading in Banbury after 1880, which was the consequence of the agricultural depression, was intensified by the failure of manufacturing industry to expand. The developments of the 1850s proved not to be a take-off into self-sustained growth.

A sense of urgency in Banbury, dictated by a rapidly rising population, brought an end to the accidie of centuries in relation to public health. The streets were paved, houses were drained, and pure water brought within reach of every citizen. Because this happened in most English towns it should not be considered something which was pre-ordained and determined. It was part of that Evangelically-inspired passion for order and good government which swept the *ancien régime* from power in the 1830s. The removal of the bow windows, doorsteps, scrapers and cellar hatches, which obstructed the streets of Banbury as they did those of Casterbridge, was as symbolic as the selling-off of the Corporation pew.[24]

Religious polarisation was a common feature of English towns in the 19th century, even if in places dominated by great estates, like Cirencester or Knutsford, Dissent was weaker than in towns which had a greater degree of independence. Religious beliefs were held in Banbury with an unusually passionate intensity. Even Banburians who had emigrated retained their zeal. In 1879 a *Times* correspondent found himself travelling in the post cart from Maritzburg to Ladysmith in the charge of a Banburian who had once driven stage coaches to Oxford, and true to Banbury's traditions, the driver expressed a particularly fierce dislike of Bishop Colenso.[25]

Society in mid-19th century Banbury was indivisible. In Victorian England, as in any other country or period, social vitality was reflected as much in cultural achievements as in economic developments or political wisdom. Banbury's rulers were not untypical of those who held authority in many towns, and they included some men of singularly narrow vision. Nevertheless they cannot be patronisingly dismissed as 'self-reliant and sensible men, good citizens in many respects, but Philistines'.[26] The cultural achievements of men like Edward Cobb, Bernhard Samuelson, William Potts, William Bigg, William Wilson and the working-class founders of the Co-operative Society were not negligible. They brought to their fellow citizens music of a high quality, a remarkable degree of knowledge of the natural sciences and of foreign countries, and an acquaintance with a wide range of literature through lectures, readings and libraries. This was a culture which has left few recognisable remains. It compares ill with that of the court of Louis XIV, or of Rembrandt's Amsterdam, but not with that of most 20th century English towns. It is possible to sense the vitality of the period in some reported speeches, like Edward Cobb's contribution to the debate on the Sabbath in 1849, and in some satirical election squibs. A society in which a reflection on the polling of Superintendent Thompson in 1859 could be a subtle parody of one of Hamlet's soliloquies, or an account of the town's politics between 1858 and 1866 could be written in 72 verses which sensitively reflect the rhythms of the Authorised Version, was not wholly Philistine.[27] How closely economic and cultural factors could interact in a market town was shown in Banbury's small neighbour, Brackley, when in 1856, after the establishment of a corn exchange and a regular monthly market, a dinner was held to celebrate the revival of the wool fair. The town's regeneration was much remarked upon, and was said to have originated with the formation of a Literary and Philosophical Society.[28] Debates, lectures and concerts were not the outcome of successful trading and manufacturing, they were part of the same vital society, the reverse of the same coin.

Nineteenth-century Banbury was shaped above all by its own history and by its sense of identity as a town. Its citizens felt themselves superior to countrymen, to the fawning deferentials of closed villages like Aynho and Thenford, to the squalid paupers who crowded into Moreton Pinkney or Middleton Cheney, and to dissolute aristocrats. This was a superiority reinforced by a vivid sense of the past. A Banburian wrote in 1833:

'Two centuries ago she was famed for her "Cakes, ale and zeal", and in not one of the three articles has she degenerated. Few men can inhabit her a week but must imbibe a portion of her zeal'.[29]

The mid-19th century was one of the most prosperous periods in Banbury's history, a period which is reflected in the main streets which are still lined by classically-proportioned shopkeepers' premises of the 1850s and '60s with their Bath stone dressings, and in such public buildings as Henry Tancred's town hall and Joseph Parker's Doric oratory. It was also a period of prosperity for the larger market towns in general, although some may retain more buildings of earlier periods of success, and some have had their Victorian character destroyed by 20th-century 'development'. Banbury provides many insights into market town societies in general because, paradoxically, it was both typical and exceptional. The economy, the religious structure, the forms of local government, the cultural pattern were similar to those which literary sources as well as other historical studies show to have been common elsewhere. Banbury was exceptional because the forces which provided the essential energy of market town communities were allowed to operate with so few constraints. While real power in Victorian England remained largely in the hands of the landed classes, Banbury was exceptional for a town dependent on agriculture in that for a certain time it was as free from aristocratic control as Manchester or Birmingham. The social class which ruled Banbury did not rule England, but within the town it retained power for 50 years. The innovative prowess of Banbury's tradesmen, the passions of its politicians, the zeal of its believers, the rationality of its sanitary reformers, the talents of its musicians and lecturers, were provided with an environment in which they could flourish. Many aspects of life in mid-Victorian Banbury, the number of carriers' carts, the number of patents taken out by local tradesmen, the intensity of religious controversies, the richness of the cultural pattern, have a sense of exaggeration about them. In some respects Banbury was a very exceptional place. There were few market towns of its size with similar attributes. But Manchester too was an exceptional place, so was Camberwell, so was Juniper Hill. By studying the athlete the physiologist comes to understand more of the workings of every human body. By examining Banbury, a good anatomical specimen of the genus market town, we gain some understanding of the whole species, and of Victorian England at large.

REFERENCES TO CHAPTERS

Chapter One

1. Mary Russell Mitford, 'Belford Regis, or Sketches of a Country Town', *Chambers's Edinburgh Review*, vol. 4 (1836), p. 170.
2. Alan Everitt, 'Town and Country in Victorian Leicestershire: the Role of the Country Carrier', in Alan Everitt, ed., *Perspectives in English Urban History* (1973), p. 216.
3. 'Cowfold', described in chapter XVI of Mark Rutherford, *The Revolution in Tanners Lane* (1887), pp. 230-50, is an example of this type of town.
4. Mark Rutherford, *Autobiography and Deliverance* (1969 ed.), pp. 26-27.
5. John Orr, *The Agriculture of Oxfordshire: a survey* (1916), p. 74.
6. John Vincent, *The Formation of the Liberal Party 1857-1868* (1966), p. 118.
7. Margaret Stacey, *Tradition and Change: a study of Banbury* (1960), p. 55.
8. *Ibid.*, pp. 11-20, for manifestations of this division in the present century.
9. G. Kitson Clark, *The Making of Victorian England* (1962), p. 126.
10. Mark Rutherford, *Autobiography and Deliverance* (1969 ed.), p. 211.
11. Elizabeth Gaskell, *Wives and Daughters* (1864-66).
12. Thomas Hardy, *The Mayor of Casterbridge* (1886).
13. George Eliot, *Scenes of Clerical Life* (1858), *The Mill on the Floss* (1860), *Silas Marner* (1861), *Felix Holt* (1866), *Middlemarch* (1871-72).
14. For a full discussion of Banbury's townships, *see* VCH, *Oxon.*, vol. 10, pp. 5, 18, 25-38, 51.
15. For a fuller discussion of sources *see* Barrie Trinder, 'Sources for the history of 19th century Banbury', *C & CH* (forthcoming). The Potts, Rusher and Walford collections are in Banbury Public Library. Messrs. Cheney & Sons, Calthorpe Street, Banbury, keep a volume of 'Specimens of Work'.
16. Collections of Rusher's *Lists and Directories* are in the Bodleian Library, Banbury Public Library, and the Oxfordshire Local Studies Library, Westgate, Oxford.
17. Information on newspapers is drawn from the British Museum Catalogue of Newspapers.
18. *BA* (3 July 1856); *BG* (20 Mar. 1856).
19. ORO, Stockton, Sons and Fortescue Collection, No. 315.
20. BPL, Political Correspondence (1832); the Correspondence of Henry William Tancred 1841-1859. The latter is reproduced in Barrie Trinder, *A Victorian MP and his Constituents* (1969).
21. For Beesley *see BG* (15 April 1847); *NH* (17 April 1847); Banbury Monthly Meeting Minutes 1824-32, 5 12 mo. 1825, ORO, B.M.M. 1/5; E. C. R. Brinkworth, 'Alfred Beesley's "History of Banbury" ', *C & CH*, vol. 2 (1962), p. 8.
22. George Herbert, *Shoemaker's Window* (1948, 1971, 1979); Regents Park College Library, Oxford, W. T. Henderson, *Recollections of His Life* (MS); T. W. Boss, *Reminiscences of Old Banbury* (1903); Sarah Beesley, *My Life* (1892); Anon. (Elizabeth Redford), *The Banbury Female Martyr* (n.d., *circa* 1863); Thomas Champness, ed., *A Memoir of Richard Edmunds of Banbury* (n.d., *circa* 1895).
23. Margaret Stacey, *Tradition and Change: a study of Banbury* (1960); *see also* Margaret Stacey, Eric Batstone, Colin Bell and Ann Murcott, *Power, Persistence and Change: a second study of Banbury* (1975); Audrey Taylor, *Gilletts: Bankers at Banbury and Oxford* (1964); Michael Mann, *Workers on the Move* (1973): Alan Crossley, ed., *The Victoria History of Oxfordshire*, vol. 10 (1972).

24. Flora Thompson, *Lark Rise to Candleford* (1939); Joseph Arch, *Joseph Arch: the Story of His Life* (1898); M. K. Ashby, *Joseph Ashby of Tysoe 1859-1919* (1961).
25. VCH *Oxon.* X, p. 6.
26. The deposition of Matthew Knight, 1604; PRO, St.Ch. 8/82/23, quoted in P. D. Harvey, 'Where was Banbury Cross?', *Oxoniensia*, vol. 31 (1966), pp. 101–106.
27. Margaret Stacey, *Tradition and Change*, pp. 8-9, VCH *Oxon.* X, pp. 68–69.

Chapter Two

1. William Mavor, *A Tour in Wales and through Several Counties of England . . . performed in the Summer of 1805* (1806), p. 162.
2. Martin Billing, *Directory and Gazetteer of Berkshire and Oxfordshire* (1854), p. 129.
3. The see of Dorchester was transferred to Lincoln in 1072.
4. George Herbert, *Shoemaker's Window* (1949), pp. 91, 97.
5. Kirsty Rodwell, ed., *Historic Towns in Oxfordshire* (1975), p. 53; M. D. Lobel, *Historic Towns*, vol. 1 (1969), p. 4.
6. G. Herbert, *op. cit.*, pp. 53, 74-75; *NH* (24 June 1843): VCH, *Oxon.* X, p. 21.
7. VCH, *Oxon.* X, p. 25.
8. VCH, *Oxon.* X, p. 5; Alfred Beesley, *The History of Banbury* (1841), p. 561, says 105 acres; T. W. Rammell, *Report on a Preliminary Inquiry into the Sewerage, Drainage and Supply of Water and the Sanitary Condition of the Inhabitants of Banbury and Neithrop* (1850), p. 7, says 300 acres but is clearly mistaken.
9. *Report of the Commissioners on the Proposed Divisions of Counties and Boundaries of Boroughs*, BPP, 1832 XI, p. 189.
10. Bod. Lib. Tithe Map 30, Parish of Banbury 1852; VCH, *Oxon.* X, pp. 21-23; the best representation of the boundary on a modern map is in M. D. Lobel, *op. cit.*, p. 14.
11. William Potts, *A History of Banbury* (1958), p. 238, *BA* (11 Nov. 1858).
12. *See* Table Two.
13. ORO, BB LV/1, Chief Rent Book for the Borough of Banbury, Lady Day 1831; VCH, *Oxon.* X, pp. 52-54.
14. *See* Table Nine; G. Herbert, *op. cit.*, p. 64.
15. *BG* (6 Jan. 1859): *OH* (23 Dec. 1837).
16. *NH* (11 Mar. 1843).
17. ORO, BB/XX/i/2b, Miscellaneous papers re Sanitation.
18. *JOJ* (17 May 1834): *NH* (19 Nov. 1836); *BG* (22 Aug. 1844; 21 May 1846; 4 June 1846).
19. *NH* (2 Feb. 1850).
20. G. Herbert, *op. cit.*, pp. 43, 49, 58, 84, 102; VCH, *Oxon.* X, p. 47.
21. G. Herbert, *op. cit.*, pp. 39, 42-46, 49.
22. Rusher's *Banbury Lists and Directories*; G. Herbert, *op. cit.*, pp. 45-46.
23. VCH, *Oxon.* X, p. 34; G. Herbert, *op. cit.*, pp. 46, 52.
24. G. Herbert, *op. cit.*, pp. 46, 50, 54-55, 59, 66, 76; VCH, *Oxon.* X, pp. 69-70; 'A Map of Banbury, 1838', *C & CH*, vol. 2 (1964), pp. 143-46.
25. VCH, *Oxon.* X, pp. 36-37.
26. *OC & CC* (23 May 1840).
27. G. Herbert, *op. cit.*, p. 45; VCH, *Oxon.* X, p. 37.
28. Audrey Taylor, *Gilletts: Bankers at Banbury and Oxford* (1964), p. 97.
29. Barrie Trinder, *Banbury's Poor in 1850* (1966), pp. 87-90, 100-103.
30. Bod. Lib., MS. D. D. Par. Banbury a.5 (R), List of Streets in Banbury and Neithrop providing a key to William Wilson's Visiting Plans, 1850.

31. ORO BL/IX/i/2, deed No. B98, 1844; BPL, RC, p. 104; PRO, HO 107, 1851 Census enumerators' returns; Rusher's *Banbury Lists and Directories*.

32. *BG* (15 May 1847).

33. PRO, HO 107, 1851 Census enumerators' returns.

34. T. W. Rammell, *op. cit.*, p. 26.

35. VCH, *Oxon.* X, pp. 29-33.;

36. G. Herbert, *op. cit.*, pp. 58, 68, 86, 94; A. Beesley, *op. cit.*, p. 553.

37. G. Herbert, *op. cit.*, pp. 42-43, 59, 61, 90-91, 97, 106-107; ORO 315, Box 71, Bundle E.

38. ORO, BB/III/i/2, BPLC Mins.; 6 Geo. IV, cap. 130.

39. B. K. Lucas, 'Banbury: Trees or Trade', *C & CH*, vol. 7 (1979), pp. 270-72; G. Herbert, *op. cit.*, pp. 54, 63, 73-74, 86; ORO, BB/III/i/2, BPLC Mins.

40. ORO, BB/III/i/2, BPLC Mins.; for the political context of these changes see below pp. 52-53.

41. ORO, BB/III/i/2, BPLC Mins.; ORO, BB/XX/i/1, Sanitary Inspector's Report; A. Beesley, *op. cit.*, p. 553.

42. ORO, BB/V/ii/1, Minutes of Banbury Watch Committee 1836-66; Bod. Lib., Oxon. 8vo., 637 (18), *Instructions for the Police Force of the Borough of Banbury* (1836); NH (25 Nov. 1837).

43. G. Herbert, *op. cit.*, p. 105; G. C. J. Hartland, 'Gas-Making in Banbury', *C & CH* vol. 4 (1969), pp. 47-53; *OH* (9 Nov. 1833; 22 Mar. 1834).

44. T. W. Rammell, *op. cit.*, pp. 14-17; Bod. Lib., Banbury Parish Registers; Sarah Beesley, *My Life* (1892), p. 32; T. W. Boss, *Reminiscences of Old Banbury* (1903), p. 9.

45. BPL, RC p. 9.

46. *BG* (17 Feb. 1848).

47. William Potts, *Banbury through One Hundred Years* (1942), p. 26; R. A. Lewis, *Edwin Chadwick and the Public Health Movement 1832-54* (1952), pp. 170-71.

48. *BG* (31 May 1849).

49. T. W. Rammell, *op. cit.*, pp. 17-18, 24-25, 32.

50. *Ibid.*, pp. 3, 11-12, 17-18, 32.

51. PRO, MH 12/139, Edward Gulson – Poor Law Commissioners, 31 Jan. 1835.

52. T. W. Rammell, *op. cit.*, pp. 17, 26.

53. *Ibid.*, p. 6.

Chapter Three

1. I. and P. Opie, *The Oxford Dictionary of English Nursery Rhymes* (1951), p. 65.

2. Alfred Beesley, *The History of Banbury* (1841), p. 559.

3. Alan Everitt, 'The Marketing of Agricultural Produce', in Joan Thirsk, ed., *The Agricultural History of England and Wales*, vol. 14, (1967), pp. 474-75; Alan Everitt, 'Town and Country in Victorian Leicestershire: the Role of the Country Carrier', in Alan Everitt, ed., *Perspectives in English Urban History* (1973), p. 216.

4. *BG* (6 July 1843).

5. PRO, MH 12/9577, Edward Gulson – Poor Law Commission, 9 March 1835.

6. For details of carriers' routes *see* Rusher's *Banbury Lists and Directories*.

7. Mary Marshall, *The Land of Britain: The Report of the Land Utilisation Survey of Britain*, pt. 56, Oxfordshire (1943), pp. 199, 203-205.

8. Arthur Young, *A General View of the Agriculture of Oxfordshire* (1813), pp. 4-5.

9. A. Young, *op. cit.*, pp. 35, 86, 106, 180-81, 269, 211-12; Clare Sewell Read, 'On the Agriculture of Oxfordshire', *JRASE*, vol. 15 (1854), pp. 189, 248.

10. A. Beesley, *op. cit.*, p. 552.

11. *Political Register* (11 Dec. 1830); *Report of the Assistant Commissioner on Hand-Loom Weavers*, BPP, 1840 XXIV, pp. 333–36.

12. William Cobbett, *Rural Rides* (ed. 1957), vol. 1, p. 248.

13. R. P. Beckinsale, 'The Plush Industry of North Oxfordshire', *Oxoniensia*, vol. 18 (1963), p. 58; Audrey Taylor, *Gilletts: Bankers at Banbury and Oxford* (1964), pp. 84–94.

14. William Felkins, *The History of the Machine-Wrought Hosiery and Lace Manufactures* (ed. 1967), p. 467; A. Beesley, *op. cit.*, p. 570; A Taylor, *op. cit.*, pp. 84, 87; George Herbert, *Shoemaker's Window* (1949), p. 123; PRO, MH 12/139, Edward Gulson — Poor Law Commission, 5 March 1835.

15. Thomas Mozley, *Reminiscences: chiefly of Towns, Villages and Schools* (1885), vol. 2, pp. 223–24; Flora Thompson, *Lark Rise to Candleford* (ed. 1957), pp. 78–79; George Herbert, *op. cit.*, pp. 122–23.

16. For Poor Law Administration in the district *see* VCH, *Oxon.* IX, pp. 23–24. 47, 65, 92, 107, 116–17, 128–29, 143, 153, 163, 179; VCH, *Oxon.* X, pp. 168, 191, 203, 246–48; for the roundsman system *see* G. Herbert, *op. cit.*, p. 48; J. D. Marshall, *The Old Poor Law 1754–1834* (1968), pp. 13–14.

17. E. J. Hobsbawm and George Rudé, *Captain Swing* (ed. 1973), pp. 112–13, 118, 136, 185–86, 303–304, 311–12; P. R. L. Horn, 'Banbury and the Riots of 1830', *C & CH* vol. 3 (1967), pp. 176–79; *JOJ* (11 Dec. 1830).

18. PRO, MH 12/9577, Edward Gulson — Poor Law Commission, 9 Mar. 1835.

19. *NH* (18 April 1845; 28 Nov. 1846; 5 Dec. 1846; 26 Dec. 1846).

20. M. K. Ashby, *Joseph Ashby of Tysoe* 1961), pp. 56, 150–51.

21. *NH* (28 April 1832; 4 May 1833; 11 May 1833), PRO, MH 12/9577, Weston & Moore — Poor Law Commission, 19 Jan. 1835.

22. T. Mozley, *op. cit.*, vol. 2, pp. 200–13, 223; *NH* (3 Aug. 1844, 27 Jan. 1849).

23. PRO, MH 12/8671, Richard Earl — Poor Law Commission, 5 May 1835.

24. *NH* (7 Jan. 1832; 11 Jan. 1834).

25. T. Mozley, *op. cit.*, vol. 2, pp. 281–82; *NH* (5 Jan. 1833, 12 Jan. 1833: 13 Jan. 1838); *BG* (14 Sept. 1876); *OH* (18 Aug. 1838); PRO, MH 12/8671, Richard Earl — Poor Law Commission, 5 May 1835.

26. *See* Map Four.

27. *BG* (17 April 1845); T. W. Boss, *Reminiscences of Old Banbury* (1903), p. 8.

28. *Report of Commissioners, Railway Gauges, Oxford, Worcester & Wolverhampton and Oxford & Rugby Railway Bills*, BPP, 1845 XI, pp. 208–209.

29. *Rusher's Banbury Lists and Directories*; T. W. Boss, *op. cit.*, p. 4.

30. *Rusher's Banbury Lists and Directories*.

31. John Drinkwater, *Inheritance, being the first book of an Autobiography* (1931), pp. 99–116; *Rusher's Banbury Lists and Directories*.

32. *Rusher's Banbury Lists and Directories*; Martin Billing, *Directory and Gazetteer of the Counties of Berkshire and Oxfordshire* (1854), p. 129.

33. Samuel Bagshaw, *History, Directory and Gazetteer of Derbyshire* (1846); H. Whellan, *History, Gazetteer and Directory of Northamptonshire* (1849); A. Everitt, 'Town and Country in Victorian Leicestershire', *op. cit.*, pp. 222–25, 232. *See also* Table One.

34. *BG* (8 July 1847).

35. PRO, MH 12/9577, Daniel Stuart — Poor Law Commission, 29 Dec. 1835.

36. *Rusher's Banbury Lists and Directories*.

37. *Rusher's Banbury Lists and Directories*.

38. *OC & CC* (14 Oct. 1837; 20 Jan. 1838; 21 April 1838); *NH* 6 Jan. 1838; 21 Jan. 1838; 24 Mar. 1838); *JOJ* (20 Jan. 1838; 16 June 1838): *BG* (28 Mar. 1844).

39. ORO, PD2/8; BPL, RC, p. 3.

40. *OH* (14 April 1838).

41. *NH* (14 April 1838); *JOJ* (14 April 1838; 6 Oct. 1838; 27 Oct. 1838); *OH* (19 May 1838); BPL, RC p. 139.

42. *NH* (1 June 1838; 15 June 1838; 18 Apr. 1840); E. T. McDermott, *The History of the Great Western Railway* (ed. 1964), vol. 1, pp. 53, 87; Rex Christiansen, *A Regional History of the Railways of Great Britain, vol. 7, The West Midlands* (1973), pp. 267–68.

43. Rusher's *Banbury Lists and Directories*.
44. A. Beesley, *op. cit.*, p. 559; Charles Hadfield, *The Canals of the East Midlands* (1966), pp. 17, 21, 25, 157; Hugh Compton, *The Oxford Canal* (1976), *passim*; Rusher's *Banbury Lists and Directories*.
45. H. Compton, *op. cit.*, pp. 106–107; Lords Select Committee to inquire into the expediency of restricting the practice of carrying goods and merchandise on Canals, Navigable Rivers and Railways on Sundays, May 1841, *House of Lords Journal* (1841) Appendix Two: *Reports from Commissioners, Railway Gauges*, BPP, 1845 XI, p. 79.
46. PRO, HO 107, 1851 Census enumerators' returns. *See also* pp. 9–10.
47. *Reports from Commissioners, Railway Gauges*, BPP, 1856 XI, pp. 62, 66, 70, 79, 392–93; C. S. Read, *op. cit.*, pp. 189–90; G. Herbert, *op. cit.*, pp. 18, 49, 69; T. W. Boss, *op. cit.*, pp. 4, 8; K. Bonser, *The Drovers* (1970), p. 194; J. Steane, *The Northamptonshire Landscape* (1974), pp. 247–49.
48. *See* Table Nine.
49. A. Taylor, *op. cit.*, p. 26.
50. R. S. Sayers, *Lloyds Bank in the History of English Banking* (1957), p. 281.
51. A. Taylor, *op. cit.*, pp. 1-15, 24-36, 38–41.
52. Dr. Williams's Library, 'Some Traditions and Historical Recollections relating to the Old Presbyterian Meeting House at Banbury by Edward Cobb' (1888), pp. 3-6.
53. J. S. W. Gibson, *Baptism and Burial Register of Banbury, Oxfordshire, pt. 2, 1653–1723* (1969).
54. Biographical details which follow are taken from the Banbury Parish Registers, Rusher's *Banbury Lists and Directories*: PRO, HO 873 1841 Census, HO 107, 1851 Census; *BG* (12 July 1860).
55. *BG* (6 Jan. 1859).
56. Regents Park College Library, Oxford, W. T. Henderson, 'Recollections of his Life'.
57. PRO, HO 107 1851 Census.
58. PRO, HO 873, 1841 Census, HO 107, 1851 Census; G. Herbert, *op. cit.*, pp. 21–23.
59. Figures from PRO, HO 873, 1841 Census, HO 107, 1851 Census. *See* Table Nine.
60. *BA* (22 Jan. 1857).
61. *BG* (25 Sep. 1845).
62. G. Herbert, *op. cit.*, p. 20.
63. Elizabeth Gaskell, *Wives and Daughters* (ed. 1971), p. 144.
64. Mark Rutherford, *Autobiography* (ed. 1969), pp. 26–27.
65. *BCR* (Feb. 1874).
66. John Vincent, *The Formation of the Liberal Party 1857-1868* (1966), pp. 100–105.
67. G. Herbert, *op. cit.*, p. 20.
68. *Ibid.*, p. 20.
69. *Taunton Courier* quoted in *BG* (30 Dec. 1847).
70. BPL, Banbury Board of Guardians Minutes 1835-36.
71. Rusher's *Banbury Lists and Directories*: PRO, HO 107, 1851 Census.
72. *BG* (13 Jan. 1848).
73. Rusher's *Banbury Lists and Directories*: PRO, HO 107, 1851 Census.
74. *BG* (15 April 1847), *OC & CC* (31 July 1841).
75. *BG* (12 Oct. 1854).
76. Rusher's *Banbury's Lists and Directories*; PRO, HO 107, 1851 Census; A. Taylor, *op. cit.*, pp. 44, 184; *BG* (22 Feb. 1849): ORO, BMM/I/5, Minutes of the Banbury Monthly Meeting of the Society of Friends, 1824-32.
77. *BG* (27 June 1850).
78. G. Herbert, *op. cit.*, p. 99, *NH* (1 Mar. 1834).
79. *BG* (27 July 1847; 11 Sep. 1879); *BA* (11 Sep. 1879).
80. *BG* (22 May 1851).
81. I. and P. Opie, *The Oxford Dictionary of English Nursery Rhymes* (1951), p. 65: E. Pearson, *Banbury Chap Books* (1890), pp. 24–25.
82. *OH* (13 Jan. 1838); *BG* (13 Mar. 1851).

83. J. S. W. Gibson, *op. cit., passim.*
84. Sir F. M. Eden, *The State of the Poor* (ed. 1938), pp. 279–80.
85. R. P. Beckinsale, 'The Plush Industry of North Oxfordshire', *Oxoniensia*, vol. 28 (1963), p. 57; P. R. L. Horn, 'The New Society of Plush Weavers: Articles, Rules and Orders, 1822', *C & CH* vol. 3 (1968), pp. 199–202; A. Aspinall, *The Early English Trade Unions* (1949), p. 19.
86. *Report of the Assistant Commission on Hand-Loom Weavers*, BPP, 1840 XXIV, pp. 333–36; A. Taylor, *op. cit.*, pp. 85–86.
87. P. R. L. Horn, 'The Banbury Weavers' Union of 1834', *C & CH*, vol. 3 (1968), pp. 203–206; *Report of the Assistant Commissioner on Hand-Loom Weavers*, BPP, 1840, XXIV, pp. 333–36; A. Taylor, *op. cit.*, pp. 79–80; R. P. Beckinsale, *op. cit.*, pp. 58–62.
88. A. Taylor, *op. cit.*, pp. 89–90.
89. PRO, HO 107, 1851 Census; Vera Hodgkins, 'The Plush Industry in Shutford', *C & CH* vol. 6, (1975), pp. 59–75; Barrie Trinder, *Banbury's Poor in 1850* (1966), pp. 110–111; A. Taylor, *op. cit.*, p. 95, R. P. Beckinsale, *op. cit.*, p. 64.
90. G. Herbert, *op. cit.*, pp. 3–5.
91. B. Trinder, *Banbury's Poor*, pp. 110–111.
92. *Report of the Assistant Commissioner on Hand-Loom Weavers*, BPP, 1840, XXIV, pp. 333–36; PRO, HO 873, 1841 Census, HO 107, 1851 Census.
93. BPL, *Banbury Cuttings 1838–42*, p. 87; *OH* (16 June 1939).
94. ORO 315, Samuelson Deeds, lease 24 Aug. 1849, A. B. Rye and Benjamin Gardner to Bernhard Samuelson, Schedule of deeds made over to Bernhard Samuelson on his purchase of the foundry from the Trustees under the will of James Gardner 1856; *NH* (5 Jan. 1839); *JRASE* vol. 6 (1845), pp. 303–23; *BG* (12 Oct. 1848; 13 Sep. 1849; 21 Nov. 1850).
95. *NH* (4 Sept. 1847); G. C. J. Hartland, 'The Vulcan Foundry, Banbury', *C & CH* vol. 3 (1968), pp. 223, 228–29; Banbury Museum, Lampitt trade notices.
96. B. Trinder, *Banbury's Poor*, pp. 111–112.
97. *BG* (21 Jan. 1847; 12 Oct. 1849; 13 Sep. 1849; 27 Sep. 1849; 18 Nov. 1858): ORO 315, Samuelson Deeds, lease 24 Aug. 1849, A. B. Rye and Benjamin Gardner to Bernhard Samuelson; *NH* (31 Mar. 1849); *Journal of the Iron and Steel Institute*, vol. 1 (1905), pp. 504–507.
98. ORO 315, Austin Papers, Temp. Box 10, Bundles F, G, H, I, K, L, M, N, O, P; ORO, BB/LIV/-11/1, Mr. Humphries's First Rate 1832; G. Herbert, *op. cit.*, p. 111; PRO, HO 107, 1851 Census.
99. Anon., *Hunt Edmunds & Co. 1896–1946*, pp. 2–5; *OC & CC* (14 Sep. 1839).
100. PRO, HO 107, 1851 Census; B. Trinder, *Banbury's Poor*, pp. 108–110.
101. Flora Thompson, *Lark Rise to Candleford* (ed. 1957), pp. 120–35.
102. PRO, HO 873, 1841 Census, HO 107, 1851 Census; G. Herbert, *op. cit.*, pp. 91–92.
103. A. Beesley, *The History of Banbury* (1841), p. 560.
104. Bod. Lib., Banbury Parish Register, 1827; *OC & CC* (6 May, 1837), *JOJ* (10 May 1834).
105. *BG* (24 Jan. 1850).
106. M. K. Ashby, *Joseph Ashby of Tysoe* (1961), p. 37.
107. A. Beesley. *op. cit.*, p. 560; *BG* (22 Oct. 1846).
108. M. K. Ashby, *op. cit.*, p. 37; *BG* (21 Oct. 1847; 19 Oct. 1848).
109. T. W. Boss, *op. cit.*, pp. 2–4.
110. *BG* (21 Oct. 1847).
111. *NH* (20 Jan. 1838); *OC & CC* (20 Jan. 1838); Asa Briggs, *Victorian Cities* (ed. 1968), pp. 88–138.

Chapter Four

1. Mark Rutherford, *Catherine Furze* (ed. 1936), p. 69.
2. *John Bull* (9 May 1831), quoted in *Diana McClatchey, Oxfordshire Clergy 1777-1869* (1960), p. 211; *OC & CC* (29 July 1837).

3. *OC & CC* (14 Aug. 1841); *OH* (29 Jan. 1842).

4. PRO, HO 129/6/163, Census Papers, Ecclesiastical Returns, Banbury, 1851.

5. W. S. F. Pickering, 'The 1851 Religious Census — a useless experiment?', *British Journal of Sociology*, vol. 18 (1967), pp. 382–407.

6. K. S. Inglis, 'The 1851 Religious Census', *Journal of Ecclesiastical History*, vol. 11 (1960), p. 74, *et seq.*

7. Nicholas Cooper, 'The Building and Furnish of St Mary's Church', *C & CH* vol. 5 (1972), p. 63. This article draws principally upon the MS Order Book kept by the Trustees (Bod. Lib. MSS. D. D. Par. Banbury, c. 6), and on the highly partial account in Alfred Beesley, *The History of Banbury* (1841), pp. 532–38, 553–56.

8. 30 Geo. III, c. 72.

9. N. Cooper, *op. cit.*, pp. 65–69.

10. *Ibid.*, pp. 69–72, 77–78.

11. *Ibid.*, pp. 67–69; BPL, PC vol. 7, p. 51; Sarah Beesley, *My Life* (1892), p. 41.

12. E. R. C. Brinkworth, 'A Nineteenth Century Vicar of Banbury: Thomas William Lancaster', *C & CH* vol. 2 (1962), pp. 57–60: *OC & CC* (25 April 1840); *Oxford Chronicle & Reading Gazette* (30 June 1849).

13. George Herbert, *Shoemaker's Window* (1949), p. 40; S. Beesley, *op. cit.*, p. 19; G. V. Cox, *Recollections of Oxford* (1868), p. 271; Shrewsbury Schools Library, Letters of Dr. Edward Burton, vol. 1, 174.

14. *BA* (3 Feb. 1881); *NH* (20 July 1839; 3 Aug. 1839; 11 July 1840).

15. *OH* (9 Aug. 1834; 27 Sep. 1834; 24, Nov. 1838): *JOJ* (24 Nov. 1838); *NH* (4 Apr. 1840).

16. *OC & CC* (23 Mar. 1840); *NH* (5 Aug. 1843).

17. BPL, RC pp. 177–78, 211, 221; *NH* (22 Jan. 1842; 3 Sep. 1842); N. Cooper, *op. cit.*, p. 72; *OH* (26 Dec. 1835).

18. *NH* (15 Aug. 1840; 30 Oct. 1841).

19. ORO, BMM I/5, Minutes of the Monthly Meeting of the Banbury Society of Friends, 1824–32, 5 Dec. 1825.

20. A. Beesley, *op. cit.*, p. 555.

21. Alfred Beesley, *Japheth, Contemplation and Other Pieces* (1834), p. vi.

22. Barrie Trinder, *Banbury's Poor in 1850* (1966), p. 116.

23. Bod. Lib. MS Ox. Dioc. b. 39.

24. 1851 Ecclesiastical Census. *See* Table Five.

25. E. P. Baker, ed., *Bishop Wilberforce's Visitation Returns for the Archdeaconry of Oxford, 1854* (1954), pp. 12–13.

26. *NH* (21 Mar. 1840); BPL, RC pp. 124, 157, 203, 217, 241–42, 247, 250; *BG* (16 Oct. 1845).

27. *JOJ* (15 Dec. 1838).

28. Bod. Lib. Oxon. 8vo, 637 (16).

29. *BG* (2 Jan. 1840); Bod. Lib. Oxon. 8vo, 637 (20).

30. Bod. Lib. Dep. d. 209, pp. 70–71, Samuel Wilberforce–Charles Forbes, 11 July 1850.

31. *BG* (28 June 1849); *Oxford Chronicle & Reading Gazette* (30 June 1849); *JOJ* (30 June 1849); *OH* (30 June 1849).

32. Amherst D. Tyssen, 'The Old Meeting House, Banbury', *Transactions of the Unitarian Historical Society*, vol. 1 (1919), pp. 274–82, 228–90; VCH, *Oxon.* X, pp. 112–113; *Christian Reformer* (1854), pp. 459–62.

33. A. D. Tyssen, *op. cit.*, pp. 290–91.

34. *Ibid.*, p. 290; *The Inquirer* (30 Jan. 1864).

35. *See* Table Five.

36. *BA* (2 July 1863).

37. VCH, *Oxon.* X, pp. 109–110.

38. ORO, BMM I/1, Minutes of the Banbury Monthly Meeting, 5 April, 1756.

39. Quoted in Elizabeth Isichei, *Victorian Quakers* (1970), pp. 178–79.

40. ORO, BMM I/6, Minutes of the Banbury Monthly Meeting 1833–45, 5 Feb. 1840.

41. E. Isichei, *op. cit.*, pp. 8–10.

42, *Ibid.*, p. 217.

43. Samuel Beesley, *Memoranda of Visits to the Borough Prison* MS *penes* D. G. W. Brown of Sunderland.

44. ORO, BMM.I/7, Minutes of the Banbury Monthly Meeting, 1845-55, 1 April 1846, 1 Aug. 1849; (A.Ll.B.Thomas), *J. Bevan Braithwaite: a Friend of the Nineteenth Century* (1909), pp. 122-23.

45. *See* Table Five.

46. VCH, *Oxon.* X, p. 117; Barrie Trinder, *The History of Methodism in Banbury* (1965), pp. 7-8.

47. *Monthly Repository* (1823), quoted in A. D. Tyssen, *op. cit.*, p. 285; B. Trinder, *History of Methodism in Banbury*, pp. 11-12; Bod. Lib. C 644.126; Marlborough Road Methodist Church, Banbury, Banbury Wesleyan Church Trust Minutes, 1813-14, Trust Accounts 1812-15, Trust Accounts 1819-49.

48. *Methodist Magazine* (1821), p. 380: Thomas Champness, ed., *A Memorial of Richard Edmunds of Banbury* (n.d., *circa* 1895), pp. 12-13, 26-27.

49. Wesleyan Methodist Church, Grimsbury, *Jubilee Souvenir*, 1871-1921 (1921), p. 3; Northamptonshire Record Office, A Register of Meeting House Certificates 1813-52.

50. Figures from *Minutes of the Methodist Conference*.

51. T. Champness, *op. cit.*, pp. 8-9.

52. Barrie Trinder, *Banbury's Poor in 1850* (1966), pp. 112-19.

53. John Petty, *A History of the Primitive Methodist Connexion* (1864), pp. 319-20; *BG* (24 Apr. 1873).

54. *Primitive Methodist Magazine* (1848), pp. 245-57; *ibid.* (1849), p. 243; *ibid.* (1851), p. 238.

55. *See* Table Five.

56. Rusher's *Banbury Lists and Directories*; *BA* (2 Feb. 1882); Marlborough Road Methodist Church, Banbury, Baptisms in the Welton (and later Banbury), Circuit of the Primitive Methodist Connexion on 1824 *et seq.*

57. PRO, RG 4, 2919, 9440, Baptismal Registers; Banbury United Reformed Church, Minutes of the Banbury Congregational Church 1868-79, copy of 'History of the Church up to his Knowledge by the Revd. Ingram Cobbin'.

58. *Evangelical Magazine* (1813), pp. 430-31; Bod. Lib. C 644.152.

59. Banbury United Reformed Church, Church Book for Banbury Independent Society, 1794 *et seq.*

60. *Evangelical Magazine* (1818), p. 399.

61. *BG* (19 Oct. 1876); VCH, *Oxon.* IX, pp. 40-41.

62. Bod. Lib. C 645.228; ORO 315, Austin Family Deeds, bundle I; *OH* (29 Mar. 1834).

63. *Baptist Magazine* (1841), pp. 127, 456, 642; Bod. Lib. C 646.115, 185; Banbury Baptist Church, Deed of Bridge Street Baptist Church, 6 April 1841; John Taylor, *The History of College Street Church, Northampton* (1897), p. 92.

64. James Cadbury, *A Tribute of Affection to the Memory of the late Caleb Clarke of Banbury* (1851): Regents Park College Library, Oxford, W. T. Henderson, *Recollections of his Life*; *BG* (27 Feb. 1851); Bod. Lib. C 647.40; BPL, PC vol. 6, p. 90.

65. *The Christian Messenger*, new series, vol. 3 (1846), pp. 570-72.

66. *See* Table Five.

67. *See* Table Six.

68. A. G. Wall, *St John's Church, Banbury* (1938), pp. 11-13; *OH* (10 Aug. 1833: 19 Dec. 1835).

69. A. G. Wall, *op. cit.*, p. 19; *BG* (7 June 1838); *OC & CC* (23 June 1838); *OH* (23 June 1838).

70. A. G. Wall, *op. cit.*, p. 18; Joseph Gillow, *A Biographical Dictionary of the English Catholics* (n.d.), vol. 5, p. 537.

71. *OH* (23 June 1838); George Harris, *The Spirit of Popery* (1838), Bod. Lib. Oxon. 8vo. (4).

72. *OC & CC* (10 Nov. 1838), *OH* (6 Oct. 1838; 27 Oct. 1838; 3 Nov. 1838; 10 Nov. 1838; 1 Dec. 1838; 8 Dec. 1838).

73. BPL, *Banbury Cuttings 1838-42*, p. 52.

74. 1851 Ecclesiastical Census, *see* Table Five.

75. A. G. Wall, *op. cit.*, pp. 19-22.

76. Catholics can be identified from Church Registers, and from A. G. Wall, *op. cit.*, p. 22.

77. BPL. RD pp. 34, 146; *OC & CC* (23 Mar. 1839; 6 Apr. 1839); BPL, *Banbury Cuttings 1832-42*, pp. 7-8; *NH* (20 Apr. 1839).
78. C. Silvester Horne, *A Popular History of the Free Churches* (1903), p. 403: H. S. Skeats and C. S. Miall, *A History of the Free Churches in England 1688-1891* (1891), p. 486.
79. BPL. *Banbury Cuttings 1838-42*, pp. 62, 72, 90–91; *NH* (25 Apr. 1840).
80. *OC & CC* (3 Apr. 1841; 24 Apr. 1841; 6 Aug. 1842); *NH* (24 Apr. 1841; 27 Apr. 1844); *Northampton Mercury* (1 May 1841).

Chapter Five

1. *NH* (19 Nov. 1831).
2. *OH* (4 Jan. 1833; 7 Dec. 1833).
3. Alfred Beesley, *The History of Banbury* (1841), pp. 539–40; William Potts, *A History of Banbury* (1958), p. 204; VCH, *Oxon.* X, p. 90.
4. *JOJ* (7 Aug. 1830).
5. *JOJ* (7 May 1831); *BG* (14 Dec. 1865).
6. A. Beesley, *op. cit.*, p. 545; Sarah Beesley, *My Life* (1892), p. 37; *JOJ* (30 Apr. 1831; 7 May 1831, 14 May 1831; 21 May 1831): *BG* (11 June 1891).
7. BPL, *Banbury Cuttings 1838-42*, pp. 128–30; PC vol. 2, p. 53.
8. *OH* (7 May 1831).
9. BPL, PC vol. 1, p. 6.
10. *Ibid.*, p. 72.
11. Pamela Horn, 'Banbury and the Riots of 1831', *C & CH* vol. 3 (1967), pp. 176–77.
12. BPL, Hurst Collection, p. 139.
13. BPL, PC vol. 1, p. 12.
14. BPL, PC vol. 5, p. 19.
15. BPL, PC vol. 1, p. 10.
16. BPL, Case V, f. 28a.
17. Sarah Beesley, *op. cit.*, p. 37.
18. *JOJ* (17 Sep. 1831; 22 Oct. 1831; 12 Nov. 1831; 3 Dec. 1831); *OH* (9 Sep. 1831; 22 Oct. 1831; 5 Nov. 1831; 21 Jan. 1832).
19. *OH* (26 May 1832; 12 Feb. 1842); *OC & CC* (12 Feb. 1842); BPL, *Banbury Cuttings 1838-42*, pp. 127–30.
20. George Herbert, *Shoemaker's Window* (1949), facing p. 116.
21. BPL. Pol. Corres. (1832), 2, W. Spurrett's Instructions to J. Munton & T. R. Cobb, 9 June 1832; *ibid.*, 3, T. R. Cobb – W. Spurrett, 10 June 1832; *OH* (16 June 1832); BPL, PC vol. 2, pp. 8, 96.
22. BPL, PC vol. 2, p. 4.
23. BPL, Pol. Corres. (1832), 2, W. Spurrett's Instructions to J. Munton & T. R. Cobb, 9 June 1832.
24. *Ibid.*, 29, T. R. Cobb – W. Spurrett, 16 June 1832; *ibid.*, 21, T. R. Cobb – W. Spurrett, 15 June 1832.
25. BPL, OC vol. 2, pp. 8, 11, 58; BPL, Pol. Corres. (1832), 5, Lyne Spurrett – T. R. Cobb, 11 June 1832.
26. BPL, Pol. Corres. (1832), 18, W. Spurrett – T. R. Cobb, 14 June 1832; *ibid.*, 28, W. Spurrett – T. R. Cobb, 16 June 1832; *ibid.*, 31, Joseph Parkes – T. R. Cobb, 17 June 1832; *ibid.*, 36 T. R. Cobb – W. Spurrett, 18 June 1832: H. W. Tancred, *A Legal Review of the origin of the System of Representation in England, and of its present state, with observations on the Reform Necessary* (1831); for Parkes *see* N. Gash, *Politics in the Age of Peel* (1953), p. 418 *et seq.*

27. ORO 315, Box 13, BRA Mins.; BPL. Pol. Corres. (1832), 34, W. Spurrett — T. R. Cobb, 18 June 1832: *ibid.*, 37, W. Spurrett — T. R. Cobb, 18 June 1832; *OH* (30 June 1832).

28. BPL, Pol. Corres. (1832), 26, T. R. Cobb — Lord Althorpe, 15 June 1832.

29. ORO 315, Box 13, BRA Mins., 22 June, 16 July 1832.

30. *Ibid.*, 15 Aug. 1832; *NH* (25 Aug. 1832); BPL, PC vol. 2, pp. 71-83.

31. BPL, PC vol. 2, pp. 5, 15, 22, 45, 61, 116; BPL, Pol. Corres. (1832), 14, W. Spurrett — T. R. Cobb, 13 June 1832.

32. BPL, PC vol. 2, p. 107.

33. *Ibid.*, p. 15.

34. *Ibid.*, pp. 1, 6, 13, 64-65, 82, 93.

35. *Ibid.*, pp. 15, 37-38, 48, 50-51.

36. *Ibid.*, pp. 47, 65, 86.

37. *Ibid.*, pp. 48, 60.

38. *Ibid.*, pp. 90, 96, 107.

39. *Ibid.*, pp. 42, 57, 107.

40. *Ibid.*, p. 15.

41. *Ibid.*, p. 87.

42. *Ibid.*, p. 111.

43. *NH* (9 Mar. 1833); *OC & CC* (5 Sep. 1842).

44. ORO 315, Box 13, BRA Mins., 10 Dec. 1832; BPL, PC vol. 2, p. 125.

45. *NH* (9 Mar. 1833; 20 Apr. 1833); *OH* (9 Mar. 1833; 20 Apr. 1833).

46. *NH* (12 Apr. 1834; 23 Aug. 1834); *OH* (20 April 1833).

47. BPL, Minutes of Banbury Board of Guardians, 1835-36, *passim*; PRO, MH 12/9577, Edward Gulson — Poor Law Commission, 9 Mar. 1835.

48. *NH* (11 Apr. 1835).

49. *NH* (26 Dec. 1835); PRO, MH 12/9577, *passim*.

50. Alfred Beesley, *op. cit.*, pp. 546-48; *OH* (2 Feb. 1833; 26 Oct. 1833, 9 Nov. 1833); *NH* (15 Aug. 1835).

51. A. Beesley, *op. cit.*, p. 548; BPL, RC p. 26.

52. *NH* (2 Jan. 1836); *OH* (26 Dec. 1835; 2 Jan. 1836).

53. *OC & CC* (9 Nov. 1839); *NH* (9 Nov. 1839; 6 Nov. 1841); *JOJ* (5 Nov. 1842); BPL, RC pp. 200, 202.

54. *BG* (18 Nov. 1847; 2 Nov. 1848); BPL, RC p. 252, PC vol. 6, pp. 64, 73-74; Bod. Lib., GA Oxon. 8vo. 993.

55. *BG* (8 Nov. 1849); BPL, PC vol. 6, pp. 78-80.

56. VCH, *Oxon.* X, pp. 76: *Report of the Royal Commission on Municipal Corporations*, BPP 1835 XXIII, pp. 9-15.

57. VCH, *Oxon.* X, pp. 79-81.

58. *NH* (25 Mar. 1836).

59. BPL, *Banbury Cuttings 1838-42*, p. 101.

60. William Potts, *op. cit.*, p. 214.

61. *NH* (13 Feb. 1836; 26 Mar. 1836; 24 Dec. 1836; 6 May 1837).

62. *NH* (12 Feb. 1842); *OC & CC* (22 Jan. 1842); *OH* (29 Jan. 1842; 12 Mar 1842); Rusher's *Banbury Lists and Directories*; Sarah Beesley, *op. cit.*, p. 47.

63. *BG* (28 Oct. 1852); VCH, *Oxon.* X, p. 88.

64. *OC & CC* (12 Nov. 1842).

65. *BG* (12 Feb. 1846).

66. *OC & CC* (22 Jan. 1842).

67. BPL, PC vol. 3, pp. 5, 10.

68. *Ibid.*, pp. 18, 24, 26.

69. *Ibid.*, p. 40; *NH* (10 Jan. 1835).

70. *OC & CC* (8 July 1837); *NH* (8 July 1837).

71. *OC & CC* (29 July 1837).

72. *OC & CC* (15 July 1837); BPL, PC vol. 4, p. 10.

73. *OC & CC* (22 July 1837; 29 July 1837); BPL, PC vol. 4, pp. 4, 21-22.

74. *OC & CC* (29 July 1837); BPL, PC vol. 4, p. 25.
75. *OC & CC* (29 July 1937; 10 Sep. 1837); BPL, PC vol. 4, p. 31.
76. *OH* (11 July 1835; 9 Sep. 1837).
77. *OC & CC* (26 Aug. 1837); BPL, RC, p. 118.
78. BPL, RC, p. 118; ORO 315, Box 16, BRA Mins. 1837-39.
79. *BG* (25 Feb. 1847).
80. ORO 315, Box 16, BRA Mins. 1837-39, 24 Nov. 1837, 15 Feb. 1839.
81. *BG* (27 Feb. 1845; 26 Feb. 1846).
82. ORO 315, Box 16, BRA Mins. 1837-39, 24 Nov. 1837.
83. *OC & CC* (3 July 1841).
84. *BG* (9 Mar. 1848).
85. *BG* (12 Dec. 1844); *NH* (14 Dec. 1844).
86. *NH* (14 Feb. 1846).
87. *NH* (14 Dec. 1844).
88. *BG* (30 Nov. 1848); *NH* (8 July 1837; 30 Sep. 1837; 9 Dec. 1837); *OC & CC* (12 Aug. 1837).
89. Quoted in Norman Gash, *Politics in the Age of Peel* (1953), p. 118.
90. ORO 315, Box 16, BRA Mins. 1837-39, 6 Sep. 1837, 4 May 1838, 26 Oct. 1838; *BG* (27 Feb. 1845; 26 Feb. 1846); *OC & CC* (3 Nov. 1838).
91. Pamela Horn, 'The Banbury Weavers' Union of 1834', *C & CH* vol. 3 (1968), pp. 203-206; *OH* (26 April 1834; 24 May 1834). For the Temperance Society *see below* pp. 70-72.
92. *OH* (20 Oct. 1838); BPL, RC, p. 98; the correspondence in PRO, HO 40, relating to disturbances in the years up to 1840 has been checked for references to the Banbury area, but there are no letters at all from Oxfordshire magistrates, and none from Warwickshire or Northamptonshire magistrates which related to the Banbury region.
93. *OH* (20 Oct. 1838).
94. *JOJ* (1 Dec. 1838); *OH* (1 Dec. 1939); *OC & CC* (1 Dec. 1838).
95. *OH* (23 April 1836).
96. *OH* (8 Dec. 1838).
97. BPL, RC, p. 123.
98. *Northern Star* (13 July 1839); *Western Vindicator* (20 July 1839); *OC & CC* (16 Mar. 1839).
99. BPL, RC, p. 152; *OC & CC* (17 Aug. 1839); BPL, *Banbury Cuttings 1838-42*, pp. 16, 46.
100. *Northern Star* (8 Feb. 1840; 28 Mar. 1840; 10 Oct. 1840; 21 Nov. 1840; 28 Nov. 1840); *OC & CC* (25 Jan. 1840); BPL, PC vol. 5, p. 26.
101. William Dorling, *Henry Vincent* (1879), p. 31; BPL, *Banbury Cuttings 1838-42*, p. 88; *OC & CC* (13 Mar. 1841); Transport House, Vincent MSS, 1/1/46, Henry Vincent – J. Miniken, 8 Mar. 1841.
102. Graham Wallas, *The Life of Francis Place* (ed. 1925), p. 379.
103. *National Vindicator* (17 July 1841); *Northern Star* (19 June 1841; 26 June 1841); W. Dorling, *op. cit.*, p. 31.
104. BPL, PC vol. 5, pp. 6, 35; *OC & CC* (3 July 1841); BPL, Case C, f. 12.
105. BPL, PC vol. 5, p. 15; vol. 11, pp. 6, 8: Case C, ff. 10, 12.
106. Barrie Trinder, *A Victorian MP and his Constituents* (1969), pp. 3-5; BPL, PC vol. 5, p. 29; *OC & CC* (26 June 1841).
107. Bod Lib. GA Oxon. 8vo. 989; BPL, PC vol. 5, pp. 1, 7.
108. BPL, PC vol. 5, p. 3.
109. BPL, PC vol. 5, pp. 10, 14, 16, 19; vol. 9, p. 8; Case C, f. 1.
110. BPL, Case C, ff. 17, 20, 119; Case D, f. 3; PC vol. 5, pp. 28, 30-34.
111. *OC & CC* (29 May 1841; 19 June 1841); BPL, PC vol. 5, p. 10; *Banbury Cuttings 1838-42*, p. 100.
112. BPL, PC vol. 5, p. 23.
113. *OC & CC* (26 June 1841); BPL, PC vol. 5, pp. 17, 32, 34, 35, 29; Case C, f. 16.
114. *OC & CC* (3 July 1841); *NH* (3 July 1841); Bod. Lib. GA Oxon. 8vo. 989.
115. *NH* (3 July 1841; 10 July 1841).
116. *National Vindicator* (17 July 1841); *Northern Star* (17 July 1841); BPL, PC vol. 5, p. 45.

117.   *JOJ* (2 Oct. 1841); *OC & CC* (23 Oct. 1841; 6 Nov. 1841); BPL, RC, p. 195; *NH* (6 Nov. 1841); R. C. Gammage, *History of the Chartist Movement 1837-1854* (ed. 1969), pp. 66–67, 187, 193.

118.   BPL, PC vol. 5, p. 26.

119.   *The Beehive* (20 Feb. 1868).

120.   G. Herbert, *op. cit.*, p. 117.

121.   *NH* (29 April 1837; 17 Mar. 1838).

122.   *National Vindicator* (12 Feb. 1842); *Northern Star* (19 Mar. 1842; 9 April 1842; 30 April 1842).

123.   *JOJ* (28 May 1842); *NH* (28 May 1842).

124.   *OC & CC* (4 June 1842); BPL, RC, p. 200.

125.   *Northern Star* (30 July 1842).

126.   *Ibid.* (31 Dec. 1842; 14 Jan. 1843; BPL, PC vol. 5, p. 28).

127.   Frederick Boase, ed., *Modern English Biography 1892-1921*, *sub* PHILP; R. G. Gammage, *op. cit.*, p. 402; BPL, Minutes of the Banbury Mechanics Institute, 27 Mar. 1843, 25 Sep. 1843; *BG* (21 Mar. 1844).

128.   Brian Harrison and Barrie Trinder, *Drink and Sobriety in an Early Victorian Country Town; Banbury 1830-1860* (1969), pp. 18–19. *See also below* p. 71.

129.   This paragraph is based on Table Twelve and pollbooks in Banbury Public Library.

130.   Norman Gash, *op. cit.*, pp. 77, 96.

131.   *BG* (23 Feb. 1843; 29 Feb. 1844; 27 Feb. 1845: 19 Feb. 1846; 26 Feb. 1846; 25 Feb. 1847); *NH* (8 Mar. 1845); B. Trinder, *Victorian MP*, pp. xx, xxi, 8, 16, 29–30, 56–57.

132.   B. Trinder, *Victorian MP*, pp. xxi, xxii, xxix, 11, 13, 23–25, 45, 121; *Oxford Chronicle and Reading Gazette* (24 June 1843).

133.   *OC & CC* (3 Dec. 1842); *BG* (12 Dec. 1844); *NH* (14 Dec. 1844).

134.   B. Trinder, *Victorian MP*, pp. xxiv–xxvi, 5, 17, 19, 31, 47, 49.

135.   *Ibid.*, pp. xxvi–xxviii, 26–27, 32–33, 41, 45–48.

136.   *Ibid.*, pp. xxviii–xxix, 53; ORO 315, Box 41, Bundle cc, Bernhard Samuelson – Sir Charles Douglas, 18 Oct. 1866; *BA* (1 Nov. 1866).

137.   B. Trinder, *Victorian MP*, pp. 5–9, 33–34; *JOJ* (23 Apr. 1842); *Oxford Chronicle and Reading Gazette* (29 April 1843; 13 May 1843); *BG* (9 May 1843; 10 April 1845; 1 May 1845; 8 May 1845); Bod. Lib. GA Oxon. 8vo. 992.

138.   *NH* (23 Mar 1839); *JOJ* (2 Oct. 1841); *OC & CC* (2 Oct. 1841); Archibald Prentice, *The History of the Anti-Corn Law League* (1853), vol. 1, p. 326, vol. 2, pp. 92, 212; *BG* (26 Feb. 1846); 25 Feb. 1847).

139.   *OH* (20 Jan. 1844); *NH* (20 Jan. 1844; 14 Feb. 1846); *BG* (14 Mar. 1844; 12 Feb. 1846; 1 April 1846).

140.   Pamela Horn, 'The Chartist Land Company', *C & CH*, vol. 4 (1968), pp. 19–23; *Northern Star* (20 June 1846; 24 April 1847; 12 June 1847, 3 July 1847; 4 Sep. 1847).

141.   BPL, PC vol. 6, pp. 44, 51, 61; B. Trinder, *Victorian MP*, pp. xxiii–xxiv, 38–39; *NH* (14 Aug. 1847).

142.   BPL, PC vol. 6, pp. 10, 22–23, 36; *BG* (22 July 1847; 29 July 1847; 5 Aug. 1847); B. Trinder, *Victorian MP*, pp. 36–37; BPL, Case C, f. 47.

143.   BPL, PC vol. 6, pp. 17, 24, 32, 34, 39; Case C, f. 6; *BG* (22 July 1847; 5 Aug. 1847); *NH* (10 July 1847; 7 Aug. 1847).

144.   This paragraph is based on Table Twelve and analysis of pollbooks for the elections concerned.

Chapter Six

1.   J. S. Mill, *Principles of Political Economy* (ed. 1876), p. 572.

2.   *See* Table Seven.

3.   Colin Bell, Eric Batstone and Anne Murcott, *Voluntary Associations in Banbury*, paper read to the South-West Branch of the British Sociological Association, Bristol, 10 July 1968.

4. Barrie Trinder, *A Victorian MP and his Constituents* (1969), p. xxi.
5. Alfred Beesley, *The History of Banbury* (1841), p. 550; *C & CC* (9 June 1838; 16 June 1838; 23 June 1838, 7 July 1838): *OH* (9 June 1838; 16 June 1838); *JOJ* (7 July 1838).
6. Sarah Beesley, *My Life* (1892), p. 51; *OC & CC* (15 Feb. 1840); BPL, *Banbury Cuttings 1838-42*, p. 54.
7. *NH* (17 Mar. 1832).
8. BPL, RC pp. 108, 134; *NH* (8 Feb. 1834); *OH* (1 Feb. 1834; 15 Feb. 1834; 5 Apr. 1834; 11 Aug. 1838); *OC & CC* (3 Feb. 1838; 10 June 1838; 4 Aug. 1838); *JOJ* (9 June 1838).
9. ORO 315, 12 AC, Minutes of the Neithrop Association for the Prosecution of Felons.
10. BPL, Cash Book and Register of the Banbury Association for the Prosecution of Felons, 1835-47; *Articles and Rules of An Association for defraying the expenses of apprehending and prosecuting Thieves and Other Offenders in Banbury and its Neighbourhood, established 1 January 1836* (1839).
11. Rusher's *Banbury Lists and Directories; see above* p. 28.
12. VCH, *Oxon.* X, pp. 121-22; and John Portergill, 'The Banbury Bluecoat Foundation', *C & CH* vol. 7 (1976), pp. 19-22.
13. A. Beesley, *op. cit.*, p. 542; BPL, RC pp. 114, 189-90, 212.
14. *Education Enquiry Abstract*, BPP, 1835 XLII, p. 740.
15. A. Beesley, *op. cit.*, p. 559; *OH* (28 Feb. 1835; 8 Aug. 1835); *NH* (20 June 1840); B. Trinder, *Victorian MP*, p. xxi. Lt. Fabian RN had lectured on the British Schools Society in Banbury in 1832, *see OH* (17 Mar. 1832).
16. BP., RC pp. 150, 157, 198; Rusher's *Banbury Lists and Directories*; George Herbert, *Shoemaker's Window* (1949), p. 33; *OH* (24 Dec. 1842); *NH* (21 Mar. 1840; 31 July 1841; 11 Mar. Mar. 1843; PRO, HO 107, 1851 Census.
17. A. G. Wall, *St John's Church, Banbury* (1938), p. 22; BPL, RC p. 42; Rusher's *Banbury Lists and Directories*.
18. Martin Billing, *Directory and Gazetteer of Berkshire and Oxfordshire* (1854), p. 129; BPL, RC p. 212; A. G. Wall, *op. cit.*, p. 22.
19. *See* Table Eight.
20. Barrie Trinder, *Banbury's Poor in 1850* (1966), p. 119.
21. BPL, MI Mins. vols. 1-3, *passim; BG* (14 Jan. 1875; 14 Mar. 1878); *OH* (6 Mar 1835; 13 Mar. 1835).
22. BPL, MI Mins., vol. 3, 23 Mar. 1850.
23. *Ibid.*, vol. 1, 9 April 1835.
24. *BG* (14 Mar. 1878).
25. *BG* (14 Jan. 1875).
26. *See above* p. 50.
27. *JOJ* (28 Mar. 1830); *OH* (11 Aug. 1832; 18 Aug. 1832; 16 Nov. 1833).
28. *JOJ* (4 May, 1838).
29. Mark Rutherford, *The Revolution in Tanner's Lane* (ed. 1887), p. 321.
30. *British and Foreign Temperance Herald* (Sep. 1834), p. 100; British and Foreign Temperance Society, *Fourth Annual Report* (1835), p. 58; Brian Harrison and Barrie Trinder, *Drink and Society in an Early Victorian Country Town: Banbury 1830-60* (1969), p. 15.
31. *OH* (23 Apr. 1836); *Preston Temperance Advocate*, July 1836, p. 53.
32. *JOJ* (31 Dec. 1836); *OH* (31 Dec. 1836); New British and Foreign Temperance Society, *First Annual Report* (1836), p. 39; *Second Annual Report* (1838), p. 54; B. Harrison and B. Trinder, *op. cit.*, pp. 16-17.
33. Beesley Papers, *penes* G. G. W. Brown, Esq., of Sunderland, Co. Durham.
34. *British and Foreign Temperance Intelligencer* (26 Feb. 1842), p. 70; (19 Mar. 1842), p. 95; (16 Apr. 1842), p. 122; (4 June 1842), p. 179; (6 Aug. 1842), p. 353; *Oxford Chronicle and Reading Gazette* (27 May 1843); B. Harrison and B. Trinder, *op. cit.*, pp. 18-19.
35. John Morley, *Life of Richard Cobden* (ed. 1881), vol. 1, p. 249.
36. *Metropolitan Temperance Intelligencer and Journal* (14 Sep. 1844; 28 Sep. 1844); *BG* (5 Sep. 1844).
37. *BG* (19 Dec. 1844).

38. *See above* p. 62.
39. B. Harrison and B. Trinder, *op. cit.*, pp. 22–24.
40. BPL, RC p. 210; B. Harrison and B. Trinder, *op. cit.*, pp. 20–23.
41. *NH* (18 Oct. 1834; 2 Mar. 1839: 15 Oct. 1842).
42. George Eliot, *Scenes of Clerical Life* (ed. 1927), p. 192.
43. BPL, RC pp. 241–42, 247, 255, 259; *NH* (3 Aug. 1839); *JOJ* (21 July 1843).
44. BPL, RC pp. 203–204, 235, 250; *NH* (12 Nov. 1842). *BG* (16 Oct. 1845).
45. BPL, RC pp. 210, 213–14, 247, 253; Rusher's *Banbury Lists and Directories*; Bod. Lib., GA Oxon. 8vo. 994.
46. *BG* (31 Oct. 1850).
47. Cheney & Sons, Specimens of Work.
48. Lou Warwick, *Theatre Unroyal* (1974), p. 149; G. Herbert, *op. cit.*, pp. 57, 97, 103.
49. L. Warwick, *op. cit.*, p. 124.
50. *OH* (3 Feb. 1838); *JOJ* (5 Feb. 1842; 26 Feb. 1842); *BG* (6 Jan. 1848).
51. BPL, Case G, ff. 43–44.
52. *BG* (18 Sep. 1845).
53. BPL, RC p. 189; Case G, f. 41; *BG* (25 Nov. 1852; 2 Dec. 1852).
54. B. Trinder, *Victorian MP*, p. 116.
55. BPL, Case G, f. 41.
56. P. H. J. H. Gosden, *Self-Help: Voluntary Associations in Nineteenth Century Britain* (1973), pp. 28–29, 39–76.
57. G. Herbert, *op. cit.*, facing p. 116.
58. *BG* (8 July 1847).
59. BPL, RC p. 198: *JOJ* (21 July 1843); *BA* (20 Aug. 1868).
60. *JOJ* (4 July 1843).
61. BPL, PC vol. 10, p. 16; *OC & CC* (25 Mar. 1837).
62. BPL, RC pp. 216, 218, 256; *JOJ* (27 Mar. 1847); BPL, PC vol. 6, p. 67.
63. *JOJ* (6 Jan. 1838); *NH* (11 July 1846).
64. *BG* (4 June 1846); *NH* (7 Nov. 1846); *BA* (28 Sep. 1876).
65. BPL, RC p. 221; *BG* (21 Mar. 1850; 11 Apr. 1850).
66. *JOJ* (19 July 1843), *BG* (14 Mar. 1843); *see below* p. 138.
67. Rusher's *Banbury Lists and Directories* shows that its officials were always teachers at the National Schools.
68. *BG* (3 Mar. 1842); B. Trinder, *Victorian MP*, p. 7.
69. *JOJ* (17 Feb. 1838); *BG* (6 Feb. 1845; 24 Feb. 1848).
70. *BG* (14 Aug. 1845).
71. *BG* (8 Aug. 1843; 25 July 1844: 22 Aug. 1844); BPL, PC vol. 6, p. 64.
72. *BG* (8 Aug. 1844; 6 Aug. 1846); *JOJ* (15 May, 1830; 13 Aug. 1842).
73. *BG* (30 July 1846).
74. G. Herbert, *op. cit.*, p. 103; *BG* (20 July 1843); A. Beesley, *op. cit*, p. 274; *see above* p. 10.
75. BPL, PC vol. 5, p. 24.
76. *See below* p. 133.
77. B. Trinder, *Victorian MP*, p. 31; *BG* (16 Sep. 1847; 16 Mar. 1848).
78. Rusher's *Banbury Lists and Directories*; *OH* (16 July 1836; 23 July 1836); *see also* pp. 142–43.
79. G. Herbert, *op. cit.*, p. 71.
80. *BG* (19 Dec. 1844).
81. J. S. Mill, *op. cit.*, p. 573.

Chapter Seven

1. Elizabeth Hemus, *Banbury – a Poem* (1854), BPL Case E1, f. 11a.
2. T. W. Boss, *Reminiscences of Old Banbury* (1903), p. 27.
3. *See* Table Two.

4. *See* Table Six.

5. E. T. McDermot, *The History of the Great Western Railway* (ed. 1964), vol. 1, p. 266.

6. *BG* (25 Apr. 1844; 11 July 1844; 7 Nov. 1844); *OH* (13 July 1844).

7. Barrie Trinder, *A Victorian MP and his Constituents* (1969), p. 15.

8. E. T. McDermot, *op. cit.*, col. 1, p. 270.

9. *OH* (13 April 1844); *BG* (30 May 1844).

10. B. Trinder, *op. cit.*, p. 16; *BG* (21 Aug. 1845; 15 Aug. 1850; 6 May 1875).

11. *BG* (21 Aug. 1845).

12. *BG* (21 Aug. 1845; 26 Mar. 1846; 9 Apr. 1847); *NH* (4 Apr. 1846; 18 Apr. 1846).

13. E. T. McDermot, *op. cit.*, vol. 1, p. 246; *BG* (14 May 1846; 4 June 1846; 29 Oct. 1846; 29 June 1848; 31 May 1849; 28 June 1849); BPL, RC p. 256; *NH* (6 Nov. 1847).

14. E. T. McDermot, *op. cit.*, vol. 1, p. 246; Bill Simpson, *The Banbury to Verney Junction Branch* (1978), pp. 9-13.

15. *BG* (2 July 1846; 26 Aug. 1847; 11 May 1848).

16. B. Simpson, *op. cit.*, p. 17.

17. Michael Robbins, 'From R. B. Dockray's Diary', *Journal of Transport History*, vol. 7 (1965), pp. 7-8; *BG* (26 April 1849; 28 Mar. 1850; 4 April 1850; 2 May 1850).

18. E. T. McDermot, *op. cit.*, vol. 1, p. 297; *BG* (5 Sep. 1850).

19. E. T. McDermot, *op. cit.*, vol. 1, p. 297; B. Simpson, *op. cit.*, pp. 13, 39-40, 43; *BG* (13 Sep. 1877).

20. Rusher's *Banbury Lists and Directories*; *BG* (2 Dec. 1858).

21. W. J. Scott, *The Great Great Western 1889-1902* (ed. 1972), p. 55.

22. Michael Robbins, *op. cit.*, p. 8.

23. *BG* (7 Nov. 1850; 2 Jan. 1851; 15 Jan. 1852); *NH* (24 June 1865).

24. *BA* (20 May 1869); *BG* (15 Feb. 1866).

25. Rusher's *Banbury Lists and Directories*; Charles Hadfield, *The Canals of the East Midlands* (1966), p. 214; Hugh Compton, *The Oxford Canal* (1976), pp. 116-117, 130-31; A. Farrant, *Rowing Holiday by Canal in 1873* (ed. Edwin Course, 1977), p. 13; *BA* (17 Sep. 1863); *BG* (23 Mar. 1862; 19 June 1873).

26. Rusher's *Banbury Lists and Directories*; *BG* (5 May 1853).

27. William Bearn, 'On the Farming of Northamptonshire', *JRASE* vol. 13 (1852), p. 47; Clare Sewell Read, 'On the Agriculture of Oxfordshire', *JRASE* vol. 15 (1854), p. 190; *BG* (23 June 1853; 10 Mar. 1846).

28. BPL, PC vol. 8, p. 27; *BG* (22 Oct. 1863; 10 Mar. 1864); *NH* (24 June 1865).

29. *See* Tables Nine and Ten.

30. Rusher's *Banbury Lists and Directories*.

31. *BG* (4 Jan. 1866); *BA* (1 Nov. 1860); *NH* (24 June 1865); BPL, PC vol. 9, p. 192.

32. Alan Everitt, 'Country Carriers in the Nineteenth Century', *Journal of Transport History*, New Ser. vol. 3 (1976), pp. 179-202.

33. *BA* (21 Oct. 1869); *BG* (15 Oct. 1863).

34. *See* Tables Nine and Ten.

35. *BG* (15 Aug. 1850).

36. G. C. J. Hartland, 'The Britannia Works from Living Memory', *C & CH* vol. 4 (1971), p. 194.

37. The obituary of the Rt. Hon Sir Bernhard Samuelson, Bt., *Journal of the Iron and Steel Institute*, vol. 1 (1905), p. 504, gives the total as 27 at the time of takeover; *BG* (27 Sep. 1849); for the earlier history of the works *see above* p. 34.

38. Archie Potts, 'Alexander Samuelson: a Victorian Engineer', *C & CH* vol. 2 (1965), p. 193; Archie Potts, 'Daniel Pidgeon and the Britannia Works', *C & CH* vol. 4 (1969), pp. 58-59.

39. *JRASE* vol. 11 (1850), pp. 464, 491-92; *BG* (2 Nov. 1850).

40. *JRASE* vol. 12 (1851), p. 633; *BG* (22 May 1851; 4 Sep. 1851; 30 Oct. 1851; 2 Sep. 1852).

41. *JRASE* vol. 12 (1851), pp. 160, 311.

42. M. K. Ashby, *Joseph Ashby of Tysoe* (1961), p. 57.

43. *BG* (1 July 1852; 29 Sep. 1852; 24 Feb. 1853; 24 Mar. 1853); *JRASE* vol. 14 (1853), pp. 359, 363; *Illustrated London News* (10 Dec. 1853), p. 490.

44. *JRASE* vol. 15 (1854), p. 373; *ibid.* vol. 16 (1855), pp. 520-21, 526; *ibid.* vol. 18 (1857), p. 442; *ibid.* vol. 19 (1859), pp. 328-29; ORO 315, Samuelson Trade Leaflets.

45. ORO 315, Samuelson Trade Leaflets: George Measom, *The Official Illustrated Guide to the Great Western Railway* (1861), p. 231; *BG* (23 Sep. 1858; 6 Jan. 1859; 7 April 1859; 22 April 1859; 23 June 1859).

46. *Journal of the Iron and Steel Institute* vol. 1 (1905), p. 504; *JRASE* vol. 22 (1861), p. 457; *ibid.* 2nd Ser. vol. 1 (1865), pp. 48, 93); *BG* (9 July 1863; 16 July 1868; 21 July 1870; 11 May 1876; 20 July 1876; 25 Jan. 1877; 17 May 1877; 7 June 1877).

47. *BG* (13 Jan. 1876) quoting *The Irish Farmer; Northern Echo* (11 May 1905).

48. 'An Early Description of the Britannia Works', *C & CH* vol. 4 (1965), pp. 60-61; G. C. J. Hartland, 'The Britannia Works from Living Memory', *C & CH* vol. 4 (1971), pp. 194-95; *BA* (10 Feb. 1872); Archie Potts, 'Ernest Samuelson and the Britannia Works', *C & CH* vol. 4 (1971), pp. 187-90.

49. ORO 315, Samuelson Trade Leaflets; *BG* (23 June 1859).

50. *BG* (2 Sep. 1852; 25 May 1854; 6 Oct. 1859; 6 July 1865; 21 July 1870; 12 Jan. 1871).

51. *BA* (23 Sep. 1858; 6 Jan. 1859); *BG* (6 Oct. 1859; 20 Oct. 1868).

52. 'An Early Description of the Britannia Works', *C & CH* vol. 4 (1965), pp. 60-61; *BG* (27 Mar. 1873); PRO, RG 10, 1871 Census.

53. *BG* (24 Jan. 1850; 2 Sep. 1852).

54. *See below* p. 137.

55. *BA* (2 Nov. 1871); *BG* (2 Nov. 1871).

56. *BA* (23 Sep. 1858); *BH* (11 Apr. 1861; 2 May 1861); *BG* (18 Jan. 1966).

57. *BG* (10 May 1866); BPL, Case W, f. 53; *NH* (14 May 1859).

58. Rusher's *Banbury Lists and Directories*; *BG* (22 April 1859; 12 July 1860; 5 Nov. 1868; 21 July 1870); *BH* (16 Oct. 1862); *BA* (3 Jan. 1868; 6 Aug. 1868); *JRASE* vol. 24 (1863), p. 497; *ibid.* 2nd Ser. vol. 7 (1871), p. 485; R. H. Clark, *The Development of the English Traction Engine* (1960), pp. 38-40; Museum of English Rural Life, Reading, Barrows & Stewart Catalogue, 1874.

59. R. H. Clarke, *op. cit.*, pp. 21-23, 96-98; PRO, RG9, 1871 Census.

60. *Journal of the Iron and Steel Institute* vol. 1 (1905), pp. 504-506; *Iron and Coal Trades Review* (12 May 1905); *Northern Echo* (11 May 1905), *The Times* (11 May 1905).

61. *BG* (18 Feb. 1864); *NH* (24 June 1865).

62. This and other information which follows is drawn from PRO, RG 10, 1871 census.

63. *BG* (19 Feb. 1857).

64. *See* Tables Nine and Ten.

65. *BG* (29 Jan. 1852; 26 Feb. 1852); BPL, PC vol. 11, p. 104.

66. *BA* (10 Sep. 1857), George Herbert, *Shoemaker's Window* (1949), p. 101.

67. BPL, PC vol. 9, pp. 256, 269; 'Weaving in the 1890s', *C & CH* vol. 3 (1968), pp. 207-209.

68. Anon, *Hunt Edmunds and Co. 1896-1946* (1946), pp. 5-8; *BG* (24 July 1856; 25 Sep. 1856; 31 Oct. 1861; 31 Aug. 1865; 28 July 1870); *BA* (25 Nov. 1869); BPL, PC vol. 9, p. 250.

69. Information on sizes of firms from PRO, RG 9, 1861 Census and RG 10, 1871 Census; *BG* (9 Aug. 1866; 23 Sep. 1875).

70. *United Kingdom First Annual Trades' Union Directory* (1861), pp. 9-10; J. R. Hodgkins, *Over the Hills to Glory* (1979), p. 37.

71. Royden Harrison, *Before the Socialists* (1965), pp. 148-49, 171-72; *BA* (6 Jan. 1859); ORO 315, Box 80, Bundle M, B. Samuelson — the Rt. Hon. Lord R. Montague, 26 Nov. 1867.

72. *BG* (2 Nov. 1871): R. Harrison, *op. cit.*, pp. 171-72; *BA* (5 Feb. 1874).

73. *United Kingdom First Annual First Trades' Union Directory* (1871), p. 9; J. R. Hodgkins, *op. cit.*, pp. 50-51.

74. *BA* (11 Aug. 1864; 11 Jan. 1872; 18 May 1873).

75. Rusher's *Banbury Lists and Directories*; Tables Nine and Ten.

76. PRO, RG 10, 1871 Census.

77. PRO, RG 9, 1861 Census.

78. *See* Tables Nine and Ten.

79. *BA* (13 Nov. 1856; 22 Jan. 1857; 13 Sep. 1860; 9 Dec. 1867; 14 Mar. 1872); *BG* (2 Sep. 1852; 10 Nov. 1864; 27 Aug. 1868; 13 Apr. 1871); BPL, PC vol. 10, pp. 9–10.

80. W. H. Lickorish, *Our Jubilee Story or Fifty Years of Co-operation in Banbury and the Neighbourhood* (1916), *passim*; F. Lamb, *A Brief History of the Banbury Co-operative Industrial Society from its commencement down to the end of the June Quarter 1887* (1887), *passim*; *BG* (12 Nov. 1868); *BA* (17 June 1869).

81. *NH* (14 June 1851); *BG* (10 Feb. 1859).

82. *BA* (28 June 1860; 5 May 1864); *BG* (5 May 1864); Tables Nine and Ten.

83. *BG* (21 Oct. 1858; 16 Oct. 1862; 20 Oct, 1870); *BA* (27 Oct. 1864; 29 Oct. 1868; 20 Oct. 1870).

84. *BG* (17 June 1857; 17 Jan. 1861; 31 Dec. 1863; 18 Jan. 1866).

85. Audrey Taylor, *Gilletts: Bankers at Banbury and Oxford* (1964), pp. 118–20.

86. *BG* (6 Feb. 1851; 7 Apr. 1853; 21 Apr. 1853); B. Trinder, *Victorian MP*, pp. xxv, 56.

87. *BG* (9 Oct. 1856; 23 Oct. 1856; 30 Oct. 1856; 6 Nov. 1856; 29 Jan. 1857; 29 Oct. 1857; 9 Dec. 1858; 6 May 1875); *BA* (1 Jan. 1857; 22 Jan. 1857; 21 May 1857; 28 May 1857; 10 Sep. 1857; ?? Sep. 1857; 29 Oct. 1857; 11 Aug. 1859); BPL, PC vol. 8, pp. 22, 28, 193; William Potts, *Banbury through One Hundred Years* (1942), p. 45; BPL, RC p. 319.

88. A. Taylor, *op. cit.*, pp. 128–62.

89. *BA* (1 April 1869).

90. BPL, PC vol. 8, pp. 122, 219.

91. *See* Tables Nine and Ten.

92. *See above* p. 31.

93. *BG* (10 Mar. 1863): *BA* (10 Mar. 1863).

94. *BA* (5 Feb. 1857); Sarah Beesley, *My Life* (1892), p. 76.

Chapter Eight

1. Report by Thomas Beesley on the first five years of the Banbury Board of Health, *BG* (13 Aug. 1857).

2. W. L. Burn, *The Age of Equipoise* (1964), p. 132

3. *See below*, pp. 119–20.

4. Rusher's *Banbury Lists and Directories*.

5. For population figures *see* Table Two.

6. T. W. Rammell, *Report on a Preliminary Inquiry into the Sewerage, Drainage and Supply of Water and the Sanitary Condition of the Inhabitants of Banbury and Neithrop* (1850); William Potts, *A History of Banbury* (1958), p. 221; *BG* (23 May 1850; 1 Aug. 1850).

7. *BG* (15 July 1852; 26 Oct. 1865).

8. BPL, PC vol. 7, pp. 54–55; *NH* (7 Aug. 1852; 14 Aug. 1852); *BG* (12 Aug. 1852).

9. Rusher's *Banbury Lists and Directories*; BPL, PC vol. 8, pp. 15–16; RC p. 320.

10. *BG* (13 Aug. 1857; 15 Apr. 1858; 22 Apr. 1858; 13 May 1858); Sarah Beesley, *My Life* (1892), pp. 77–82.

11. *BG* (8 Aug. 1850).

12. *BG* (11 Feb. 1858); BPL, PC vol. 9, p. 12; ORO, BB/X/i/1 B of H Mins., *passim*.

13. ORO, BB/X/i/1-2, B of H Mins., 13 Dec. 1858, 3 Sep. 1861, 9 Feb. 1863: *BG* (16 Nov. 1854; 27 Feb. 1862).

14. ORO, BB/X/i/2, B of H Mins., 22 Sep. 1862; BB/X/iii/1, 28 July 1871, 27 Oct. 1873, 17 Nov. 1873; BB/X/i/3, 1 July 1878.

15. ORO, BB/X/i/2, B of H Mins., 7 Aug. 1865, 25 Sep. 1865.

16. ORO, BB/X/iii/1, B of H Mins., 17 Nov. 1873: BB/X/i/3, 14 Aug. 1876; *BA* (22 Dec. 1881 and *passim*); *BG* (22 Dec. 1881 and *passim*); BPL, RC p. 320.

17. *BG* (18 May 1854; 13 July 1854; 24 Aug. 1854; 13 Aug. 1857).
18. ORO, BB/X/iii/1, B of H Mins., 9 May 1858, 5 Sep. 1858; *BG* (21 Sep. 1865); W. P. Johnson, *The Stranger's Guide through Banbury* (1859), p. 4.
19. ORO, BB/X/i/1, B of H. Mins., 3 Sep. 1861; BB/X/i/2, 27 Nov. 1865, 23 Mar. 1866, 9 Oct. 1866; BB/X/iii/1, 17 Apr. 1871, 27 Oct. 1871, 20 Nov. 1871; *BG* (19 July 1866; 25 June 1866; 25 June 1868; 13 Apr. 1871; 16 Nov. 1871); *BA* (19 Dec. 1867).
20. *BG* (17 Mar. 1871; 12 May 1870: 8 Sep. 1870; 13 Jan. 1875); *Salopian Journal* (11 Oct. 1871).
21. BPL, PC vol. 7, p. 94; *BG* (28 Sep. 1854, 2 July 1857; 6 Aug. 1857; 25 Mar. 1858).
22. BPL, PC vol. 9, pp. 126–29, 145, 152–53; *BA* (21 Jan. 1864); ORO, BB/X/i/2, B of H Mins., *passim*.
23. G. C. J. Hartland, 'Gasmaking in Banbury', *C & CH* vol. 4 (1969), pp. 47–49; BPL, PC vol. 7, p. 85.
24. *BG* (30 Sep. 1852; 14 Oct. 1852; 28 Oct. 1852; 2 Dec. 1852; 13 Aug. 1857); ORO, BB/X/i/2, B of H Mins., 17 Apr. 1865.
25. ORO, BB/X/i/2, B of H Mins., 28 Jan. 1867; *BG* (13 Aug. 1857).
26. *BG* (6 Feb. 1851); for freehold land societies *see* S. D. Chapman and J. N. Bartlett, 'The Contribution of Building Clubs and Freehold Land Societies to Working Class Housing in Birmingham', S. D. Chapman, ed., *The History of Working Class Housing* (1971), pp. 223–46.
27. *BG* (6 Feb. 1851; 10 Apr. 1851; 7 Apr. 1853; 21 Apr. 1853; 22 Feb. 1855); Barrie Trinder, *A Victorian MP and his Constituents* (1969), p. 74.
28. *BG* (7 Apr. 1853); ORO, 315/M/3/24, Plan of the Property of Banbury Freehold Land Society situate at Grimsbury, Northamptonshire, 1853.
29. *Ibid.*; ORO, BB/X/i/1, B of H Mins., *passim*.
30. PRO, RG 9, 1861 Census, RG 10, 1871 Census; William Potts, *Banbury through One Hundred Years* (1942), pp. 98–99.
31. PRO, RG (, 1861 Census; *BG* (28 Mar. 1872); T. W. Boss, *Reminiscences of Old Banbury* (1903), pp. 18–19.
32. PRO, RG (, 1861 Census, RG 10, 1871 Census; Ordnance Survey first edition 25 in. map; *BG* (28 Mar. 1872); ORO, BB/X/iii/1, B of H Mins., 15 Dec. 1873; BB/X/i/1, 28 Dec. 1863.
33. Sarah Gosling, '57–129 Causeway, Banbury', in Crispin Paine *et al.*, 'Working Class Housing in Oxfordshire', *Oxoniensia*, vol. 43 (1978), pp. 201–204.
34. ORO, BB/X/iii/1, B of H Mins., 28 Apr. 1873; Ordnance Survey first edition 25 in. map.
35. *BG* (23 Dec. 1852).
36. ORO, 315/m/3/13, Plan of the Property of the Banbury Freehold Land Society: ORO, BB/X/i/1, B of H Mins., 7 May 1858; *BA* (1 Apr. 1869); *BG* (25 Aug. 1853; 24 Mar. 1864).
37. PRO, RG 10, 1871 Census.
38. W. P. Johnson, *Stranger's Guide*, p. 21; ORO, BB/X/i/1, B of H Mins., 1 July 1861; BB/X/iii/1, 7 Mar. 1870; *BG* (25 Sep. 1862); *BA* (23 July 1868).
39. George Herbert, *Shoemaker's Window* (1949), p. 45; *BG* (6 Sep. 1855; 27 Feb. 1862); *BA* (19 Oct. 1855); ORO, BB/X/i/2, B of H Mins., 21 Apr. 1863; BB/X/i/3, *passim*; PRO, RG 10, 1871 Census; Ordnance Survey first edition 25 in. map.
40. *BA* (5 Feb. 1865); ORO, BB/X/i/2, B of H Mins., 26 Mar. 1866: BB/X/iii/1, 7 Mar. 1870.
41. ORO, BB/X/i/1, B of H Mins., 8 Apr. 1861, 10 Sep. 1866; ORO 315/71 Bundle B, Cobb Papers.
42. *BG* (13 May 1852; 28 Apr. 1853); PRO, RG 10, 1871 Census, *see above* p. 28.
43. *BH* (3 Jan. 1861; 4 Apr. 1861); ORO, 315/M/1/6, Plan of a 'New Road' from Oxford Road to the GWR station, 1860; VCH, *Oxon*. X, p. 37.
44. *BG* (12 Jan. 1854; 26 Aug. 1861); *NH* (11 Feb. 1854); ORO, BB/X/i-ii, B of H Mins., *passim*.
45. *BG* (17 Nov. 1870).
46. *BG* (14 Apr. 1870); ORO, BB/X/i/1-2, B of H Mins., *passim*.
47. ORO, BB/X/i/1-2, B of H Mins., *passim*.
48. B. Trinder, *Victorian MP*, p. xxvi; *BG* (25 Apr. 1860; 17 May 1860: *BA* 17 May 1860).
49. *NH* (20 Apr. 1853); *BG* (14 July 1859).
50. *BG* (4 Apr. 1878; 13 June 1878; 28 Nov. 1878; 17 July 1879); BPL, RC p. 314.

51. *BG* (18 Nov. 1858; 22 Sep. 1859; 23 Nov. 1866).

52. *BG* (5 Jan. 1860); *BA* (5 Jan. 1860; 4 Nov. 1875; 16 Dec. 1875); ORO, BB/V/ii/1-2, Minutes of Banbury Watch Committee.

53. *BG* (23 May 1861; 15 May 1862).

54. *BG* (17 Apr. 1851; 13 July 1854).

55. BPL, BVF/ED, Memo to accompany the General Return of the 1870 Education Act; *see* Table Eight.

56. William Potts, *Banbury through One Hundred Years* (1942), pp. 80-82.

57. *BA* (22 Dec. 1870); BPL, RC p. 381.

58. ORO, BB/XI/vii/ 2, Log Book of Banbury British School, Boys, 1862-89; BPL, PC vol. 9, pp. 56, 121; *BA* (3 Oct. 1878); Sarah Beesley, *op. cit.*, p. 118; Michael Argyles, *From South Kensington to Robbins: An Account of English Technical and Scientific Education since 1851* (1964), pp. 26, 31-33, 136.

59. Paul Harvey and Barrie Trinder, *New Light on Banbury's Crosses*, (1967), pp. 192-196.

60. ORO, BB/X/iii/1, B of H Mins., 9 June 1873.

61. *BA* (26 June 1873); ORO, BB/X/i/2, B of H Mins., 21 May 1866.

62. *BG* (17 Nov. 1870).

Chapter Nine

1. Regents Park College Library, Oxford, W. T. Henderson, *Recollections of his Life.*

2. *BG* (28 June 1849); *JOJ* (30 June 1849); *OH* (30 June 1849); R. G. Wilberforce, *The Life of Samuel Wilberforce* (1880-82), vol. 2, pp. 30-34.

3. *NH* (3 Nov. 1849; 17 Nov. 1849; 22 Dec. 1849; 13 July 1850); *BG* (12 Nov. 1849; 24 Jan. 1850; 15 April 1858).

4. R. G. Wilberforce, *op. cit.*, vol. 2, pp. 30-34; *BG* (28 Feb. 1850).

5. Bod. Lib. MS. Oxon. Dioc. Pprs., d. 178, pp. 44, 439.

6. Bod. Lib. MS. D.D. Par. Banbury a.5 (R), St Mary's Banbury, List of Church Officers, &c., Visiting Plans, 1850; Oxon. Dioc. Pprs. b. 70; Barrie Trinder, *Banbury's Poor in 1850* (1966), *passim*; *BG* (19 Dec. 1850).

7. BPL. PC vol. 7, p. 51; *BG* (27 May 1852; 10 Feb. 1853); E. P. Baker, *Bishop Wilberforce's Visitation Returns for the Archdeaconry of Oxford 1854* (1954), pp. 12-13.

8. Charles Forbes, *Address to Parishioners in South Banbury on the present time* (1850), Bod. Lib. Oxon, 8vo. (20); Box. Lib. MS Oxf. Dioc. Pprs. d. 550, 22, 26; R. K. Pugh, *The Letter Books of Samuel Wilberforce 1843-68* ((1970), pp. 190, 194-96.

9. *BG* (20 Nov. 1851; 19 Feb. 1852; 16 Sep. 1852; 24 Feb. 1853; 2 Oct. 1879); *NH* (21 Feb. 1852; 18 Sep. 1852; 26 Feb. 1853); BPL, PC vol. 9, p. 259; *BA* (24 Jan. 1880; 30 Sep. 1880).

10. E. P. Baker, *op. cit.*, Bod. Lib. Oxf. Dioc. Pprs. d. 180.

11. E. P. Baker, *op. cit.*, pp. 13-14; *Church Times* vol. 7 (1 Oct. 1869), p. 363 (29 Oct. 1869), p. 417.

12. BPL, PC vol. 6, pp. 81-84; *BG* (20 Dec. 1849).

13. *BG* (11 Apr. 1850).

14. *BG* (14 Mar. 1850; 8 May 1851; 12 Jan. 1854).

15. *BG* (30 Sep. 1858); *BA* (23 Sep. 1858).

16. VCH, *Oxon.* X, p. 104: *BA* (17 Feb. 1881).

17. *BG* (3 Jan. 1867; 14 Feb. 1867; 9 May 1867): BPL, PC vol. 9, p. 267; Sarah Beesley, *My Life* (1892), pp. 114–115.

18. *BA* (25 Aug. 1869; 23 Sep. 1869); S. Beesley, *op. cit.*, pp. 127, 137; BPL, PC vol. 10, p. 11.

19. *BG* May 1873), *passim*; *BA* (14 Jan. 1875).

20. *BG* (30 May 1878; 10 Oct. 1878; 7 Nov. 1878; 14 Nov. 1878; 9 Jan. 1879).

21. *BG* (27 July 1873); *BA* (1 July 1880).

22. W. T. Henderson, *Recollections*; *BG* (1 May 1851).

23. W. T. Henderson, *Recollections*; *BG* (29 Nov. 1855).

24. *BG* (26 Mar. 1857; 3 July 1862; 8 Oct. 1863); *BA* (26 Mar. 1857; 8 Oct. 1863).

25. *BH* (27 Mar. 1862); *BA* (13 Sep. 1955; 16 July 1856; 31 Mar. 1864).

26. *BA* (31 Mar. 1864).

27. W. T. Henderson, *Recollections; Evangelical Magazine* (1854), p. 101; *BG* (10 Nov. 1853); Albert Dawson, *Joseph Parker, DD: His Life and Ministry* (1901), p. 38.

28. *BG* (29 Dec. 1853; 3 Jan. 1854; 25 May 1854); *Evangelical Magazine* (1852), p. 419; A. Dawson, *op. cit.*, p. 40; Joseph McCabe, *The Life and Letters of George Jacob Holyoake* (1908), pp. 224-27; Joseph Parker, *A Preacher's Life* (ed. 1903), pp. 248-51.

29. Banbury United Reformed Church, Church Book, 1853-57; J. Parker, *op. cit.*, p. 140; *BG* (3 Aug. 1854).

30. *BG* (25 Sep. 1856; 9 Apr. 1857); *BA* (9 Apr. 1857); *Evangelical Magazine* (1856), p. 661; *ibid.* (1857), p. 291; J. Parker, *op. cit.*, p. 137.

31. *Evangelical Magazine* (1857), p. 291; *BG* (2 Oct. 1856).

32. Joseph Parker, *Short Arguments on the Sabbath, Drummond Tract No. 526* (1855) in BPL, PC vol. 7, p. 107.

33. BPL, PC vol. 7, pp. 108, 111.

34. *Ibid.*, p. 114.

35. *Ibid.*, pp. 118-20.

36. J. Parker, *Preacher's Life*, p. 135; W. T. Henderson, *Recollections*.

37. Thomas Hardy, *The Mayor of Casterbridge* (ed. 1978), p. 262.

38. *BG* (20 Mar. 1856); *BA* (6 Mar. 1856; 27 Mar. 1856); *see above* p. 000.

39. BPL, PC vol. 7, pp. 128-32.

40. W. T. Henderson, *Recollections*; *BG* (8 June 1857; 17 June 1858); *Evangelical Magazine* (1858), p. 430; J. Parker, *Preacher's Life*, p. 145; A. Dawson, *op. cit.* p. 46; Banbury United Reformed Church, Church Book, 1857-69.

41. Amherst D. Tyssen, 'The Old Meeting House, Banbury', *Transactions of the Unitarian Historical Society*, vol. 1 (1919), pp. 292-93; *BG* (13 Sep. 1849; 20 June 1850; 22 Aug. 1850); *The Inquirer* (30 Jan. 1864); Memorial to Edward Cobb, formerly in Church Church Chapel, Banbury; Order of Service for the Opening of Christ Church Chapel, Banbury, BPL, Case M (Unpaginated).

42. A. D. Tyssen, *op. cit.*, p. 294; BPL, PC vol. 7, pp. 40-44.

43. *BA* (2 July 1863); *BG* (20 April 1865); *BH* (12 June 1861); BPL, PC vol. 9, p. 109; A. D. Tyssen, *op. cit.*, p. 297.

44. *Banbury Guardian Almanacks* (1852, 1853); *BG* (9 Nov. 1857).

45. *BG* (21 June 1877).

46. Anon. (Julia Redford), *The Banbury Female Martyr* (n.d.), *passim*; *BA* (3 Apr. 1856; 12 July 1866); *BG* (7 Mar. 1864; 14 Mar. 1864; 12 July 1866).

47. Banbury United Reformed Church, Church Book, 1853-57; *BG* (17 June 1858); Rusher's *Banbury List and Directory* (1862).

48. *NH* (11 Jan. 1851; 19 April 1851).

49. ORO, BMM/I/7-8, Banbury Monthly Meeting Minutes, 1845-55, 1855-70, *passim*.

50. *See* Table Four.

51. A. G. Wall, *St John's Church, Banbury* (1938), pp. 24, 29; *BG* (22 Mar. 1855; 28 Sep. 1876).

52. A. G. Wall, *op. cit.*, p. 23; *BH* (17 Jan. 1861); *BA* (23 Aug. 1860).

53. *BA* (4 Feb. 1869); *BG* (8 May 1856).

54. Marlborough Road Methodist Church, Banbury Wesleyan Circuit Quarterly Meeting Minutes, 1842-74.

55. Marlborough Road Methodist Church, Banbury Primitive Methodist Circuit Schedules, 1851-73; *BA* (20 Sep. 1855; 24 June 1857; 5 July 1857; 11 June 1863; 25 July 1867; 7 May 1868; 9 May 1872). *BG* (30 Apr. 1868).

56. *BG* (29 July 1858; 16 Jan. 1879); *BA* (5 Nov. 1874).

57. *BA* (7 May 1857); *BG* (8 May 1862; 7 May 1868; 11 Aug. 1870; *Primitive Methodist Magazine* (1862), p. 428; *ibid.* (1866), p. 111.

58. *BG* (18 Dec. 1851; 24 Dec. 1851).

59. *BG* (27 May 1852; 29 July 1852; 10 Feb. 1853; 23 Mar. 1854).

60. Rusher's *Banbury List and Directory* (1855), *BG* (25 Nov. 1852; 2 Dec. 1852; 17 Mar. 1853); *NH* (18 Dec. 1852).

61. Marlborough Road Methodist Church, Banbury Wesleyan Circuit Quarterly Meeting Minutes 1842-74; Banbury Wesleyan Circuit Plan, winter 1862-63: Banbury Wesleyan Circuit Schedules; statistics are drawn from *Minutes of the Wesleyan Methodist Conference.*

62. Marlborough Road Methodist Church, Minutes of Windsor Terrace Sunday School, 1851-54; Banbury Wesleyan Circuit Plan, 1851; E. A. Knight, *A Century and a Quarter of Sunday School Work* (1933), pp. 10-11.

63. *BG* (21 Jan. 1858. 1 June 1871); Barrie Trinder, *The History of Grimsbury Methodist Church* (1962), pp. 8-9; Marlborough Road Methodist Church, Banbury Wesleyan Circuit Plans, 1851, 1855; Banbury Wesleyan Prayer Leaders' Plan 1845 (Brailsford Collection); Banbury Wesleyan Local Preachers' Minute Book, 1827-47.

64. Marlborough Road Methodist Church, Banbury Wesleyan Circuit Plan, 1862; Banbury Wesleyan Circuit Schedules; *BG* (8 Oct. 1868; 1 June 1871; 9 Nov. 1871; 27 Apr. 1876; 6 July 1876; 4 July 1878).

65. Marlborough Road Methodist Church, Banbury Wesleyan Circuit Qiarterly Meeting Minutes, 1842-74; *BA* (7 June 1860; 5 Feb. 1863); *BH* (13 June 1861); *BG* (29 May 1862; 3 Sep. 1863).

66. Marlborough Road Methodist Church, Banbury Wesleyan Church Accounts, 1849-73; *BG* (5 May 1864; 19 May 1864; 11 May 1864); *BA* (10 May 1864).

67. Marlborough Road Methodist Church, Conveyance, 18 May 1880; *BA* (7 Feb. 1878; 8 Jan. 1880); Barrie Trinder, *The History of Methodism in Banbury* (1965), pp. 24-26.

68. *Methodist Recorder* (31 May 1900); *BG* (17 Nov. 1865; 7 June 1900).

69. Marlborough Road Methodist Church, Banbury Wesleyan Circuit Minutes 1842-74; Banbury Wesleyan Chapel Trustees Minutes 1848 *et seq.*

70. *BA* (1 June 1871); *BG* (25 May 1871; 25 April 1878).

71. Banbury United Reformed Church, Church Book, 1869-79; *BG* (26 Oct. 1871; 24 April 1873; 19 Oct. 1876).

72. *BA* (21 May 1874).

73. *BG* (25 Mar. 1869); *BA* (1 Apr. 1869; 20 May 1869); ORO, 315, Box 79b, George St Clair-Bernhard Samuelson, 1 Oct. 1868; Janet Sutterby, *Saints Below: a history of the Baptist Church meeting at Bridge Street Chapel, Banbury* (1973), p. 18.

74. Banbury United Reformed Church, Church Book, 1857-69.

75. M. K. Ashby, *Joseph Ashby of Tysoe 1859-1919* (1961), p. 27.

76. Banbury United Reformed Church, Church Book, 1857-69; *BG* (3 Feb. 1870).

77. *BG* (4 Feb. 1875; 21 June 1877); *BA* (22 Sep. 1877); Barrie Trinder, 'Revivalism in Banbury 1860', *C & CH* vol. 3 (1966), pp. 75-77; BPL, PC vol. 9, p. 45.

78. *BA* (2 Feb. 1860; 15 Mar. 1860); *BG* (23 Feb. 1860).

79. *BA* (4 May 1871; 3 July 1873; 10 Feb. 1874); *BG* (3 July 1863; 15 April 1869; 16 June 1870; 12 Feb. 1874); George Warner, *A Memoir of the Life and Labours of the late Kenrick Kench, Town Missionary of Banbury* (1874).

80. *BG* (27 May 1880; 3 June 1880; 14 June 1888; 21 June 1888; 28 June 1888; 26 July 1888).

81. *BA* (30 Mar. 1882; 13 Apr. 1882; 7 Dec. 1882).

82. *BG* (23 Mar. 1871; 20 Nov. 1873; 5 Sep. 1878; 30 Jan. 1879; 22 April 1880); *BA* (22 Jan. 1874; 26 Feb. 1880; 5 Oct. 1882).

83. *BA* (1 July 1880), *BG* (1 July 1880); *see* Table Fifteen.

84. W. T. Henderson, *Recollections;* *BG* (14 April 1853); *NH* (16 April 1853); *BA* (14 May 1857); BPL, PC vol. 7, pp. 63-70, 79.

85. *BG* (18 Jan. 1855; 22 April 1858; 13 Dec. 1866); *BH* (13 Mar. 1862).

86. *NH* (10 Dec. 1853); *BG* (27 May 1852; 27 Oct. 1853; 18 May 1854; 13 Dec. 1855); *BA* (13 Sep. 1855; 10 Oct. 1855; 15 Nov. 1855; 13 Dec. 1855); Sarah Beesley, *My Life* (1892), p. 81; BPL, PC vol. 7, pp. 99-103.
87. *BA* (17 Jan. 1856; 24 Jan. 1856).
88. Barrie Trinder, *A Victorian MP and his Constituents* (1969), p. xxxi, *BG* (12 Aug. 1858; 8 Sep. 1859); BPL, PC vol. 9, p. 29; ORO, BB/X/ii/1, Minute Book of the Burial Board of the Banbury Local Board of Health.
89. BA (29 Oct. 1868).

Chapter Ten

1. John Bright's description of Banbury in the House of Commons on 31 March 1859, *BA* (31 Mar. 1859).
2. *Edinburgh Review*, vol. 52 (1853), p. 58.
3. H. J. Hanham, *Election and Party Management: Politics in the Time of Disraeli and Gladstone* (1959), pp. 41, 55.
4. *BG* (24 June 1852; 3 June 1858; 10 June 1858; 22 Nov. 1858); BPL, PC vol. 6, pp. 9, 17, vol. 8, pp. 13-14; John Vincent. *The Formation of the Liberal Party 1857-1868* (1966), p. 103.
5. Barrie Trinder, *A Victorian MP and his Constituents* (1969), pp. xxi-xxii, xxv-xxviii, 56, 79, 87, 95-99, 116-117, 119-120; *BG* (9 July 1857).
6. B. Trinder, *Victorian MP*, pp. xxx-xxxi; *BA* (28 May 1857; 13 Aug. 1857); *see also above* p. 120.
7. *BG* (17 June 1852; 24 June 1852); BPL, PC vol. 7, pp. 3, 5, 7, 11, 18-19; B. Trinder, *Victorian MP*, pp. 70-71.
8. *BA* (17 Jan. 1856; 24 Jan. 1856); *see also above* p. 120.
9. *BA* (18 Sep. 1856; 2 Oct. 1856); BPL, PC vol. 8, pp. 1-4.
10. *BG* (20 Nov. 1856; 12 Mar. 1857; 19 Mar, 1857; 26 Mar. 1857; 2 Apr. 1857); *BA* (12 Mar. 1857; 26 Mar. 1857; 2 Apr. 1857; 11 Nov. 1858); ORO 315, Temp. Boxes P. R. O, Austin family papers; BPL, PC vol. 8, pp. 34, 39-40, 46-47, 61; *ibid.*, vol. 9, p. 143; Regents Park College Library, Oxford, W. T. Henderson, *Recollections of his Life*.
11. *BA* (2 Apr. 1857); BPL, Pollbooks.
12. B. Trinder, *Victorian MP*, pp. xxv, xxxv, 115, 122-23, 147; *BG* (20 Nov. 1856; 27 Nov. 1856; 29 Ape. 1858); BPL, PC vol. 8, pp. 95-100; British Museum, Add. MS. 38396, ff. 96-97.
13. B. Trinder, *Victorian MP*, pp. xxxvi-xxxvii, 123-31; *Law Times* (25 Aug. 1860), pp. 282-83; *ibid.* (1 Sep. 1860, pp. 294-95; *BA* (23 Aug. 1860); *BG* (23 Aug. 1860).
14. BPL, PC vol. 8, pp. 101, 103, 105, 107-108, 111, 113-114, 118, 121, 127, 130-31, 145, 148, 153, 165, 179, 191, 193; *BG* (29 Oct. 1858; 4 Nov. 1858; 11 Nov. 1858; 18 Nov. 1858; 9 Dec. 1858; 16 Dec. 1858; 23 Dec. 1858; 6 Jan. 1859; 13 Jan. 1859; 3 Feb. 1859; 10 Feb. 1859); *BA* (4 Nov. 1858; 11 Nov. 1858; 18 Nov. 1858; 10 Feb. 1859; 31 Mar. 1859); *BA* (4 Nov. 1858; 11 Nov. 1858; 18 Nov. 1858; 10 Feb. 1859; 31 Mar. 1859); *NH* (5 Feb. 1859; 26 Mar. 1859); B. Trinder, *Victorian MP*, pp. 121, 124; Arthur Miall, *The Life of Edward Miall* (1884), pp. 217-18; *The Nonconformist* (10 Feb. 1859); W. T. Henderson, *Recollections*; Sarah Beesley, *My Life* (1852), p. 85.
15. *BG* (7 Sep. 1876).
16. BPL, Pollbooks.
17. *The Times* (11 Feb. 1859); BPL, Brooks Collection, p. 160.
18. BPL, PC vol. 8, pp. 204-205, 211-212, 218-220, 229, 235, 243; *BG* (5 May 1859); W. T. Henderson, *Recollections*; *NH* (7 May 1859; 14 May 1859); B; Trinder, *Victorian MP*, p. 135.

19. BPL, PC vol. 9, pp. 237, 241.
20. BPL, PC vol. 9, p. 55; *BG* (7 Feb. 1861; 21 Feb. 1861; 19 Feb. 1863); *BA* (1 Sep. 1864); J. Vincent, *op. cit.*, p. 75.
21. W. T. Henderson, *Recollections*; BPL, PC vol. 9, pp. 146, 166, 171-73, 175, 178, 184, 187, 192, 217; *BG* (4 Aug. 1864; 25 May 1865; 1 June 1865; 6 July 1865; 13 July 1864; 20 July 1865).
22. *BG* (13 July 1865; 20 July 1865); BPL, PC vol. 9, pp. 208-209, 216.
23. ORO, 315, Box 80, Samuelson Election Correspondence.
24. ORO 315, Box 80, Bundle M, Samuelson Election Correspondence. *BG* (22 Feb. 1866; 26 Apr. 1866; 3 May 1866; 10 May 1866; 17 May 1866; 31 May 1866); *BA* (1 Mar. 1866; 17 Ma 1866).
25. BPL, PC vol. 9, pp. 228, 251, 256, 269; for the Reform League *see* Royden Harrison, *Before the Socialists* (1965), pp. 78-136; *BG* (22 Nov. 1866; 2 May 1867); *BA* (22 Nov. 1866; 2 May 1867).
26. ORO 315, Box 79b, Box 80 Bundle M, Samuelson Election Correspondence; BPL, RC p. 371; PC vol. 9, p. 270; Case W, ff. 2-4, 6, 11-13, 16, 20, 23-25, 30-34, 38-39, 58, 63; *BG* (8 Oct. 1868; 15 Oct. 1868; 29 Oct. 1868; 5 Nov. 1868; 12 Nov. 1868; 19 Nov. 1868); Royden Harrison, *op. cit.*, pp. 148-49, 164, 171; H. J. Hanham, *op. cit.*, pp. 353-54.
27. BPL, Pollbooks; *see* Tables Thirteen and Fourteen.
28. *BG* (15 Oct. 1868; 22 Oct. 1868; 29 Oct. 1868); ORO 315, Box 79b, Samuelson Election Correspondence; BPL, Case W, ff. 17, 22.
29. Quoted in Royden Harrison, *op. cit.*, p. 184.
30. BPL, Pollbooks.
31. BPL, Pollbooks; *see* Tables Thirteen and Fourteen.
32. *BG* (8 Oct. 1868; 29 Oct. 1868); BPL, PC vol. 9, p. 10.
33. BPL, Case W, f. 22.

Chapter Eleven

1. *BA* (13 Oct. 1859).
2. John Randall, *Broseley and its Surroundings* (1879), p. 94.
3. T. W. Boss, *Reminiscences of Old Banbury* (1903), p. 27.
4. John Vincent, *The Formation of the Liberal Party 1857-1868* (1966), p. 27.
5. Regent's Park College Library, Oxford, W. T. Henderson, *Recollections of his Life.*
6. *BG* (27 Aug. 1857; 30 Sep. 1858; 30 April 1863); *BA* (7 Jan. 1858); Barrie Trinder, *Banbury's Poor in 1850* (1966), p. 103.
7. *BG* (2 Jan. 1868); *BA* (9 Jan. 1868).
8. *BA* (8 Nov. 1855; 21 Oct. 1858; 10 Mar. 1859); *BG* (21 Oct. 1858); for York *see* Frances Finnegan, *Poverty and Prostitution: a study of Victorian Prostitutes in York* (1979).
9. *BG* (6 Jan, 1859).
10. *BG* (11 Apr. 1861; 5 Sep. 1861; 14 Nov. 1861).
11. *BA* (9 July 1863; 20 Feb. 1868); *BG* (24 Mar. 1864).
12. *BH* (2 May 1861); *BG* (31 May 1866); ORO, T/SL/102/i, Log Book of Banbury National School; BB/XI/vii/2, Log Book of Banbury British School.
13. *BA* (28 July 1855; 28 July 1864); *BG* (25 July 1861; 31 July 1862; 30 July 1864); *BH* (25 July 1861).
14. *BG* (25 July 1861; 23 July 1863); *BH* (24 July 1862); *BA* (21 July 1864); *see above* p. 75.
15. *BA* (11 Nov. 1875); *BG* (9 Nov. 1865; 8 Nov. 1866).
16. *BG* (10 April 1860).

17. *BG* (4 April 1867).
18. James Cadbury, *A New History of Banbury before and after the passing of a Maine Liquor Law* (n.d.), BPL PC vol. 9, p. 279: *BG* (29 April 1852; 20 April 1854); Brian Harrison, 'The British Prohibitionists 1853-72: a biographical analysis', *International Review of Social History*, vol. 15 (1970), pp. 376, 451.
19. *The Alliance* (24 Feb. 1855), p. 226; Brian Harrison and Barrie Trinder, *Drink and Sobriety in an Early Victorian Country Town: Banbury 1830-60* (1969), p. 25; *BG* (3 Apr. 1857: 28 Mar. 1867).
20. *BA* (6 Sep. 1855, 27 Sep. 1855); B Harrison and B. Trinder, *op. cit.*, p. 25.
21. *BG* (12 July 1866; 10 Jan. 1867; 17 July 1870).
22. *BG* (28 June 1866).
23. *BG* (16 Mar. 1858; 6 May 1858; 15 July 1858; 1 Sep. 1859; 8 Sep. 1859); *BA* (25 Mar. 1858).
24. *BG* (21 Feb. 1856; 6 May 1858; 1 Aug. 1861).
25. *BA* (28 April 1864; 2 Dec. 1869); *BG* (31 Mar. 1864).
26. *BA* (4 Feb. 1864; 31 Jan. 1867); *BG* (23 Nov. 1865; 11 July 1867; 21 May 1868; 18 June 1868; 23 July 1868).
27. *BA* (19 May 1870); *BG* (18 April 1867; 14 April 1870; 19 May 1870).
28. *BG* (13 July 1854; 25 Oct. 1855).
29. *BA* (29 Mar. 1866); *BG* (18 Jan. 1866; 29 Mar. 1866).
30. BPL, MI Mins., 25 Mar. 1850; 31 Mar. 1851; *BG* (28 Mar. 1850).
31. BPL, MI Mins., 29 Mar. 1852, n.d. Oct. 1852; n.d. Oct. 1854, 20 Apr. 1858, 29 Sep. 1858; *BG* (30 Apr. 1857; 15 Oct. 1857; 22 Apr. 1858; 30 Sep. 1858).
32. BPL, MI Mins., 4 Oct. 1865, 28 Mar. 1866, 20 Sep. 1866; *BG* (3 Oct. 1867).
33. BPL, MI Mins., 3 Jan. 1854, 20 Apr. 1858; William Potts, *Banbury through One Hundred Years* (1942), p. 83; *see also* pp. 104-105.
34. BPL, MI Mins., 4 Oct. 1864, 4 Oct. 1864; William Potts, *op. cit.*, pp. 83-84; Sarah Beesley, *My Life* (1892), p. 115.
35. *BG* (3 June 1852; 18 Nov. 1856; 11 Feb. 1858); BPL, MI Mins., 29 Sep. 1851, 29 Mar. 1852.
36. *BG* (6 Jan. 1876; 13 Jan. 1876; 30 Mar. 1876).
37. *BG* (13 Feb. 1862); BPL, MI Mins., 2 Apr. 1855.
38. *BG* (2 Oct. 1862); BPL, MI Mins., 29 Sep. 1864.
39. BPL, MI Mins., 2 Nov. 1854, 13 Aug. 1858, 10 Oct. 1860, 22 Mar. 1865.
40. BPL, MI Mins., 31 May 1865, 29 Sep. 1866, 29 Sep. 1868, 9 Aug. 1869; *BG* (27 Aug. 1868); BPL, PC vol. 10, p. 9.
41. BPL, PC vol. 10, p. 2.
42. *BA* (24 Dec. 1874); *BG* (7 Jan. 1875; 14 Jan. 1875; 11 Feb. 1875; 8 Feb. 1877; 29 Nov. 1877; 14 Nov. 1878).
43. *BG* (24 Jan. 1850; 9 Jan. 1851; 5 Aug. 1852; 2 Sep. 1852; 9 Sep. 1852; 26 Sep. 1852; 9 Apr. 1857).
44. *BG* (1 Apr. 1858; 8 Apr. 1858; 13 May 1858; 20 May 1858; 8 July 1858; 12 Aug. 1858; 2 Sep. 1858); *BA* (1 Oct. 1857; 12 Aug. 1858).
45. *BA* (27 Feb. 1868; 25 Mar. 1869).
46. *BG* (4 Oct. 1866).
47. *BG* (20 July 1876; 30 Aug. 1877; 22 Aug. 1878; 26 Aug. 1880).
48. *BG* (21 July 1870; 28 July 1870); *Banbury Beacon* (29 July 1870).
49. *BG* (4 July 1867); *BA* (4 July 1867); ORO, T/SL/102/i, Log Book Of Banbury National School.
50. *BG* (8 July 1852; 9 July 1857; 8 July 1858; 7 July 1859); *BA* (7 July 1850).
51. *BG* (5 July 1866; 28 Sep. 1876).
52. *BG* (30 June 1859; 7 July 1859; 27 June 1861; 3 July 1862; 6 July 1865).
53. *BG* (8 July 1852; 21 June 1866; 5 July 1866); *BA* (24 June 1869; 8 July 1869).
54. *BG* (1 July 1858; 29 July 1858); *BA* (2 Feb. 1860; 21 June 1860; 13 Aug. 1868).
55. W. H. Lickorish, *Our Jubilee Story, or Fifty Years of Co-operation in Banbury and the Neighbourhood* (1916), *passim*.

56. *BG* (26 May 1859; 26 June 1863; 22 June 1865; 4 Jan. 1866; 12 July 1866; 2 Aug. 1866; 11 Oct. 1866; BPL, PC vol. 9, p. 56; ORO, T/SL/102/i, Log Book of Banbury National School; Ian Beckett, 'The Amateur Military Tradition: new tasks for the local historian', *Local Historian* vol. 13 (1979), pp. 476-81.

57. *BG* (31 Oct. 1850; 15 Jan. 1852; 26 Oct. 1854); Barrie Trinder, *A Victorian MP and his Constituents* (1969), p. xxvi.

58. *BG* (24 Nov. 1856); *BA* (16 April 1857); *see above* p. 92.

59. *BA* (13 Oct. 1859).

60. W. H. Lickorish, *op. cit.; see above* p. 69.

61. William Dorling, *Henry Vincent* (1879), p. 31; R. C. Gammage, *The History of the Chartist Movement* (ed. 1969), pp. 401, 411; *BG* (14 May 1863).

62. *BA* (12 Dec. 1860); *see above* pp. 56-61.

63. Asa Briggs, *Victorian Cities* (ed. 1968), pp. 195-200; *BA* (21 Oct. 1958).

64. *NH* (1 Feb. 1851); *Illustrated London News* (8 June 1850), p. 413.

65. *BG* (3 Mar. 1854; 13 Apr. 1854).

66. *BA* (28 May 1868; 28 Oct. 1869); *BG* (18 Feb. 1858; 28 May 1868).

67. *BG* (25 Nov. 1858).

68. *BG* (8 Apr. 1852; 17 Feb. 1859; 24 Feb. 1859; 2 Nov. 1865).

69. W. P. Johnson, *A Stranger's Guide through Banbury* (1859), p. 6.

70. *BG* (13 Mar. 1855; 15 Apr. 1858).

71. *BG* (18 Nov. 1853).

72. George Eliot, *Middlemarch* (ed. 1965), p. 246: Barrie Trinder, 'The Distant Scene: Banbury and the United States in the Mid-Nineteenth Century', *C & CH*, vol. 7 (1978), pp. 163-74.

73. *BG* (14 June 1855).

74. *BG* (10 Mar. 1863; 28 May 1863).

75. *BA* (2 Feb. 1860).

76. *BG* (16 Apr. 1857); *BA* (2 Apr. 1857).

77. *BG* (27 Oct. 1859).

78. *BA* (13 Feb. 1873; 16 Oct. 1873); *BG* (13 Feb. 1873; 16 Oct. 1873).

79. *BG* (5 Feb. 1857; 3 Apr. 1857; 17 Sep. 1857; 21 Jan. 1858; 11 Feb. 1858; 30 Apr. 1858; 24 Dec. 1868); *BA* (18 Feb. 1858); *BH* (6 Mar. 1862); B. Trinder, *Victorian MP*, p. 116.

80. *BG* (17 Dec. 1857; 20 Jan. 1859); *BA* (20 Jan. 1857).

81. *BG* (1 Apr. 1857; 27 Feb. 1862; 3 Nov. 1864); *BH* (13 Mar. 1862).

82. *BG* (15 Dec. 1850; 9 Mar. 1861; 3 Dec. 1868).

83. *BG* (19 Jan. 1871; 15 Aug. 1872); *BA* (7 Jan. 1869).

84. *BA* (29 Apr. 1858); *BG* (22 Apr. 1858).

85. *BG* (24 Oct. 1850; 17 Aug. 1854; 26 Sep. 1861; 9 Oct. 1862; 17 Sep. 1868); *BA* (26 June 1856; 9 Oct. 1858: 11 Oct. 1866; 20 Oct. 1870).

86. *BG* (30 Sep. 1858); *BA* (21 July 1850; 1 Nov. 1860; 8 Nov. 1860; 28 May 1863).

87. *BG* (25 Oct. 1855); *BA* (21 Oct. 1858; 16 Aug. 1860; 1 Oct. 1863; 25 Aug. 1869).

88. *BG* (17 Jan. 1850; 9 Jan. 1857).

89. *BG* (5 July 1855; 25 Oct. 1855; 22 Sep. 1858).

90. *BA* (23 Oct. 1856; 20 Oct. 1858); *BG* (24 Oct. 1861; 16 Oct. 1862).

91. *BG* (18 Nov. 1856; 5 April 1860); *BA* (7 Apr. 1864; 14 Apr. 1864).

92. Lou Warwick, *Theatre Un-Royal* (1974), pp. 176-79. 187; *BG* 22 Jan. 1853; 29 Jan. 1853; 5 Feb. 1863).

93. *BG* (10 Aug. 1854; 3 May 1855; 15 May 1859; 3 May 1866; 17 Sep. 1868; 19 Feb. 1880); *BH* (27 Mar. 1862; 25 June 1863); *BA* (13 Dec. 1855).

94. *BH* (14 Mar. 1861); *BG* (2 Feb. 1854; 22 Jan. 1863; 29. Jan. 1863; 5 Feb. 1863).

95. *BG* (22 Aug. 1857; 16 Aug. 1866); *BA* (27 Aug. 1863).

96. *BG* (3 Sep. 1857; 16 Sep. 1858; 6 Sep. 1887); *BA* (26 Aug. 1858); *NH* (24 June 1854; 18 Nov. 1854; 20 Jan. 1855; 14 June 1856).

97. *NH* (13 July 1850; 18 Aug. 1851); *BG* (28 Mar. 1850).

98. *BG* (25 June 1857).

99. *BA* (5 Aug. 1858); *BG* 13 Aug. 1868); *BH* (13 June 1861).

100. *BG* (28 Mar. 1861).
101. *BA* (13 Sep. 1855); *BG* (22 June 1865).
102. *BG* (4 June 1857; 7 Apr. 1870).
103. *BG* (15 Oct. 1863); *BA* (17 Mar. 1864).
104. *BG* (28 Dec. 1864; 6 Apr. 1865); *BA* (11 Oct. 1866); R. C. K. Ensor, *England 1870-1914* (1936), pp. 164-65.
105. *BG* (16 Oct. 1879).
106. *BG* (21 June 1855; 4 Oct. 1855; 15 Nov. 1855; 26 July 1866; 30 Apr. 1868); W. Potts, *op. cit.*, p. 120.
107. *BG* (3 Mar. 1864; 28 Apr. 1864; 4 Feb. 1875); *BA* (5 Aug. 1869; 26 Aug. 1869; 1 Feb. 1877).
108. *BG* (20 May 1875; 2 Aug. 1877; 1 Aug. 1878; 4 Sep. 1879); *BA* (28 May 1874; 20 Nov. 1879; 24 Dec. 1879).
109. *BA* (18 June 1863).
110. *BH* (5 July 1861; 12 July 1861); *see above* p. 117.
111. James Obelkevich, *Religion and Rural Society: South Lindsey 1825-1875* (1976), pp. 59-60.
112. *BG* (24 Jan. 1850); *BA* (18 Nov. 1869).
113. W. Henderson, *Recollections*.
114. Mark Rutherford, *The Revolution in Tanner's Lane* (Popular ed., n.d.), p. 162.

Chapter Twelve

1. Richard Jefferies, *Hodge and his Masters* (ed. 1966), vol. 2, p. 127.
2. *Ibid.*, vol. 1, p. 36.
3. John Orr, *The Agriculture of Oxfordshire; a Survey* (1916), pp. 195-98; P. J. Perry, *British Farming in the Great Depression 1870-1914: an Historical Geography* (1974), pp. 24-25.
4. *BA* (3 Oct. 1872; 6 Jan. 1881; 5 Jan. 1882); *BG* (22 July 1875; 3 May 1877).
5. *Report of HM's Commissioners on Agriculture*, BPP, 1882 XV, pp. 72-73.
6. *Preliminary Reports from HM's Commissioners on Agriculture*, BPP, 1881 XVI, p. 280; *BA* (7 Oct. 1880; 26 Oct. 1882).
7. *Preliminary Reports of HM's Commissioners on Agriculture*, BPP, 1881 XVI, pp. 267, 275-77, 309-11; J. Orr, *op. cit.*, p. 88.
8. J. Orr, *op. cit.*, pp. 70-71; Agricultural Economics Research Institute, Oxford, *Country Planning: a study of rural problems* (1944), pp. 29-30.
9. *See* Table Two.
10. *BG* (24 Oct. 1878).
11. J. Orr, *op. cit.*, p. 70; *Country Planning*, p. 5.
12. *BA* (16 May 1872; 20 Mar. 1873; 6 May 1875); *BG* (23 Jan. 1873; 13 Feb. 1873; 20 Feb. 1873; 17 Mar. 1873); for the disastrous consequences of migration to Brazil in this period *see* A. Milward and S. B. Saul, *The Industrial Development of Continental Europe* (1973), p. 153.
13. *See* Table Two.
14. Rusher's *Banbury Lists and Directories*.
15. *BA* (20 Jan. 1881; 27. Jan. 1881).
16. *BG* (9 Jan. 1879; 16 Jan. 1879; 6 Feb. 1879).
17. *BG* (27 Nov. 1879; 11 Dec. 1870); *BA* (24 Dec. 1879; 1 Jan. 1880; 29 Apr. 1880).
18. Audrey Taylor, *Gilletts: Bankers at Banbury and Oxford* (1964), p. 165; *BG* (4 Apr. 1878).
19. S. B. Saul, 'The Market and the Development of the Mechanical Engineering Industries in Britain, 1860-1914', *Economic History Review* 2nd Ser., vol. 20 (1967), pp. 118-119; Archie Potts, 'Ernest Samuelson and the Britannia Works', *C & CH* vol. 4 (1971), pp. 187-93; David Alderton and John Booker, *The Batsford Guide to the Industrial Archaeology of East Anglia* (1980), *passim*.

20. Anon., *Hunt Edmunds & Co. 1896-1946* (1946), pp. 5-9.

21. *Views & Reviews, special edition, Banbury* (1897), reprinted in 'Weaving in the 1890s', *C & CH* vol. 3 (1968), pp. 207-10; *BG* (3 Feb. 1876; 6 Feb. 1879); William Potts, *Banbury through One Hundred Years* (1942), pp. 39-40.

22. *BG* (6 June 1872; 11 Feb. 1875; 5 Oct. 1876; 7 June 1877); *BA* (1 Jan. 1874; 29 Aug. 1878; 28 Aug. 1879; 1 Jan. 1880; 8 Jan. 1880; 2 Sep. 1880); J. H. Russell, *The Banbury and Cheltenham Direct Railway 1887-1962* (1978), pp. 8-10; J. M. Dunn, *The Stratford-upon-Avon and Midland Junction Railway* (1952), pp. 7-9.

23. Audrey Taylor, *op. cit.*, pp. 163-82.

24. W. H. Lickorish, *Our Jubilee Story* (1916), pp. 6-7; Frederick Lamb, *A Brief History of the Banbury Co-operative Industrial Society* (1887), *passim*; *BCR* (Oct. 1871).

25. *BCR* (Feb. 1872; Dec. 1872; Feb. 1874; Mar. 1874); *BG* (22 Dec. 1870; 13 July 1871); *BA* (23 Sep. 1880).

26. Joseph Arch, *The Autobiography of Joseph Arch* (ed. 1966), pp. 42-45; Pamela Horn, *Joseph Arch* (1971), pp. 44-47, 54, 63-67, 102-106, 141.

27. *BA* (2 May 1872; 16 May 1872: 6 June 1872).

28. J. R. Hodgkins, *Over the Hills to Glory* (1978), pp. 68-69.

29. *BA* (15 Aug. 1872); *BG* (3 Apr. 1873).

30. *BG* (27 Mar. 1873).

31. *BA* (8 May 1873; 30 Apr. 1874; 8 Oct. 1874); *BG* (30 Apr. 1874).

32. *BG* (1 May 1879), *BA* (6 Mar. 1879); J. R. Hodgkins, *op. cit.*, p. 76.

33. Earl Jowitt, *A Dictionary of English Law* (ed. 1959), vol. 2, p. 1820.

34. *BG* (10 Aug. 1871); *BA* (17 Aug. 1871).

35. *BA* (11 July 1872; 18 July 1872; 22 Aug. 1872; 5 Sep. 1872).

36. *BA* (15 Jan. 1874; 23 July 1874; 29 Oct. 1874); ORO, T/SL/102/i, Log Book of Banbury National School.

37. *BG* (8 July 1873; 13 Jan. 1876; 27 Jan. 1876); *BA* (9 Mar. 1876; 17 June 1876; 24 June 1876).

38. *BG* (22 June 1874; 1 Mar. 1877).

39. *BG* (21 Sep. 1876; 28 Sep. 1876).

40. *BG* (22 June 1876); *BA* (9 Mar. 1876).

41. *BG* (14 Feb. 1878); *BA* (21 Feb. 1878).

42. BPL, RC pp. 281, 340; *BG* (20 Nov. 1879).

43. *BG* (17 April 1879).

44. *BG* (25 July 1878); *BA* (25 July 1878).

45. *BA* (31 Jan. 1880; 27 May 1880; 5 Aug. 1880).

46. *BG* (21 Sep. 1876).

47. *The Sportsman*, quoted in *BA* (10 June 1880).

48. *BA* (6 Jan. 1876); *BG* (6 Jan. 1876).

49. *BA* (16 Mar. 1871; 7 Oct. 1875; 21 Sep. 1876); *BG* (19 Aug. 1875; 17 Aug. 1876; 28 Sep. 1876; 4 Apr. 1878; 12 Dec. 1878); BPL, RC, p. 235.

50. *BA* (11 Jan. 1871); *BG* (14 Oct. 1875).

51. *BG* (28 Oct. 1875; 4 Nov. 1875).

52. *BA* (17 Apr. 1873); *BG* (18 May 1876).

53. *BA* (21 Jan. 1871; 29 Sep. 1871; 11 July 1872; 14 Nov. 1872; 17 Apr. 1873; 22 Feb. 1877; 13 May 1880).

54. *BA* (11 Jan. 1871; 21 Dec. 1871); *BG* (21 Aug. 1873).

55. *BA* (19 May 1870; 2 Mar. 1871); *BG* (19 May 1870; 21 Aug. 1873).

56. *BA* (3 Oct. 1872).

57. *BG* (26 June 1873); *BA* (26 June 1873).

58. *BG* (24 July 1873; 31 July 1873); *BA* (21 Aug. 1873).

59. *BG* (2 Mar. 1871; 11 Feb. 1873; 29 Jan. 1874).

60. *BG* (26 Oct. 1871; 14 Mar. 1872; 25 Mar. 1875); *BA* (26 Oct. 1871: 25 Apr. 1872).

61. *The Shield* (July 1874), pp. 142-44; *BA* (5 Feb. 1874; 4 June 1874).

62. *BG* (11 Mar. 1875; 12 April 1877).

63. *BG* (28 Apr. 1870; 24 Jan. 188); *BA* (25 Sep. 1879; 6 Nov. 1879; 24 Jan. 1880).
64. P. Horn, *op. cit.*, p. 67; *BA* (15 May 1872; 4 July 1872).
65. W. H. Lickorish, *op. cit.*, p. 8.
66. *BA* (10 Aug. 1876). *NG* (13 Nov. 1875).
67. *BCR* (Oct. 1871).
68. *BCR* (Apr. 1873).
69. *BA* (3 Oct. 1872); P. Horn, *op. cit.*, p. 67; *see also above* p. 149.
70. *BCR* (Oct. 1871).
71. *Ibid.*
72. *BG* (5 Nov. 1876; 9 Jan. 1879); *BA* (12 Oct. 1876).
73. *BG* (4 Jan. 1877).
74. *BCR* (July 1873); *BA* (18 Dec. 1873).
75. Walter Bagehot, *The English Constitution* (ed. 1963), p. 161.
76. *BA* (22 Dec. 1870; 29 Jan. 1874); BPL, RC p. 381.
77. BPL, Case W, ff. 1-5.
78. *BA* (5 Feb. 1874); *BG* (5 Feb. 1874); BPL, Case W. f. 7.
79. *BA* (5 Feb. 1874); *BG* (5 Feb. 1874); BPL, Case W, f. 17.
80. *BA* (5 Feb. 1874); *BG* (5 Feb. 1874).
81. *BA* (5 Feb. 1874); *BG* (5 Feb. 1874); BPL, Case W, f. 14; Table Fourteen.
82. *BA* (5 Feb. 1874; 12 Feb. 1874; 26 Feb. 1874); *BG* (5 Feb. 1874; 12 Feb. 1874; 26 Feb. 1874; 22 Oct. 1874).
83. *BG* (27 June 1876; 14 Sep. 1876); *BA* (14 Sep. 1876).
84. *BG* (21 Sep. 1876; 30 Nov. 1876; 1 Feb. 1877; 7 June 1877); *BA* (29 Sep. 1877).
85. *BG* (25 July 1878; 10 Oct. 1878).
86. *BG* (27 Feb. 1879; 16 Oct. 1879); *BA* (5 Dec. 1878; 6 Nov. 1879); BPL, RC, p. 281.
87. *BA* (4 Mar. 1880; 11 Mar. 1880).
88. *BA* (19 Feb. 1880); L. E. Naylor, *The Irrepressible Victorian* (1965), pp. 62-66.
89. *BG* (11 Mar. 1880; 18 Mar. 1880).
90. *BG* (11 Mar. 1880; 18 Mar. 1880; 25 Mar. 1880).
91. *BA* (25 Mar. 1880; 1 Apr. 1880); *BG* (25 Mar. 1880; 1 April 1880).
92. *BG* (18 Mar. 1880; 1 Apr. 1880).
93. Table Fourteen.
94. *BA* (1 Apr. 1880).
95. *BA* (8 Apr. 1880; 22 Apr. 1880; 15 July 1880).
96. *BA* (1 Dec. 1881; 9 Mar. 1882; 29 June 1882); W. Potts, *op. cit.*, pp. 124-26.

Chapter Thirteen

1.   Richard Jefferies, *Hodge and his Masters* (1966 ed.), vol. 1, p. 119.
2.   J. L. Langley, 'Memories of Late Victorian Banbury', *C & CH*, vol. 2 (1963), pp. 51-56; 'Banbury at the Turn of the Century', *ibid.*, vol. 5 (1972), pp. 23-40.
3.   Margaret Stacey, *Tradition and Change; a study of Banbury* (1960).
4.   Barrie Trinder, 'Fifty Years On: Banbury in 1931', *C & CH*, vol. 8 (1981), pp. 117-37.
5.   M. Stacey, *op. cit.*, p. 12.
6.   *Ibid.*, p. 11.
7.   *Ibid.*, p. 31.
8.   *Ibid.*, pp. 54-58.
9.   Thomas Hardy, *The Mayor of Casterbridge* (1978 ed.), p. 64.
10. R. Jefferies, *op. cit.*, vol. 1, p. 119.

11. *Ibid.*, vol. 1, p. 120.
12. *See* Table One.
13. M. K. Ashby, *Joseph Ashby of Tysoe* (1961), pp. 56, 150-51.
14. R. Jefferies, *op. cit.*, pp. 120-26.
15. John Prest, *The Industrial Revolution in Coventry* (1960), pp. 28-31.
16. *OH* (7 Dec. 1833).
17. George Eliot, *Felix Holt the Radical* (Blackwood ed., n.d.), pp. 29, 42, 214.
18. *OH* (11 Jan. 1833).
19. Mark Rutherford, *The Revolution in Tanner's Lane* (1887 ed.), p. 233.
20. David Alderton and John Booker, *The Batsford Guide to the Industrial Archaeology of East Anglia* (1980), pp. 184-85, *et passim*.
21. *Seventh Report of the Medical Officer of the Privy Council*, Appendix, Six BPP, 1864 XXVI, p. 201.
22. Martin Billing, *Directory and Gazetteer of the Counties of Berkshire and Oxfordshire* (1854), pp. 65-72; *NH* (12 Aug. 1854).
23. *NH* (20 Oct. 1855).
24. Thomas Hardy, *op. cit.*, p. 62.
25. *BG* (19 Apr. 1879).
26. G. W. Trevelyan, *English Social History* (1944), p. 493.
27. BPL, PC, vol. 8, p. 243, *ibid.*, vol. 11, p. 10.
28. *NH* (12 July 1856).
29. *OH* (11 Jan. 1833).

Table One

A Comparison of some Midlands Market Towns

Source: Sundry trade directories

The purpose of this table is to give an indication of the place of Banbury in the scale of Midlands market towns, by comparing the numbers of journeys made each week by carriers to a selection of towns, and the numbers of tradesmen in occupations particularly linked with market functions. The table is arranged in order of the totals of carrier journeys per week. Due allowance should be made for the varying dates of the directories, and for the different conventions used by directory publishers.

Town	Date	Carrier journeys per week	Population in 1851	Linen Drapers	Grocers	Ironmongers	Public houses
Birmingham . . .	1856	524	232,841	87	170	64	1,597
Reading	1854	513	21,456	24	74	16	212
Derby	1846	465	40,609	25	42	5	232
Leicester . . .	1835	454	60,584	25	82	9	369
Banbury	1851	446	8,793	16	19	16	80
Bury St Edmunds . .	1844	340	13,900	14	21	21	75
Northampton . . .	1849	290	26,657	17	39	11	162
Oxford	1854	290	27,843	15	52	11	233
Coventry . . .	1856	287	36,812	20	43	10	239
Ipswich	1844	250	32,914	18	43	10	168
Nottingham . .	1835	235	57,407	37	82	11	390
Cirencester	1859	160	6,096	11	26	5	56
Wolverhampton . .	1851	142	49,985	23	80	18	320
Newark	1835	123	11,330	13	22	6	78
Shrewsbury . . .	1851	116	19,681	18	38	11	155
Newbury	1854	106	6,574	15	27	9	80
Daventry	1849	96	4,430	6	14	4	41
Warwick	1856	92	10,973	10	16	4	71
Chesterfield . . .	1846	90	7,101	12	17	5	49
Abingdon	1854	71	5,954	5	18	4	71
Hereford	1851	69	12,108	15	36	7	87
Cheltenham . . .	1859	63	35,051	32	56	19	202
Sleaford	1842	54	3,729	7	12	4	26
Leamington . .	1856	52	15,962	15	28	6	82
Wantage	1854	52	2,951	6	9	4	28
Melton Mowbray . .	1835	48	4,391	7	16	2	46
Stratford on Avon .	1835	40	3,372	7	8	2	37
Worksop	1854	33	6,058	6	12	2	43
Huntingdon . . .	1854	31	6,219	9	8	4	31
Witney	1854	30	3,009	7	17	4	43
Ashbourne	1846	26	2,418	11	13	4	35
Stafford	1851	25	11,829	12	32	6	84
Lichfield	1851	24	7,012	9	18	6	65
Barton on Humber .	1842	18	3,866	—	12	2	16
Rugby	1835	20	6,317	4	8	3	41
Leek	1851	20	8,877	8	12	3	47
Bridgnorth . . .	1851	16	7,610	4	16	3	73
Bicester	1854	16	3,054	5	8	4	22
Chipping Norton . .	1854	15	2,932	3	6	3	26
Leominster	1859	13	5,214	7	13	4	61
Brackley	1849	12	2,157	3	9	2	17
Bishop's Castle . .	1851	9	1,961	2	5	3	11
Deddington	1854	9	2,178	3	9	2	9
Chipping Campden .	1859	5	2,351	4	4	4	15

Table Two

The Population of Banbury and the Banbury Union in the Nineteenth Century

Source: Census Returns

	Banbury borough	Neithrop	Grimsbury	Total population of Banbury parish	Population of other parishes in Banbury PL Union	Total population of Union	Percentage of Union population in Banbury
1801	2,755	1,055	260	4,070	15,737	19,807	20.5
1811	2,869	1,332	248	4,449	16,434	20,883	21.3
1821	3,396	1,851	426	5,673	19,362	25,035	22.7
1831	3,737	2,169	521	6,427	20,278	26,705	24.1
1841	3,736	2,850	655	7,241	21,231	28,471	25.5
1851	4,035	4,185	573	8,793	20,995	29,788	29.3
1861	4,055	5,072	1,111	10,238	19,923	30,161	33.0
1871	4,114	5,749	1,905	11,768	19,440	31,208	37.1
1881	3,600	6,060	2,467	12,127	17,994	30,121	40.3
1891	3,638	6,153	3,031	12,822	16,673	29,495	43.5
1901	3,394	6,617	3,015	13,026	15,527	28,553	45.6

Table Three

Traffic on Main Roads in the Banbury Area: 1845

Source: Reports from Commissioners on Railway Gauges, Oxford, Worcester & Wolverhampton and Oxford & Rugby Railway Bills, BPP, 1845, XI, p. 209.

Route between Banbury and:	Passengers with Post horses 14 days	Passengers with flys, gigs &c. 14 days	Passengers in vans, spring carts &c. 14 days	Total passengers 14 days	Passengers per day
Stratford upon Avon . . .	286	2,262	3,224	5,772	412
Bicester . . .	390	3,432	3,042	6,864	490
Oxford . . .	832	3,926	5,018	9,776	698
Southam . . .	442	3,900	6,812	11,154	797

	General Merchandise tons p.a. (estimated)	Agricultural and building products tons p.a. (estimated)	Total freight tons p.a. (estimated)
Stratford . .	1,118	1,508	2,626
Bicester . . .	1,534	1,352	2,886
Oxford . . .	2,626	1,482	4,108
Southam . . .	3,458	1,508	4,966

Table Four

Migration.into Banbury from the Hinterland 1851 and 1871

Source: 1851 and 1871 Census enumerators' returns

The Index figure is obtained by dividing the population of the parish concerned in 1851 and 1871 by the number of migrants from the parish recorded in Banbury in the same year..

Parish and distance from Banbury (in miles)	1851 Migrants in Banbury	Index figure	1871 Migrants in Banbury	Index figure
Drayton—2	23	10.22	51	30.18
Bodicote—2	104	15.45	142	20.97
Broughton—3	15	8.33	27	17.76
North Newington—3 . . .	45	10.32	39	8.88
Wroxton—3	49	6.21	48	6.52
Hanwell—3	31	10.30	64	25.10
Adderbury—4	110	8.16	109	8.52
Bloxham—4	120	8.99	113	7.65
Tadmarton—4	27	6.00	43	9.91
Milton—4	12	7.32	13	8.84
Horley—4	26	6.62	44	13.02
Shotteswell—4	20	6.09	25	8.12
Cropredy—4	47	7.89	39	7.29
Chacombe—4	23	10.87	59	13.08
Middleton Cheney—4 . . .	120	8.37	121	9.79
Kings Sutton—4	36	2.79	21	5.34
Barfords—5	18	3.25	21	5.34
Milcombe—5	18	7.47	13	5,06
Swalcliffe—5	8	2.18	22	6.18
Shutford—5	21	5.05	30	7.94
Alkerton—5	3	1.58	8	3.98
Hornton—5	31	5.25	37	6.60
Mollington—5	15	3.79	28	8.64
Wardington—5	60	6.96	59	7.86
Thenford—5	5	3.79	13	9.92
Deddington—6	72	3.30	96	4.66
South Newington—6	37	8.83	29	7.80
Wigginton—6	7	2.87	21	6.77
Shennington—6	17	3.89	30	8.04
Warmington—6	14	3.97	34	8.25
Farnborough—6	20	5.73	17	3.99
Claydon and Clattercote—6 .	18	5.31	19	5.65
Edgcote—6	3	3.89	5	5.21
Thorpe Mandeville—6 . . .	9	5.96	13	8.55
Marston St Lawrence—6 . .	10	1.85	10	1.95
Farthinghoe—6	19	4.33	31	7.67
Charlton and Newbottle—6 .	13	2.97	23	4.63
Aynhoe—6	19	3.10	25	4.03
Worton—7	4	2.72	8	5.93
Sibford—7	30	3.34	63	8.32
Epwell—7	16	4.85	24	7.89

Continued on next page—

Table Four—*continued*

Parish and distance from Banbury (in miles)	1851 Migrants in Banbury	Index figure	1871 Migrants in Banbury	Index figure
Ratley and Upton—7 . . .	17	3.61	11	2.96
Avon Dassett—7	4	1.95	12	4.46
Aston le Wells—7	14	8.33	10	8.33
Appletree—7	3	3.49	7	11.11
Chipping Warden—7	26	5.00	30	6.25
Culworth—7	10	1.46	21	3.53
Greatworth—7	9	6.66	8	3.83
Hinton in the Hedges—7 . .	3	1.91	—	—
Souldern—7	10	1.62	27	4.59
North Aston—8	4	1.30	4	1.46
Duns Tew—8	7	1.55	10	2.65
Great and Little Tew—8 . .	15	1.93	14	1.80
Swerford—8	11	2.50	9	2.06
Hook Norton—8	48	3.21	48	3.81
Tysoe—8	19	1.81	17	1.53
Radway—8	12	3.49	19	5.41
Fenny Compton—8	19	2.37	24	6.72
Boddington—8	28	3.86	26	3.67
Eydon—8	20	3.22	20	3.77
Sulgrave—8	24	2.97	21	3.66
Croughton—8	7	1.20	12	2.03
Somerton—8	3	0.88	5	1.37
Steeple and Middle Aston—9 .	3	0.43	12	1.42
Westcot Barton—9	5	1.79	4	1.41
Middle Barton—9	7	—	17	1.78
Sandford St Martin—9 . . .	8	1.52	8	1.68
Brailes—9	18	1.38	50	3.23
Wormleighton—9	1	0.51	4	1.98
Byfield—9	17	1.66	13	1.55
Helmdon—9	10	1.66	9	1.37
Brackley—9	35	1.54	60	2.55
Evenley—9	4	0.60	6	1.02
Fritwell—9	4	0.78	4	0.72
Great and Little Rollright—10 .	3	0.63	4	0.99
Whichford—10	2	0.27	8	1.87
Cherrington—10	1	0.29	—	—
Oxhill—10	8	2.50	8	2.13
Kineton—10	16	1.26	33	2.18
Gaydon—10	4	1.40	—	—
Priors Hardwick—10	1	0.33	8	2.39
Woodford—10	9	1.13	8	2.39
Moreton Pinkney—10 . . .	8	1.39	13	2.54
Lois Weedon and Weston—10 .	5	0.92	4	0.74
Whitfield—10	2	0.61	—	—
Turweston—10	1	—	1	0.27
Cottesford—10	—	—	1	0.41
Stratton Audley—10	3	0.98	—	—
Heyford—10	15	1.49	11	1.02

Table Five

Attendances at Church Services in Banbury, 30 March, 1851

Source: PRO, HO 129/6/163, Census Papers, Ecclesiastical Returns, Banbury, 1851.

	Highest attendances	Proportion of total of highest attendances	Total attendances	Proportion of sum of total attendances
St Mary's Parish Church	1,300	42.03	3,300	47.69
Wesleyan Methodist .	558	18.04	1,146	16.56
Primitive Methodist .	212	6.85	515	7.44
Presbyterian/Unitarian	212	6.92	417	6.09
Independent . . .	120	3.88	220	3.18
Baptist, Bridge Street	200	6.47	400	5.78
Baptist, West Bar.. .	70	2.26	120	1.73
Baptist, South Bar .	109	3.52	223	3.22
Quaker	60	1.95	99	1.43
Roman Catholic . .	250	8.08	480	6.94
Totals . .	3,093		6,920	
Total Methodists . .	770	24.89	1,661	24.00
Total Old Dissent . .	713	23.05	1,380	19.91

Table Six

Immigration into Banbury

Source: 1851 and 1871 census enumerators' returns

People born in:	Number living in Banbury 1851	Proportion of total population (8,746) (1)	Number living in Banbury 1871	Proportion of total population (11,692) (1)	
Bedfordshire . . .	37	0.42	67	0.57	
Berkshire	74	0.85	132	1.13	
Buckinghamshire . .	167	1.91	277	2.37	
Cambridgeshire . .	6	0.07	22	0.19	
Cheshire	6	0.07	15	0.13	
Cornwall	9	0.10	9	0.08	
Cumberland . . .	5	0.06	5	0.04	
Derbyshire	11	0.12	15	0.13	
Devon	19	0.22	39	0.33	
Dorset	4	0.04	24	0.21	
Durham	8	0.09	8	0.07	
Essex	35	0.40	61	0.52	
Gloucestershire . .	127	1.45	137	1.17	(2)
Hampshire and I.o.W.	27	0.31	34	0.29	
Herefordshire . . .	5	0.06	16	0.14	
Hertfordshire . . .	28	0.32	21	0.18	
Huntingdonshire . .	3	0.03	6	0.05	
Kent	32	0.36	37	0.32	
Lancashire	30	0.34	58	0.50	
Leicestershire . . .	43	0.49	55	0.47	
Lincolnshire . . .	12	0.14	36	0.31	
London	158	1.81	257	2.20	(3)
Middlesex	39	0.45	17	0.15	(4)
Norfolk	21	0.24	30	0.26	
Northamptonshire .	651	7.44	940	8.04	(5)
Northumberland . .	5	0.06	5	0.04	
Nottinghamshire . .	10	0.11	11	0.09	
Rutland	2	0.02	4	0.03	
Salop	10	0.11	26	0.22	
Somerset	25	0.29	50	0.43	
Staffordshire . . .	31	0.35	97	0.83	
Suffolk	11	0.12	21	0.18	
Surrey	38	0.43	24	0.21	(4)
Sussex	7	0.08	22	0.19	
Warwickshire . . .	481	5.50	780	6.67	(6)
Westmoreland . . .	0	0.00	4	0.03	
Wiltshire	48	0.55	73	0.62	
Worcestershire . . .	64	0.73	89	0.76	
Yorkshire	44	0.50	46	0.39	
Unknown but English	69	0.79	19	0.16	
Scotland	24	0.27	49	0.42	
Wales	24	0.27	34	0.29	
Ireland	78	0.89	68	0.58	
Abroad	37	0.43	49	0.42	
Total from other counties and abroad	2,562	29.29	3,989	32.41	
Oxfordshire . . .	1,935	16.43	1,935	16.56	
Total born outside Banbury	3,999	45.72	5,924	50.67	

Notes: (1) The hamlet of Nethercote is excluded. (2) Excludes Shennington. Includes Bristol where Somerset is not specified. (3) Both Middlesex and Surrey portions. (4) Excludes London. (5) Excludes Grimsbury. (6) Includes all persons born in Shipston on Stour.

Table Seven

Dates of Foundation of Voluntary Societies active in Banbury between 1830 and 1850

Sources: Rusher's *Banbury Lists and Directories* and contemporary newspapers

Quasi-governmental bodies

Neithrop Association for the Prosecution of Felons	Before	1819
Banbury General Association for the Prosecution of Felons		1835
Mendicity Society		1834

Philanthropic Societies

Old Charitable Society		1782
Bank for Savings		1818
Visiting Charitable Society		1820
Labourer's Friend Society		1833
Banbury and Neithrop Clothing Society		1831
Medical Aid Society	By	1838
Dorcas Society		1842
Refuge Society		1845
Small Savings Society		1847

Friendly Societies

Weavers Arms		1832
Conservative Friendly Society		1837
White Horse Friendly Society		1837
Reindeer Club	By	1838
United Smiths	By	1838
Cock & Greyhound, Old Club	By	1838
White Hart	By	1838
Loyal Wellington Oddfellows, Independent Order	By	1839
United Christian Benefit Society		1840
Mutual Aid Society		1843
Reformers' Friendly Society	By	1843
Millwrights Arms		1840
British Queen Oddfellows, Independent Order	By	1843
Fountain of Liberty Oddfellows, Independent Order	By	1843
Rechabites		1844
Tradesmens Benefit Society	By	1844
Buck and Bell	By	1845
British Queen Oddfellows, Manchester Unity Order		1848

Religious Societies

British and Foreign Bible Society Auxiliary		1817
Society for the Propagation of the Gospel	By	1832
Church Missionary Society		1835
London Association for Promoting Christianity amongst the Jews		1842
Society for Promoting Christian Knowledge	By	1846
Protestant Institute		1845
Naval and Military Bible Society	By	1846
China Missionary Society	By	1849
Church Choir		1835

Musical Societies

Amateur Music Society	By	1835
Brass Band		1836
Harmonic Society		1840
Church Singers Society	By	1841
Temperance Brass Band		1844
Choral Society		1844
Philharmonic Society		1847

Continued on following page

Table Seven — *continued*

Educational and Cultural Bodies
    National Schools Society 1817
    Infants School 1835
    Mechanics' Institute 1835
    British Schools 1839
    Flori- and Horticultural Society 1847

Political and Social Reforming Bodies
    Anti-Slavery Association 1832
    Temperance Society 1834
    Agricultural Association 1834

Sports Club
    Cricket Club 1836

Table Eight

Occupations of Children in Banbury in 1851 and 1871 (percentages)

Source: 1851 and 1871 Census enumerators' returns

Age Group	1851			1871		
	Home	School	Work	Home	School	Work
2	73.21	26.79	—	97.10	2.90	—
3	54.31	45.60	—	64.29	35.71	—
4	44.55	55.45	—	45.49	54.51	—
5	31.60	68.40	—	31.73	68.27	—
6	21.35	78.65	—	30.55	69.45	—
7	19.16	80.84	—	25.54	74.46	—
8	22.12	77.40	—	21.72	78.28	—
9	18.85	80.63	—	19.43	79.76	—
10	17.01	78.35	4,64	20.00	78.21	1.79
11	19.02	73.37	7.61	23.26	73.61	3.13
12	22.16	65.27	12.57	18.00	68.80	13.20
13	19.51	54.64	25.85	20.83	54.17	25.00
14	23.27	34.59	42.14	17.31	37.31	45.38
15	18.72	18.72	62.56	20.40	20.40	59.20
16	18.33	6.28	75.39	13.52	8.20	78.28
17	13.17	2.40	84.43	14.22	4.89	80.89
18	19.53	0.59	79.88	12.70	2.46	84.84
2–10	19.53	65.54	0.60	40.74	58.99	0.27
5–10	21.80	77.29	0.91	25.08	74.50	0.42
11–14	20.84	57.48	21.68	19.94	58.86	21.20
11–18	19.44	32.70	47.86	17.69	34.93	47.38
7–11	19.27	78.21	2.52	22.06	76.76	1.18
2–18	27.55	51.18	21.27	30.59	48.39	21.02

Table Nine

Banbury: Occupational Structure in 1851

Source: 1851 Census enumerators' returns

	Total	Proportion of working population	Total	Proportion of working population	Total	Proportion of working population
1. Leisured class					113	2.74
2. Professional					183	4.44
3. Civil and Borough Service . .					46	1.11
4. Agricultural traders					66	1.60
5. Transport, accommodation and food					434	10.52
5.1 Transport			184	4.46		
5.2 Drink trade			231	5.60		
5.3 Other accommodation and food			19	0.46		
6. Retail trade					442	10.71
6.1 Food			244	5.91		
6.2 Textiles.			75	1.82		
6.3 Miscellaneous			123	2.98		
7. Crafts and Manufactures . . .					1,384	33.55
7.1. Small scale crafts &c. .			870	21.09		
7.1.1 Metal	95	2.30				
7.1.2 Leather	200	4.85				
7.1.3 Clothing	394	9.55				
7.1.4 Wood	96	2.33				
7.1.5 Fine crafts	56	1.36				
7.1.6 Miscellaneous	29	0.70				
7.2. Building trade			229	5.55		
7.2.1 Construction . . .	184	4,45				
7.2.2 Manufacture and sales .	45	1.09				
7.3. Larger scale manufactures			285	6.91		
7.3.1 Textiles	195	4.73				
7.3.2 Engineering	90	2.18				
8. Agriculture and Horticulture .					306	7.42
9. Domestic service					735	17.81
10. *Miscellaneous*					417	10.10
10.1 Hawkers, scavengers &c. .			50	1.21		
10.2 Unclassified occupations .			355	8.60		
10.3 Non-local occupation . .			12	0.29		
Totals					4,126	100

Table Ten

Banbury: Occupational Structure in 1871

Source: 1871 Census enumerators' returns

		Total	Proportion of working population	Total	Proportion of working population	Total	Proportion of working population
1.	Leisured class					149	2.87
2.	Professional					269	5.18
3.	Civil and Borough Service . .					51	1.18
4.	Agricultural traders					77	1.48
5.	Transport, accommodation and food					445	8.57
	5.1 Transport			172	3.31		
	5.2 Drink trade			249	4.80		
	5.3 Other accommodation and food			24	0.46		
6.	Retail trade					601	11.58
	6.1 Food			307	5.91		
	6.2 Textiles.			135	2.60		
	6.3 Miscellaneous			159	3.07		
7.	Crafts and Manufactures . . .					1,866	35.94
	7.1. *Small scale crafts &c.* . .			843	16.24		
	7.1.1 Metal	104	2.01				
	7.1.2 Leather	170	3.27				
	7.1.3 Clothing	341	6.57				
	7.1.4 Wood	138	2.66				
	7.1.5 Fine crafts	68	1.31				
	7.1.6 Miscellaneous	22	0.42				
	7.2. *Building trade*			426	8.20		
	7.2.1 Construction	364	7.01				
	7.2.2 Manufacture and sales .	62	1.19				
	7.3. *Larger scale Manufactures*			597	11.50		
	7.3.1 Textiles	102	1.97				
	7.3.2 Engineering	495	9.53				
8.	Agriculture and Horticulture .					216	4.16
9.	Domestic service					928	17.87
10.	*Miscellaneous*					580	11.17
	10.1 Hawkers, scavengers &c. .			59	1.13		
	10.2 Unclassified occupations .			490	9.44		
	10.3 Non-local and unknown occupations			31	0.60		
	Total					5,192	100

Table Eleven

The Party Balance on Banbury Borough Council 1836–1880

Source: Rusher's *Banbury Lists and Directories*

									Liberals	*Conservatives*
1836	.	.	.	.	.	.	.	.	16	0
1837	.	.	.	.	.	.	.	.	16	0
1838	.	.	.	.	.	.	.	.	16	0
1839	.	.	.	.	.	.	.	.	16	0
1840	.	.	.	.	.	.	.	.	16	0
1841	.	.	.	.	.	.	.	.	16	0
1842	.	.	.	.	.	.	.	.	16	0
1843	.	.	.	.	.	.	.	.	16	0
1844	.	.	.	.	.	.	.	.	16	0
1845	.	.	.	.	.	.	.	.	16	0
1846	.	.	.	.	.	.	.	.	16	0
1847	.	.	.	.	.	.	.	.	16	0
1848	.	.	.	.	.	.	.	.	14	2
1849	.	.	.	.	.	.	.	.	14	2
1850	.	.	.	.	.	.	.	.	12	4
1851	.	.	.	.	.	.	.	.	12	4
1852	.	.	.	.	.	.	.	.	12	4
1853	.	.	.	.	.	.	.	.	14	2
1854	.	.	.	.	.	.	.	.	14	2
1855	.	.	.	.	.	.	.	.	14	2
1856	.	.	.	.	.	.	.	.	14	2
1857	.	.	.	.	.	.	.	.	12	4
1858	.	.	.	.	.	.	.	.	11	5
1859	.	.	.	.	.	.	.	.	11	5
1860	.	.	.	.	.	.	.	.	10	6
1861	.	.	.	.	.	.	.	.	10	6
1862	.	.	.	.	.	.	.	.	9	7
1863	.	.	.	.	.	.	.	.	8	8
1864	.	.	.	.	.	.	.	.	12	4
1865	.	.	.	.	.	.	.	.	12	4
1866	.	.	.	.	.	.	.	.	15	1
1867	.	.	.	.	.	.	.	.	15	1
1868	.	.	.	.	.	.	.	.	13	3
1869	.	.	.	.	.	.	.	.	11	5
1870	.	.	.	.	.	.	.	.	11	5
1871	.	.	.	.	.	.	.	.	11	5
1872	.	.	.	.	.	.	.	.	11	5
1873	.	.	.	.	.	.	.	.	10	6
1874	.	.	.	.	.	.	.	.	10	6
1875	.	.	.	.	.	.	.	.	10	6
1876	.	.	.	.	.	.	.	.	9	7
1877	.	.	.	.	.	.	.	.	9	7
1878	.	.	.	.	.	.	.	.	9	7
1879	.	.	.	.	.	.	.	.	9	7
1880	.	.	.	.	.	.	.	.	12	4

These figures show the state of the parties in January of each year, usually the result of elections held in the previous November. No allowance is made for by-elections, or for the various factions within the Liberal Party in Banbury. Party affiliation, if not made explicit at a council election, is judged from the way the councillor habitually voted in general elections.

Table Twelve

Banbury Election Statistics 1835–1847

(i)   Class composition of the Liberal vote in Banbury 1835–1847 (percentages)

Source: Pollbooks, Banbury Public Library

		1835	*1837*	*1841*	*1847*
1.	Leisured Class	1.48	3.31	4.03	2.05
2.	Professional	7.39	10.50	10.48	10.51
3.	Civil and Borough Service . . .	—	—	—	0.51
4.	Agricultural Traders	4.93	3.87	5.65	2.82
5.1	Transport	0.98	0.55	—	0.77
5.2	Drink Trade	13.30	13.81	11.29	14.36
5.3	Other accommodation &c.. . . .	—	—	0.81	1.03
6	Retailers.	30.54	26.52	25.81	27.44
7.1	Crafts	23.64	24.31	22.59	20.51
7.2	Building Trade.	5.42	7.74	8.87	8.72
7.3.1	Textile Manufacture	2.46	2.76	4.03	1.80
7.3.2	Engineering.	1.48	0.55	1.61	1.28
8.	Agriculture and Horticulture . .	4.93	4.97	3.22	6.92
9.	Domestic Service	—	—	—	—
10.	Miscellaneous and Unknown . .	3.45	1.11	1.61	1.28
		100	100	100	100

(ii)   Class composition of the Conservative vote in Banbury 1835–1847 (percentages)

Source: Pollbooks, Banbury Public Library

		1835	*1837*	*1841*	*1847*
1.	Leisured Class	4.65	1.33	5.00	1.22
2.	Professional	20.90	10.67	12.00	12.20
3.	Civil and Borough Service . . .	—	—	—	0.61
4.	Agricultural Traders	2.33	6.67	4.00	1.22
5.1	Transport	—	—	—	0.61
5.2	Drink Trade	13.96	22.67	23.00	18.90
5.3	Other accommodation &c.. . . .	—	—	—	0.61
6.	Retailers.	18.61	20.00	20.00	26.22
7.1	Crafts	6.98	17.33	13.00	14.02
7.2	Building Trade.	9.31	6.67	6.00	10.98
7.3.1	Textile Manufacture	—	—	—	4.26
7.3.2	Engineering.	—	—	1.00	2.44
8.	Agriculture and Horticulture . .	16.27	13.33	16.00	4.88
9.	Domestic Service	—	—	—	—
10.	Miscellaneous and Unknown . .	6.98	1.33	—	1.83
		100	100	100	100

Table Twelve continued on following pages

Table Twelve – *continued*

Banbury Election Statistics 1835-1847

(iii) Class composition of the Chartist vote in Banbury 1841 (percentages)

Source: Pollbooks, Banbury Public Library

		1841
1.	Leisured Class	—
2.	Professional	1.96
3.	Civil and Borough Service	—
4.	Agricultural Traders	5.88
5.1	Transport	—
5.2	Drink Trade	17.65
5.3	Other accommodation &c.	1.96
6.	Retailers.	21.57
7.1	Crafts	35.29
7.2	Building Trade.	3.92
7.3.1	Textile Manufacture.	—
7.3.2	Engineering.	—
8.	Agriculture and Horticulture	11.77
9.	Domestic Service	—
10.	Miscellaneous and Unknown	—
		100

(iv) The Liberal share of the vote of each social class in Banbury elections 1835-1847 (percentages)

Source: Pollbooks, Banbury Public Library

		1835	*1837*	*1841*	*1847*
1.	Leisured Class	60.00	85.71	50.00	75.00
2.	Professional	62.50	70.37	50.00	51.22
3.	Civil and Borough Service	—	—	—	50.00
4.	Agricultural Traders	90.91	58.33	50.00	81.82
5.1	Transport	100.00	—	—	66.67
5.2	Drink Trade	81.82	59.52	30.43	44.64
5.3	Other accommodation &c.	—	—	50.00	75.00
6.	Retailers.	88.57	76.19	50.79	59.81
7.1	Crafts	94.12	77.19	47.47	71.25
7.2	Building Trade.	73.33	73.68	57.89	47.06
7.3.1	Textile Manufacture.	100.00	100.00	50.00	100.00
7.3.2	Engineering.	100.00	100.00	66.67	75.00
8.	Agriculture and Horticulture	58.82	47.37	15.38	29.63
9.	Domestic Service	—	—	—	—
10.	Miscellaneous and Unknown	70.00	66.67	100.00	60.00
	Total share of vote	82.52	70.70	45.09	57.95

Table Twelve continued on following page

Table Twelve — *continued*

Banbury Election Statistics 1835-1847

(v)   The Conservative share of the vote of each social class in Banbury elections 1835-1847 (percentages)

Source: Pollbooks, Banbury Public Library

		1835	1837	1841	1847
1.	Leisured Class	40.00	14.29	50.00	25.00
2.	Professional	37.50	29.63	46.15	48.78
3.	Civil and Borough Service	—	—	—	50.00
4.	Agricultural Traders	9.09	41.67	28.57	18.18
5.1	Transport	—	—	—	33.33
5.2	Drink Trade	18.18	40.48	50.00	53.36
5.3	Other accommodation &c.	—	—	—	25.00
6.	Retailers	11.43	23.81	31.75	40.19
7.1	Crafts	5.88	22.81	22.02	28.75
7.2	Building Trade	26.67	26.32	31.58	52.94
7.3.1	Textile Manufacture	—	—	50.00	—
7.3.2	Engineering	—	—	33.33	25.00
8.	Agriculture and Horticulture	41.18	52.63	61.54	70.37
9.	Domestic Service	—	—	—	—
10.	Miscellaneous and Unknown	30.00	33.33	—	40.00
	Total share of vote	17.48	29.30	36.36	42.05

(vi)   The Chartist share of the vote of each social class in the Banbury election of 1841 (percentages)

Source: Pollbooks, Banbury Public Library

		1841
1.	Leisured Class	—
2.	Professional	3.85
3.	Civil and Borough Service	—
4.	Agricultural Traders	21.43
5.1	Transport	—
5.2	Drink Trade	19.75
5.3	Other accommodation &c.	50.00
6.	Retailers	17.46
7.1	Crafts	30.51
7.2	Building Trade	10.53
7.3.1	Textile Manufacture	—
7.3.2	Engineering	—
8.	Agriculture and Horticulture	23.08
9.	Domestic Service	—
10.	Miscellaneous and Unknown	—
	Total share of vote	18.55

Table Thirteen

Banbury Election Statistics 1857–1865

(i)   The 'Old Liberal' Share of the vote of each social class in Banbury elections 1857–1865 (percentages)

Source: Pollbooks, Banbury Public Library

		1857 Tancred	Feb. 1859 Samuelson	Apr. 1859 Samuelson	1865 Samuelson
1.	Leisured Class	100	66.67	33.33	20.00
2.	Professions	93.55	42.59	41.51	33.33
3.	Civil and Borough Service	—	50.00	33.33	16.67
4.	Agricultural Traders	100	35.00	33.33	60.00
5.1	Transport	100	75.00	80.00	71.43
5.2	Drink Trade	88.37	53.02	64.79	50.00
5.3	Other accommodation &c.	50.00	22.22	40.00	42.86
6	Retail	70.77	27.35	38.60	30.16
7.1	Crafts	65.00	25.93	38.96	35.71
7.2	Building Trade	84.62	42.31	54.17	35.48
7.3.1	Textile Manufacture	50.00	40.00	50.00	66.67
7.3.2	Engineering	100	81.25	85.72	76.92
8.	Agriculture and Horticulture	69.23	15.15	25.93	25.80
9.	Domestic Service	—	50.00	—	—
10.	Miscellaneous and Unknown	88.24	40.00	60.00	43.21
	Share of total vote	78.83	37.57	45.85	38.80

(ii)   The Conservative share of the vote of each social class in Banbury elections 1857–1865 (percentages)

Source: Pollbooks, Banbury Public Library

		Feb. 1859 Hardy	Apr. 1859 Douglas (Voters classed as Conservatives)	1865 Bell
1.	Leisured Class	33.33	22.22	20.00
2.	Professions	46.30	93.62	39.22
3.	Civil and Borough Service	25.00	33.33	50.00
4.	Agricultural Traders	35.00	33.33	20.00
5.1	Transport	25.00	—	28.57
5.2	Drink Trade	33.73	18.31	32.32
5.3	Other accommodation &c.	44.45	20.00	14.28
6	Retail	43.12	28.07	35.71
7.1	Crafts	28.39	12.99	25.00
7.2	Building Trade	30.77	16.67	32.26
7.3.1	Textile Manufacture	20.00	—	—
7.3.2	Engineering	—	7.14	—
8.	Agriculture and Horticulture	66.67	55.55	61.29
9.	Domestic Service	50.00	100	—
10.	Miscellaneous and Unknown	40.00	20.00	23.46
	Share of total vote	37.36	24.66	31.07

Table Thirteen — *continued*

Banbury Election Statistics 1857–1865

(iii) The Radical share of the vote of each social class in Banbury elections 1857–1865 (percentages)

		1857 Yates	1859 Miall	April 1859 Douglas (Voters classed as Liberal or uncommitted)	1865
1.	Leisured Class	—	—	44.45	60.00
2.	Professions	6.45	11.11	18.87	27.45
3.	Civil and Borough Service . . .	—	25.00	33.33	50.00
4.	Agricultural Traders	—	30.00	33.33	20.00
5.1	Transport	—	—	20.00	—
5.2	Drink Trade	11.63	13.25	16.90	17.65
5.3	Other accommodation &c.. . . .	50.00	33.33	40.00	42.86
6.	Retail	29.23	29.36	33.33	34.13
7.1	Crafts	35.00	45.68	48.05	39.29
7.2	Building Trade.	15.38	26.92	29.16	32.26
7.3.1	Textile Manufacture	50.00	40.00	50.00	33.30
7.3.2	Engineering.	—	18.75	7.14	23.08
8.	Agriculture and Horticulture . .	30.77	18.18	18.52	12.91
9.	Domestic Service	—	—	—	—
10.	Miscellaneous and Unknown . .	11.76	20.00	20.00	33.33
	Share of total vote . .	21.17	25.05	29.04	30.13

(iv) Class composition of the 'Old Liberal' vote in Banbury 1857–1865 (percentages)

		1857 Tancred	Feb. 1859 Samuelson	Apr. 1859 Samuelson	1865 Samuelson
1.	Leisured Class	0.92	2.26	1.51	0.49
2.	Professional	13.43	12.99	11.06	8.25
3.	Civil and Borough Service . . .	—	1.13	0.05	0.49
4.	Agricultural Traders	4.17	3.96	2.51	4.37
5.1	Transport	1.39	3.39	4.02	2.43
5.2	Drink Trade	17.60	24.86	23.11	16.50
5.3	Other accommodation &c.. . .	0.46	1.13	1.01	1.46
6.	Retail	21.29	16.95	22.11	18.45
7.1	Crafts	18.06	11.86	15.07	14.65
7.2	Building Trade.	5.09	6.22	6.53	5.43
7.3.1	Textile Manufacture	0.92	2.26	1.51	1.94
7.3.2	Engineering.	5.56	7.34	6.03	4.85
8.	Agriculture and Horticulture . .	4,17	2.83	3.52	3.88
9.	Domestic Service	—	0.56	—	—
10.	Miscellaneous and Unknown . .	6.94	2.26	1.51	16.99

Table Thirteen – *continued*

Banbury Election Statistics 1857–1865

(v)   Class composition of the Conservative vote in Banbury, 1859–1865 (percentages)

		1857	Feb. 1859 Hardy	April 1859 Douglas (voters classed as Conservatives)	1865 Bell
1.	Leisured Class		1.13	1.87	0.61
2.	Professions		14.21	19.63	12.12
3.	Civil and Borough Service . . .		0.57	0.93	1.21
4.	Agricultural Traders		3.98	4.67	1.82
5.1	Transport		1.31	—	1.21
5.2	Drink Trade		15.91	12.15	13.33
5.3	Other accommodation &c. . . .		2.27	0.93	0.61
6.	Retail		26.71	29.92	27.27
7.1	Crafts		13.07	9.35	12.72
7.2	Building Trade		4.55	3.74	6.06
7.3.1	Textile Manufacture		1.13	—	—
7.3.2	Engineering		—	0.93	—
8.	Agriculture and Horticulture . .		12.50	14.02	11.52
9.	Domestic Service		0.52	0.93	—
10.	Miscellaneous and Unknown . .		2.27	0.93	11.52

(vi)   Class composition of the Radical vote in Banbury 1857–1865 (percentages)

		1857 Yates	Feb. 1859 Miall	April 1859 Douglas (voters classed as Liberals and uncommitted)	1865 Douglas
1.	Leisured Class	—	—	3.13	1.88
2.	Professions	3.45	5.08	7.81	8.75
3.	Civil and Borough Service . . .	—	0.85	0.78	1.88
4.	Agricultural Traders	—	5.08	3.91	1.88
5.1	Transport	—	—	1.56	—
5.2	Drink Trade	8.62	9.32	9.38	7.50
5.3	Other accommodation &c. . . .	1.72	2.55	1.58	1.88
6.	Retail	32.76	27.12	29.69	26.87
7.1	Crafts	36.20	31.37	28.90	20.62
7.2	Building Trade	3.45	5.93	5.47	6.25
7.3.1	Textile Manufacture	3.45	3.39	2.34	1.25
7.3.2	Engineering	—	2.54	0.78	1.88
8.	Agriculture and Horticulture . .	6.90	5.08	3.91	2.50
9.	Domestic Service	—	—	—	—
10.	Miscellaneous and Unknown . .	3.45	1.69	0.78	16.86

Table Fourteen

Results of Parliamentary elections in Banbury 1868–1880

Source: Pollbook for 1868, Banbury Public Library; *Banbury Guardian* 5 Feb. 1874.
          1 April 1880

	1868	1874	1880
Votes cast for Samuelson (Liberal)	772	760	1,018
Liberal share of poll (percentage)	66.04	52.93	63.59
Votes cast for Conservatives (Stratton, Wilkinson, Bowles) . .	397	676	583
Conservative share of poll (percentage).	33.96	47.07	36.41
Bad Votes	—	5	9
Neutral Voters.	355	309	238
Total number of registered electors	1,524	1,750	1,848
Proportion of electorate who voted (percentages)	76.71	82.34	87.12

Table Fifteen

*Numbers of Sunday School children from congregations in Banbury attending the Sunday
School Centenary demonstration on 29 June 1880*

Sources: Banbury Advertiser, Banbury Guardian, 1 July 1880.

Church of England:		
St Mary's	601	
Christ Church	280	
Temperance Hall	95	
Total		976
Methodist:		
Marlborough Road Wesleyan	600	
Grimsbury Wesleyan.	400	
Primitive Methodist	165	
Total		1,165
Dissenting:		
Society of Friends	66	
Unitarian	34	
Bridge Street Baptist.	220	
Ebenezer Calvinistic Baptist	46	
Disciples of Christ	30	
Congregationalist	275	
Total		671
Non-Denominational		
Neithrop Mission	160	
Wood Green Lodge Class	34	
Workhouse	53	
Total	247	
Sum total	3,059	

The Procession also included children from villages around Banbury who are not included in these figures.

Literary Appendix I

BANBURY FAIR

They came from Broughton's lordly halls,
From Wroxton's ancient fane,
From Tew, and Aston on the Walls
And from the Barfords twain.

From Abthorpe and from Appletree,
From Adstone old and grey,
From Buckingham and Coventry
And Bilston far away.

From Burton Dassett's height they came,
From Leamington's proud town,
From Birmingham that place of fame,
And Croughton on the Down.

From Burford and from Burdrop too,
From Chipping Norton's soil,
The Hanwell beauties you may view,
And those from Hampton Poyle.

From Hornton and from Horley,
And some from Hill of Edge,
From Deddington in Crowds they came,
And Hinton in the Hedge.

From Astons three and Marstons two,
From Adderbury vales,
From Culworth you the crowds may view,
From Shotteswell and Brailes.

From Charwelton where Cherwell springs,
From Moreton Marsh they came,
From Alkerton and Shennington,
And Toddenham by name.

From Tadmarton and Tackley,
From Sibford of renown,
And Bodicote and Brackley
And Shipston's ancient town.

They come from East, they come from West,
From North and South they're there,
The lads and lassies in their best
To visit Banbury Fair.

Banbury Advertiser (21 Oct. 1869).

Literary Appendix II

A RECAPITULATION: 'FACTS ARE STUBBORN THINGS'

Tune (and Principles) *The Vicar of Bray*

In eighteen hundred and forty eight I came into this town, Sirs,
And finding here a shop to let; I quickly settled down, Sirs,
The place I thought well suited was, for this my speculation;
And time has proved, as you all know, 'twas no miscalculation.
    And this is right, as 'twill be seen and all must say it's true Sirs,
    That Banbury would have better been without this Foundree S(crew) Sirs.

In eighteen hundred and fifty eight, Old Tancred he retired, Sirs;
To add an M.P. to my name, was my ambition fired, Sirs,
So Draper, Munton, Cobb and Co., I force to my assistance;
Tho' Whig and Rad., and Hardy too, says 'Sammy keep your distance'.

I shirked the Ballot, you all know, when some few wanted Miall;
I saw that was too straight for me, so I would not give it trial,
No! No! that game won't do for me, Fair Play was not what I meant;
I got elected, just by one, to wit, the Superintendent.

Then Charley Douglas was brought down and gave me such a hiding;
I caused a row about my town, and sent my friends a kicking;
They smashed the windows of all those, who thus did me dismember,
And Charley honoured my late seat, and proved a better member.

An Alien! Bell tried me to prove, but of this I great care took;
I found (?) my Grandpa's name inscribed in a poor old Jew's Prayer Book,
And by this f(act), I proved 'd'ye see', my Naturalisation;
No Court of Law, would this accept, in any other nation.

With Mewburn too, I next assayed, to fight 'gainst borough's wishes;
But Poor Old Mew was sold by One all through my Loaves and Fishes;
I took my seat in Westminster; this should be well in mind born,
I spoke to the Permissive Bill, was snubbed by Bernal Osborne.

A sudden dissolution came, while I was out a yachting;
And Wilkinson so shook my seat, in fact he nearly got in;
For a five days canvass, he, so nearly me defeated;
I've had the horrors ever since, for fear I'll be unseated.

It's oft been questioned what I've done for this my little Borough;
For once, I will be quite sincere, be candid, and be thorough,
I've sought my own aggrandisement, on each and every purpose,
And brought Rascality and Crime to fill your Jail and Workhouse.

(continued overleaf)

213

A Recapitulation — continued

>   I patronise in all I can, the Civil Service Stores, Sirs,
>   Aye! even to my Horse Corn (while Tradesmen fail in scores) Sirs;
>   Co-operation I support, and preach it beneficial,
>   But won't apply it to my works! That would be prejudicial.
>
>   And now that Bowles is brought down here and giving me the heartache
>   He's making friends too fast, I fear; he shakes me like an earthquake;
>   For Independent Temperance Men, Pubs, Anti-Vaccinators,
>   They won't believe that I'm sincere, and almost call me Traitor.
>
>   I think I know a trick or two to try upon your flank, Sirs;
>   I will put on the Foundree S(crew) and run upon the Bank, Sirs;
>   I'll sell the Shop; I'll let the Grange; (that's just what we expected)
>   So help me Cot! tish rat I'll do! If I'm not re-elected.
>
>   A few more words, and thus I'll close me re-capitulation;
>   There's not a line, I here disclose that needs corroboration;
>   Electors! Working Men, and all, prove to your Nation true, Sirs;
>   And vote for Bowles and Liberty from this Old Borough s(crew), Sirs.

Rusher Collection, p. 303.

Literary Appendix III

A correct rendering of a Chapter of Eastern History of the Town where Cakes are made for the Queen's People. By Libra.

1.   And it came to pass that one of the great Queen's grave counsellors gave up the ghost, and he was buried with his father, and the golden box in which he kept the dust for his nose was buried with him, but his image was placed in the Council Chamber of the ancient town wherein cakes are made for all the great Queen's people.

2.   Then the Queen's ministers sent a writ under the seals to the chief clerk, saying call together the elders of the town and choose a discrete man to sit in the seat of him who is gone to sleep with his fathers, and he did so.

3.   But when the Queen's proclamation was made, straightway divers men who thought themselves leaders of the people, and who were puffed up, said amongst themselves, it is our right to choose the new counsellor for the great Queen; and they grew angry with other men, every man of them angry with his neighbour who did not bow down to their word.

4.   Then came forth a great man, learned in the laws of the land, wearing on the crown of his head horse hair, done up according to custom, and a silken robe flowing from his shoulders to his heels which had been given him in the Queen's Courts to do him honour, that he might appear before the Queen in her glory.

5.   So he said to the people of the town where cakes are made, as he stood over against the goodly cross, I will serve you well, for I am learned in the law, and my honour shall be your honour and your glory my glory.

6.   Then a few wise men and discreet did cleave unto him and said hail!

7.   Then came also another man, and he was one of those who sing hymns, and he said O ye righteous people harken unto me. I have served the great Queen many days and my name is known in the land, send me to be your counsellor before the Queen, and those who worshipped without rites and ceremonies did cleave unto him and said we will send you.

8.   Then came another man and he was rich from his birth, whose fathers had lived among the nobles of the land and much people took hold of the hem of his garment and said this man is fit to go before the great Queen, for he doth ride in a chariot drawn by horses.

9.   While these things were spoken in the Market Place, behold there came also yet another man, and he was of the Hebrew nation and circumcised, a notable man of the family of Tubal Cain, which be cunning artificers in iron and brass.

10.   Now he thought in his heart that he could make laws as well as implements of husbandy for the tillers of the field, and the men who wrought in his place of fires and forges and the sound of hammers gave a great shout, and said our master shall go to the Queen's Courts, and whosoever saith nay shall be evil entreated.

11.   Then said the son of Tubal Cain in his heart, I will try to win those men who are puffed up, and some of the great amongst them said, we will cleave to you, but they straightway went secretly to the north, the south, the east and the west to find a man after their own heart, but they could not. So it came to pass when they saw this they said, let us respect the circumcised and make him a great man and our servant, and they conspired together.

12.   As the time drew nigh when the great Queen's writ must be obeyed, there were running to and fro and much tumult amongst the people. And it came to pass when the man learned in the law saw the iniquity of those who were puffed up and called themselves whigs, and the strength of those who caught the right man by the hem of his garment and the straitness of those who sing hymns, and heard the noise and revelries of those who work in iron and brass, he called together those few wise men who did cleave

215

to him, and said, tomorrow about the time of the rising of the sun I shall depart from this town where cakes are made for the Queen's people, for they do not desire that knowledge and wisdom should rule amongst them.

13.   The sun was going down so he embraced his few friends and bid them farewell. But a greater town nigh to the Queen's palace chose him to be their law maker, and shortly after the great Queen made him one of her ancient judges, for he was a learned man and is he not a judge amongst the people unto this day?

14.   Then the blindness of the people in the town where cakes are made was shown to all the nation, for it came to pass on the day when the writ was obeyed there were great and grievous tumults amongst the people, many men playing fast and loose to get gain and have rule over others.

15.   About noon on that day much people played false with those who be called righteous, so he whom they had chosen left the town, and the strife was between he who was born rich and the son of the Hebrew Tubal Cain, who had much people who served and lived on his bread and drank deep draughts of stuff called beer, which maketh those who drink thereof, like those who are possessed with a devil whose name is Legion.

16.   And when the lots were taken, the worker in iron and brass had one more than he who was born rich, given by a man in blue raiment who carries a staff, so the chief clerk sent him to the Courts of the Nation.

17.   After he who was circumcised took his seat amongst the Queen's law makers he did nothing worthy of note, neither did he open his mouth; and many of those who served with him were corrupt, and the Queen's wrath was kindled against her counsellors, and she sent an officer with a black rod at the advice of her ministers, and scattered that assembly.

18.   And when the cry throughout the land was for worthier men, there came to the Town of Cakes he who had sat in the seat of the honourable for seven weeks, and he said to those who are puffed up, and those who worked at his fires and forges and those who got gain out of his works of iron and brass, make me a counsellor of the nation once more, for I am a man with much tin.

19.   And behold there came also a sprig of the house of the noble who had often served the great Queen in her courts, and those who were friends of the learned man of the law who was made one of the Queen's judges, and those who sang hymns according to custom, and those who took hold of the hem of the rich man's garment united as one man, and they made the sprig of the nobles the lawmaker for the town where cakes are made for the Queen's people.

20.   Then there were the workers in iron and brass, and those who got gain out of the son of Tubal Cain, exceeding wrath; and they made a great tumult and fiercely assaulted with filthy weapons of riotous men all those who cast lots against them.

21.   Verily they were wild like beasts of the wilderness — or men possessed with the devil — they did yell and howl, and evilly entreat all whom they caught in the streets, and they stormed the tents of those who did not cast lots for gain, and grievous was the confusion and ruin which they wrought against their neighbours.

22.   About the time of the going down of the sun the wrath of Tubal Cain's offspring waxed hot against his chief men and those sons of Belial who were drunken, and he cried aloud in his wrath and agony, let every man go to his own house and be quiet or he shall not more taste of my beer nor finger my tin, nor work in my foundry of iron and brass, for if this riot continues my hope in the future will be snuffed out.

23.   Then they were quiet and surly, and began to devise mischief; but the sprig of the house of the nobles served the great Queen faithfully and without reward, except a good conscience, as many years as the other had served weeks, even unto the time when the courts dissolve according to the laws.

24.   It came to pass when new writs were sent from the Queen throughout the land to certain cities and towns, one came to the Town of Cakes and the chief clerk made proclamation in the Market Place.

25.   Then said the chief men of the town, who had respect to the nobles of the land and the ancient customs, if we divide the people who work in iron and brass and those who sing hymns, and keep our band together, for we have waxed stronger, and bring forth a great merchant, we shall make ourselves heard in the courts of the kingdom, and they did so, for it was known to some of them that the artificer was an alien.

26.   And when the sprig of the nobles saw what was done, he would not join the tumult, but like the man learned in the law, whom the Queen made one of her judges, he went to his own house and there abode, but his friends said nay, we will stand or fall by our faith. And they did so.

27.   Now it was known to certain men that the artificer and the great merchand had both much tin, which is stuff of a shining colour, and when melted and spread over base things it maketh them to shine for a season, but it soon weareth and showeth the base stuff baser than before.

28.   In the night season the melting of tin was done. On the day of trial and rumult there were many workers of iron and brass and wood, and many others of divers trades, through the influence of those who puffed up, did fun about to and fro, shining as if beautiful with tin, and before the sun went down, the artificer was declared by the chief clerk the cake which should be sent to the courts of the nation from the Town of Cakes. Then the merchant and his friends protested before the judges and claimed the seat of honour.

29.   In due time the judges sat in judgment, and said this artificer is a circumcised subject of the Queen, for he saith his grandfather was born in her capital city, and he produceth a book of doubtful character containing a record thereof, and as it is the custom of the courts of the kingdom to give the prisoner the benefit of the doubt, we follow the same. So the artificer hath the seat.

30.   When this was known in the town, behold there was a great cry of rejoicing, beating of brazen instruments, and blastings of culcan powder and drinking of much beer as is their custom.

———————

The above verses describe the politics of Banbury between 1859 and 1865. The characters and groups can readily be identified in chapter ten. The remaining 42 verses describe in detail the celebrations on 9 May 1866 when Samuelson's victory in the electoral court was celebrated.

BIBLIOGRAPHY

All of the works from which information on Banbury during the period under review has been taken are listed below, but works quoted for purely comparative purposes, standard reference works and novels have not been included. In the 19th century it is sometimes difficult to make a clear distinction between manuscript and other sources, and several collections listed as documentary sources consist largely or in part of printed ephemera.

I. Documentary Sources

OXFORD

1. Bodleian Library

(i) Manuscripts.

    (a) Banbury Parish Records:
        Tithe Map 30: Parish of Banbury, 1852;
        William Wilson's Visting Plans, 1850, D. D. Par. Banbury a.5 (R);
        Map of Banbury, *circa* 1838;
        Parish rate books.

    (b) Oxford Diocesan Records:
        Letter Books of Samuel Wilberforce, Dep. d. 209;
        Diocesan Book, C. 327, d. 178, 549–50;
        Nonconformist registration certificates, c. 644–47.

(ii) Printed sources.

    Banbury election addresses, posters &c., 1831–68, G A Oxon., b. 101;
    Collection of newspaper cuttings relating to Banbury 1839–48, G A Oxon. 8vo, 989–94;
    Volume of pamphlets relating to Banbury, Oxon. 8vo, 637.

2. Oxfordshire Record Office

    (a) Stockton, Sons and Fortescue Collection (No. 315):
        Banbury Paving and Lighting Commission papers and accounts;
        Banbury Reform Association minute books;
        Bernhard Samuelson, business papers;
        Banbury Freehold Land Society, plans for estate in Grimsbury;
        Thomas Draper, plans for property development &c.;
        Neithrop Association for the Prosecution of Felons, minutes &c.;
        Austin's Brewery, sundry papers, accounts &c.;
        Sundry property deeds.

    (b) Banbury Borough Corporation Collection:
        Banbury Paving and Lighting Commission, minutes;
        Banbury Board of Health, minutes;
        Banbury Watch Committee, minutes;
        Banbury British Schools, log books.

2. *Oxfordshire Record Office — continued*

   (c) Other collections:
   Banbury Monthly Meeting of the Society of Friends, minutes &c.;
   Banbury National School, log books;
   Banbury Library (Arkell) Collection, deeds &c.

3. *Regent's Park College Library*

   W. T. Henderson, Recollections of his Life (MS).

4. *Manchester College Library*

   Sundry accounts &c. relating to Banbury Unitarian Church.

LONDON

5. *Public Record Office*

   1841 census enumerators' books, HO 873;
   1851 census enumerators' books, HO 126/6/163;
   1861 census enumerators' books, RG 9;
   1871 census enumerators' books, RG 10;
   Poor Law Commission correspondence, MH 12/139, 8671, 9677–78;
   Non-Parochial Registers, RG 2/2919, 9440.

6. *Dr. Williams's Library*

   Edward Cobb, Some Traditions and Historical Recollections relating to the Old Presbyterian
   Meeting House at Banbury, 1888 (MS).

7. *Transport House Library*

   Vincent MSS.

BANBURY

8. *Banbury Public Library*

   (a) Manuscripts:
   The Correspondence of Henry William Tancred, MP, 1841–59;
   Banbury Mechanics' Institute, minutes, accounts, sundry papers;
   Banbury Board of Guardians, minutes 1835–36;
   Banbury and Neithrop Clothing Society, minutes;
   Banbury Association for the Prosecution of Felons, minutes &c.;
   Memorandum to accompany the General Return on the 1870 Education Act.

   (b) Collections consisting principally of printed ephemera:
   Potts Collection (11 volumes);
   Rusher Collection;
   Brooks Collection;
   Walford Collection;
   Hurst Collection;
   Cases A, B, C, D, E, E1, E2, F, G, M, W;
   Banbury Cuttings, 1838–42;
   Grangerised version of Alfred Beesley, *History of Banbury* (1841), 12 volumes.

9. *Marlborough Road Methodist Church, Banbury*

Records of Banbury Wesleyan Circuit, minutes of quarterly meetings and local preachers' meetings,
schedules, preaching plans, baptismal registers;
Records of Banbury Primitive Methodist Circuit, baptismal registers, schedules &c.;
Records of Banbury Wesleyan Church, property deeds, trust minutes and accounts, Sunday School
registers &c.;
Records of Grimsbury Wesleyan Church; Neithrop Wesleyan Mission Hall, Windsor Street Branch
Sunday School, Calthorpe Street Mission, Banbury Primitive Methodist Church-
Brailsford Collection of printed ephemera.

10. *Banbury United Reformed Church*

Church Book, Banbury Independent Church, 1794;
Church Account Book, 1822–47;
Church Minutes and Accounts 1853 *et seq.*;
Baptismal Registers.

11. *Baptist Church, Banbury*

Property deeds, portraits, &c. relating to Bridge Street Chapel.

12. *Cheney & Sons, printers, Calthorpe Street, Banbury*
Volume of Specimens of Work.

ELSEWHERE

13. *Baptist Church, Middleton Cheney*
Lists of members, registers &c.

14. *Northamptonshire Record Office, Delapre Abbey, Northampton*
A Register of Meeting House Certificates, 1813–52 (Diocese of Peterborough).

15. *Birmingham Roman Catholic Diocesan Record Office*
Journal of the Revd. P. J. Hersent, with notes of Baptisms at Banbury.

16. *Shrewsbury Schools Library*
Letters of Dr. Edward Burton.

17. *D. G. W. Brown, Esq., Sunderland*
Samuel Beesley, Memoranda of Visits to the Borough Prison, Banbury;
Samuel Beesley, account books.

18. *Museum of English Rural Life, Reading*
Samuelson and Barrows & Stewart Trade catalogues, &c.

II.   **Official Publications**

Parliamentary Papers:

Report of the Commissioners on the Proposed Division of Counties and Boundaries in Boroughs,
1832, XI;
Report of the Royal Commission on Municipal Corporations, 1835, XXXIII;

II. Official Publications — Parliamentary Papers — continued

Education Enquiry Abstract, 1835, XLII;
Report of the Assistant Hand Loom Weavers Commissioners, 1840, XXIV;
Report of Commissioners on Railway Gauges, Oxford Worcester and Wolverhampton, and Oxford and Rugby Railway Bills, 1845, XI;
Second Report of the Children's Employment Commission, 1864, XXII;
Preliminary Reports from HM's Commissioners on Agriculture, 1881, XV, XVI;
Report from HM's Commissioners on Agriculture, 1882, XIV, XV, XVI.

House of Lords, Select Committee to inquire into the expediency of restricting the practice of carrying goods and merchandise on Canals, Navigable Rivers and Railways on Sundays, *House of Lords Journal*, 1841, Appendix Two.

Hansard, *Parliamentary Debates.*

III. Newspapers and Periodicals

1. Local Newspapers and Journals:

Banbury Advertiser;
Banbury Beacon;
Banbury Beehive;
Banbury Co-operative Record;
Banbury Guardian;
Banbury Herald;
Jackson's Oxford Journal;
Northampton Herald;
Northampton Mercury;
Oxford City and County Chronicle (subsequently *Oxford Chronicle and Reading Gazette*);
Oxford Herald.

2. National Publications:

The Alliance;
The Baptist Magazine;
The Beehive;
The British and Foreign Temperance Herald;
The British and Foreign Temperance Intelligencer;
The Christian Messenger;
The Church Times;
The Evangelical Magazine;
The Illustrated London News;
The Journal of the Royal Agricultural Society of England;
The Law Times;
The Methodist Magazine;
The Metropolitan Temperance Intelligencer and Journal;
The Minutes of the Primitive Methodist Conference;
The Minutes of the Wesleyan Methodist Conference;
The National Vindicator of the West and Wales;
The Nonconformist;
The Northern Star;
The Preston Temperance Advocate;
The Primitive Methodist Magazine;
The Shield;
The Times;
The Western Vindicator.

IV. Printed Works

1. Books published before 1920 and modern editions of documentary sources:

C. B. Andrews, ed., *The Torrington Diaries* (1954);

E. P. Baker, ed., *Bishop Wilberforce's Visitation Returns for the Archdeaconry of Oxford*, 1854 (ORS, XXV, 1954);

Joseph Arch, *The Story of His Life Told by Himself* (1908);

Alfred Beesley, *The History of Banbury* (1841);

—— *Japheth: Contemplation and other poems* (1834);

Sarah Beesley, *My Life* (1892);

Martin Billing, *Directory and Gazetteer of the Counties of Berkshire and Oxfordshire* (1854);

Thomas Ward Boss, *Reminiscences of Old Banbury* (1903);

C. J. Bowen, *Catholicity in Banbury since the Reformation* (1898);

James Cadbury, *A Tribute of Affection to the Memory of the late Caleb Clarke of Banbury* (1851);

Thomas Champness, ed., *A Memoir of Richard Edmunds of Banbury* (n.d., *circa* 1895);

G. V. Cox, *Recollections of Oxford* (1868);

Albert Dawson, *Joseph Parker: His Life and Ministry* (1901);

William Dorling, *Henry Vincent* (1879);

Eleanor Draper, *Notes on Calthorpe Manor House, Banbury, and its Inhabitants* (1915);

Sir F. M. Eden, *The State of the Poor* (ed. 1938);

A. Farrant, *Rowing Holiday by Canal in 1873* (ed. Edward Course, 1977);

William Felkins, *The History of the Machine Wrought Hosiery and Lace Manufacture* (ed. S. D. Chapman, 1967);

Charles Forbes, *An Address to Parishioners in South Banbury* (1850);

R. C. Gammage, *The History of the Chartist Movement 1837-54* (ed. 1969);

J. S. W. Gibson, ed., *The Baptism and Burial Register of Banbury*, vol. 2, 1653-1723 (BHS IX, 1969);

—— *The Baptism Register of Banbury*, vol. 3, 1723-1812 (BHS XVI, 1978);

—— *The Marriage Register of Banbury*, vol. 3, 1790-1837 (BHS V, 1963);

Joseph Gillow, *A Biographical Dictionary of the English Catholics* (n.d.);

George Harris, *The Spirit of Popery* (1838);

Elizabeth Hemus, *Banbury: a poem* (1854);

George Herbert, *Shoemaker's Window* (ed. C. R. Cheney, 1949; ed. C. R. Cheney and Barrie Trinder, 1973, 1979);

W. P. Johnson, *A Stranger's Guide to Banbury* (1859);

—— *A History of Banbury* (n.d., *circa* 1863);

H. B. Kendall, *The Origins and History of the Primitive Methodist Church* (n.d.);

Frederick Lamb, *A Brief History of the Banbury Co-operative Industrial Society from Its Commencement . . . to 1887 (1887);*

W. H. Lickorish, *Our Jubilee Story or Fifty Years of Co-operation in Banbury and the Neighbourhood* (1916);

Joseph McCabe, *The Life and Letters of George Jacob Holyoake* (1908);

Edward Marshall, *Religious Changes since the Institution of our Society* (the Banbury Clerical Association), (1903);

William Mavor, *A Tour in Wales and through Several Counties of England . . . in the Summer of 1805* (1806);

George Meason, *The Official Illustrated Guide to the Great Western Railway* (1861);

Arthur Miall, *The Life of Edward Miall* (1864);

Thomas Mozley, *Reminiscences: chiefly of towns, villages and churches* (1885);

John Orr, *The Agriculture of Oxfordshire: a survey* (1916);

Joseph Parker, *A Preacher's Life* (ed. 1903);

—— *Short Arguments on the Sabbath* (1855);

—— *A Soldier's Retrospect, being a narrative of the events in the life of William Nightingale of Banbury* (1854);

IV. Printed works — Books before 1920 — continued

Edwin Pearson, *The Banbury Chap Books* (1890);

John Petty, *The History of the Primitive Methodist Connexion* (1864);

Archibald Prentice, *The History of the Anti-Corn Law League* (1853);

R. K. Pugh, ed., *The Letter Books of Samuel Wilberforce 1843-68*, ORS, XLVIII (1970);

T. W. Rammell, *Report on a Preliminary Inquiry into the Sewerage, Drainage and Supply of Water and the Sanitary Condition of the Inhabitants of Banbury and Neithrop* (1850);

(Elizabeth Redford), *The Banbury Female Martyr* (n.d., *circa* 1863);

J. G. Rusher, *Cries of Banbury and London* (1843);

—— *Rusher's Banbury Lists and Directories* (1798-1881);

Henry Tancred, *A Legal Review of the origin of the System of Representation in England, and of its present state with observations on the Reform Necessary* (1831);

James Taylor, *The History of College Street Church, Northampton* (1897);

Barrie Trinder, *A Victorian MP and his Constituents: the correspondence of Henry William Tancred 1841-59*, BHS VIII (1969);

United Kingdom First Annual Trades Directory (1861);

Views and Reviews: Special Edition, Banbury (1897);

Graham Wallas, *The Life of Francis Place* (ed. 1925);

George Warner, *A Memoir of the Life and Labours of the late Kenrick Kench, Town Missionary of Banbury* (1874);

Wesleyan Methodist Church, Grimsbury, *Jubilee Souvenir 1871-1921* (1921);

R. G. Wilberforce, *The Life of Samuel Wilberforce* (1880-1882);

Arthur Young, *A General View of the Agriculture of Oxfordshire* (ed. 1969).

2. Books Published since 1920:

Agricultural Economics Research Institute, Oxford, *Country Planning: a study of Rural Problems* (1944);

K. J. Allison, M. W. Beresford and J. C. Hurst, *The Deserted Villages of Oxfordshire* (1965);

M. Argyles, *From South Kensington to Robbins; An Account of English Technical and Scientific Education since 1851* (1964);

M. K. Ashby, *Joseph Ashby of Tysoe 1859-1919*, (1961);

A. Aspinall, *The Early English Trades Unions* (1949);

K. Bonser, *The Drovers* (1970);

E. R. C. Brinkworth, *The Borough of Banbury 1554-1954* (1954);

—— *Old Banbury* (1958);

C. R. Cheney, *John Cheney and his Descendants* (1936);

Rex Christiansen, *A Regional History of the Railways of Great Britain, vol. 7: The West Midlands* (1973);

R. H. Clark, *The Development of the English Traction Engine* (1960);

Hugh Compton, *The Oxford Canal* (1976);

John Drinkwater, *Inheritance; being the first book of an Autobiography* (1931);

J. M. Dunn, *The Stratford-upon-Avon and Midland Junction Railway* (1952);

A. M. Everitt, ed., *Perspectives in English Urban History* (1973);

Frank Emery, *The Oxfordshire Landscape* (1974);

Charles Hadfield, *The Canals of the East Midlands* (1966);

Brian Harrison, *A Dictionary of British Temperance Biography* (1973);

—— *Drink and the Victorians* (1971);

Brian Harrison and Barrie Trinder, *Drink and Sobriety in an early Victorian Country Town: Banbury 1830-69* (1969);

Royden Harrison, *Before the Socialists* (1965);

Paul Harvey and Barrie Trinder, *New Light on Banbury Crosses* (1967);

E. J. Hobsbawm and George Rude, *Captain Swing* (ed. 1973).

J. R. Hodgkins, *Over the Hills to Glory; Radicalism in Banburyshire 1832-1945* (1978);
Pamela Horn, *Joseph Arch* (1971);
— *Agricultural Trade Unionism in Oxfordshire 1872-1881*, ORS XLVIIII (1974);
— *Labouring Life in the Victorian Countryside* (1976);
Anon., *Hunt Edmunds & Co. 1896-1946* (1946);
Elizabeth Isichei, *Victorian Quakers* (1970);
E. Agnes Knight, *A Century and a Quarter of Sunday School Work 1808-1933* (1933);
E. R. Lester, *John Kalebergo of Banbury* (1975);
M. D. Lobel, ed., *Historic Towns*, vol. 1 (1969);
Diana McClatchey, *Oxfordshire Clergy 1777-1869* (1960);
E. T. McDermott, *The History of the Great Western Railway* (1927);
Michael Mann, *Workers on the Move* (1973);
Mary Marshall, *The Land of Britain: the Report of the Land Utilisation Survey of Britain, Pt. 56, Oxfordshire* (1943);
L. E. Naylor, *The Irrepressible Victorian: Thomas Gibson Bowles* (1965);
I. and P. Opie, *The Oxford Dictionary of English Nursery Rhymes* (1951);
P. J. Perry, *British Farming during the Great Depression 1870-1914: an Historical Geography* (1974).
William Potts, *A History of Banbury* (1958);
— *Banbury through One Hundred Years* (1942);
Kirsty Rodwell, *Historic Towns in Oxfordshire: a Survey of the New County* (1975);
J. H. Russell, *The Banbury and Cheltenham Railway 1887-1962* (1978);
R. S. Sayers, *Lloyds Bank in the History of English Banking* (1957);
W. J. Scott, *The Great Great Western 1889-1902* (ed. 1972);
Bill Simpson, *The Banbury-Verney Junction Branch* (1978);
Margaret Stacey, *Tradition and Change: a Study of Banbury* (1960);
Margaret Stacey, Eric Batstone, Colin Bell and Anne Murcott, *Power, Persistence and Change: a Second Study of Banbury* (1975);
John Steane, *The Northamptonshire Landscape* (1974);
Janet Sutterby, *Saints Below: a History of the Baptist Church meeting at Bridge Street, Chapel, Banbury* (1973);
Audrey Taylor, *Gilletts: Bankers at Banbury and Oxford* (1964);
Joan Thirsk, ed., *The Agrarian History of England and Wales, vol. 4, 1500-1640* (1967);
A. Ll. B. Thomas, *J. Bevan Braithwaite: a Friend of the Nineteenth Century* (1909);
A. Ll. B. Thomas and Elizabeth Emmott, *William Charles Braithwaite: Memoirs and Papers by his Children* (1931);
Flora Thompson, *Lark Rise to Candleford* (ed. 1957);
Barrie Trinder, *The History of Grimsbury Methodist Church* (1962);
— *The History of Methodism in Banbury* (1965);
— *Banbury's Poor in 1850* (1966);
Victoria History of the County of Oxford, vol. 9, Bloxham Hundred, ed. M. D. Lobel and Alan Crossley (1969);
Victoria History of the County of Oxford, vol. 10, ed. Alan. Crossley (1972);
A. G. Wall, *St John's Church, Banbury* (1938);
Lou Warwick, *Theatre Unroyal* (1974).

3. Articles

William Bearn, 'On the Farming of Northamptonshire', *JRASE*, vol. 23 (1852);
I. W. F. Beckett, 'The Amateur Military Tradition: New Tasks for the Local Historian', *Local Historian*, vol. 13 (1979);
R. P. Beckinsale, 'The Plush Industry of North Oxfordshire', *Oxoniensia*, vol. 28 (1963);
Colin Bell, Eric Batstone and Anne Murcott, 'Voluntary Associations in Banbury', paper read to

the South-West branch of the British Sociological Association, 1968;

E. C. R. Brinkworth, 'A Nineteenth Century Vicar of Banbury: Thomas William Lancaster', *C & CH*, vol. 2 (1962);

—— 'Alfred Beesley's "History of Banbury" ', *C & CH*, vol. 4 (1967);

C. R. Cheney, 'Cheney and Sons: Two Centuries of Printing in Banbury', *C & CH*, vol. 4 (1967).

Nicholas Cooper, 'The Building and Furnishing of St Mary's Church, Banbury', *C & CH*, vol. 5 (1972);

Alan Everitt, 'The Banbury's of England', *Urban History Year Book 1974*, ed. H. J. Dyos (1974); vol. 8 (1982).

Alan Everitt, 'The Primary Towns of England', *Local Historian*, vol. 11 (1975);

—— 'Country Carriers in the Nineteenth Century', *Journal of Transport History*, new series, vol. 3 (1976);

Peter Fashon, 'Banbury Castle: A Summary of Excavations in 1972', *C & CH*, vol. 6 (1973);

Sarah Gosling, '57-129 Causeway, Banbury', in Crispin Paine *et al.*, 'Working Class Housing in Oxfordshire', *Oxoniensia*, vol. 43 (1978);

Brian Harrison, 'The British Prohibitionists 1853-72: A Biographical Analysis', *International Review of Social History*, vol. 15 (1970);

G. C. J. Hartland, 'Gas-Making in Banbury', *C & CH*, vol. 4 (1969);

—— 'The Vulcan Foundry, Banbury', *C & CH*, vol. 3 (1968);

—— 'The Britannia Works from Living Memory', *C & CH*, vol. 4 (1971);

P. D. Harvey, 'Where was Banbury Cross?', *Oxoniensia*, vol. 31 (1966);

Vera Hodgkins, 'The Plush Industry in Shutford', *C & CH*, vol. 7 (1979);

Pamela Horn, 'Banbury and the Riots of 1830', *C & CH*, vol. 3 (1967);

—— 'The Banbury Weavers' Union of 1834', *C & CH*, vol. 3 (1968);

—— 'The Chartist Land Company', *C & CH*, vol. 4 (1968);

—— 'The New Society of Plush Weavers: Articles, Rules & Orders, 1822', *C & CH*, vol. 3 (1968);

K. S. Inglis, 'The 1851 Religious Census', *Journal of Ecclesiastical History*, vol. 11 (1960);

B. K. Lucas, 'Banbury: Trees or Trade?' *C & CH*, vol. 7 (1979);

W. S. F. Pickering, 'The 1851 Religious Census – a Useless Experiment?' *British Journal of Sociology*, vol. 18 1967);

John Portergill, 'The Banbury Bluecoat Foundation', *C & CH*, vol. 7 (1976);

Archie Potts, 'Alexander Samuelson: a Victorian Engineer', *C & CH*, vol. 2 (1965);

—— 'Daniel Pidgeon and the Britannia Works', *C & CH*, vol. 4 (1969);

—— 'Ernest Samuelson and the Britannia Works', *C & CH*, vol. 4 (1971);

C. S. Read, 'On the Agriculture of Oxfordshire', *JRASE*, vol. 15 (1854);

Michael Robbins, 'From R. B. Dockray's Diary', *Journal of Transport History*, vol. 7 (1965);

Kirsty Rodwell, 'Excavations at Banbury Castle 1973-74: an interim report', *C & CH*, vol. 5 (1974);

(Bernhard Samuelson), Obituaries, *Journal of the Iron and Steel Institute*, vol. 1 (1905); *Northern Echo* (11 May 1905); *The Iron and Coal Trades Review* (12 May 1905); *The Times* (11 May 1905);

Barrie Trinder, 'Revivalism in Banbury, 1860', *C & CH*, vol. 3 1966);

—— 'Joseph Parker, Sabbatarianism and the Parson's Street infidels', *C & CH*, vol. 1 (1960);

—— 'The Distant Scene: Banbury and the United States in the Mid-Nineteenth Century', *C & CH*, vol. 7 (1978);

—— 'An Early Description of the Britannia Works', *C & CH*, vol. 4 (1965);

—— 'Fifty Years on – Banbury in 1931', *C & CH*, vol. 8 (1981);

—— 'Schisms and Divisions; the Origins of the Dissenting Congregations in Banbury 1772-1860', *C & CH* vol. 8 (1982).

—— 'Victorian Banbury: a Review of the Sources', *C & CH* (forthcoming);

Amherst D. Tyssen, 'The Old Meeting House, Banbury', *Transactions of the Unitarian Historical Society*, vol. 1 (1919).

INDEX

226